Studies in Renaissance Literature

Volume 33

THOMAS TRAHERNE AND
SEVENTEENTH-CENTURY THOUGHT

Studies in Renaissance Literature

ISSN 1465-6310

General Editors
David Colclough
Raphael Lyne
Sean Keilen

Studies in Renaissance Literature offers investigations of topics in English literature focussed in the sixteenth and seventeenth centuries; its scope extends from early Tudor writing, including works reflecting medieval concerns, to the Restoration period. Studies exploring the interplay between the literature of the English Renaissance and its cultural history are particularly welcomed.

Proposals or queries should be sent in the first instance to the editors, or to the publisher, at the addresses given below; all submissions receive prompt and informed consideration.

Professor David Colclough, School of English and Drama, Queen Mary, University of London, Mile End Road, London, E1 4NS

Dr Raphael Lyne, Murray Edwards College, Cambridge, CB3 0DF

Professor Sean Keilen, Literature Department, UC Santa Cruz, 1156 High St, Santa Cruz, CA 95060, USA

Boydell & Brewer Limited, PO Box 9, Woodbridge, Suffolk, IP12 3DF

Previously published volumes in this series are listed at the back of this volume

THOMAS TRAHERNE AND SEVENTEENTH-CENTURY THOUGHT

Edited by

Elizabeth S. Dodd and Cassandra Gorman

D. S. BREWER

First published 2016
D. S. Brewer, Cambridge

ISBN 978-1-84384-424-2

D. S. Brewer is an imprint of Boydell & Brewer Ltd
PO Box 9, Woodbridge, Suffolk IP12 3DF, UK
and of Boydell & Brewer Inc.
668 Mt Hope Avenue, Rochester, NY 14620-2731, USA
website: www.boydellandbrewer.com

A catalogue record for this title is available
from the British Library

The publisher has no responsibility for the continued existence or accuracy of URLs
for external or third-party internet websites referred to in this book, and does not
guarantee that any content on such websites is, or will remain, accurate or appropriate

This publication is printed on acid-free paper

Typeset by Fakenham Prepress Solutions, Fakenham, Norfolk NR21 8NN

CONTENTS

Contributors   vii

Acknowledgements   x

Conventions and Abbreviations   xi

Foreword by Julia Smith: Traherne and Historical Contingency   xiii

Introduction: 'A lover of all Things … An Active ey' (Select Meditations
    I.82): Traherne in Context   1
Elizabeth S. Dodd and Cassandra Gorman

PART I: PHILOSOPHIES OF MATTER AND SPIRIT

1   'The Lanthorns Sides': Skin, Soul and the Poetry of Thomas Traherne 31
    Phoebe Dickerson

2   No Things But In Thoughts: Traherne's Poetic Realism   48
    Kathryn Murphy

3   Thomas Traherne and 'Feeling Inside the Atom'   69
    Cassandra Gorman

4   'Consider it All': Traherne's Revealing of the Cosmic Christ in
    The Kingdom of God   84
    Alison Kershaw

PART II: PRACTICAL AND PUBLIC DEVOTION

5   Crossing the Red Sea: *The Ceremonial Law*, Typology and the
    Imagination   107
    Warren Chernaik

6   Sectarianism in *The Ceremonial Law*   130
    Carol Ann Johnston

Contents

7   Thomas Traherne and the Study of Happiness   154
    Ana Elena González-Treviño

8   'Innocency of Life': The Innocence of Thomas Traherne in the
    Context of Seventeenth-Century Devotion   172
    Elizabeth S. Dodd

Afterword by Jacob Blevins   193
Chronology of Traherne's Life and Contemporary Intellectual
    Developments   197
Bibliography   200
Index   214
Index of Biblical References   221

CONTRIBUTORS

Jacob Blevins is Professor of English at McNeese State University. He is the author/editor of five books, including *Catullan Consciousness and The Early Modern Lyric* (2004); *An Annotated Bibliography of Thomas Traherne Criticism* (2005); *Re-Reading Thomas Traherne: A Collection of New Critical Essays* (2007); *Dialogism and Lyric Self-Fashioning* (2008) and *Humanism and Classical Crisis* (2014). Blevins is also the editor of Volume 9 of *The Works of Thomas Traherne: The Notebooks*, which will be published in 2018. He is the current editor of the comparative literature journal, INTERTEXTS.

Warren Chernaik is Emeritus Professor of English, University of London, and Visiting Professor at King's College London. He was the founding Director of the Institute of English Studies (IES), University of London, and is now a Senior Research Fellow of the IES. He is the author of *The Myth of Rome in Shakespeare and his Contemporaries* (2011), *The Cambridge Introduction to Shakespeare's History Plays* (2007), a study of *The Merchant of Venice* (2005), *Sexual Freedom in Restoration Literature* (1995), *The Poet's Time: Politics and Religion in the Work of Andrew Marvell* (1983), and essays on such seventeenth-century authors as Marvell, Milton, Jonson, Herbert, Rochester and Behn, as well as co-editing books on topics as diverse as detective fiction, changes in copyright law, and Andrew Marvell. He is completing a book on Milton entitled *Milton and the Burden of Freedom*, to be published by Cambridge University Press, and has recently published essays on Shakespeare in *Cahiers Élisabéthains*, *Medieval and Renaissance Drama in England* and *English*.

Phoebe Dickerson is a student at Pembroke College, Cambridge. She is currently writing up her Ph.D. thesis, which explores the dermal aspects of seventeenth-century English verse (from the shifting nakedness of Edenic bodies, to blushing mistresses and scarred souls) and aims to draw scholarly attention to the period's previously unrecognised interest in skin. Since September 2015, she has also been teaching English at St Paul's Girls' School, London, where she has dedicated time and energy to converting seventeen-year-olds to the joys of reading early modern devotional poetry.

Elizabeth S. Dodd is Associate Programme Leader for the MA in Theology, Imagination and Culture and Programme Leader for the Ministry MA at Sarum College, Salisbury. She is the author of *Boundless Innocence in Thomas Traherne's Poetic Theology: 'Were all Men Wise and Innocent ...'* (2015), and has published chapters and articles on Traherne. She completed her doctoral dissertation on Thomas Traherne at Cambridge University, under the supervision of Professor David Ford, and co-organised the symposium on 'New Directions in Traherne Studies' with Cassandra Gorman in December 2012. Her main research interests are in literature and theology, particularly seventeenth-century metaphysical poetry and the theme of innocence in Christian literature. She has an interest in theological aesthetics, in particular the uses of genre theory, and her next project will explore the lyric voice in English theology.

Ana Elena González-Treviño is professor of seventeenth- and eighteenth-century English literature at the National Autonomous University of Mexico. She wrote her doctoral dissertation on Thomas Traherne (Queen Mary, University of London) and has subsequently published several articles about him and about other Restoration and eighteenth-century authors in English and in Spanish. She has also translated several works by Traherne into Spanish. She is a member of the Digital Humanities Seminar and the Critical Theory Seminar. She currently directs a seminar on seventeenth- and eighteenth-century culture and literature in English and French.

Cassandra Gorman co-organised the symposium 'New Directions in Traherne Studies' with Elizabeth Dodd in 2012. She completed her Ph.D. in English at the University of Cambridge in 2014, and has since taught early modern literature at the University of Birmingham, Anglia Ruskin University and the University of Oxford. She is currently Lecturer in English and Director of Studies at Trinity College, University of Cambridge. Her research explores ways in which the imaginative literature of the seventeenth century was not only responsive to but a part of scientific progress, with a particular interest in the reciprocal influence between early modern atomism and theological thought. She has published chapters on Traherne in collections of essays and an article on Lucy Hutchinson's 'Soteriological Materialism' in The Seventeenth Century (2013), and is working now on her first monograph: *Trusting in Indivisibles: Early Modern Literature and Atomism.*

Carol Ann Johnston earned her Ph.D. from Harvard University and is Martha Porter Sellers Chair of Rhetoric and the English Language and

Professor of English at Dickinson College. She teaches courses on early modern literature, Southern literature, and visual poetry. Her essays on various subjects from Eudora Welty to printing and lyric poetry have appeared in *Criticism*, *Mississippi Quarterly*, *The American Poetry Review* and *Re-Reading Thomas Traherne*, as well as poems in *Shenandoah*, *The Drunken Boat* and elsewhere. She is currently completing a manuscript on visual traditions in Traherne's work and writing an opera libretto about the English clockmaker John Harrison.

Alison Kershaw received her Ph.D. from the University of Western Australia (UWA), having submitted her thesis 'The Poetic of the Cosmic Christ in Thomas Traherne's *The Kingdom of God*'. Formerly a librarian at UWA and the University of Western Australia, she is currently writing a book of prayers based on the Lectionary and practicing as an artist. She is also co-founder of Hallowell Press, a small artisan publishing project on the south coast.

Kathryn Murphy is Fellow and Tutor in English Literature at Oriel College, Oxford. She works mainly on early-modern prose and poetry, and their relationship to the philosophical shifts of the seventeenth century. Recently published articles include 'Thomas Traherne, Thomas Hobbes, and the Rhetoric of Realism', in *The Seventeenth Century*, and work on Fulke Greville, Francis Bacon, Thomas Browne and Robert Burton. She is editing Bacon's *Sylva Sylvarum* and Browne's *Urne-Buriall* and *Garden of Cyrus* for Oxford University Press, as well as the *Penguin Book of Renaissance Prose*, and writing a book entitled *The Tottering Universal: Metaphysical Prose in the Seventeenth Century*.

Julia J. Smith is an independent scholar, and general editor of the Oxford Traherne, a fourteen-volume fully annotated edition of the Collected Works of Thomas Traherne, commissioned by Oxford University Press. Her research interests include manuscript studies, textual editing, and early modern religious literature, and she has published extensively on Traherne and his associates, including Susanna Hopton and other seventeenth-century authors. She is currently completing a biography of Traherne.

ACKNOWLEDGEMENTS

This collection emerged out of an academic symposium entitled 'Future Directions for Traherne Studies', which was held in December 2012. This was the first international conference on Traherne in fifteen years. It marked a new stage in the reception and interpretation of Traherne in anticipation of the first full publication of his corpus, from Boydell and Brewer and Oxford University Press. Thanks must go first and foremost to the Arts and Humanities Research Council and the Cambridge University Divinity Faculty, which funded the conference, and to Selwyn College, Cambridge, which hosted it.

Thanks are also due to all those involved in the symposium, for their participation and contribution to the ongoing study and enjoyment of Traherne. One participant deserves a particular mention. Dr Denise Inge was a key figure in the promotion and dissemination of thought and scholarship on Traherne, having been involved in the early reception and interpretation of the Lambeth Palace manuscript from 1997 onwards. Her contribution was significant and her passion was inspiring. Unfortunately this collection came too late to include her final word on Traherne. However, her incisive questions, creative connections and pursuit of new avenues of interpretation enlivened the conversations and debates that gave birth to this volume. It is hoped that her voice can still be heard through its pages.

CONVENTIONS AND ABBREVIATIONS

WORKS BY THOMAS TRAHERNE

With the exception of Traherne's notebooks, *Roman Forgeries* and *Christian Ethicks*, all quotations from his work are taken from Boydell & Brewer's *The Works of Thomas Traherne*, ed. Jan Ross, 6 vols to date (Cambridge, 2005–14):

Vol. I: *Inducements to Retirednes, A Sober View of Dr Twisses his Considerations, Seeds of Eternity or the Nature of the Soul, The Kingdom of God*

Vol. II: *Commentaries of Heaven*, Part I

Vol. III: *Commentaries of Heaven*, Part II

Vol. IV: *Church's Year-Book, A Serious and Pathetical Contemplation of the Mercies of GOD, in Several Most Devout and Sublime Thanksgivings for the Same* [*Meditations on the Six Days of the Creation*]

Vol. V: *Centuries of Meditations, Select Meditations*

Vol. VI: Poems from the Dobell Folio, *Poems of Felicity, The Ceremonial Law*, Poems from the Early Notebook

We quote from the following for the remainder of Traherne's published works:

Thomas Traherne, *Christian Ethicks: Or, Divine Morality. Opening the Way to Blessedness, By the Rules of Vertue and Reason*, ed. Carol L. Marks and George R. Guffey (Ithaca, 1968)

Thomas Traherne, *Roman Forgeries* (London, 1673)

We quote from the manuscripts for Traherne's as yet unpublished works:

Commonplace Book (Oxford, Bodleian Library, MS Eng. Poet. c. 42)

Early Notebook (Oxford, Bodleian Library, MS Lat. misc. f. 45)

Ficino Notebook (London, British Library, MS Burney 126)

Text from the *Commentaries of Heaven* are cited by volume and page number; texts from the *Centuries of Meditations* and *Select Meditations* are cited by century and meditation number; the poems are cited by page and line number. All other works by Traherne are referenced by page number.

ABBREVIATIONS

edn	edition
fol./fols	folio(s)
MS/MSS	Manuscript(s)
ODNB	*Oxford Dictionary of National Bibliography*, ed. H. C. G. Matthew and Brian Harrison, 60 vols (Oxford, 2004); online edition at < http://www.oxforddnb.com/>
OED	*Oxford English Dictionary*; online edition at < http://www.oed.com/>
PMLA	*Publications of the Modern Language Association of America*
TLS	*The Times Literary Supplement*

All quotations from the Bible, unless specified otherwise, are taken from *The Bible: Authorized King James Version with Apocrypha*, ed. Robert Carroll and Stephen Prickett (Oxford, 1997).

Foreword

TRAHERNE AND HISTORICAL CONTINGENCY

Julia J. Smith

Traherne's persona as an author is almost entirely a creation of the twentieth century. The seemingly miraculous sequence of the rediscovery of his unpublished manuscripts over the century from 1897 to 1997, utterly divorced in both time and location from the context in which they were created, has from the first promoted ahistorical readings of his life and work. This tendency has been further reinforced by the fact that Traherne's literary reputation during the seventeenth century, based only on the publication of *Roman Forgeries* (1673) and *Christian Ethicks* (1675), was slight, and as a result there is a lack of contemporary comment on his writing, which might otherwise have guided interpretation of his work in relation to the current events that shaped it. The nature and content of the earliest manuscript discoveries, published as *Poetical Works* (1903), *Centuries of Meditations* (1908) and *Poems of Felicity* (1910), contributed to confirm the sense of temporal dislocation by at once defining as the key themes in Traherne's writing the re-creation of Adam in Eden, the celebration and loss of childhood innocence, the recovery of felicity, and the mystical experiences of solitude.[1] These emotionally accessible images had a universal appeal, which made instantly perceived parallels with Blake, Wordsworth and Whitman seem more relevant than the historical context in which they were created. The lack of knowledge about Traherne himself and the difficulty of finding documentary evidence also meant that the poems and *Centuries* were immediately exploited as a source of biographical information, leading to over-literal and naive interpretations of his work, and in some cases to anachronistic and inaccurate

---

[1]   *The Poetical Works of Thomas Traherne, B.D., 1636?–1674*, ed. Bertram Dobell (London, 1903); *Centuries of Meditations*, ed. Bertram Dobell (London, 1908); *Traherne's Poems of Felicity*, ed. H. I. Bell (Oxford, 1910).

assumptions about his life. Thus, within a few years of his rediscovery, the preoccupations that were to govern Traherne criticism for most of the next century had been established.

Literary criticism of Traherne is, however, as historically contingent as his own writing, and the persistence of these themes throughout the first decades of the twentieth century reflects more than the intrinsic qualities of the first manuscript discoveries. His poems and the *Centuries* were published during an era when to be a 'joyful and happy soul' did not seem impossible, and Edwardian critics were keenly responsive to the celebration of innocence and physical beauty.[2] Nor was the attraction of Traherne's re-creation of a childhood Eden undermined by the devastating events of the First World War; on the contrary, it was reinforced in the Twenties by the nostalgia of survivors for their own pre-war childhoods. That Traherne too was separated from his childhood by a horrific war did not however suggest itself as a means of interpreting his work.

The literary critical trends of the early twentieth century did not tend to a more sophisticated and contextual interpretation of Traherne. The New Criticism that developed from the 1920s onwards led to a dramatic re-evaluation of seventeenth-century poets, from which Traherne did not benefit: he was anachronistically grouped with the metaphysical poets of the earlier seventeenth century, and thus further divorced from the Restoration period to which as a writer he properly belonged; and then denigrated as an unsatisfactory example of the metaphysical mode, described by T. S. Eliot merely as 'a remarkable curiosity'.[3] In fact, Traherne's work does not respond well to a 'words on the page' reading, which tends to lead precisely to the perception that his writing does not have the difficult or complex qualities so valued by Modernism. The kind of close reading that Traherne's work does repay is contextually informed and historically nuanced, and this was not likely to be favoured by Modernist critics whom recent history had given every reason for seeing disassociation from the past as desirable.

There are unfortunately few periods of history in which the human tragedy does not create a longing for a lost Eden, and the early parameters established for Traherne criticism were to remain hugely influential and tenacious. It is not a coincidence that it was during the Second World War that Gladys Wade powerfully endorsed the representation of Traherne as 'one of the most radiantly, most infectiously happy mortals this earth

---

[2]   *Centuries*, ed. Dobell, p. xvi.

[3]   T. S. Eliot, 'Mystic and Politician as Poet: Vaughan, Traherne, Marvell, Milton', *The Listener* 3.2 (April 1930), 590–1, at 591.

has known', adding to the long-standing image of his rural idyll a trope which echoed that of so many patriotic wartime songs: Traherne had won through 'a period of bitterest, most brutal warfare' to achieve the equivalent of the anticipated time of 'love and laughter/ And peace ever after' for which a war-torn society yearned.[4] Nor is it a coincidence that it was at the height of the Cold War and in the shadow of the atomic bomb that Traherne was most strongly reproved by the next generation of critics for his 'facile, expansive, emotional optimism'. Indeed, Carol Marks explicitly commented in 1966 that 'Traherne's joyful optimism crashes today against the Berlin wall, the Vietnamese war.'[5]

The belief of the pre-war decades in innocence has never been regained, and as the concept has declined in both credibility and attractiveness, there has been a very slow movement of Traherne scholarship away from its earlier preoccupations towards a more historically based interpretation of his work. This has not however been without strong contrary currents. For example, during the 1960s Marks laid a foundation for contextualised criticism by her meticulous research into the contemporary sources of Traherne's notebooks.[6] But shortly before she began work, Margoliouth's Oxford edition of the *Centuries, Poems, and Thanksgivings* (1958) had been published, a work that was to remain the standard edition for the next fifty years, but which by excluding *Roman Forgeries*, *Christian Ethicks*, the Commonplace Book, *Church's Year-Book*, the Early Notebook and the Ficino Notebook both embodied the principle that they were to be considered peripheral to Traherne studies, and in practical terms ensured their continued inaccessibility to a wide audience.[7]

It was also during this period that a second sequence of rediscoveries of Traherne's unpublished manuscripts, no less remarkable than the first, was inaugurated by the identification of the Osborn Manuscript in 1964.[8] Although it was first announced with the assertion that it 'meets the

[4]   Gladys I. Wade, *Thomas Traherne: A Critical Biography* (Princeton, 1944), p. 3.
[5]   Douglas Bush, *English Literature in the Earlier Seventeenth Century*, 2nd edn (Oxford, 1962), p. 158; Carol L. Marks, 'Traherne's Church's Year-Book', *Papers of the Bibliographical Society of America* 60 (1966), 31–72, at 72.
[6]   Carol L. Marks, 'Studies in the Reading of Thomas Traherne', B. Litt. thesis, University of Oxford (1962); Carol L. Marks, 'Thomas Traherne's Commonplace Book', *Papers of the Bibliographical Society of America* 58 (1964), 458–65; Marks, 'Traherne's Church's Year-Book'; Carol L. Marks, 'Thomas Traherne's Early Studies', *Papers of the Bibliographical Society of America* 62 (1968), 511–36; Carol Marks Sicherman, 'Traherne's Ficino Notebook', *Papers of the Bibliographical Society of America* 63 (1969), 73–81.
[7]   *Centuries, Poems, and Thanksgivings*, ed. H. M. Margoliouth, 2 vols (Oxford, 1958).
[8]   James M. Osborn, 'A New Traherne Manuscript', *TLS* (8 October 1964), 928.

expectations' of Traherne's readers in its portrayal of the innocence of childhood and other related themes, it was soon realised to be a work deeply and explicitly engaged with contemporary events. Traherne scholars were perhaps slow to realise the implications of this engagement for the interpretation of his other works, but the announcement in 1982 of the discovery of *Commentaries of Heaven* was to provide evidence of the most substantial kind of Traherne's interest in public affairs, new philosophy and religious controversy.[9] Also in 1982, a seminal article by Nabil Matar demonstrated through detailed analysis of 'A Thanksgiving and Prayer for the Nation' that Traherne's concern for national affairs is apparent not only in explicit statement, but also in biblical allusions, and choice of imagery and vocabulary. This was followed by a series of articles by other scholars that placed Traherne in very specific contexts of late-seventeenth-century religion, politics and devotional practice, and that both urged the necessity and demonstrated the benefits of historically informed criticism.[10]

The 1980s were a fruitful time for Traherne criticism, in spite of its very slight interaction with the meteoric rise of literary theory during this period.[11] They were also the decade of Thatcherism, and in the 1990s Traherne studies were in their own way to respond to this, giving rise to academic – and historically informed – criticism which saw Traherne's works as providing a critique of the market economy, and also to an increasing number of general readers who sought in Traherne a spiritual guide who could offer an alternative to the materialism and individualism of the 1980s.[12] This latter use of Traherne's works is undoubtedly one which he himself would have approved, but it is in its nature ahistorical. Nonetheless, it perhaps also gave an impetus to academic studies of Traherne, which by the end of the 1990s had increased significantly in

---

9   Elliot Rose, 'A New Traherne Manuscript', *TLS* (19 March 1982), 324; Allan Pritchard, 'Traherne's *Commentaries of Heaven* (With Selections from the Manuscript)', *University of Toronto Quarterly* 53 (1983), 1–35.

10   Nabil I. Matar, 'Prophetic Traherne: "A Thanksgiving and Prayer for the Nation"', *Journal of English and Germanic Philology* 81.1 (1982), 16–29; Christopher Hill, 'Thomas Traherne, 1637–74', in *The Collected Essays of Christopher Hill*, vol. I: *Writing and Revolution in 17th Century England* (Brighton, 1985), pp. 226–46; Richard Douglas Jordan, 'Thomas Traherne and the Art of Meditation', *Journal of the History of Ideas* 46 (1985), 381–403; Julia J. Smith, 'Attitudes towards Conformity and Nonconformity in Thomas Traherne', *Bunyan Studies* 1.1 (1988), 26–35; Julia J. Smith, 'Thomas Traherne and the Restoration', *The Seventeenth Century* 3.2 (1988), 203–22.

11   A. Leigh DeNeef, *Traherne in Dialogue: Heidegger, Lacan, and Derrida* (Durham, NC, 1988) is the most prominent example of engagement with critical theory.

12   David Hawkes, 'Thomas Traherne: A Critique of Political Economy', *Huntington Library Quarterly* 62 (1999), 369–88.

prominence. 1997 was an *annus mirabilis* of Traherne scholarship, which saw the first international conference devoted to Traherne, the first publication of *Select Meditations* thirty-three years after its discovery, and most importantly the identification of two major new manuscripts, *The Ceremonial Law* and the Lambeth Manuscript, the latter in particular further increasing awareness of both the range and the intellectual depth of Traherne's work.[13] There was a sense in that year that the momentum behind Traherne studies was unstoppable.

The potential, however, of contextual interpretation of Traherne has never been fully realised. As I wrote in the late 1980s, 'Traherne is only very slowly being restored to his proper social, intellectual, and political context', and this has unfortunately remained largely true in the intervening years.[14] There have been many reasons why this has been so, some more easily addressed than others. For much of this period, the new manuscript material has been relatively inaccessible, giving at least a pretext to the many articles that have continued to focus their attention on a handful of lyrics. There has also been a continuing lack of the sound factual basis that must underpin any contextual study. The paucity of documentary sources for Traherne's life has given lasting currency to a variety of biographical myths created by Gladys Wade; this in turn has meant that there has been no adequate information for dating his works, thus denuding them of a precise context. Nor has there been any rigorous scholarly analysis of the evidence for the attribution of works doubtfully ascribed to Traherne. A particularly persistent problem has been the purveyance of outdated information by standard reference works, some of which remain largely in a 1940s time warp: the current editions of both *The Concise Oxford Companion to English Literature* and *The Cambridge Guide to Literature in English*, for example, perpetuate views of Traherne that have been known for decades to be inaccurate.[15]

---

[13] *Select Meditations*, ed. Julia J. Smith (Manchester, 1997); Julia J. Smith and Laetitia Yeandle, '"Felicity disguisd in fiery Words": Genesis and Exodus in a Newly Discovered Poem by Thomas Traherne', *TLS* (7 November 1997), 17; Jeremy Maule, 'Five New Traherne Works: The Lambeth Manuscript', unpublished paper, delivered at the Thomas Traherne Conference, Brasenose College, Oxford, 30 July 1997; Denise Inge and Calum MacFarlane, 'Seeds of Eternity: A New Traherne Manuscript', *TLS* (2 June 2000), 14.

[14] Smith, 'Thomas Traherne and the Restoration', 203.

[15] Wade, *Thomas Traherne*; 'Thomas Traherne (1637–74)', in *The Concise Oxford Companion to English Literature*, ed. Dinah Birch and Katy Hooper, 4th edn (Oxford, 2012); 'Thomas Traherne 1637–74', in *The Cambridge Guide to Literature in English*, ed. Dominic Head, 3rd edn (Cambridge, 2006); also outdated are 'Thomas Traherne (1637–74)', in *The Oxford Companion to English Literature*, ed. Dinah Birch, 7th edn (Oxford, 2009); and 'Thomas Traherne (1637–74)', in *The Oxford Companion to British History*, ed. John Cannon (Oxford, 2009).

Traherne scholars however are now better placed to engage in the detailed and contextualised interpretation of his writing than their predecessors. The ten manuscripts that have been identified to date give us not only a wealth of information about Traherne's practices of composition and compilation, but also many hitherto unknown works in which the evidence of Traherne's interest in the new science, theological controversy and political philosophy is overwhelming. At the same time, these works are being made more accessible than ever before through the publication of Jan Ross's edition, and the fully annotated edition commissioned by Oxford University Press that is currently under way.[16]

There are also broader scholarly and cultural trends which may mean that the time is now ripe for the historical recontextualisation of Traherne to succeed. Of particular relevance to Traherne scholarship is the massive burgeoning of manuscript studies since the groundbreaking publication in 1993 of both Harold Love's *Scribal Publication in Seventeenth-Century England* and the final volume of Peter Beal's *Index of English Literary Manuscripts*.[17] These offer a means of interpreting the very specific milieu in which Traherne's unique corpus of autograph manuscripts were produced, and enable us to see in great detail the ways in which even the act of writing for Traherne was socially engaged. Emphasis on accurate identification of the hands that contribute to the manuscripts, analysis of the process of collaboration, the chronology of the manuscripts' compilation, and evidence of their purpose will hugely augment our understanding of Traherne's social, geographical and cultural context.

These contexts, of course, cannot be understood without more knowledge of Traherne's life and the places in which he spent it than was available to the twentieth century. Another cultural change of recent years has been the huge increase of academic interest in both life-writing and biographical research, spearheaded by that most impressive of scholarly projects, the *Oxford Dictionary of National Biography*, published in 2004. New biographical work on Traherne himself has already uncovered much information and refuted many of the myths about his life, including that of his intellectual and spiritual isolation, and this in turn can provide an accurate context both for interpreting his thought, and for freeing his

---

[16] *The Works of Thomas Traherne*, ed. Jan Ross, 9 vols (Cambridge, 2005–); the Oxford Traherne is under the general editorship of Julia J. Smith, has an international and interdisciplinary team of editors, and will be published in fourteen volumes.

[17] Peter Beal, *Index of English Literary Manuscripts*, vol. I: *1450–1625*, parts 1 and 2 (London, 1980); vol. II: *1625–1700*, parts 1 (London, 1987) and 2 (London, 1993); Harold Love, *Scribal Publication in Seventeenth-Century England* (Oxford, 1993).

work from the overly autobiographical readings of the last century.[18] A parallel increase of interest in local and regional culture may also help us to understand how Traherne's writing is precisely located in Herefordshire and the Welsh Marches: Herefordshire must surely to date be the most under-studied county in England, but it is increasingly apparent that this, and not Teddington or London, was the site of Traherne's creativity, and that it influenced much more than his perception of landscape.

Also of significance has been a re-evaluation of literary periods, entailing the rejection of the traditional watershed of 1660, and a corresponding resurgence of interest in the Restoration period. This has great benefits for the proper understanding of Traherne, who both chronologically and intellectually is indeed a Restoration writer, but who fits very ill with twentieth-century stereotypes of 'Restoration literature'. Bridging the gap between pre- and post-Restoration literature has also enabled a shift from a scholarly preoccupation with radicals, puritans and nonconformists towards the perception that 'conformists' to the established political and ecclesiastical order can be equally interesting, and also that, as is indeed the case with Traherne himself, the distinction between conformists and nonconformists is by no means always clear-cut, and that allegiances throughout the period were often shifting and uneasy.

Finally, the highly politicised culture in which we now live can and should make us more alert to the political charge that can lie behind everyday words and images. This heightened sensitivity to the political implications of language would have been very recognisable to authors of the mid-seventeenth century, and should warn us against failing to see that Traherne's language too carries precise contemporary and local resonances, as well as universal meaning.

Thomas Traherne and Seventeenth-Century Thought once again makes the case for a detailed recontextualisation of Traherne, challenging afresh the perversely persistent images of a naive writer isolated from the complex intellectual currents of his time. It demonstrates a variety of ways in which Traherne responded to the intellectual preoccupations of the later seventeenth century, its subject matter ranging from Bacon, Hobbes and atomism, to typology and devotional literature. In doing so it hints at many more possibilities for future study of other aspects of Traherne's engagement with contemporary science, politics, devotional trends and ecclesiastical controversy, and for understanding Traherne as an early modern thinker and theologian as well as poet. Traherne's intellectual,

---

[18] Julia J. Smith, 'Thomas Traherne (*c.*1637–1674)' in *ODNB*; Julia J. Smith, *Thomas Traherne: A Life* (forthcoming).

political and religious views must now be given the serious attention by scholars for which exponents of Milton and Marvell do not have to argue. Traherne wrote in the *Centuries* of his own desire as a child for 'a Book from Heaven' to be brought to him by an angel, and also of his maturer realisation that the Bible, a book with a context and a history, had already answered his desire 'in a far better maner then I was able to imagine' (III.27).[19] Traherne's works too are richer, more intellectually challenging and more worthy of study because he and they have a history.

[19]   Quoted from Ross, V, p. 107.

Introduction

'A LOVER OF ALL THINGS … AN ACTIVE EY' (*SELECT MEDITATIONS*, I.82): TRAHERNE IN CONTEXT

Elizabeth S. Dodd and Cassandra Gorman

'COMING TO THE MATTER': A MAN OF HIS TIME

Readers have long considered the concerns of Thomas Traherne's writings to be out of this world, but the author himself was based firmly within it, as an eclectic who drew on all the intellectual resources of his time, and as a priest fully participating in the activities of social and religious life. The essays of the current collection challenge a long-standing assumption that this poet and theologian was unconcerned with his social, political and intellectual surroundings and was somehow – rather unrealistically – 'out of his time'.[1] This volume seeks to recontextualise Traherne, and to reconsider the most significant themes that characterise his writings within their seventeenth-century background. Revealing the author's debts to his cultural influences is not to undermine the remarkable originality

---

[1]   Criticism on Traherne has persisted in arguing, in the words of Richard Douglas Jordan, that the writer was not 'a modern man'. A. L. Clements opened his study of Traherne's mysticism with the claim that 'though contemporary movements surely had some effect on him', the context for his study should be 'the rich and complex Christian contemplative or mystical tradition' of late antiquity and medievalism. Though such a reading of Traherne undoubtedly has strong merits, it presents a limited view of the author's intellectual contexts by neglecting the substantial 'effect' of contemporary theologies and philosophies on his work. More recently, Susan Stewart has claimed that Traherne's poetry in particular demonstrates 'the synonymity of aspects of seventeenth-century lyric with aspects of the medieval'. Richard Douglas Jordan, *The Temple of Eternity: Thomas Traherne's Philosophy of Time* (Port Washington, 1972), p. 55; A. L. Clements, *The Mystical Poetry of Thomas Traherne* (Cambridge MA, 1969), p. 13; Susan Stewart, *Poetry and the Fate of the Senses* (Chicago, 2002), p. 242.

of his work, but rather to affirm it: never has there been a better time to defend Traherne against accusations of mediocrity, or shallow learning.[2] Autograph manuscript discoveries of recent years have brought striking revelations that challenge long-standing assumptions about his philosophical, doctrinal and social interests. The Traherne that emerges is an early modern polymath, fascinated, as he declared on his frontispiece to the *Commentaries of Heaven*, by 'ALL THINGS'.[3]

About halfway through *The Kingdom of God*, an encyclopaedic survey of the natural and celestial world, Traherne dedicates a section to the 'Moon and Stars, their Magnitude and Distance, Influences, Aspects, and Motions' (Ross, I, p. 362).[4] He opens with a series of similitudes, establishing clearly that the subjects for study are observable from a human vantage point: 'The World is like Heaven, God like the Sun, the Moon and the Stars like Saints and Angels.' Each point of comparison reads as an early modern theological commonplace: earth is made in heaven's likeness and its form bestows the mortal inhabitant with the closest impression of the divine realm; God is a fountain of light, accommodated for human understanding in the sun's beams; humanity can feel awe at the glory of the immortal saints by looking up at the blazing stars. At first glance, Traherne's accommodative analysis of the visible cosmos seems unoriginal and unworldly, as does his follow-up point:

---

[2]   Writing on the *Centuries*, Carol L. Marks considered Traherne's presentation of the 'physical world' as a substance that merits 'study (such as the Royal Society supported and Traherne may have dabbled in)', implying that his interest in natural knowledge was casual at the very least; indeed, she argued that her suggestion was based on the 'slender evidence' of his philosophical imagery. Admittedly, Marks was writing before the discovery of the later Traherne manuscripts, in which the writer's scientific leanings are most clearly realised. However, in a paper discussing the *Commentaries*, Finn Fordham argued that the clergyman's writings 'frequently show a weak absorption of scientific discoveries'. The evidence for Traherne's reading in natural philosophy points towards a rather strong absorption, as the studies in this volume will reveal (see especially the chapters by Kathryn Murphy and Cassandra Gorman). Carol L. Marks, 'Thomas Traherne and Cambridge Platonism', *PMLA* 7 (1966), 521–34, at 527; Finn Fordham, 'Motions of Writing in the Commentaries of Heaven: The "Volatilitie" of "Atoms" and "ÆTYMS"', *Re-Reading Thomas Traherne*, ed. Jacob Blevins (Tempe, 2007), pp. 115–34, at p. 116.

[3]   *Thomas Traherne and Seventeenth-Century Thought* owes much to the rolling publication of Traherne's complete works by Boydell & Brewer, as edited by Jan Ross. The *Commentaries of Heaven* is published in Ross, *The Works of Thomas Traherne*, 9 vols (Cambridge, 2007), vols II–III. For Ross's transcription of the frontispiece, see II, p. 3. All further references to and quotations from the *Commentaries* in this book will be taken from this edition, and cited by volume and page number in the text.

[4]   All further references to and quotations from *The Kingdom of God* will be taken from this edition of *The Works of Thomas Traherne*, ed. Jan Ross (Cambridge, 2005), vol. I, and cited by page number in the text.

The Similitude of his Wisdom, Goodness, and Glory, of his Purity and
Beauty, Greatness and Majesty, is aptly Typified in this Material Tabernacle.
(p. 362)

But a characteristic priority of Traherne's thought shines through this
statement. The magnificent qualities of the Godhead are 'Typified' not
just in the scripture of the Old Testament, or in abstracted emblems of
recognisable things, but in a live 'Tabernacle' that is constantly moving
and transforming as it provides a home for mortal creatures. Traherne's
emphasis on the temporary dwelling of the natural world as an apt
'Similitude' merges with and absorbs his biblical typology; he is also, of
course, comparing his material surroundings to the tent that protected the
Ark of the Covenant and gave sanctuary to the Israelites in the wilderness.[5]
In this metaphor, however, it is the scriptural figure of the 'Tabernacle'
that forms the vehicle for understanding the value of the wider world. The
world and its movements are of primary importance. He continues:

> But leaving the Allegorie, and Coming to the Matter, we may Contemplat
> how Wonderfull God is in his House, and Famelie […] Here is a Visible
> World, a World of Treasures on Earth to be Enjoyed: a visible Inheritance,
> and a Present possession imparted to the Soul […] The Sun that is one
> Hundred Sixty times bigger than the Earth, by the best Computation, is
> four Millions, three Hundred twenty Nine Thousand Miles higher than the
> Earth. Of the Plannets two move between the Moon and it: Three between
> it and the fixed stars: The Earth is 22600 2/22 Miles in Compass; and yet
> many of those Stars, that seem little Sparkles are abundantly Greater: Their
> Multitude is Innumerable, their Distances both from the Earth and from
> Each other, unconceivable: yet are all these in respect of GOD, but a litle
> Point. (p. 363)

It is in the 'Matter' itself, Traherne urges, that we shall come closest to
God. In moving on from the 'Allegorie' of ancient typologies, he establishes
himself as a theologian primarily interested in the material experience of
the here and now. The Traherne of *The Kingdom of God* is undeniably of
the same voice as the author of the *Centuries of Meditations* – 'You never
Enjoy the World aright, till the Sea it self floweth in your Veins, till you
are clothed with the Heavens, and Crowned with the Stars' (*Centuries
of Meditations*, Ross, V, I.29) – but he combines ecstatic wonder at the
mysteries of creation with a scientific study of measurements and distances,
drawn from his reading of the early modern astronomers Copernicus and

---

[5]   For further work on Traherne's typology, see the chapters by Warren Chernaik,
'Crossing the Red Sea', and Carol Ann Johnston, 'Sectarianism in *The Ceremonial Law*',
in this volume (both essays focus on Traherne's use of typology in *The Ceremonial Law*).

Hevelius, amongst others.[6] The combinations of his thought should not come as a surprise, given that he was writing at the time of Baxter and Browne, but they do: Traherne emerges as a highly original thinker in his own right; one who was knowledgeable of current affairs and interests, who addressed them in surprising combinations and pushed interpretations in novel directions.

Until fairly recently, it was customary in Traherne criticism to develop a portrait of the author as solitary and solipsistic. In the words of Denise Inge, he has traditionally been considered a thinker with his 'head in the clouds and feet in paradise'.[7] This enduring evaluation was not without its merits, though Inge's phrase 'head in the clouds' aptly exposes a limiting and somewhat derogatory understanding of the writer. Traherne's reflections on the kingdoms of Heaven and Earth ultimately steer towards the conclusion that 'ALL THINGS' – 'Created and Increated' – merge into one when the soul meditates on the infinite, immortal Godhead (*Commentaries*, II, p. 3). Time becomes a meaningless and limiting concept, and the thinker outgrows his mortal circumstances to measure 'Heaven with a Span' and to esteem 'a thousand yeers as but one Day' (*Centuries*, I.19). The rewards of this yearning are nevertheless only possible if human beings pause to 'take in' the information that surrounds them. If Traherne has his 'feet in paradise', it is a world of infinite variety that whets his appetite for further objects of knowledge – and no object of knowledge is considered too large, or too small. For Traherne, metaphysical voyages into the distant universe and close studies of recent philosophical treatises are not mutually exclusive. Though his extreme positivism would be remarkable in any period of history, he was educated in the scholarship of seventeenth-century Europe, and the theologian who saw a 'World of Treasures on Earth to be Enjoyed' included its contemporary theological, philosophical and scientific theories amongst its riches.

It is the aim of the present collection to overcome the critical tendency to understand Traherne as a socially and intellectually isolated and, at worst, a naive thinker. Each of the essays in this volume considers this early modern writer in the complex intellectual currents of his time. They challenge aspects of Traherne studies that, though not new, have long

---

[6] All further references to and quotations from the *Centuries of Meditations* will be taken from this edition of *The Works of Thomas Traherne*, ed. Jan Ross (Cambridge, 2013), vol. V, and cited in the text by century and meditation number. Traherne acknowledges his reading of 'Modern Divines and Philosophers' including Copernicus and Hevelius two chapters later in *The Kingdom of God*, p. 377.

[7] Denise Inge, *Wanting Like a God: Desire and Freedom in Thomas Traherne* (Norwich, 2009), p. 1.

lain dormant or seemingly 'settled': his theory of 'Felicity', his desire for innocence, his attitudes to solitude and society, and his understandings of the body and the soul. Several chapters posit new ways of reviewing the author's beliefs in the light of contemporary intellectual influences such as radical religion, materialism and devotional culture, and two of the essays focus in detail on the most newly discovered of Traherne's works, *The Ceremonial Law*, published for the first time in 2014.[8]

'TO ENTERTAIN THE UNKNOWN GOOD' (*CENTURIES*, III.26): INTERPRETING THE NEW MANUSCRIPTS

A thorough recontextualisation of Traherne has been made possible by the unexpected emergence of new manuscripts. Jeremy Maule found and identified the pre-mentioned Lambeth Palace manuscript in 1997.[9] In addition to its lengthiest work, *The Kingdom of God*, its contents include a discourse on the nature of the soul (*Seeds of Eternity*), a critical analysis of the Calvinist and Arminian opinions, respectively, of Robert Sanderson and Henry Hammond (*A Sober View of Dr Twisses his Considerations*), and a treatise on retirement (*Inducements to Retirednes*). Out of all of Traherne's works, it is arguably *A Sober View* that best demonstrates his educated interest in contemporary theological debates about election and free will. He prepared his treatise meticulously, dividing his critical evaluation into twenty-eight chapters and inviting another reader to leave feedback in the margins. Section XVI opens with the bald statement 'We Study Truth and *not Parties*', which sums up Traherne's attitude to the debate: his eventual position falls somewhere in between Hammond's and Sanderson's, with the conclusion that there are 'two Sorts of Elect', those 'that voluntarily repent and believ', and those 'of a set and determined Number … whom God is resolved to convert in their Rebellion and Bring to Salvation' (*Sober View*, Ross, I, p. 132, pp. 184–5).[10] If we were seeking to

---

[8]   *The Ceremonial Law* is the most recently published of all Traherne's works, appearing for the first time in 2014 in Ross's sixth volume of the *Works* (which also includes poems from the Dobell folio and Early Notebook, and the Poems of Felicity.) All further references to and quotations from the poems and *The Ceremonial Law* will be taken from this edition of *The Works of Thomas Traherne*, ed. Jan Ross (Cambridge, 2014), vol. VI, and cited in the text by page and line number.

[9]   For details of the discovery, see Denise Inge and Calum MacFarlane, 'Seeds of Eternity: A New Traherne manuscript', *TLS* (2 June 2000), 14.

[10] All further references to and quotations from *A Sober View of Dr Twisses his Considerations,* as well as *Seeds of Eternity* and *Inducements to Retirednes*, will be taken from this edition of *The Works of Thomas Traherne*, ed. Jan Ross (Cambridge, 2005), vol. I, and cited in the text by page number.

compile a bibliography of Traherne's reading from his works, the research that went into *A Sober View* would reveal underappreciated political and social interests. The discovery of *Seeds of Eternity* adds tomes of ancient philosophy to the list – in addition to Aristotle (*De Anima*) he references Augustine, St Denise and St Jerome, Justin Martyr, Gregory of Nyssa, Plato, Theophrastus, Plotinus, Chalcidius, Proclus and many more – but the author's accompanying study of the body's 'Contexture and form' clearly draws on the work of early modern 'Chimists and Physicians' (*Seeds*, Ross, I, pp. 238–9 and p. 240).

In *Inducements to Retirednes* we find a work that, rather than supporting the traditional view of Traherne as an isolated thinker, on the contrary confirms his investment in the activities of the wider world and his opinions on the importance of sociability. The treatise is a defence of the spiritual value of personal meditation. He explains the benefits of such a retreat: 'Our Soul entereth not [Eternity] till Eternity entereth into us', a state of being that can be achieved by 'Recollection of Mind, which is a Retirement of Soul, or Thought into it self' (*Inducements*, Ross, I, p. 7). *Inducements to Retirednes* is not a denial of the 'Joys of Societie' or the 'Divine Enjoyment' of friendship (pp. 7, 14), but a knowing rejection of the more cloying properties of human company, and a practical guide to what can be achieved – for the good of others as well as one's self – from solitary reflection. In retirement 'we are able to live in Peace, and Enjoy a Million' (p. 7). Contrarily to what we might expect, retirement is in fact a sociable activity:

> for Man is made a Sociable Creature, and is never Happy till his Capacities are filled with all their Objects, and his Inclinations hav attained their proper Ends. But these Objects are Wide and many, their fountains are Dispersed, and lie abroad: they cannot therfore but in Retirement be at once Enjoyed. (p. 12)

Nor is the Traherne of *Inducements to Retirednes* communing with the world only in a timeless, metaphysical sense. Parish records, and autobiographical statements dispersed throughout his works, paint a portrait of the author as a caring, involved parish priest; he vows here to love 'evry person in the whole World, with as near and violent affection, as I would my Wife, or my Dearest Friend' (p. 15). He was moreover one who spent his solitary time in study of fashionable and at times progressive subjects. Traherne explains that he has not withdrawn to master the skills of any single art, such as 'Chymistrie', or to become an 'Exact Historian' or 'Grammarian' (p. 13), but to pursue all these disciplines and others within the divine. The writer who lists examples of the social, political and intellectual benefits of retirement is one who knows how the world works:

Do not Men in Retirement prepare Illustrious Scenes for the Theatre? [...]
Are not all the Great Transactions of the World managed in Privat before
they appear? Even Solomons Temple was prepared in the Solitudes. Sermons
Preached by Bishops, the Glory of the most famous Conventions, the
Prosperity of Kingdoms, is provided in Retirement. And all the Miraculous
Effects of Government in War and Peace, are Secretly Hammered at the
Council Table. Yea, and as if that were not Secret Enough, evry man alone
in His Closet, and within Himself first meditateth, what there he proposeth.
(p. 12)

Further evidence, if needed, that Traherne was engaged with the politics
and scholarship of his time is in his description of 'Doing Good' as the
'Highest Epicurism' (p. 14). Referring here to the Epicurean philosophy
that declared pleasure the highest good, he responds with open-minded
ambivalence to a school of thought that propelled early modern material
science but horrified many of his theological contemporaries, a response
that we can read as anticipatory of his spiritual 'A treatice of Atoms' in *The
Kingdom of God* (pp. 341–7).

Traherne took his interest in atoms further in a second major encyclopaedic work, greater still in its ambition than *The Kingdom of God*
– the *Commentaries of Heaven*. The initial finding of this manuscript was
perhaps the most sensational to date of all the posthumous discoveries:
in 1967 it was rescued from a burning rubbish tip in Lancashire, and it
continued to rest for a further fifteen years in a Canadian attic before
it was finally attributed to Traherne in 1982.[11] *Commentaries of Heaven*
was Traherne's attempt to define 'ALL THINGS', one by one, in an alphabetically ordered treatise dedicated to the 'Satisfaction of Atheists, and the
Consolation of Christians' (II, p. 3). It is a testimony to the magnitude of
his undertaking that the existing manuscript runs to about 300,000 words,
but only makes it as far as the letter 'B'. As with nearly all of Traherne's
works, the *Commentaries* resists firm dating, but can be attributed with
some confidence to the early 1670s – the most productive literary period
of the author's life.[12] Traherne expands upon and further develops his
meditations on – and quest for the obtainment of – 'Felicity', the desired
end of all of his writings; there are specific cross-references between the

---

[11] For further details, see Elliot Rose, 'A New Traherne Manuscript', *TLS* (19 March 1982),
324 and Ross, II, p. xi.

[12] In the commentary on 'Aristotle', Traherne copies from Theophilus Gale's 'Excellent
Description' of the philosopher (*Commentaries*, III, p. 188) in Gale, *Court of the Gentiles*
(London, 1670), pp. 360–6; in the commentary on 'Antichrist', when discussing his
opinions on the 'Counterfeit' Catholic church, Traherne refers his reader to a forthcoming work, *Roman Forgeries* (London, 1673): 'a whole Tract upon that theme, (an
intire volume) fit to be published' (*Commentaries*, III, p. 110). See also Ross, II, p. xvii.

Commentaries and subjects discussed in three of his most substantial prose works: the *Centuries*, *The Kingdom of God* and *Select Meditations*. It is tempting to read the *Commentaries* as the pinnacle of Traherne's insatiable quest for knowledge, both natural and divine. In this work Traherne advanced his lifelong experimentation with literary form, producing a text that closely resembled his Commonplace Book but incorporated features of an up-and-coming genre – the dictionary – and the systematically organised encyclopaedia.[13] The *Commentaries* was very much a product of its historical moment, in form and in content: abstract topics such as 'Abhorrence' and 'Affection' rub shoulders with 'Air', 'Aristotle' and the 'Ant'; as with *The Kingdom of God*, interjections from the ancient philosophers and the patricians combine with references to modern scholars including Francis Bacon and Theophilus Gale; Traherne considers (and refutes) the opinions of various religious sects, most notably Anabaptism and Socianism; the section on the 'Atom', likely to have been prepared at a very similar time to its corresponding chapter in the Lambeth Palace manuscript, is one of the longest in the entire work.[14]

The late-twentieth-century discoveries are undeniably significant in the new revelations they make of Traherne as a thinker and a theologian, but they also encourage us to expand upon our understanding of Traherne as a poet. Many of his longer prose works feature original poetry. In the *Centuries*, the writer turns to verse in the Third Century, when prompted by reflections on personal experience; further verse accompanies thoughts on King David and the poetic voice of the psalms.[15] The poetry of *Select Meditations* is explicitly devotional in tone, and accords with the shift inwards that prompted the opening of the work as we have it: 'When I retire first I seem to Com in my selfe as to a Centre, in that Centre I find Eternitie and all its Riches' (*Select Meditations*, I.81).[16] This introspective, devotional focus is still present in the *Commentaries of Heaven*, but these verses bear the additional significance of contributing to the knowledge sought and explored in its pages. It becomes clear that the 'Centre'

---

[13]　See Ross, II, p. xxxiii. There are significant similarities in content, and cross-references between Traherne's Commonplace Book and the *Commentaries*, notably on the topics of Atom, Capacity, Charitie, Divinity, Freedom, Friendship, Grace, Incarnation, Infinit, Intercession, Liberty, Light, Matter, Motion, Soul and World. See the appendices to Ross, II, pp. 523–8.

[14]　Traherne rants against the Anabaptists in the commentary on 'Baptism' (III, p. 452) and criticises the 'Absurditie' of Socinianism in 'Atonement' (III, p. 372).

[15]　There are poems in the Third Century in meditations 4, 19, 21, 26, 47, 49, 50 and 69.

[16]　All further references to the *Select Meditations* will be taken from this edition of *The Works of Thomas Traherne*, ed. Jan Ross (Cambridge, 2013), vol. V, and will be cited in the text by century and meditation number.

of Traherne's individual is considered equidistant to 'ALL THINGS' in heaven and earth, and that this soul is able to absorb all objects in the search for higher meaning and felicity.[17] The vast majority of sections in the *Commentaries* conclude with a poem. In these poetical reflections, Traherne brings together items of information from the preceding commentary, contracts their meaning and draws a moral from his study. Occasionally he is conscious that his passion and ambition override this purpose for the concluding poem – as at the end of his section on the 'Atom', when he considers 'Whether it be not best leav out some of these Poems' (III, p. 363). For Traherne, poetry is both devotional, as it is for Herbert, and a more expansive means for study by, paradoxically, tightening his focus on a subject to draw evaluations from it. His poems ought to be reconsidered as works of philosophical poetry, in addition to examples of seventeenth-century Protestant lyric.[18]

Traherne has not been substantially considered alongside the great philosophical poet of his age, John Milton, since Louis Martz's seminal study from the 1960s, *The Paradise Within: Studies in Vaughan, Traherne and Milton*.[19] Further work on the two authors might now be possible – and indeed desirable – following the discovery in 1997 of a long poem by Traherne, *The Ceremonial Law*. Consisting of around 1800 lines in heroic couplets, the work is an unfinished typological poem based on events from Genesis and Exodus. As with the *Commentaries of Heaven*, evidence suggests that Traherne intended his work to be of a much greater length and to cover further ground; a note in another, seventeenth-century hand appears on an early leaf of the manuscript with the advice: 'I like this mightily but I pray prosecute it … I would you would goe thorow the whole Sacred Story' (Ross, VI, p. xxxii). Julia Smith and Laetitia Yeandle, the discoverer of the manuscript, claimed in their *TLS* article announcing the find that *The Ceremonial Law* is, 'unlike the *Commentaries of Heaven*

---

[17] For more on this absorbent power of Traherne's soul, see Phoebe Dickerson, '"The Lanthorns Sides": Skin, Soul and the Poetry of Thomas Traherne' in this volume.

[18] On this note, allusions to Lucretius in the metaphors of Traherne's 'Atom' poems suggest that he had read *De Rerum Natura* – see Gorman's chapter in this volume, p. 77. Barbara Lewalski discussed Traherne in *Protestant Poetics and the Seventeenth-Century Religious Lyric*, but undervalued the richness of his verse: she argued that Traherne's poetry was less successful than that of other religious lyricists of the century because 'his version of the Protestant aesthetic involved approaching language as a transparent medium pointing to essences rather than as a densely and complexly suggestive poetic matrix'. Barbara Kiefer Lewalski, *Protestant Poetics and the Seventeenth-Century Religious Lyric* (Princeton, 1979), p. 367.

[19] Louis L. Martz, *The Paradise Within: Studies in Vaughan, Traherne and Milton* (New Haven, 1964).

... not addressed to an elite audience'. The *Commentaries* requires its reader to cover the same scholarly ground, and make the same educated connections, as its author. While the objectives of his encyclopaedic work are intolerant of ignorance, Traherne's poem delivers its messages in ways that, as Smith and Yeandle remark, 'he could have intelligibly preached to his rural congregation at Credenhill in Herefordshire'.[20] As Warren Chernaik's essay in this volume will go on to suggest, *The Ceremonial Law* reveals another, social side to Traherne's poetical intentions. The typological subjects of his longer poem are displayed and interpreted for an entire Christian flock, an all-inclusive 'we', rather than solely for the poet's isolated meditative purposes. Traherne's rhyming couplets accumulate to develop a didactic tone, which becomes more emphatic in the sections of the poem that invite the reader to learn about God through shared, physical observation. (The section on 'Noahs Rainbow', for example, opens by explaining that God 'sends down Salvation from ye Skies' in response to the offering *up* of a 'Sacrifice'. Traherne's vocabulary here moreover stresses that the offering to God is a communal exercise: 'From Earth we offer up ...'; *Ceremonial Law*, p. 200, lines 2–3.) The *Ceremonial Law* therefore provides us with greater insight into a social, worldly consciousness within Traherne's theological practice that is all too often overlooked. Considering the revelations of its author's theology still further, the poem is also, as Carol Ann Johnston will argue in her contribution to this volume, suggestive of influences from radical Protestantism in Traherne's belief. He was of course educated at the puritanical stronghold of Brasenose College, Oxford, and there are striking parallels to be traced between the poem's typological images and certain signs and expressions associated with the more radical sectarian churches.

Like the news yearned for by the infant in 'On News' (*Centuries*, III.26), the new manuscripts serve to illuminate treasures that are already present by shedding light on the known works. The essays of this collection discuss all of the newly discovered works, but also include fresh criticism on nearly all of Traherne's most well-known writings, including the *Centuries*, *Christian Ethicks*, the Dobell poems and the Poems of Felicity, the *Select Meditations*, and the *Thanksgivings*. Following these preliminary words on Traherne's world and works, the remainder of this introduction will now shift focus to address more closely the critical reception of his writings, and the impact of the new discoveries upon the field of Traherne studies.

---

[20] Julia Smith and Laeticia Yeandle, '"Felicity disguised in fiery Words": Genesis and Exodus in a Newly Discovered Poem by Thomas Traherne', *TLS* (7 November 1997), 17.

'TO TELL THINGS AS THINGS WERE': THE HISTORICAL TURN

The appearance of this volume is timely: we are in the midst of what can be defined as a 'historical turn' in Traherne criticism, a growing critical consensus that supports a thorough re-evaluation of the man and his works in the light of his context. The contributions of this volume owe much to the legacy of this historical turn, but are founded upon a much longer critical history.

An initial wave of enthusiasm accompanied the identification and first publication of the Dobell poems and *Centuries* by Bertram Dobell in 1903 and 1908, after W. T. Brooke discovered the manuscripts in a book barrow in 1896–97.[21] Critics lauded Traherne primarily as a new, undiscovered or rediscovered poet, and he would soon be classified as a metaphysical writer alongside George Herbert, John Donne, Henry Vaughan and Richard Crashaw.[22] He also quickly became identified as a mystic, and was co-opted into a broader genealogy of English mysticism.[23] It was not until later that he would be classed among the Anglican latitudinarian divines, and his distinctively Anglican identity would be explored.[24] Established as both a mystic and a metaphysical, Traherne was easily divorced from his time.[25] Those who situated him within a long mystical tradition often considered the contemporary influences on his thought to be negligible.[26] Those who praised him for his unique perspective saw Traherne as a poet of retreat

---

[21]   *The Poetical Works of Thomas Traherne, B.D., 1636?–1674: Now First Published from the Original Manuscripts*, ed. Bertram Dobell (London, 1903); *Centuries of Meditations: Now First Printed from the Author's Manuscript*, ed. Bertram Dobell (London, 1908).

[22]   See, for example, Bertram Dobell, 'An Unknown Seventeenth-Century Poet', *Athenaeum* 3780, 3781 (7, 14 April 1900), 433–5, at 466; Anon., 'A Rediscovered Poet', *The Academy* 64 (1903), 359–60; Anon. 'A Newly-Discovered Poet', *TLS* (27 March 1903), 94–5; Anon., 'A New, Old Poet', *Harper's Weekly* (3 November 1906), 1559; W. D. Maclintock, 'A Re-Discovered Poet', *The Dial* 34 (16 June 1903), 395–8. The first major study of Traherne as a metaphysical poet was by J. B. Leishman, *The Metaphysical Poets: Donne, Herbert, Vaughan, Traherne* (Oxford, 1934); this was swiftly followed by Helen C. White, *The Metaphysical Poets: A Study in Religious Experience* (New York, 1936).

[23]   See Louise Collier Willcox, 'A Joyous Mystic', *The North American Review* 193.667 (1911), 893–904; W. K. Fleming, *Mysticism in Christianity* (London, 1913), pp. 178–93; Walter Lock, 'An English Mystic', *Constructive Quarterly* 1 (1913), 826–36; Caroline F. E. Spurgeon, *Mysticism in English Literature* (Cambridge, 1913), pp. 72–80; Elbert N. S. Thompson, 'Mysticism in Seventeenth-Century English Literature', *Studies in Philology* 18.2 (1921), 170–231.

[24]   See, for example, William J. Wolf, 'The Spirituality of Thomas Traherne', in *Anglican Spirituality*, ed. William J. Wolf (Wilton, CT, 1982), pp. 49–68.

[25]   For a study that combines both, see Itrat-Husain, *The Mystical Element in the Metaphysical Poets of the Seventeenth Century* (Edinburgh, 1948).

[26]   For example, Elbert N. S. Thompson compares Traherne with the Romantics and

from the world, not concerned with poetic conventions or contemporary philosophical debates.[27]

Despite such timeless evaluations of his thought, there was a strong interest in Traherne's biography, although its sources were patchy at best. This gave rise to one attempt at a major study of his life, and several narrower investigations into his career and movements.[28] By the 1960s attention was paid to more detailed source criticism, which aimed to locate Traherne more precisely within the movements of metaphysical poetry, Christian Platonism and latitudinarian devotion.[29]

It was on this basis that scholarship from the 1980s onwards was able to turn and situate Traherne more clearly within his various contemporary philosophical, religious, political, social and cultural contexts.[30] These included re-evaluating Traherne in relation to contemporary religious movements, or placing him within the political and religious context of Restoration England, exploring the nature and extent of his royalism and his devotion to the national church.[31] More recent studies

---

situates him within a broad tradition of mystical Platonism, 'The Philosophy of Thomas Traherne', *Philological Quarterly* (1929), 97–112.

[27] Arthur Quiller-Couch, *Felicities of Thomas Traherne* (London, 1934), pp. viii–xxviii.

[28] Gladys Irene Wade, *Thomas Traherne: A Critical Biography* (Princeton, 1944); Angela Russell, 'The Life of Thomas Traherne', *Review of English Studies* 6.21 (1955), 34–43; Richard Lynn Sauls, 'Traherne's Hand in the Credenhill Records', *The Library* 24 (1969), 50; see also the introduction to *Thomas Traherne: Centuries, Poems, and Thanksgivings*, ed. H. M. Margoliouth, 2 vols (Oxford, 1958), vol. I.

[29] See, for example, Gertrude Roberts Sherer, 'More and Traherne', *Modern Language Notes* 34.1 (1919), 49–50; Frances L. Colby, 'Thomas Traherne and Henry More', *Modern Language Notes* 62 (1947), 490–2; Carol L. Marks, 'Thomas Traherne and Hermes Trismegistus', *Renaissance News* 19.2 (1966), 118–31; George Robert Guffey, *Traherne and the Seventeenth-Century English Platonists, 1900–1966*, Elizabethan Bibliographies, Supplements, No. 11 (London, 1969).

[30] See, for example, Graham Parry, *Seventeenth-Century Poetry: The Social Context* (London, 1985), pp. 116ff; Michael Ponsford, 'The Poetry of Thomas Traherne in Relation to the Thought and Poetics of the Period', Ph.D. thesis, University of Newcastle upon Tyne (1983); Janice C. B. Ross, 'The Placing of Thomas Traherne: A Study of the Several Seventeenth-Century Contexts of his Thought and Style', Ph.D. thesis, University of Cambridge (1983).

[31] See, for example, Nabil Matar, 'A Note on Thomas Traherne and the Quakers', *Notes and Queries* 226 (1981), 46–7; consider an earlier, although less compelling, comparison between Traherne and another contemporary expression of radical religion, Ernst Lehrs, *Der Rosenkreuzerische Impuls im Leben und Werk von Joachim Jundius und Thomas Traherne* (Stuttgart, 1962); Julia J. Smith, 'Attitudes towards Conformity and Nonconformity in Thomas Traherne', *Bunyan Studies* 1.1 (Autumn 1988), 26–35; Julia J. Smith, 'Thomas Traherne and the Restoration', *The Seventeenth Century* 3.2 (1988), 203–22; Nabil Matar, 'The Anglican Eschatology of Thomas Traherne', *Anglican*

have expanded their gaze to include various other contemporary intellectual influences upon his thought: Baconian experimentalism, atomism, Christian humanism, religious polemic, scholastic Aristotelianism and Pythagoreanism.[32] This expanding interpretive framework provides a broad foundation upon which to reassess Traherne in the light of the recently discovered manuscripts.

In his seminal *Defense of Poesy* (1595), Philip Sidney followed Aristotle in distinguishing between history, which deals with particularities and is tied to events as they happened, and philosophy, which deals with universal principles and expresses itself in abstract precepts. For Sidney, poetry unites and surpasses these two forms of learning because it is both connected to the material world without being shackled to it, and is concerned with universal truths without withdrawing into flights of fancy. Poetic interpretations of Traherne arguably prevent the historical turn from becoming a thin account of 'things as things were.'[33] The contributions to this volume pay attention to his use of language and find new avenues of interpretation into Traherne and his context through investigations of his poetics.[34] The historical turn does not exclude philosophical or poetic investigations into Traherne's thought, but provides a firmer basis for their conclusions.

Combined with the historical turn, the discovery of new manuscripts has created further opportunities for revisiting – and challenging – longstanding themes in Traherne studies. As a precursor to outlining the volume's objectives and structure, the following sections comment on recent and enduring critical trends in Traherne scholarship, both literary

---

Theological Review 74.3 (Summer 1992), 289–303; Nabil Matar, 'The Political Views of Thomas Traherne', *Huntingdon Library Quarterly* 57.3 (Summer 1994), 241–53.

[32] Examples include: J. J. Balakier, 'Thomas Traherne's Dobell Series and the Baconian Model of Experience', *English Studies* 70 (1989), 233–47; Stephen Clucas, 'Poetic Atomism in Seventeenth-Century England: Henry More, Thomas Traherne and "Scientific Imagination"', *Renaissance Studies* 5 (1991), 327–40; John Spencer Hill, *Infinity, Faith and Time: Christian Humanism and Renaissance Literature*, McGill-Queen's Studies in the History of Religion (Montreal and Kingston, 1997), pp. 40–66; Susan E. Jones, 'Fighting Words: Clashes of Discourse in Three Seventeenth-Century Anglican Writers: Henry Vaughan, Jeremy Taylor, and Thomas Traherne', Ph.D. thesis, University of Florida (1997); Paul Cefalu, 'Thomistic Metaphysics and Ethics in the Poetry and Prose of Thomas Traherne', *Literature and Theology* 16.3 (September 2002), 248–69; Jacob Blevins, 'Finding Felicity through the "Pythagorean Eye": Pythagoreanism in the Work of Thomas Traherne', *Classical and Modern Literature* 25.1 (2005), 41–51.

[33] Philip Sidney, *The Defense of Poesy* (London, 1595), sig. D3v.

[34] See especially the chapters by Dickerson and Kershaw. For a previous study of Traherne's poetic language, see Kenneth John Ames, *The Religious Language of Thomas Traherne's Centuries* (New York, 1978).

and theological, in relation to key overlapping themes that recur within and between the chapters of this volume: the relationship between spirit and matter; the concept of infinity, borders and boundaries; and the pursuit of happiness and holiness. These are not only central subjects for Traherne, but also important issues in the broader context of seventeenth-century thought.[35]

'THAT LITLE WORLD WITHIN IT SELF': SPIRIT AND MATTER

Traherne's concern with the spiritual world has naturally been a key subject among mystical interpretations of his thought. Whether interpreted through a universal mystical framework or a particular one, Traherne has been frequently and influentially abstracted from his historical context. Some studies have identified Traherne with a universal mystical impulse that stems from standard structures of psychological development, and so have compared him with sources as various as Zen Buddhism and Vedic poetics.[36] Earlier studies that situated Traherne within a peculiarly English tradition of Christian mysticism also tended to look elsewhere for their evaluative frameworks.[37] Keith Salter influentially found him wanting according to Evelyn Underhill's mystical categories, which are modelled on high medieval mysticism.[38] He traced Traherne's spiritual progress through the five hierarchical stages of spiritual awakening, purification, illumination, annihilation of the self and mystical consummation with the divine. He concluded that Traherne only reached the stage of illumination, stopping short of St John of the Cross's dark night of the soul in which the ego is erased, and of the final and absolute unity with the divine.[39] Later literary studies retreated from such attempts to classify the mystical

---

[35] See, for example, *The Cambridge History of Seventeenth-Century Philosophy*, ed. Daniel Garber and Michael Ayers (Cambridge, 1998), chapters 8, 18, 19, 23, 24 and 36.

[36] See, for example, David Golz, 'Thomas Traherne and the Zen Poet of "On Believing in Mind"', *Studia Mystica* 13.1 (1990), 56–66; James J. Balakier, 'Thomas Traherne's "Thoughts" Poems and the Four Levels of Speech in Vedic Poetics', *Consciousness, Literature and the Arts* 7.3 (December 2006). See also Franz K. Wöhrer, *Thomas Traherne: The Growth of a Mystic's Mind. A Study of the Evolution and the Phenomenology of Traherne's Mystical Consciousness* (Salzburg, 1982), pp. 99–135; Robert Ellrodt, *Seven Metaphysical Poets: A Structural Study of the Unchanging Self* (Oxford, 2000), pp. 91–8.

[37] See, for example, Percy Osmond, *The Mystical Poets of the English Church* (New York, 1919), pp. 195–249; cf. Rufus M. Jones, *Spiritual Reformers in the Sixteenth and Seventeenth Centuries* (London, 1914), who places Traherne within a more immediate context of radical spirituality.

[38] Evelyn Underhill, *The Mystics of the Church* (London, 1925).

[39] Keith William Salter, *Thomas Traherne. Mystic and Poet* (London, 1964), pp. 43–6.

psychology of his works and focused on the mystical imagery of his poetry, reading his depictions of spiritual experience as little more than poetic licence.[40]

Consideration of spirit naturally leads on to questions about Traherne's attitude towards the material world. His reverence for the material world in general and the human body in particular has long been recognised. Early criticism saw a praise of nature as one of the major themes of his poetry of felicity, alongside his devotion to childhood. Many of these early readings, coloured by anticipation of the emerging secular Enlightenment, saw Traherne as a pantheistic nature-mystic.[41] These interpretations evolved into Henry McAdoo's attempt to reclaim the Christian theological foundations of Traherne's naturalism as a 'mysticism through nature' rather than a 'nature-mysticism'.[42] More recently, they have culminated in ecological or 'green' readings of the world as 'gift' in his theological philosophy.[43]

The relationship between Traherne's preoccupation with spirit and his praise of matter can only be addressed by a thorough understanding of his intellectual context and his interpretation of his sources. The influence of Christian Neoplatonism on Traherne is clear, through the works of Cambridge and Oxford Platonists such as Thomas Jackson and Theophilus Gale. However the nature of his response to its legacy of metaphysical dualism has been long contested. Platonist and Augustinian readings of Traherne see in him a mystical ascent into the divine, away from the material world.[44] Investigations of his Anglican spirituality, by contrast, emphasise his cataphaticism or incarnational sacramentalism, which affirms the value of mundane or worldly things against the flight into pure spirit of the *via negativa*.[45] Following the latter interpretations,

---

[40] Clements, *Mystical Poetry*; Alison J. Sherrington, *Mystical Symbolism in the Poetry of Thomas Traherne* (St Lucia, Queensland, 1970).

[41] See, for example, Leishman, *Metaphysical Poets*, p. 197.

[42] Henry R. McAdoo, *The Spirit of Anglicanism: A Survey of Anglican Theological Method in the Seventeenth Century* (London, 1965), p. 116.

[43] Robert N. Watson, *Back to Nature: The Green and the Real in the Late Renaissance* (Philadelphia, 2006), pp. 297–323.

[44] Sarah Hutton, 'Platonism in Some Metaphysical Poets: Marvell, Vaughan and Traherne', in *Platonism and the English Imagination*, ed. Anna Baldwin and Sarah Hutton (Cambridge, 1994), pp. 163–77, at p. 169; cf. Donald Allchin, *Participation in God: A Forgotten Strand in Anglican Tradition* (London, 1988), which identifies mystical ascent with the Anglican tradition.

[45] See A. M. Allchin, 'The Sacrifice of Praise and Thanksgiving', in *Profitable Wonders: Aspects of Thomas Traherne*, ed. A. M. Allchin, Anne Ridler and Julia Smith (Oxford, 1989), pp. 22–37.

recent literary criticism increasingly emphasises the non-dualist or sacramental aspects of his language, in the tradition of mystics such as Julian of Norwich and Meister Eckhart, or as rooted in a religious perspective that was increasingly menaced by the advance of secular empiricism.[46] Historicist studies find in Traherne's poetry a genuine interest in the 'new science' and an attempt to communicate scientific knowledge in a way that reveals humanity's underlying spiritual glory.[47] Turning to the influence of contemporary scholastic Aristotelianism and the anti-Hobbesian reaction, Kathryn Murphy does not see a preoccupation with the spiritual-intellectual world of 'thoughts' alone, but a realism that values 'All Things', in the words of the *Commentaries of Heaven*, through a concretisation of the abstract in 'nesses, tudes and tides'.[48] Inspired by the 'new science' and devoted to the world around him, Traherne used language to infuse matter with spiritual light.

Interpretation of the newly discovered manuscripts will further inform these debates. For example, Traherne's treatise on the soul, *Seeds of Eternity*, encapsulates the ambiguous relationship between matter and spirit. On the one hand 'the Body is but the Case of the Soul', but Traherne is also keen to 'repell that opinion as a vulgar Error, that maketh it the impediment and prison of the mind'. He views it instead 'as a glorious Instrument and Companion of the soul' (*Seeds*, p. 240). The body here is distinct from and inferior to spirit, but Traherne recognises the dangers of dualism embedded in this philosophical principle. The following paragraph goes further, elevating the body, which, because it contains all the elements that are within the world, is a 'litle World within it self, made to rule and possess the Greater' (p. 240). He then proceeds with an avowedly poetic, rather than scientific, description of the body. Leaving precision and accuracy to 'Chimists and Physicians' he describes the retina as the 'Curtain spread abroad to receive Ideas, and represent them to the mind' (p. 240). There is in this passage a symbiosis of body and spirit that underpins his attitude towards the material world.

The significance of matter in Traherne's thought takes on a more tangible

---

[46]   See James Charleton, *Non-Dualism in Eckhart, Julian of Norwich and Traherne* (London, 2012); Gary Kuchar, '"Organs of thy Praise": The Function and Rhetoric of the Body in Thomas Traherne', in *Religion in the Age of Reason: A Transatlantic Study of the Long Eighteenth Century*, ed. Kathryn Duncan (New York, 2009), pp. 59–81.

[47]   Jonathan Sawday, *The Body Emblazoned: Dissection and the Human Body in Renaissance Culture* (London, 1995), pp. 256–9.

[48]   Kathryn Murphy, '"Aves Quaedam Macedonicae": Misreading Aristotle in Francis Bacon, Robert Burton, Thomas Browne and Thomas Traherne', Ph.D. thesis, University of Oxford (2009); Kathryn Murphy, 'Thomas Traherne, Thomas Hobbes, and the Rhetoric of Realism', *The Seventeenth Century* 28.4 (2013), 419–39.

texture in the light of recent scholarly interest in material texts.[49] There is an increasing recognition of the importance of the construction and circulation of his texts during his lifetime.[50] Additions, crossings out and the use of amanuenses indicate the processes involved in creative production. Formatting suggests whether the text might have been prepared for publication or circulation. Gaps intimate the unfulfilled intentions of the writer. Annotations by external commentators reveal the reactions of the first intended readers.

The process through which thoughts were incarnated into words carries significance for an assessment of the man and his work. According to Finn Fordham, Traherne's editing of the *Commentaries* demonstrates a yearning for perfection even in the imperfect medium of material prose.[51] For Tanya Zhelezcheva, the unfinished works are not failures but a distinctive 'non-finito' genre that expresses the inconclusiveness of existence.[52] In some ways, the circumstances of the material texts have been integral to Traherne criticism from the start. The stories of Traherne's rediscovery carry such strong appeal, perhaps, because of the real danger in which the texts were placed. Found in a book barrow and rescued from a burning rubbish tip, with burn marks, missing pages and editorial amendments in other hands, the manuscripts themselves highlight the corporeal fragility of human creativity.

The contributions to this volume revisit themes of matter and spirit in the light of an in-depth reading of the recently published texts. Elizabeth Dodd and Ana Elena González-Treviño look at the spiritual life, exploring the public manifestations of private devotion. Cassandra Gorman and Phoebe Dickerson are concerned with bodies, among other material things, and address the paradoxical glory and shame of nakedness. As Dickerson argues, it is not the boundaries between spirit and matter with which Traherne is concerned, but the doors through which they communicate with each other. The unification of matter and spirit might be expressed through the Hermetic model of the soul as a human *hymenaus* between earth and heaven; the Chalcedonian

---

[49] Consider the work of the Centre for Material Texts, Cambridge University <http://www. english.cam.ac.uk/cmt/> [accessed January 2015]; or the material texts series of the University of Pennsylvania Press.

[50] See, for example, Tomohiko Koshi, 'The Rhetoric of Instruction, and Manuscript and Print Culture in the Devotional Works of Thomas Traherne', Ph.D. thesis, University of Reading (2004); Cedric C. Brown and Tomohiko Koshi, 'Editing the Remains of Thomas Traherne', *Review of English Studies*, 57.232 (November 2006), 766–82.

[51] Fordham, 'Motions of Writing', *Re-Reading Thomas Traherne*, ed. Blevins, pp. 115–134.

[52] Tanya Zhelezcheva, 'The Poetics of the Incomplete in the Works of Thomas Traherne (ca. 1638–1674)', Ph.D. thesis, Northeastern University (2011).

definition of Christ as a unity of divinity and humanity (which is applied equally to the human Adam); or the definition of atoms as 'Material Spirits' and emblems of the soul (*Seeds*, p. 238; *Commentaries*, II, pp. 22, 222; *Commentaries*, III, p. 351). Without denying the Platonic trajectory of spiritual ascent in, for example, *Select Meditations* I.90 (section xxxi) or *Inducements to Retirednes*, there is also an incarnational movement expressed in figures such as *The Kingdom of God*'s Celestial Stranger, discussed by Alison Kershaw, and the atom, discussed by Gorman. While the Celestial Stranger descends from heaven to earth in wonder at its glory, the atom, which originates in the sun, plunges into the 'mire' of material existence. These divergent trajectories meet in an incarnational theology and a material philosophy that attempts to encompass 'All Things'.

CENTRE EVERYWHERE AND CIRCUMFERENCE NOWHERE: INFINITY, BORDERS AND BOUNDARIES

The theme of infinity raises issues of cosmology, theology and politics, but is also intimately linked with Traherne's poetics. Its most obvious critical framework is the seventeenth-century cosmological transition from the medieval sphere of the heavens to the modern universe, which Alexander Koyré identified as a movement from an enclosed to a truly infinite world.[53] Marjorie Nicolson placed Traherne's understanding of circulation within this interpretive framework, and saw the effect of the infinite universe in a poetics insatiable for infinite expansion.[54] Rosalie Colie identified infinity as a moral as well as a philosophical concept, wherein the vocation to infinite goodness is actualised through desire, and sin presents a threat of infinite decline.[55] On the foundation of these studies, Traherne's predilection for infinity has often been identified with this modernising cosmological shift and this secularising intellectual transformation.[56]

---

[53] See Alexander Koyré, *From a Closed World to the Infinite Universe* (Baltimore, 1957).

[54] Marjorie Hope Nicolson, *The Breaking of the Circle: Studies in the Effect of the 'New Science' Upon Seventeenth Century Poetry* (Evanston, 1950), pp. 120, 173–9.

[55] Rosalie L. Colie, 'Thomas Traherne and the Infinite: The Ethical Compromise', *Huntingdon Library Quarterly* 21.1 (1957), 69–82.

[56] See, respectively, Matthew P. Akers, 'From the Hexameral to the Physico-Theological: A Study of Thomas Traherne's *Meditations on the Six Days of the Creation* and *The Kingdom of God* Focusing upon the Cosmological Controversy', Ph.D. thesis, Drew University, Madison, NJ (2008); Marie-Dominique Garnier, 'The Mythematics of Infinity in the *Poems* and *Centuries* of T. Traherne: A Study of its Thematic Archetypes', *Cahiers Élisabéthains* 28 (1985), 61–71.

Nevertheless, Traherne encompasses the modern universe within the medieval cosmos, retaining the Neo-Plotinian imagery of the infinite sphere whose centre is everywhere and circumference nowhere, and defining infinity as a divine attribute.[57] In the *Centuries* the infinite love of God is 'both ways infinit', at once in all eternity and in each moment, so that it may fill the soul which is 'an Infinit Sphere in a Centre' (II.80). In *The Kingdom of God* the soul is modelled on God's infinity. The 'Circuit of Heaven' or the infinity of God's Kingdom is seen through the infinite glory and belovedness of humanity: 'And of This Circle does the sphere of felicitie Consist' (p. 279). Traherne's concern in this treatise is with the indivisible and expansive infinity of goodness. This is seen in the soul, which is 'a living Sphere of Infinit Blessedness', and in its holy freedom: 'It is only Sin that Crumples up the Soul, which were it freely Spread abroad, would be as Wide and as large as the Univers' (pp. 276, 305). Through the lens of the cosmic sphere Traherne contains the modern 'infinitization of the universe' within the realm of devotion.[58]

Traherne's appeal to infinity also echoes the boundless devotion of patristic ascetics. The excessive style of his poetic language has been interpreted as a form of *epektasis*, modelled on Gregory of Nyssa's theology of praise in which the overflowing soul is drawn through infinite expansion into the divine.[59] This is made possible through the transgressive voice of poetry, whose creative imagination enables a new vision of the world.[60] Traherne's poetics leads from time into eternity, just as the *Centuries* move the reader from the sensory experience of numbered meditations to pure contemplation of the infinite, as Susan Stewart attests.[61] This poetic impulse expresses the 'virtue' of covetousness or avarice, whereby the soul sinlessly yearns for the infinite glory for which it was created. The poem for 'Avarice' describes this desire:

> Hydropick Nature thirsteth after all,
> And still retains its Primitive Desire.
> Altho it erres and deviates since the Fall,
> Tis mindful of its End; and doth aspire

---

[57] See Don Parry Norford, 'Microcosm and Macrocosm in Seventeenth-Century Literature', *Journal of the History of Ideas* 38.3 (1977), 409–28.

[58] Koyré, *Infinite Universe*, p. 2.

[59] David Ford, *Christian Wisdom: Desiring God and Learning in Love* (Cambridge, 2007), pp. 235–7.

[60] See Ames, *Religious Language*, p. 56; John Stewart Allitt, *Thomas Traherne: Il Poeta-Teologo della Meraviglia e della Felicità* (Milan, 2007); Stanley S. Stewart, *The Expanded Voice: The Art of Thomas Traherne* (San Marino, 1970), pp. 170–213.

[61] Stewart, *Poetry and the Fate of the Senses*, pp. 227–42.

Unto that one vast Object of Delight
Which Satisfies in being Infinite. (*Commentaries*, III, p. 411)

In this poem the transgressive nature of desire is redefined according to its pure and primitive origins, which properly thirst after what is true and infinite.

For John Spencer Hill, Traherne's infinity signifies freedom or capacity. It is part of a high Christian humanist anthropology and a 'symbol of the breathtaking possibilities open to man's [*sic*] spirit'.[62] Infinity as freedom inevitably evokes a consideration of its opposite, of borders and boundaries. Traherne's childhood dislike for the 'hedges, ditches, limits, bounds' of private property has been interpreted as a primitivist reflection of contemporary radical egalitarianism, modelled by Levellers and Quakers[63] ('Wonder', VI, p. 6, 56–72). The intuition that property justly belongs to all is linked to the radical virtue of covetousness, 'implanted in us that we might desire Treasure and rejoyce in it' (*Sober View*, p. 62). Jacob Blevins views this intuition as a betrayal of the infinite, as it accepts the boundaries of finitude by attempting to articulate the sublime through the conventional language of ownership.[64] By contrast, Diane Kelsey McColley agrees with Hill, seeing not a covetous desire but a principle of 'non-ownership' that is part of Traherne's love of the natural world. She therefore concludes that he 'allies himself to the generative earth by urging enjoyment of nature's riches without possession'.[65] In this volume, Carol Ann Johnston provides an interesting contribution to these debates, as she asserts that the language of infinite freedom in *The Ceremonial Law* reveals a radical notion of human agency. This interpretation defines the soul in terms of activity rather than capacity, and finds a way to overstep the boundaries of finitude through the notion of infinite freedom.

Elsewhere in this volume, infinity takes different forms. It adopts a Christological shape in Kershaw's discussion of the infinite sphere in the context of the new science, as the comprehensive cosmic Christ who fills all things after the manner of Ephesians 1.23. Both Warren Chernaik and Johnston explore the linguistic construction of an eternal present in *The Ceremonial Law*; Johnston through the repetitive mode of typology, which creates a synchronicity of space and time, and Chernaik through

[62] Hill, *Infinity, Faith and Time*, pp. 41, 47.

[63] Christopher Hill, *The English Bible and the Seventeenth-Century Revolution* (London, 1993), pp. 134–5, 202–3.

[64] Jacob Blevins, 'Infinity is Thine: Proprietorship and the Transcendental Sublime in Traherne and Emerson', *ANQ* 25.3 (2012), 186–9.

[65] Diane Kelsey McColley, *Poetry and Ecology in the Age of Milton and Marvell* (Aldershot, 2007), pp. 55–6.

the dissolution of boundaries between first, second and third persons.[66] Dickerson is concerned with the spirit's transgressive nature, in which 'The material limits of things give them *access to* (they are 'the only way to') 'a real infinity' (pp. 39–40). Dodd shows how the notion of innocence transgresses the boundaries placed upon it by later criticism. The atom is also an expansive object, which despite its penetrative capacity has inner integrity. According to Gorman it is 'a contraction of eternity – a minute space in which the divine is lodged though not contained' (p. 83). These various modes of infinity form part of the rich tapestry of Traherne's work, in which overlapping thoughts combine in kaleidoscopic forms to provide a source for a multitude of interpretations.

'HIM, THAT STUDIETH HAPPINESS': HAPPINESS AND HOLINESS

Of all of Traherne's concerns, felicity has perhaps the best claim to be the most central. Since the printing of the *Poems of Felicity* in 1910, originally prepared for publication by Traherne's brother Philip, felicity has frequently been named as 'a' if not 'the' core theme in his thought.[67] His focus on felicity has commonly been identified with his enjoyment of the material and spiritual world.[68] This is attached to a predilection for praise and thanksgiving that has been attributed to a psychological or mystical optimism often viewed in pejorative terms, as evidence of a shallow 'deistic sentimentalism'.[69] Evidence of a joyful perspective on existence is found in poems such as 'The Rapture', which portrays happiness not as a

---

[66] Compare Richard Douglas Jordan's concept of 'eternity-time' in *The Temple of Eternity*, pp. 12–30.

[67] Thomas Traherne, *Poems of Felicity* (London, British Library, MS. Burney 392); first published as *Poems of Felicity*, ed. H. Bell (London, 1910). All further references to and quotations from the *Poems of Felicity* will be taken from *The Works of Thomas Traherne*, ed. Jan Ross (Cambridge, 2014), vol. VI, and cited in the text by page and line number. On felicity, see Thomas O. Beachcroft, 'Traherne and the Doctrine of Felicity', *Criterion* 9 (January 1930), 291–307; Renée Grandvoinet, 'Thomas Traherne and the Doctrine of Felicity', *Études de Lettres* 13 (1939), 164–77; Willis Barnstone, 'Two Poets of Felicity: Thomas Traherne and Jorge Guillén', *Books Abroad* 42.1 (Winter 1968), 14–19; Barry Spurr, 'Felicity Incarnate: Rediscovering Thomas Traherne', *Discovering and (Re)covering the Seventeenth Century Religious Lyric*, ed. Eugene R. Cunnar and Jeffrey Johnson (Pittsburgh, PA, 2001), pp. 273–89.

[68] See, e.g. Justin Miller, 'Love and Pain in the Poet of Felicity', *Historical Magazine of the Protestant Episcopal Church* 49.3 (September 1980), 209–20; Margaret Willy, 'Thomas Traherne: "Felicity's Perfect Lover"', *English* 12 (Autumn 1959), 210–15, at 213.2–215.1.

[69] Douglas Bush, *English Literature in the Earlier Seventeenth Century*, 2nd edn revised (Oxford, 1962), pp. 156–8; see also Francis Towers, 'Thomas Traherne: His Outlook on Life', *The Nineteenth Century and After* 87 (1920), 1024–30.

philosophical ideal but an embodied experience expressed through the rhetorical devices of short exclamations and insistent questions:

> O Heavenly Joy!
> O Great and Sacred Blessedness
> Which I possess!
> So great a Joy
> Who did into my Armes convey! (Ross, VI, p. 16, 8–12)

Traherne's joyful outlook has also been identified with a high theological anthropology that follows Pelagius rather than Augustine, emphasising humanity's glory and capacity for goodness in continuity with humanism and Cambridge Platonism.[70] This aspect of Traherne's thought is easily associated with a modernising trend and thereby abstracted from its time.[71] In the most recent substantial interpretation of Traherne's felicity there is an apparent tension between assessing the contemporary sources for Traherne's experience and identifying the universal psychological processes in which it participates. J. J. Balakier sees Traherne's felicity as influenced by models of Baconian experimentalism, but also defines it according to modern neuroscientific categories as a 'state of advanced cognitive development'; a fourth mode of consciousness or visionary state of awareness.[72]

Interpreting the pursuit of felicity as the *summum bonum* or the good that is the consummation of existence highlights Traherne's eschatological perspective. It privileges the yearning for a happy future state that is found in his evocative depictions of paradise and Eden.[73] Straightforward scholastic readings of this theme have been joined by more imaginative comparisons with contemporary psychology and philosophy.[74] Source criticism has traced Traherne's vision of felicity not only to Aristotle, but also to a Neoplatonist notion of *eudaimonia* as perfection and to an

---

[70] See, for example, Michael Ponsford, 'Traherne's Apostasy', *Durham University Journal* 76 (1984), 177–85.

[71] For example, Ronald E. McFarland looks forward through Traherne to the Enlightenment in 'Thomas Traherne's Thanksgivings and the Theology of Optimism', *Enlightenment Essays* 4.1 (1973), 3–14, at 3.

[72] J. J. Balakier, *Thomas Traherne and the Felicities of the Mind* (Amherst, 2010), pp. ix–xi, 105.

[73] On felicity as the desired end in Renaissance Christian epics, see J. Steadman, 'Felicity and End in Renaissance Epic and Ethics', *Journal of the History of Ideas* 23.1 (1962), 117–32.

[74] Compare Paul Cefalu, 'Thomistic Metaphysics'; James Skeen, 'Discovering Human Happiness: Choice Theory Psychology, Aristotelian Contemplation, and Traherne's Felicity', *Quodlibet Journal* 5.2-3 (2003) <http://www.quodlibet.net/articles/skeen-choice.html> [accessed January 2012].

Augustinian notion of *beatitudo* or enjoyment of the world.[75] Martz looks to Bonaventure as well as to Augustine for Traherne's model of felicity as a restoration of the 'paradise within'.[76] Felicity is also pursued in the anticipated consummation of desire, expressed in conceits that echo the eroticism of medieval mysticism, such as the Amazon Queen wooed by God in the final chapter of *The Kingdom of God* (pp. 502–3). Chernaik highlights the appearance of this latter theme in *The Ceremonial Law*, where the desire for the absent paradise is part of the journey to felicity through the wilderness.[77]

What prevents Traherne's felicitous perspective from being purely future-oriented, and what ties it to his context, is its partnership with holiness. As Inge has argued, he was not a 'mystical hedonist', but happiness and holiness are inseparable for Traherne.[78] So in the *Centuries* felicity is attained through virtuous living; the wise man 'generaly held, that Whosoever would enjoy the Happiness of Paradice must put on the Charity of Paradice. And that Nothing was his Felicity but his Duty' (IV.22). *Inducements to Retirednes* similarly intimates a realised eschatology wherein the bliss of heaven is possible on earth through retirement from evil: 'Retirement is therfore Necessary to him, that Studieth Happiness, becaus it is the Gate that leadeth therunto [to the life of angels here on earth].' This process links felicity with infinity as it continues: 'For in Retirement alone can a Man approach to that which is Infinit and Eternal. Infinity and Eternity are only to bee seen by the Inward Ey' (p. 5). This passage supports interpretations that link felicity with contemplation or a state of mind, but also interpretations of felicity as a devotional or mystical way.[79]

In this volume, González-Treviño explores the nature of Traherne's

---

[75] See Verena Olejniczak Lobsien, 'Felicity: Thomas Traherne's Art of Life', *Transparency and Dissimulation: Configurations of Neoplatonism in Early Modern English Literature* (Berlin, 2010), pp. 156–84; see also, R. G. Howarth, '"Felicity" in Traherne', *Notes and Queries* 193 (1948), 249–50, who argues that Traherne writes more from the Latin tradition of 'blessedness' than the Aristotelian tradition of 'felicity'.

[76] Martz, *Paradise Within*, p. 39.

[77] On this theme, see also Belden C. Lane, 'Thomas Traherne and the Awakening of Want', *Anglican Theological Review* 81.4 (Autumn 1999), 651–64; Inge, *Wanting Like a God*.

[78] Denise Inge, *Happiness and Holiness: Thomas Traherne and His Writings* (Norwich, 2008); Anthony Low, 'Thomas Traherne: Mystical Hedonist', *Love's Architecture: Devotional Modes in Seventeenth-Century English Poetry* (New York, 1978), pp. 259–93.

[79] E.g. J. J. Balakier, 'Thomas Traherne's Concept of Felicity, the "Highest Bliss," and the Higher States of Consciousness of Maharishi Mahesh Yogi's Vedic Science and Technology', *Modern Science and Vedic Science* 4.2 (1991), 137–75; M. V. Seetaraman, 'The Way of Felicity in Thomas Traherne's "Centuries" and "The Poems"', in *Critical Essays on English Literature*, ed. V. S. Seturaman (Bombay, 1965), pp. 81–104.

pursuit of felicity on earth and its link with moral education, specifically through the idea of 'studying felicity' against the background of early modern happiness 'guidebooks'. She places felicity in a didactic and an ethical frame, as an aspect of spiritual life and development as well as the final goal of perfection. This interpretation is entirely suitable for a theologian who in his *Christian Ethicks* chose to treat only of virtue and nothing of vice, fixing his gaze on what would conduce to felicity in this life (see *Ethicks*, p. 207). Dodd similarly places happiness in the context of holiness, by discussing innocence through contemporary devotional culture as a feature of the holy life and a means to felicity on earth. The other contributions to this volume also demonstrate sensitivity to Traherne's devotional and religious contexts. Chernaik and Johnston acknowledge the formative influence of contemporary devotion upon his thought, while Gorman, Murphy and Kershaw recognise the integral place of theology within his philosophies of matter and spirit. These contributions uncover the happy fusion of philosophy, theology and ethics that characterises much of the work of this eclectic intellectual, poet and priest, 'a Philosopher a Christian and a Divine' (IV.3).

THOMAS TRAHERNE AND SEVENTEENTH-CENTURY THOUGHT

This volume aims to reignite discussion on settled readings of Traherne's work, to reconsider issues in Traherne studies that have long lain dormant and to supplement our picture of the man and his writings through new discoveries and insights. The collection is organised into two sections. Each of the essays in Part I, 'Philosophies of Matter and Spirit', reconsiders Traherne's notions of spirit and matter, and the borders between them, in the light of his response to contemporary intellectual contexts. Phoebe Dickerson opens the collection with a reinvestigation of Traherne's idea of the soul from the perspective of his references to skin and surfaces. In relation to the theories laid out by Jean-Luc Nancy in his essay 'The Soul', she rethinks the vitality of physical borders in Traherne's work. She argues that while other devotional poets of the period (notably Crashaw, Herbert and Vaughan) call for empathy with the vulnerability of Christ's skin, torn and rent asunder, Traherne pays closer attention to his own skin – not in disparagement of vanity or the sins of the flesh, but as the site at which his lyric voice articulates experience of self and soul. The skin offers security, not imprisonment, and she sees in Traherne's account of its activity a way of constituting the soul *as* experience: a means to enfold a universe of potential, in and beyond the limits of the body.

The following three chapters offer varying assessments of Traherne's attitudes towards the material world. Kathryn Murphy complicates critical readings of Traherne's Aristotelianism by revealing his response to contemporary experimental science and the influence of Francis Bacon upon his study of nature. In her essay she examines the 'thinginess' of Traherne's writings, arguing that his repetitive and enumerative attention to 'things' is a deliberate strategy for working through a concern with ontology: what is real, and what constitutes a thing? Murphy traces Traherne's response to Aristotle's *Categories* and Bacon's *De augmentis*, and shows how he follows Bacon in drawing attention away from things conceived as substances, to accidents – the passing states of the substance – conceived as things. According to Traherne's metaphysics, accidents assume a higher level of reality than 'naked' substances. Although an accident can only be considered a 'thing' in the mind, Murphy shows how Traherne moves on from Bacon to posit the reality of things in thoughts over objects in the world.

Cassandra Gorman also looks at the impact of seventeenth-century natural philosophy upon Traherne, examining his interpretation of atomism within the context of spiritual accommodation. She argues that Traherne expands upon the common theological reception of seventeenth-century atomism – which dwelt, more or less, on atoms as examples of mortal frailty and corporeal worthlessness – to create a means for the obtainment of 'Felicitie' and grace. As an entity, he claims a single atom encompasses the span of 'ALL THINGS'. Gorman shows that this 'Atom' is more than a distanced literary symbol for the recognition of human frailty, or the greatness of God; it comes to function as a model for the 'insatiable' Christian soul, which in Traherne's theology is ever seeking to explore 'All in All'. By reconciling ourselves to the atom, Traherne claims, we come to know our soul.

Lastly, Alison Kershaw follows Murphy and Gorman by arguing that Traherne accommodates ancient theological principles – namely, the image of the incarnate Christ, often overlooked in interpretations of Traherne as a pantheistic nature mystic – in his response to the expanding cosmology of the 'new science'.[80] Traherne holds to a 'cosmic Christology', comparable to that of the twentieth-century theologian Teilhard de Chardin but part of a long Christian tradition, within the context of the new infinite world. Her chapter focuses on *The Kingdom of God*, delving into Traherne's diverse contemporary influences. It discusses in detail the trope of the Celestial Stranger in Chapter 25 as a way into Traherne's incarnational Christology. The new world is infused by the cosmic Christ,

---

[80] See Peter Kennedy Maitland, 'Thomas Traherne's Path to Felicity: The Missing Christ', M.A. thesis, Carleton University (1994).

who is the infinite sphere of hermetic philosophy. Christ subsists in the world not as an exterior judge but as an implicit presence, not only as the incarnate first-born of all creation, but as implicated in the world through the act of creation itself. This presence is not spiritual only, but a bodily and organic fullness.

Part II, 'Practical and Public Devotion', groups together essays that challenge long-standing assumptions about Traherne in the light of his participation in contemporary devotional culture. They investigate common notions of Traherne as an isolated and solipsistic nature-mystic, a conformist or loyal Anglican, and a lover of childhood. Responding to previous interpretations of Traherne as a meditative poet, Warren Chernaik reinterprets Traherne's devotion as both sociable and practical in his study of *The Ceremonial Law* – a recently published work that has been little read, and even less subjected to scholarly examination. Chernaik takes the reader on a chronological journey through this poem, exploring its poetic and thematic structures in comparison with Traherne's better-known works. Through Traherne's use of the pronouns 'I', 'we', 'they' and 'you', Chernaik explores the character of the poem by considering the communal construction of experience through poetry and the appro-priation of scriptural narrative and its didactic function. The porous boundaries between the personae reflect those between self, community and eternity, leading to a meditation on the nature of the church as both a visible and spiritual fellowship. This chapter highlights the tensions between Traherne's typological and narrative interpretations of scripture in this poem, concluding that his distinctive approach to the narrative and typology of scripture lies in the unbounded activity of the imaginative eye, which draws on all the resources of memory to recreate the experience of the Israelites in the individual believer.

Carol Ann Johnston's chapter also focuses on *The Ceremonial Law*, but brings to light another way of reading Traherne's typology. Drawing Traherne's most recently discovered work into comparison with the *Select Meditations* – and arguing the likelihood that these works were composed at a similar date – she challenges long-standing critical assumptions of the author's conservative Anglicanism. Johnston's close reading of *The Ceremonial Law* reveals hitherto unexplored evidence for Traherne's sympathies with radical Protestantism. She shows how the typological emphasis of the poem focuses on images and characters that were prominent in radical Protestant writings of the period, most notably the figure of Moses and the 'burning bush'. The newly discovered work opens up new possibilities for a political reading of Traherne: Johnston reveals an author who was experimenting with broad theological ideas between manuscripts, and who, in *The Ceremonial Law*, entertained typologies of radical sectarianism.

Ana Elena González-Treviño re-evaluates the central theme of happiness in Traherne's work, arguing that he locates the attainment of bliss in social engagement. For the writer of the *Poems of Felicity* and *Thanksgivings*, happiness is clearly a central theme. Traherne sought happiness through study, and set himself up as a tutor in felicity. So much is known already, but González-Treviño chooses to take Traherne at his word and to investigate the 'curriculum' for his study of felicity. She situates him within the contemporary trend for manuals or guidebooks to happiness, and sets him against Hobbesian scepticism. She addresses not only the well-known *Christian Ethicks*, *Select Meditations* and *Centuries of Meditations*, but also the less-read *Inducements to Retirednes* and *Commentaries of Heaven*. She discusses the pursuit of happiness as an aspect of holiness, and so as allied to meditation, but also explores the integral role of reason in the study of felicity, as rooted in faith and assurance. The writing of texts is shown to be an integral part of the pursuit of happiness, which is inherently communicative.

Finally, Elizabeth Dodd critiques the persistent tendency to interpret Traherne's idea of innocence in light of the child of Romantic literature, looking instead to the context of seventeenth-century devotion. Within the notion of 'innocency of life', drawn from Thomas Wilson's popular *Christian Dictionary*, Dodd explores different models of innocence that appear both in contemporary spiritual literature and in Traherne's works: scriptural, ethical, devotional and sacramental. She discusses *The Ceremonial Law* and the scriptural theme of innocent sacrifice in the Christological typology of the lamb, in relation to questions of sin and salvation. *Christian Ethicks* expresses the moral innocence of the Christian life as an activity of both preservation and pursuit that unites the inner and outer self. Similarly, *Inducements to Retirednes* reveals the differences between private and public innocence, and the *Church's Year-Book* demonstrates the incorporation of innocence into the language of public devotion. The cultic ritual connotations of washing one's hands in innocence, mentioned in *Inducements to Retirednes* and the *Thanksgivings*, connect innocence with worship and summarise the priestly duty to an innocent life. Finally, *A Sober View* provides a sacramental model of innocence that suggests the importance of baptism for, and the inherence of grace in, the innocence of the Christian life.

Together, these contributions show that interpreting Traherne as a man of his time does not close down the possibilities of interpretation but rather opens up new and exciting avenues for investigation. They demonstrate the importance of taking proper account of the impact of the more recently discovered manuscripts and of fully integrating them into our overall picture of Traherne. The breadth and novelty of discussion displayed here indicates that Traherne studies remain just as vibrant as they were in the wake of the very first manuscript discoveries and that there is still much more to explore.

I

PHILOSOPHIES OF MATTER AND SPIRIT

Chapter 1

'THE LANTHORNS SIDES': SKIN, SOUL AND THE POETRY OF THOMAS TRAHERNE

Phoebe Dickerson

In one of the many icons from Francis Quarles's popular didactic work of 1635, *Emblemes*, a small figure stands, clad in a belted smock, his hands clasped in prayer. His arms emerge, as if through the bars of a prison cell, from between the ribs of a skeleton, which in turn sits in cross-legged contemplation, propping its skull-head on an osseous hand. Beneath the image runs a motto taken from Romans 7.24: 'O wretched man that I am, who shall deliver me from the body of this death?'[1]

Where the soft-featured, monkish figure represents the soul, the emblem's extended epigram demands that this skeletal 'body of death' be read as a true likeness of man's living flesh:

> Behold thy darling, which thy lustfull care
> Pampers; for which thy restlesse thoughts prepare
> Such early cates: for whom thy bubbling brow
> So often sweats […]
> Behold thy darling, whom thy soul affects
> So dearly; whom thy fond indulgence decks
> And puppets up in soft, in silken weeds.[2]

The repeated invocation that the reader 'behold [his] darling' insists that he recognise the discrepancy between his besotted affections and the degraded object on which he is loading them: namely, his mortal frame. Where the icon conspicuously flays the body back to unrelenting bone, the

---

[1] Francis Quarles, 'Rom. VII. XXIV. O wretched man that I am! Who shall deliver me from the body of this death?', in *Emblemes Divine and Moral* (London, 1635), Book V, VIII, p. 273.

[2] Ibid., lines 1–4, 9–11.

31

infatuated reader and the soul (who stand as one interlocutor) cosset the body's edges, enveloping them in 'silken weeds'. In detailing this passion for the body, Quarles directs considerable attention to the very sensate superficies of which the icon has been stripped: the reader 'decks' and 'puppets' the body in 'soft', 'silken' weeds, while his own skin breaks a sweat in an agitation of affection so great that his brow 'bubbles'.

Quarles's emblem is typical of a prevalent early modern tendency to equate the outsides of things with deception and the distractions of worldly vanity: the emblem's pictorial excoriation of the body seeks to assert episte-mological control over the dangers of smooth skin and sensuous affections by reframing the body's tender and concupiscent composition as unfor-giving bars of bone, and reducing its rich tissues to thin air. In 'The Person', Thomas Traherne, writing in the latter half of the seventeenth century, similarly asserts the worthlessness of fine accoutrements: he renounces 'fals Ornaments' (Ross, VI, p. 40, 51) and 'Gilded Manicles' (p. 40, 60) and likewise recommends the 'taking [...] away' of 'Paint [...] Cloath [and] Crown' (p. 39, 16–17).[3] Unlike Quarles, however, whose purpose is to disabuse the reader of his body's worth, Traherne promises to 'Glorify' (p. 39, 16) the person, body and soul together. Treating dress and jewels as rhetorical figures, he writes that 'Naked Things [...] do best reveal [their worth],/ When we all Metaphores remove' (p. 39, 19, 25–6). In Traherne's hands, nakedness lends the body a stark dignity. He asks that the reader 'Survey the Skin, cut up the flesh, the Veins/ Unfold' (p. 40, 31–2) so that he might truly apprize God's gifts. In Traherne's hands, a true appraisal of the body's beauty calls for a penetrative imagining – an anatomical exami-nation – thereof, and yet, strikingly, the poem frames this very process as one that *clothes* the person:

> A Deep Vermilion on a Red,
> On that a Scarlet I will lay,
> [...]
> With Robes of Glory and Delight
> Ile make you Bright.
> Mistake me not, I do not mean to bring
> New Robes, but to Display the Thing. (p. 39, 8–9, 12–15)

The garb that Traherne's poem confers on the body – that he lays down in layered Red, Vermilion and Scarlet – is borne up from within that body: anatomy becomes a means of accommodating the person, clothing it outwardly in its own inward and sanguinary brightness. It is worth

---

[3] Unless otherwise stated, I will quote the Dobell manuscript variant when referring to the poems.

observing that Traherne does not command the 'cutting' of the skin: rather, he tells the reader to 'survey' it. The skin hovers, smooth to our regard, implicitly (if we pursue the episode to its logical conclusion) broken, but semantically left untouched and intact.

'The Person' is unusual among Traherne's own poems for its vivid attention to the corporeal. The poem assuredly communicates Traherne's desire – as expressed, also, in *Seeds of Eternity* – to 'repell that opinion as a vulgar Error, that maketh [the body] the impediment and prison of the mind', arguing instead that it is 'a glorious Instrument and Companion of the soul' (Ross, I, p. 240). And yet, in his poetry, this notion does not correspond to rich evocations of the corporeal body: Traherne's concern is more the unrestrictedness of the soul than the body as 'glorious instrument'. In 'My Spirit', he recalls an infant state of feeling 'no Dross nor Matter in [his] Soul,/ No Brims nor Borders, such as in a Bowl/ We see' (p. 26, 8–9): such scope of spiritual experience knows neither impediment nor prison and, in the process, dissolves material boundaries, overstepping limits.

When John Donne addresses his own soul in 'The Second Anniversarie', he accuses it of being infected and locked in by the body: he considers death a release, writing:

> Thinke thy sheel broke, thinke thy Soule hatch'd but now.
> And thinke this slow-pac'd soule, which late did cleave
> To'a body, and went but by the bodies leave,
> Twenty, perchance, or thirty mile a day,
> Dispatches in a minute all the way
> Twixt heaven, and earth.[4]

By Donne's account, the body dictates and defines the exploits of the soul. This is not the case in Traherne's poetry, where the soul (or the mind) is able to take such journeys unhindered: thoughts 'even in the Brest,/ Rove ore the World with Libertie' ('Thoughts. I', p. 64, 71–2). The narrow scope of man's breast cannot determine the reach of the soul's activity.

One might infer that Traherne's soul – in its ideal mode – does not know the body: in 'The Preparative', which describes an original state of unmediated spirituality, he writes, 'Then was my Soul my only All to me' (p. 11, 13). He talks of being 'Unbodied and Devoid of Care' (p. 12, 41). And yet, this claim to being without a body complicates the state of being that Traherne sets out in the first verse of this poem:

---

[4] John Donne, 'The Second Anniversarie', in *The First Anniversarie An Anatomie of the World* (London, 1612), p. 47.

My Body being Dead, my Lims unknown;
     Before I skild to prize
     Those living Stars mine Eys,
Before my Tongue or Cheeks were to me shewn,
Before I knew my Hands were mine,
Or that my Sinews did my Members joyn,
When neither Nostril, Foot, nor Ear
As yet was seen, or felt, or did appear;
     I was within
A House I knew not, newly clothd with Skin. (p. 11, 2–11)

The experience that Traherne describes is not one of total disembod-
iment, but rather of possessing a body before having knowledge of the
fact. The insistent use of possessive pronouns, together with Traherne's
allusive assembly of body parts ensures that the reader is made vividly
aware of the material body – a body that is 'his'. While Traherne tells us
that the recollected 'I' had not been 'shewn' the fabric of his body, the
speaker nonetheless displays to the reader its constituent parts – the
tongue, hands, sinews and other organs that make up his corporeality.

Traherne does not simply and entirely conjure a condition of bodily
insensitivity. The body that he boldly describes as 'Dead' in the first line
notably has 'living Stars' for eyes. Most striking, however, are the last two
lines of this verse – 'I was within/ A House I knew not, newly clothd with
Skin' – there is a shift in voice: while every other line describes a state *not
yet experienced* by the subject, here our attention is drawn positively to
this prior condition. The simple statement, 'I was within', seems to denote
a felt experience: read together with the following line, however, the
speaker appears to un-know this withinness, or at least to be unfamiliar
with the nature of the 'House' ('A House I knew not') that renders that
withinness possible. The skin, in that small clause hung on the end of the
verse like a slight garment or an afterthought, hovers with the condition
of inwardness: together they are spared any explicit dismissal as unseen or
unfelt. The possibility of the subject's self-awareness hovers in the speaker's
inability to excise these two codependent ideas from any conjuring of
human experience, however spiritual: inwardness ('within') is connoted at,
or by, the edge ('Skin').

Traherne denies the body – body as flesh, as corpus, as 'other' – a
significant place in his poetry, and yet he insists that the reader recognise
the spiritual experience as one of being 'within'. The word 'within' occurs
seventy, and 'inward' twenty times in his poems: by contrast, 'outward' and
'without' together appear only thirty times. Such a lexical imbalance alone
is not particularly telling: indeed, it is typical of the Protestant mode of
meditative interiority or introspection so prevalent during the seventeenth

century. What is more conspicuously idiosyncratic, and more worthy of investigation, is the degree to which Traherne conjures this inwardness by means of those very limits whose involvement in the soul's activity he recurrently disavows. In 'Fullnesse', he talks of 'A Spiritual World Standing within,/ An Univers enclosd in Skin.' (p. 30, 8–9). In the following poem, 'Nature', he writes; 'A Secret self I had enclosd within,/ That was not bounded with my Clothes or Skin' (p. 32, 19–20). The same terms – 'Skin', 'within', 'enclosed' – operate to seemingly contradictory effect: whereas in 'Fullnesse', Traherne appears to evoke what Robert Watson terms an 'instatic' experience of the world, in 'Nature', the self moves outward beyond the skin.[5] In each case, the skin's role in arbitrating the activity of the soul is more complicated than it might appear and requires closer contextualised consideration. To turn attention to Traherne's allusions to the skin, and to his particularly suggestive engagement with dynamics of enclosure, is to trace a vital and (as yet) unexplored way of considering the character of the soul in Traherne's verse.

If this essay is to engage fully with Traherne's deployment of the skin, it must be sensitive to the elasticity of his conceptualisation of the soul and to the paradoxes at play in his transactions with it: in an attempt to make it so, I will consider Traherne's writing alongside the thinking of the modern French philosopher Jean-Luc Nancy. In his 1994 lecture, 'On the Soul', Nancy deconstructs traditional assumptions about body and soul. Just as the soul that Traherne articulates is neither easily, nor helpfully, conformable to the little body that Quarles ensconces in its mortal cage, so Nancy dismisses the idea of the soul as a 'little person, a little angel [...] a more subtle body' trapped in the 'prison of the body': it is, he argues, erroneous to think of the soul as 'anything other than the body'.[6] Rather, to talk of the soul, by Nancy's account, is to talk of 'the body's relation with itself', insofar as it is a relation to the outside – the state of being out.

> The soul is the body's difference from itself, the relation to the outside that the body is for itself. In other words [...] the soul is the difference from itself that makes the body.[7]

With this complex configuration of soul and body, Nancy demands that the reader discard her customary assumptions about these terms' distinction

---

[5] Robert N. Watson, *Back to Nature: The Green and the Real in the Late Renaissance* (Philadelphia, 2006), p. 297.

[6] Jean-Luc Nancy, 'On the Soul', in *Corpus*, trans. Richard A. Rand (New York, 2008), pp. 122–35, at p. 126.

[7] Ibid.

from one and another: soul and body are mutually dependent, constitutive aspects of one another.

Nancy's writing calls attention to the complexities of distinguishing inside from out, in regards to the human experience. If Nancy asks us to consider the soul as the body's 'being out', then this is, in part, with the aim of disturbing the notion of the body as 'something closed, full, on its own and in itself'. Such a thing – something 'gathered up in itself, penetrated with self and penetrated within itself such that, precisely, it is impenetrable' – is not, Nancy contends, a body, but a mass.[8] A mass has no scope for extension: it cannot stretch beyond itself or display itself. Mass exists without relation, neither conscious of, nor susceptible to, the influences of the world beyond itself. By contrast, the body is 'open and infinite': it is, he suggests, 'the opening of closure itself, the infinite of the finite itself'.[9] In Nancy's hands, the idea of the soul becomes subsumed into his treatment of the body, in ways that Traherne would and could not have accepted. Nonetheless, Nancy's paradoxical configuration of closure and openness stimulates a new reading of Traherne's contact between skin and soul.

SKIN: TEARING AND TOUCHING

When the devotional poets of the seventeenth century consider the skin as anything more than a garment, betokening the superficiality of worldly existence, they tend to subject it to trials that see its customary wholeness sensibly problematised. Of inevitably central importance is Christ's skin, which invites attention as the site at which his suffering speaks itself, and through whose scourged and ruptured margin his salvific blood flows. In the poems of Richard Crashaw (c.1612–c.1652), Christ's skin is, as Richard Rambuss says, covered with wounds, 'variously metaphorized as "eye[s] that weep" and mouths that kiss'.[10] The skin, ill-equipped to contain Christ's illimitable spirit or to close off his person, is discomposed as his effusive wounds invite intimate devotion. So broken is his skin that it becomes something of an anti-skin, a texture of orifices, promising passionate access of a type that the whole, unified skin routinely denies.

---

8 Ibid., p. 123.

9 Ibid., p. 122.

10 Richard Crashaw, 'On the Wounds of Our Crucified Lord', in *Steps to the Temple* (London, 1646). Richard Rambuss argues that '[w]hat excites adoration here is the notion that Christ's body is exposed to be all openings and valves; no surface on it is completely sealed. Everywhere open, utterly accessible, this body presents no unbreachable borders of permeability and impermeability.' See 'Christ's Ganymede', in *Closet Devotions* (Durham, 1998), p. 30.

From the open/ed body of Christ, to the troubled integument of the tormented sinner: in 'The crazed Soule being almost in dispaire', John Davies of Hereford (c.1565–1618) describes the 'scars' of his sin, renewed and opened by incessant sinning:

> And what the *Balmes of Grace* had clos'd before,
> I, through the itch of *sinne,* have opened wide:
> Which, through corruption, now are growne so sore
> That scarse I can so sore a *Cure* abide.
>
> The *Skinne,* which growing over, hid my *Wounds*
> Through breaking out of the *corruption,* gape:
> For, *sinne* the *grace* once granted quite confounds:
> So that I feare I hardly can escape.[11]

The speaker's compulsive addiction to the itch of sin, aggravates his scars to gape afresh: the skin of Davies's 'crazed soul' is at once open and closed. Syntactical awkwardness amplifies the sense of physiological incoherence, as in lines 9–10, where it seems to be the skin, rather than the wounds that the skin is growing over, which 'gapes'. 'Confounded' by sin, incapable of 'escape', the speaker is paradoxically hidebound by his broken skin.[12]

While Protestant sectarian or Anglican lyric poets of the period tend to dedicate less attention to Christ's wounds, moving away from the meditative practice of empathically writing oneself into the scene of Christ's passion, their poetry nonetheless reveals an engagement with the figurative significance of markings and woundings in the evocation of inward anguish.[13] In George Herbert's introspective poem 'Affliction [IV]', the speaker considers how his thoughts agitate his soul:

> Wounding my heart
> With scattered smart
> As wat'ring pots give flowers their lives.

[11] John Davies, 'The crazed Soule being almost in dispaire', in *The Muses Sacrifice* (London, 1612), pp. 67–8, lines 5–12.

[12] The figurative connotations of the term 'hidebound' – denoting mental restrictedness of one type or another – derive from a physiological condition of 'Having the skin tight and incapable of extension' (*OED, adj.,* sense 2).

[13] Michael Schoenfeldt argues that 'Protestant lyric devotion in seventeenth-century England move[d] away from identification with the spectacularly gruesome suffering of the crucified Christ [...] A renewed emphasis in Reformed religion on the Davidic and Pauline notions that the only sacrifice God desires occurs neither in sanctified architectural space, nor in explicit corporal suffering, but rather in the interior spaces of the believer'. See '"That Spectacle of Too Much Weight": The Poetics of Sacrifice in Donne, Herbert and Milton', in *Seventeenth-Century British Poetry, 1603–1660,* ed. John P. Rumrich and Gregory Chaplin (New York, 2006), pp. 890–907, at p. 890.

Nothing their fury can control
While they do wound and pink my soul.[14]

In their homely way, Herbert's thoughts are analogous to Christ's wounds: the pain that they scatter gives life, just as Christ's suffering makes possible the believer's eternal salvation. Thus, Herbert configures his soul's sensitivity in terms of a punctured or perforated integument, pinked by penetrating thoughts.[15]

The skin, then, commonly appears – whether explicit or suggested – as a rent or aggravated membrane, whose subjection to tactile disturbance is figurative of the sinner's sensitivity to his own corruption and expressive of a desire for empathic access to Christ's suffering. In Traherne's hands, however, the skin functions in ways that are markedly different. He does not present the skin as a vehicle for the effusion of feeling, nor in rough or ambivalent counterpoint to Christ's skin: it does not stand, blank, in antagonistic relation to internal, psychological discord; it does not respond to, or have cause to resist, the ticklish stimuli of the external world.

Only in one poem, 'An Infant-Ey', is the skin brought into explicit contact with the external world, and in this instance, it is treated as an *article*, an *object* of the speaker's infatuation, not part of his own sensory equipment:

> A House, a Woman's Hand, a piece of Gold,
> A Feast, a costly Suit, a beauteous Skin
> That vy'd with Ivory, I did behold;
> And all my Pleasure was in Sin:
> [...]
> O dy! dy unto all that draws thine Ey
> From its first Objects. (p. 98, 43–6, 49–50)

H. M. Margoliouth argues that 'An Infant-Ey' is an 'inferior' poem to those that precede it, due to the 'moralizing self-appeal' with which it is resolved, and the fact that it 'laments the loss of the 'Infant-Ey' [rather] than dwell[ing] on its joys'.[16] Part of the poem's inadequacy, I would add, lies in the fact that Traherne's speaker is notably detached from the very things that supposedly disturb his tranquility. Listed as they are, the physical distractions that he so comfortably itemises appear to hold no power over

---

[14] George Herbert, *The Temple* (London, 1633), pp. 82–3, lines 7–12.

[15] The verb 'to pink' refers to a mode of ornamenting cloth or leather 'by cutting or punching eyelet holes, slits, etc.' (*OED*, *v.* 1, sense 1). By association, it can mean 'to pierce, stab, or prick with a pointed weapon or instrument' (*OED*, *v.* 1, sense 2.b).

[16] *Thomas Traherne: Centuries Poems and Thanksgivings*, ed. H. M. Margoliouth, 2 vols (Oxford, 1958), II, p. 361.

him: he 'beholds' them, a verb that likewise takes possession of an act of looking. Likewise, the only sense-organ seemingly alert in this poem – even when confronted with the tactile and gustatory delights of Traherne's list – is the eye. The beauteous skin he describes excites no response in the speaker's *own* skin: this is the beautiful skin of *another* body (a body that, tellingly, receives no more description) and, although the Sin that chases on the heels of this ivory vision gestures toward the speaker's lust, Traherne's speaker makes no mention of his skin's potentially charged zone: the poem leaves it undisturbed. For a poet so concerned with the skin, Traherne's explicit thoughts about touch here are not unusual: he does not describe the vivid contacts between bodies, or go into the tingling particulars of the skin's mediation of the fraught distinction between inside and out. The quality of touch, however, if not the activity per se, pervades his writing.

Thinking back to Nancy's claim that the body is 'the opening of closure itself, the infinite of the finite itself', it might seem that John Davies describes a body that conforms to this very paradoxical state, its skin gaping through sins, yet shut tight with their scars. However, the openness of this body lies in its disruption, and this disruption, as such, traps the infinite soul and renders it finite: in other words, it operates a reversal of the terms Nancy sets out. Indeed, Nancy's lecture goes on to illuminate what is inherent in this opening of the body; namely, touch: 'to touch on what is closed is [...] to open it. [...] And to open – to touch – is not to tear, dismember, destroy.'[17] According to this claim, the body opens with the touch that recognises, and does not seek to disturb, that body's closure. Nancy argues that, 'if I penetrate the form of a body, I destroy it, I dissolve it [...] and make it into a mass' (p. 127). Just so, in Davies's hands, the sin-riddled skin denies the soul access to the world around it. The touch, as distinct from tearing, does not disrupt the limits of that which is closed: rather, it consolidates them, and in so doing, turns those limits into the site where the infinite is felt.

Traherne does not speak explicitly about touch in terms of grappling fingers, or of skin on skin: indeed, he consciously excludes the influences of other bodies from his evocation of his unmediated spirit. And yet, the quality of touch is nonetheless implicit in his articulation of the relational aspect of all human (as embodied) experience. In the *Centuries of Meditations*, Traherne famously avers that 'infinit Worth shut up in the Limits of a Material Being, is the only way to a Real Infinity. GOD made Nothing infinit in Bulk, but evry thing there where it ought to be' (Ross, V, III.20). Were any one thing infinite in form and scale, it would,

---

[17]   Nancy, 'On the Soul', p. 122.

by necessity, crowd all other things out of existence: it would, by Nancy's logic, be a mass.[18] In spite, then, of Traherne's oft-reiterated claim that 'a man [...] thinks not of Walls and Limits till he feels them and is stopt by them', it is these very walls and limits that allow participation in infinity. To return to Traherne's claim – that 'infinit Worth shut up in the Limits of a Material Being, is the only way to a Real Infinity' (III.20) – is to observe that the relationship between 'infinite worth' and 'real infinity' is not one of simple identity. The material limits of things give them *access to* (they are 'the only way to') 'a real infinity'. Likewise, their 'infinite worth is shut up *in*' [my italics], not *by*, the limits of their materiality. This small word, 'in', embraces the possibility that the point of limit – the edge that materiality confers on things – is, at least in part, the *site* of this infinite worth, rather than the boundary that prohibits its experience. Traherne's is a philosophy of nearness and access: it is here, at the unbroken edge, that 'inwardness' knows itself, and at which the body becomes the 'opening of closure'.

THE LANTHORNS SIDES

As Nancy insists that to tear the body is to destroy the very notion of that body, so Traherne actively distances his speaker's soul from any contact that might pose a threat to the coherence of his being. In 'Silence', he describes how his original, Adamic innocence had not yet experienced the advances of sin:

> No rotten Soul, did like an Apple, near
> My soul approach. There's no Contagion here. (p. 25, 59–60)

These lines appear strikingly altered in the version prepared for *Poems of Felicity*: the apple is gone and the whole dynamic of corruption is changed:

> No rotten Seed, or Bitterness of Gall,
> Tainted my Soul. (p. 154, 58–9)

Although the apple in the Dobell version necessarily calls to mind that Paradisiacal fruit ('whose mortal taste', as Milton tells us, 'Brought death into the world, and all our woe'[19]), the notions of rottenness, of contagion, and the verb 'approach', come together to evoke a dynamic of proximity and external influence. The focus is not on the ingestion of the fruit: rather, we see the rotten soul as a rotten apple, whose closeness

---

[18] Nancy argues that God himself might be termed a 'mass', a mass being – by his definition – 'the impenetrable, in the sense of something penetrated without remainder or limit' ('On the Soul', p. 123).

[19] John Milton, *Paradise Lost*, ed. Alastair Fowler, 2nd edn (Harlow, 2007), I.3, p. 57.

breeds inward corruption with other fruit by external association.[20] By contrast, where sin is articulated as a 'seed', it is immediately understood as something planted *in* the soul: where 'contagion' acts between bodies, this 'taint' manifests internally.[21] Gone too is the rhyme of 'near' and 'here', which subtly affirms the externality of this process.

When Traherne goes on to claim that – in contradistinction to this later corrupted existence – 'the World was more in me, then I in it' (p. 26, 81, Dobell; p. 155, 80, *Poems of Felicity*), the effect is not the same in both versions. In *F*, sin is experienced immanently: as such, in the treatment of the sinful and the innocent soul, the object of the poetic eye appears, likewise, to be inward, the scope of its concerns contiguous with – and bounded by – the limits of the soul or individual. In the Dobell version, by contrast, Traherne shifts the axis of his attention from the external to the internal. As a result, the acknowledgment that the world is not entirely enclosed by him – that the world is '*more* [my italics] in me then I in it', as opposed to being, simply, 'in me' – participates in the poem's wider evocation of the individual as a diffuse experience of being at, or beyond, an edge that mediates different modes of infinity.

In *The Poetics of Space*, Gaston Bachelard asserts that

> Outside and inside are both intimate – they are always ready to be reversed, to exchange their hostility. If there exists a border-line surface between such an inside and outside, the surface is painful on both sides.[22]

What for Bachelard is posed as a site of painful and intimate interchange, Traherne treats as the site of the enjoyment of infinity. In Traherne's hands, inside and outside appear endlessly reversed, subject to incessant reorientation. As he writes in The Fifth Century,

> The Infinity of God is our Enjoyment, because it is the Region and Extent of his Dominion. [...] It surroundeth us continualy on evry side, it filles us, and inspires us. It is so Mysterious, that it is Wholy within us, and even then it wholly seems, and is, without us. It is more inevitably and constantly, more neerly and immediately our Dwelling Place, then our Cities and Kingdoms and houses. Our Bodies themselves are not so much ours, or within us as that is. (*Centuries*, Ross, V.2)

---

[20] This sense is corroborated by the fact that apples are not uniformly synonymous with sin in Traherne's verse: in fact, in 'The Enquirie', Traherne refers to 'The Glories of his [God's] Attributes' as 'dangling Apples' (p. 44, 31–2). He refers, also, to the 'Apple' of his eye in 'My Spirit' (p. 28, 66), immediately, immanently, enjoying the glories of his spirit.

[21] The *OED* defines 'contagion' primarily as 'the communication of disease from body to body by contact direct or mediate'. It also offers it in its figurative sense, as a 'hurtful, defiling, or corrupting contact' (sense 4.a).

[22] Gaston Bachelard, *The Poetics of Space*, trans. Maria Jolas (Boston, 1994), p. 217.

That which surrounds, likewise fills us: that which is within us, is 'wholly' without us. Perhaps most striking of these paradoxes is the final claim of this passage, namely that 'our Bodies are not so much ours, or within us, as [the Infinity of God] is': such phrasing *externalises* the human experience, explicitly upturning that accepted notion with which this essay set out, namely, that the body is a closed vessel, within which we are carried through life. Traherne's comfortable claim that our bodies are, instead, 'within us', frames the soul as that which is without, as that which encompasses the body.

Nancy argues that to speak of the soul is to talk of the presence of the body: it is 'its position, its "stance", its "sistence" as being *out-side* (ex)'. He says:

> It's through my skin that I touch myself. And I touch myself from outside, I don't touch myself from inside. [...] The phenomenological analyses of 'self-touching' always return to a primary interiority. Which is impossible. To begin with, I have to be in exteriority in order to touch myself. And what I touch remains on the outside. I am exposed to myself touching myself.

Acknowledging the work done by phenomenologists, Edmund Husserl and Maurice Merleau-Ponty, Nancy nonetheless argues that they wrongly perpetuate the traditional model, whereby all such touching reaffirms interiority. Instead, he concludes that the soul is a name for the body's capacity to extend from and in itself. He goes on to claim that the soul is 'nothing other than the experience of the body. [...] *Experiri*, in Latin, is precisely going outside, leaving without a destination, crossing through something without knowing whether we will return from it.'[23]

In 'Nature', a poem to which I alluded earlier, Traherne writes:

> A secret self I had enclosd within,
> That was not bounded with my Clothes or Skin,
> Or terminated with my Sight, the Sphere
> Of which was bounded with the Heavens here:
> But that did rather, like the Subtile Light,
> Securd from rough and raging Storms by Night,
> Break through the Lanthorns sides, and freely ray
> Dispersing and Dilating evry Way. (p. 32, 19–26)

The self is 'secret', 'enclosd', but paradoxically bright and radiant, free to 'disperse' and 'dilate' who knows where. Analogous to the light, the self breaks through the skin, which in turn is framed as the 'lanthorns sides'. This image is not unique to Traherne. It is used by his near contemporary, the early American devotional poet Edward Taylor, in '135. Meditation.

---

[23] Nancy, 'On the Soul', p. 134.

Can. 6.4. Terrible as an Army with Banners': 'Thy Body's like a golden Lanthorn trim/ Through which the lamps of Grace shine from within'.[24] In each instance, the light requires the lantern if it is to shine: without its sides, the light would be extinguished or go unseen in the violent night.

In Taylor's hands, this simile is part of a meditation on the church militant, allegorised via an emblazoned and glorified body: its eye balls fling 'fiery bullets, Graces flaming Darts'; its mouth is a bow and arrow ('thy Tong's the string/ That shoots his Arrows'); its hands 'cast out like lightening sharp and Thunder', and all is clad in undinted 'Coate of Male'.[25] The focus is all on this impenetrable and emissive body, whose effulgence is just one aspect of its violent effusiveness. And yet, all attention is on the body that thus shoots out power, rather than on the transmission of its radiance. By contrast, the skin is all that Traherne conjures of the body: the 'lanthorns sides' are conjured solely as the means of this spiritual dilation, whose activity he goes on to describe:

> It did encompass, and possess rare Things,
> But yet felt more, and on its Angels Wings
> Pierc'd through the Skies immediately. (p. 32, 29–31)

The body left behind, that 'Secret self [...] enclos'd within', takes on dermal qualities: like the skin through which it breaks, it 'encompasses [...] rare Things';[26] like the skin, it is receptive to feeling and sensation. As when he writes in 'Silence' that 'The world was more in me then I in it', we see the self enfolding the world, becoming, as Nancy puts it, 'the being outside'; not just of the body, but of the universe. In turn, this secret self 'pierces through the skies', an act that makes a skin of the sky's fabric.

Such is the nature of experience: if Traherne's 'Secret self' is not bounded by his 'Clothes or skin', in spite of its 'enclosure', it is because these limits become the site of the opening of closure. Traherne's writing posits all experience as witness to an involvement of interior with exterior, with inside and outside folded within one another. According to Robert Watson, 'the inward and the outward are not distinguishable in Traherne's philosophy [...]. Things [...] are present essentially within him, but this renders them so vivid that the ego nearly dissolves into the given universe.' Watson argues that in Traherne's writing we encounter him 'surrendering

---

24 Edward Taylor, *Edward Taylor's 'Gods Determinations' and 'Preparatory Meditations': A Critical Edition*, ed. Daniel Patterson (Kent, 2002), pp. 456–7, lines 11–12.

25 Ibid., lines 20–1, 27, 31.

26 The word 'rare', as used in this instance, probably denotes near-immateriality, or faintness, as opposed to scarcity: the soul is sensitive to – and capable of enfolding – ungraspable, intangible entities.

the ego-barrier.'[27] I contend, rather, that the ego is defined in the crossing of barriers: it exists *as* experience, as the 'going outside, leaving without a destination, crossing through something'. In turn, where experience configures itself via membranes, all of the world, together with the self or soul that accommodates that world, must – at various points – likewise become skins.

Antonia Birnbaum, writing about Jean Luc Nancy, remarks that his is 'a thinking that is always eager to cross borders, to suffer no restriction, to leave nothing self-enclosed: not even to leave the soul cloistered and confined in a prison intended as the envelope for its corporeal existence'.[28] The same might be said of Traherne, who – as I have shown – recurrently treats the skin's seeming closure as an invitation to consider infinite reach. Perhaps the most conspicuous instance of Traherne 'crossing borders' arises at the end of one of his best-known poems, 'Shadows in the Water'. The speaker gazes into a puddle, and, looking on the sky and 'second selves' reflected therein, contemplates the existence of other worlds. In the final lines, he meditates upon those joys in heaven that are

> Laid up in store for me;
> To which I shall, when that thin Skin
> Is broken, be admitted in. (p. 171, 78–80)

The 'thin Skin' in question is at once the surface of the water and, of course, the speaker's own skin, whose dissolution or 'brokenness' denotes death's erasure of a corporeally delimited inwardness. Death is the final act of 'going outside, [of] leaving without a destination' (Nancy), from which there is no return. In *Christian Ethicks*, Traherne explains that 'the *Skin* importeth Death for as much as it cannot be fleyed off, without the destruction of the Creature' (p. 130). If the skin 'imports Death' because its removal *causes* death, then it must equally denote Life, because it is vital to the business of living. And not merely because the skin protects an interior, corporeal space, but rather – as I hope to have shown – because it necessitates the very acts, of overstepping, of crossing over, that are constitutive of human experience. Only through contact with the edge, can you know yourself to be inside or out.

[27] Watson, *Back to Nature*, p. 297.
[28] Antonia Birnbaum, 'To Exist Is to Exit the Point', in Jean Luc-Nancy, *Corpus*, trans. Richard A. Rand (New York, 2008), pp. 145–50, at p. 146.

NAKEDNESS

The skin lends itself to the articulation of a soul that can infold a universe of potential, but that can likewise be pressed out towards that universe in the naked experience of it. Steven Connor, in a paper entitled 'A Skin that Walks', has argued that

The skin is not a part of the body, because it is the body's twin, or shadow [...]. The very wholeness that the skin possesses and preserves [...], means that it is always in excess of, out in front of the body. The skin is thus always part immaterial, ideal, ecstatic.[29]

I would add that, not only is the skin not a part of the body, but it is also more – or less – than itself, for the skin has what Traherne might term the 'infinite Capacitie' to absorb into itself the quality of its encounters; to thrill with its transgressions, such that it can become both essential and abstracted.

In Chapter 24 of *The Kingdom of God*, entitled 'Of all the Emanations and Influences', Traherne says that 'all Bodies Ray, and [...] their Essences and Spirits mingle together: [...] they exceed themselves and ever flow unto Each other' (Ross, I, p. 381). In numerous of his poems, such a fluidly involved universe of spirits can be felt, perhaps counter-intuitively, in the surface-bound word 'naked'. While 'naked' suggests the unmediated condition of something perceived ('the naked Truth', for instance, that Traherne promises to convey with 'transparent Words' in his prefatory poem, 'The Author to the Critical Peruser', p. 84, 1–3), it also necessarily calls to mind an unclothed state: a 'naked body' is, of course, a bare-skinned one. In Traherne's hands, however, the term inevitably appears in conjunction with abstract terms, with no reference to the body: in 'The Preparative', he writes of being 'A Naked Simple Pure *Intelligence*' (p. 11, 22), and later – in the same poem – of being 'A Disentangled and a Naked Sence' (p. 13, 68). In 'My Spirit', he opens the poem thus:

> My Naked Simple Life was I.
> That Act so Strongly Shind
> Upon the Earth, the Sea, the Skie,
> It was the Substance of My Mind.
>   The Sence itself was I.
> I felt no Dross nor Matter in my Soul,
> No Brims nor Borders, such as in a Bowl
> We see, My Essence was Capacitie.
>   That felt all Things (p. 26, 2–10)

---

[29] Steven Connor, 'A Skin That Walks', paper given at the Humanities and Arts Research Centre, Royal Holloway University of London, 13 February 2002 <http://stevenconnor.com/skinwalks.html> [accessed December 2015].

In each instance, Traherne's speaker depicts himself as an abstract state of being: he does not merely possess intelligence, sense, life. Rather, he *is* intelligence, sense, life. The word 'naked' tells the reader that he is all of these things in their unadulterated, unmediated state, but it also lends these abstract conditions a material quality, compelling the reader's attention to the edge of being where they make themselves known. In the same instance, it converts that half-configured skin into 'Essence and Spirit' (*Kingdom of God*).

In 'My Spirit', this autonomous and naked life 'exceeds itself' in just the manner that Traherne describes in *The Kingdom of God*: the self-consti-tuting 'sence' is born from the radiance of his 'Naked Simple Life' and its perceptual mingling with Earth, Sea and Sky. His 'Essence was Capacitie./ That felt all Things': we see no brims nor borders perhaps, but capacity necessarily denotes fullness, or the point at which something becomes full, and this is a concept that requires limits. That this very fullness should become consummately sensate compels us to consider it in terms of surface contact and extension.

In Nancy's *Corpus*, he self-consciously reflects on the business of writing, and of the touching that happens 'in writing all the time':

> Writing in its essence touches upon the body. [...] Writing touches upon bodies *along the absolute limit* separating the sense of the one from the nerves of the other. Nothing *gets through*, which is why it touches.[30]

Nancy makes a point of distancing this articulation from association with inscribed or tattooed flesh: he likewise assures the reader that he does not invoke the notion of 'touching' writing, in the sense of moving or emotive words. It is the business of all writing, according to Nancy, to touch: it cannot help itself.

In the context of Traherne's work, what Nancy says of writing might be applied instead to the type of reading that his poems invite: to read his poetry is to become aware of just such absolute limits as Nancy describes. Traherne's reader is not invited to inhabit the body, or to participate in the experiences that his speaker evokes. It is not his poetry's aim to stimulate empathic self-awareness in its reader. Indeed, Traherne's poems are strikingly devoid of the kind of invocations to self-scrutiny that abound elsewhere in early modern devotional poetry. Rather, his poems position the reader externally, together with the speaker, who conjures his retro-spective meditations on an original and ideated state from a position of being outside. And it is there that the reader stands, just beyond the skin:

---

[30]   Nancy, 'On the Soul', p. 11.

in contact with the speaker, she feels the infinity of inwardness in the immediacy of the naked, absolute edge. As Nancy's theories illuminate, body and soul are located in the refusal to see the skin as a terminating integument. For Traherne, like Nancy, the living skin is the site where what is closed is opened; opened in such a way that the skin – intact and secure – forgets its association with mortal clay and becomes indispensible in the articulation of divine human experience.

Chapter 2

NO THINGS BUT IN THOUGHTS: TRAHERNE'S POETIC REALISM

Kathryn Murphy

Traherne was a poet preoccupied with things. He liked lists; one critical article refers to his 'cataloguing style'.[1] Less positively, Christopher Hill complained that 'Traherne's poems can degenerate into boring catalogues.'[2] Some lines consist wholly of the naming of parts:

> Thy Gifts O God alone Ile prize,
> My Tongue, my Eys,
> My cheeks, my Lips, my Ears, my Hands, my Feet
> ('The Person', Ross, VI, p. 41, 63–5.)

Moreover, the words 'Thing' or 'Things', almost always capitalised, are an unusually frequent and emphatic occurrence in his poetry:

> Things fals are forcd, and most Elaborate,
> Things pure and true are Obvious unto Sence;
> The first Impressions, in our Earthly State,
> Are made by Things most Great in Excellence. ('Ease', p. 34, 7–10)

Of the seventy-five separate poems in the two major poetic manuscripts, only seven do not contain either word.[3]

Yet this raises a critical paradox. It has frequently been considered a flaw

---

[1] Carl M. Selkin, 'The Language of Vision: Traherne's Cataloguing Style', *English Language Review* 6 (1976), 92–104.

[2] 'Thomas Traherne', *The Collected Essays of Christopher Hill*, vol. I: *Writing and Revolution in Seventeenth-Century England* (Brighton, 1985), pp. 226–46, at p. 228.

[3] 'The Rapture', 'The Apprehension', 'The Return', 'Bells', 'Churches', 'The Image', 'The Evidence'. The two manuscripts are the Dobell manuscript, Bodleian, MS. Eng. poet. c. 42, and British Library, MS. Burney 392, entitled 'Poems of Felicity'. In counting, I treated versions of poems that appear in both MSS as a single poem.

in Traherne's poems that they are 'generic', 'diffuse', and lack a 'distinctive impression'.[4] One editor claimed that 'Traherne almost never mentions by name an item of flora or fauna – there are flowers in his poems but no violets or daffodils. [... P]articulars as things in themselves do not interest him.'[5] Traherne is thus apparently concerned with things both too much and not enough.

The problem is at once aesthetic and philosophical. This essay aims to resolve it by justifying Traherne's repetitive and enumerative attention to 'things' as a deliberate strategy, and part of his attention to how philosophical commitments are enacted in genre and rhetoric. This, of course, runs against old clichés that read Traherne's poems as 'facile, expansive, emotional optimism', a position much more difficult to hold after the discovery and publication of discursive prose works such as *The Kingdom of God* and the *Commentaries of Heaven*.[6] All of the judgements given above were based on limited evidence, through no fault of the critics: they wrote when only a fraction of Traherne's works had been discovered, and fewer published. The prose enables us to place Traherne's poetic – or apparently anti-poetic – 'things' in the context both of the Aristotelian grounding of his education, and the rethinking of it by figures such as Francis Bacon and his followers in the Royal Society, with their rallying cry to attend to 'the things themselves'. After attending more closely to Traherne's use of 'things' and lists in the first part of this chapter, the next two sections address these philosophical contexts, while the fourth traces Traherne's eclectic and idiosyncratic engagement with them in the *Commentaries*. The remainder of the essay turns to how Traherne's writings encourage the reader, as he puts it in the *Centuries*, 'to study all Things in the best of all possible Maners' (V, I.133).

TRAHERNE'S VAGUE THINGS

The paradox in the critical tradition echoes the ambivalence of the word 'thing' itself. On the one hand, the *OED* tells us, 'thing' is a specifying

---

[4] Patrick Grant, 'Irenaean Philosophy and Thomas Traherne', *The Transformation of Sin: Studies in Donne, Herbert, Vaughan and Traherne* (Montreal, 1974), pp. 170–97, at pp. 172–3; Margaret Bottrall, 'Traherne's Praise of the Creation', *Critical Quarterly* 1 (1959), 126–33, at 128–9; Selkin, 'Language of Vision', 92; see also Douglas Bush, *English Literature in the Earlier Seventeenth Century, 1600–1660*, 2nd edn revised (Oxford, 1962), pp. 156–8.

[5] Dick Davis, 'Introduction', *Selected Writings of Thomas Traherne* (Manchester, 1988), p. 13.

[6] Bush, *English Literature*, p. 158.

gesture towards an emphatically existing object: a 'thing' is 'that which exists individually [...]; that which is or may be in any way an object of perception, knowledge, or thought; an entity, a being'.[7] To call something a thing is to make a claim about its status as real, and also to suggest it can be separated from the rest of reality and made an object of thought. Traherne uses 'thing' in this sense: in the section on Aristotle in the *Commentaries of Heaven*, he asserts that 'Good men are Things as well as any', reifying persons as appropriate objects of contemplation (III, p. 188). And yet 'thing' is also '[u]sed indefinitely to denote something which the speaker or writer is not able or does not choose to particularize, or which is incapable of being precisely described'.[8] It is a placeholder for something not quite known, or a deliberate gesture of vagueness.

This sense too appears in Traherne. In 'Solitude', the speaker seeks comfort from he knows not what: 'Nor could I ghess/ What kind of thing I long'd for' (p. 115, 33–4). 'Thing' here names a specificity of felt desire that cannot name or know its object. The mute refusal of the various world to yield him satisfaction causes the speaker to exclaim 'Ye sullen Things!/ Ye dumb, ye silent Creatures, and unkind!' (p. 115, 41–2). It is not that there are no things, but that none of the many things is *the* thing, the object of the speaker's longing.

This use of 'Things' to mark the stubborn opacity of stuff, its reluctance to relinquish meaning, is frequent. In several poems, to speak of 'Things' is to draw attention to the dismaying variety of particulars. 'The Inference I' complains of a wasted world: 'Ten thousand thousand Things are dead;/ Ly round about me; yet are fled' (p. 182, 31–3). In 'Christendom', attention is directed away from 'ten thousand things' offering empty stimulation (p. 124, 23). In 'Desire', the natural world is busy but vacant:

> Alass, all these are poor and Empty Things,
>   Trees Waters Days and Shining Beams
> Fruits, Flowers, Bowers, Shady Groves and Springs,
>   No Joy will yeeld, no more then Silent Streams.
>   These are but Dead Material Toys. (p. 72, 37–41)

'Things' here are *mere* things.

Of course, as the poems demonstrate, this is not always Traherne's mode; in 'Insatiableness II', the speaker desires a world 'Enrich with infinit Variety' (p. 188, 17). But even where variety provokes not anxiety but pleasure, the same imprecision in the meaning of 'things' remains. In 'Poverty', the speaker misses 'Ten thousand absent things', a plenitude that would allow

---

7   *OED, s.v.* thing, *n.*1, sense 8.
8   *OED, s.v.* thing, *n.*1, sense 8.c.

him to appreciate the 'Infinit' bounty of God (p. 119, 39, 43): it is precisely in not knowing what things these are that the desire and its insatiability consists. In 'Christendom', the speaker 'long[s] to know what Things did ly behind/ That *Mystic Name*' (p. 123, 13–14), hankering after access to a reality 'behind' mystery or appearance, not yet available to articulation.

Even in the most obvious counter to the suggestion of a lack of particularity in Traherne – in his lists of nouns – the same issue emerges. Though Traherne, despite the critics, emphatically names items of flora and fauna, the suggestion that he pays little attention to things themselves is fair. In *The Kingdom of God*, Traherne tells his reader that 'The Earth even beneath its Surface is filled with Inhabitants. Frogs, Moles, Worms, Ants, Addars, Woodlice, Spiders, Bettles, Askars, Dormice, with Innumerable others' (I, p. 421). The capacious et cetera of 'Innumerable others' suggests that this list of creeping things is not, nor could be, comprehensive. The creatures mentioned are significant not in themselves, but in the cumulative impression of tiny teeming insect life. The *Thanksgivings* consist almost entirely of lists of things for which to be grateful:

> Apples, Citrons, Limons, Dates, and Pomgranates,
> Figs, Raisins, Grapes, and Melons,
> Plumbs, Cherries, Filberts, Peaches,
> Are all thy riches; for which we praise and bless thy Name. (IV, p. 350)

In lines unmetrical, unrhymed, and rhetorically bare, Traherne uses *mise-en-page* and lineation to formalise the list as a literary mode. But these strategies of organisation highlight the arbitrariness of the individual members of the lists. Not even metre or rhyme justifies their inclusion; it is not the thing itself which is at stake. The fruits of the cornucopia are 'all thy riches', but not 'all of thy riches'. The impossibility of such a comprehensive list is in fact the point.

The issue is partly grammatical: Traherne's lists of nouns name not individual things, but species or classes. Even where some qualification seems to be offered, adjectives or deixis that would make a thing particular, something is awry. 'The Salutation' enumerates body parts:

> I that so long
> Was Nothing from Eternitie,
> Did little think such Joys as Ear or Tongue,
> To Celebrat or See:
> Such Sounds to hear, such Hands to feel, such Feet,
> Beneath the Skies, on such a Ground to meet. (p. 3, 16–21)

The function of 'such' is usually to specify the qualities of one thing with regard to another already known, or to place the noun it qualifies in a kind, class, or category already mentioned. The repetition gives an impression of deictic insistence. Yet Traherne neglects to supply a category or prior object to which these joys, sounds, hands, ground, feet are to be related. Similarly, in 'Wonder', Traherne invites the reader to see while giving them nothing – no thing – to visualise:

Rich Diamond and Pearl and Gold
In evry Place was seen;
Rare Splendors, Yellow, Blew, Red, White and Green,
Mine Eys did evry where behold. (p. 4, 47–50)

In 'The World', 'The choicest Colors, Yellow, Green, and Blew/ Did all this Court/ In comly sort/ With mixt varieties bestrew' (p. 110, 73–6). These are fields of pure colour unattached to any object. Traherne's gestures of specification remain no more than gestures.

There is indeed then something odd at work in Traherne's treatment of things: though the word 'Thing', and classes of things, abound, they remain unqualified and unparticularised. Rather than poetic naivety, however, this reflects Traherne's preoccupation with the ontological problem of what 'things' actually are: what is fundamentally real, and how a manifold world of various things can come together as a unity. In foregrounding such concerns, Traherne was typical of his time; the next sections consider how he made use of his intellectual context.

THEORIES OF THINGS: ARISTOTLE

Thinking about things was in fact the first step of the university arts course, leading to a BA, that Traherne studied at Brasenose College, Oxford, from 1653 to 1656. That education began with the study of Aristotelian logic; and the study of logic began with the analysis of things.[9] The point is stressed in logic textbooks written in Oxford in the earlier part of the century, and popular during Traherne's student days. Richard Crakanthorpe, a fellow of the Queen's College, wrote that '*Rerum ipsarum cognitio*', the cognition of things themselves, was the foundation of logic; a marginal note emphasises that '*Logicus Res considerat*' ('The Logician considers Things').[10] Robert Sanderson, a Fellow of Lincoln College, began his textbook by asserting that '*Finis* [logicae] vero unicus, Cognitio *sc.* rerum' ('there is in truth a single end [of logic]: the cognition

---

[9] Students might also study rhetoric in their first year, but the study of logic, through Aristotle or Porphyry, was specified.

[10] Richard Crakanthorpe, *Logicæ Libri Quinque*, 2nd edn (London, 1641), sig. A6r.

of things').[11] Thinking rightly about things was both the beginning and the end of logic, and thus the first step of every student's university studies.

Before learning to argue, then, students learned how to form concepts of things, and the 'simple terms' used to describe them.[12] The source text was Aristotle's *Categories*, the first part of his *Organon* or logical works. The *Categories* divided the description of things into ten 'predicaments': substance, quantity, quality, relation, place, time, position, state, action, and affection.[13] Substance contains individual entities ('things') and the species to which they belong, such as human beings, animals, flowers, stones. It is the only category whose members exist independently; the others exist in, or as descriptions of, substance. Etymologically, 'substance' is what underlies everything else; the remaining nine categories are 'accidents', passing states that befall the substance. Within substance itself, there is a further hierarchical division. Primary substances are individuals: Socrates, for example, or this lion, that oak tree. Secondary substances are the species and genera to which the primary substances belong: man, lion, oak, animal, etc. For Aristotle, the primary substances were the foundation of reality: without them, neither secondary substance nor accidents could exist.[14]

Within the context of the *Organon*, the purpose of the *Categories* was to analyse 'things', so that the names given them – the 'signa Rerum', or 'signs of things', as Crakanthorpe put it – would be apt, and could do duty within the argumentative structure of the syllogism. But the *Categories* also imply metaphysical commitments about the fundamental structure of reality: a world composed of primary substances categorised by species and genus, and qualified by fleeting accidents. Particulars have real existence, and universals and 'predicables' – things and words that can exist or be true simultaneously in many different things, like 'animal', 'man', 'white' – can only exist dependently, instantiated in particular things.

Traherne's debts to his Aristotelian education have been emphasised by scholars countering the prevailing view of him as a Platonic mystic.[15]

---

[11]   Robert Sanderson, *Logicæ Artis Compendium*, 2nd edn (Oxford, 1640), p. 1.

[12]   Sanderson, *Logicæ artis compendium*, p. 3: 'Logicæ tres sunt partes [...] quarum *Prima* dirigit primum actum Mentis, sc. *Conceptum simplicem*; & est *de Simplicibus terminis*: quo pertinent introductio Porphyriana, & Liber Categoriarum Aristotelis.' ('There are three parts of logic [...] of which the first directs the first act of the mind, that is to say the *simple concept*; and concerns itself with *simple terms*: the subject of Porphyry's *Isagoge*, and Aristotle's book of the *Categories*.' My translation.)

[13]   These provide answers to questions: what is it; how many, how much, how large is it; what is it like; what is it in relation to; where is it; when is it (was it, will it be); how is it placed; what state is it in (Aristotle provides the examples 'has shoes on', 'has armour on'); what is it doing; and what is happening to it?

[14]   As expressed in the *Categories* 2^b5.

[15]   Paul Cefalu, 'Thomistic Metaphysics and Ethics in the Poetry and Prose of Thomas

The *Commentaries of Heaven* contains entries both for 'Aristotle' and 'Of Aristotles Philosophie', describing Aristotle as 'the Greatest Philosopher in Nature' (III, p. 188), and 'the Greatest Master of Methods in the World' (III, p. 189).[16] Significantly, it is precisely for Aristotle's attempt 'to set forth the Nature of things' that Traherne praises him, emphasising that this is also his own 'design' in the *Commentaries*, since 'clear and perfect Apprehensions of all Objects, in their Several Classes, in all their Circumstances' are 'the most immediate Way to Philosophie and Happiness' (III, p. 201). Traherne is referring to the *Categories*: 'Classes' refers to the apparatus of genus and species, and 'Circumstances' to accidents. 'Apprehension', too, has a technical sense: *apprehensio* is the power by which, through the senses and the intellect, 'rerum notitiam percipimus', we perceive the 'notes' or marks of things; the first step of the process of cognition by which we analyse the stuff of the world.[17] Traherne wrote poems entitled 'Misapprehension' and 'Right Apprehension', and the phrase 'clear and perfect apprehensions' is used again in *Christian Ethicks*, where they are the only thing lacking in the failure of man to come to terms with God.[18] What he found most sympathetic in Aristotle, then, was his concern in the *Categories* with the true apprehension of the nature of things: indeed, Traherne saw their aims as common.

Nonetheless, there are already traces in these examples of Traherne's poetry of a dissatisfaction with Aristotle's ontological picture. The purpose of 'Logick', Traherne writes, is to see 'Things methodized, divided and defind,/ Marshald in Classes' (III, p. 204). The speaker's perplexity in 'Christendome' about how to attribute the things of the world to 'kinds', and the complaint in 'Solitude' at the 'unkind' refusal of the world to resolve into categorised sense, express a felt inadequacy in logic's strategies. To know a thing, for Aristotle, was to know what kind of thing it was, to be able to place a substance within a hierarchy of genus and species. That the things of the world are 'unkind' suggests that this method was not entirely adequate to Traherne's purpose. For such dissatisfaction, he had a strong contemporary example.

Traherne', *Literature and Theology* 16 (2002), 248–69; David Hawkes, 'Thomas Traherne: A Critique of Political Economy', *Huntington Library Quarterly* 62 (1999), 369–88.

16   Here Traherne quotes Theophilus Gale, whose *Court of the Gentiles* provided much of the text of 'Aristotle'.

17   See Rudolph Goclenius, *Lexicon Philosophicum* (Frankfurt, 1613), p. 120.

18   Traherne, *Christian Ethicks*, p. 37.

THEORIES OF THINGS: BACON

Though the Aristotelian framework was still the dominant mode of transmitting the logical tradition at the universities, the seventeenth century saw it increasingly attacked. Traherne was certainly aware of this: his engagement with Thomas Hobbes would have exposed him to explicit attacks on 'Aristotelity', and his years at Brasenose coincided with controversies over the teaching of Aristotle involving prominent figures in the university.[19] Most significantly, while at Oxford, in the same context in which he received his education in logic, Traherne was also reading Francis Bacon, an adamant anti-Aristotelian whose works were intended to supply a *Novum Organum*, a new organon to replace the old. The earliest example of Traherne's writing we have is the Early Notebook, a volume of notes from reading used by Traherne and his brother Philip. It contains in Thomas's hand 'Flores Elegantissimae' excerpted from Bacon's *De dignitate et augmentis scientiarum* (1623).[20]

One of Bacon's preoccupations in *De augmentis*, and throughout his works of the 1620s, was a reorientation of his readers' understanding of things. In his introduction to the *Novum Organum*, Bacon objected that the 'human Intellect' had hitherto neglected to find appropriate remedies for its propensity to error, 'whence comes manifold Ignorance of Things, and from the Ignorance of Things countless disadvantages'. Thus, he claimed, 'every effort should be directed to seeing how the commerce between the *Mind*, & *Things* [...] could be restored'.[21] In other words, the foundations of logic, methods of *cognitio rerum*, needed to be reformed. To discover 'the nature of the real world itself', Bacon insisted, 'everything should be sought from the things themselves'.[22] His purpose was not simply to demand that natural historians and philosophers pay closer attention to objects, but also that they reconceive the nature of things.

There is no direct evidence that Traherne knew the *Novum Organum*, but a distinction in ways of perceiving things is explicit in *De augmentis*. The '*Physique* of the *variety of things*' – the study of the teeming world of particulars – divides, Bacon writes, into two categories:

---

[19] On Hobbes, and other controversies, see Kathryn Murphy, 'Thomas Traherne, Thomas Hobbes, and the Rhetoric of Realism', *Seventeenth Century* 28.4 (2013), 419–39.

[20] Bodleian, MS. Lat. misc. f. 45. The excerpts occupy fols 69–170, though non-continuously. See Carol L. Marks, 'Thomas Traherne's Early Studies', *Papers of the Bibliographical Society of America* 62 (1968), 511–36, at 520–33.

[21] Francis Bacon, 'Franciscus de Verulamio sic cogitavit', in *Novum organum*, ed. and trans. Graham Rees (Oxford, 2004), p. 3 (translation amended).

[22] Bacon, *Novum Organum*, p. 37; see also pp. 17, 21, 45, 255.

into Physique of concrets; and into Physique of Abstracts: or into Physique of Creatures; and into Physique of *Natures*. The one (to use the termes of Logique) inquires of *Substances* with all the variety of their Adjuncts; the other of *Accidents*, or Adjuncts through all the variety of substances. *For example*, if the enquiry be of a *Lion*, or of an *Oak*, these are supported by many and diverse Accidents: Contrariwise if the inquiry be made of *Heate*, or *Heavinesse*, these are in many distinct substances.[23]

Bacon offers two ways of parsing the world. The '*Physique of concrets*' is a way of seeing in which the world consists of '*Substances*', such as a lion, or an oak, which are stable in kind; the '*variety of things*' derives from the multiversity of their accidents. It names the Aristotelian world populated by substances that persist under a changing surface of contingent accidents. The '*Physique of Abstracts*', however, sees the world differently. The universals of redness, heat, or heaviness are the stable forms to be investigated. Substances like a lion or an oak sink into the background, as the contingent bearers of accidents.

The 'termes of Logique' to which Bacon refers are the apparatus of substance and accident derived from Aristotle's *Categories*. Bacon, in advocating the '*Physique of Abstracts*', reverses the hierarchies of Aristotelian ontology. Bacon thus proposes a strong form of realism (in the sense opposed to nominalism), asserting not just the existence, but the ontological priority, of universals such as redness or heaviness, the 'forms' of which should be the proper arena of the natural investigator's attention. Bacon is conscious that this runs counter to common sense:

if any man thinks that our forms [...] mix and conjoin things unrelated – for the heat of the heavens and of fire seem not to be at all alike; neither do the fixed red of a rose and so on, and the apparent red of a rainbow or rays from an opal or diamond [...] – such a man must learn that custom, the unanalysed appearances of things [*integralitas rerum*], and mere opinion enslave his intellect.[24]

The *integralitas rerum* is the apparent wholeness, integrity, individuality of 'things'. Bacon's imaginary objector must learn instead to see 'things' as aggregates or 'concrets' of simpler natures, and thus 'grasp [...] the unity of nature beneath the surface of materials which are very unlike'.[25] Bacon aims to train the reader's attention to see a world in which

---

[23] Francis Bacon, *Of the Advancement and Proficience of Learning [...] IX Bookes*, trans. Gilbert Wats (Oxford, 1640), pp. 144–5.

[24] Bacon, *Novum organum*, p. 255.

[25] Bacon, *Novum organum*, p. 203.

apparent accidents are in fact the ground of the real. The same reorientation is part of Traherne's discussion of 'things' in the *Commentaries of Heaven*.

TRAHERNE'S ACCIDENTS

In the *Commentaries*, the manuscript title-page tells the reader, 'ALL THINGS' are 'Discovered to be Objects of Happiness', 'EVRY BEING […] Alphabeticaly Represented […] In the Light of GLORY', and 'the highest Objects of the Christian faith' displayed 'in their Realitie and Glory' (II, p. 3). The entries begin with the common, earthly definition of the word or thing under attention, which is then gradually redefined *sub specie aeternitatis*. The emphatic terms of the title – 'THINGS', 'BEING', 'Objects', 'Realitie' – show the *Commentaries*' concern with ontology, with what is real and what it means to be a thing. The purpose of many of the entries is to insist on the reality of things that Hobbesian nominalism would consign to nonsense.[26] A central strategy throughout is thus reification: the making of abstract nouns, spiritual entities, adjectives, and unpromising topics like 'Abhorrence' and 'Bastard' – the titles of the first and last extant entries – into things worthy of contemplation.

Nowhere is this more obvious, or more relevant to Traherne's 'Things', than in 'Accident', one of a series of entries directed at concepts from Aristotelian logic and metaphysics.[27] Traherne initially draws attention to the non-technical sense of accident, describing it as 'a Thing that befalleth another by Chance'. However, it is the sense 'among Philosophers' (II, p. 108) in which he is particularly interested. He begins with Aristotle's *Categories*, and an orthodox stress on the distinction between substances and accidents: while a substance is 'a Thing that subsisteth of it self, under many Accidents', an accident 'is a Thing which cannot subsist alone, but needeth another to sustain it in its Being. As Redness in a Rose, Brightness in the Sun, Roundness in a Globe &c' (II, p. 109). This follows Aristotle's account of the priority of being, but Traherne's articulation of it shifts towards realism. Traherne already assumes that there is such a 'Thing' as red*ness*, bright*ness*, round*ness*. His nominalisation of the adjectives is also reification: an assertion of the existence of universals as things. The syntax suggests a reversal of priority similar to Bacon's: the substances rose, sun, and globe qualify their accidents,

---

[26] See Murphy, 'Thomas Traherne, Thomas Hobbes, and the Rhetoric of Realism', esp. 424–34.

[27] Others include 'Act', 'Action', 'Activity', 'Art', 'Aspect'.

rather than vice versa. The inclusion of 'Accident' as an entry had indeed already begged the question, since it must belong among the category of 'ALL THINGS' named by the title-page: an assertion of the thingliness, the reality, of accidents.

Traherne's realism becomes more insistent as 'Accident' continues. Much debate was expended in medieval philosophy on the status of accidents; even the most ardent realists tended to suggest that some of the categories – action, passion, and relation in particular – could only have dependent existence, or describe 'modes' of actually existing things.[28] But Traherne includes 'Action' as an entry in the *Commentaries*, and insists in 'Accident' that 'The Relation of a father to His son, of a freind to his Friend, of a Wife to her Husband is a Real Being' (II, p. 110). This emphatic realism leads inevitably towards a questioning of the priority of substances:

> Substances that are Divested of all Accidents, are Naked Existences. Of which we cannot say What they are, When they are, How they are, nor any thing. Nay rather such Existences [...] would be Impossible. for that a Thing should be made without the Circumstance of Time befalling it, wherin it was made; or of Place Where; or of Maner, How; is Impossible [...] Can any Thing be, that is Neither Alive nor Dead; Corporeal nor Spiritual; Coloured, nor Uncoloured; finit, nor Infinit? All things that are, must be one of these; & therfore Subject to Accidents. (II, pp. 110–11)

It was a common position that the defective human intellect could only perceive substances through their accidents. Traherne goes further, however, to equalise the Aristotelian hierarchy.

Traherne is thus in harmony with Bacon's reorientation, agreeing that the focus on substance is a distraction from the true object of attention:

> Gross Apprehensions are apt to look for all Goodness in Substances. It must be Wine, or Oyl, or Gold, or som such Thing: els it cannot be Delightfull. I am sure it was my Mistake a great while. but now I am taught to look for all Glory & Delight among Accidents. (II, p. 111)

Traherne's reference to 'som such Thing' recalls Bacon's objection to the apparent *integralitas rerum*. Traherne wants to remedy the same 'Mistake', and correct 'Gross' – unsubtle – 'Apprehensions'.

Given what we know of Traherne's reading, it is possible that Bacon was one of those who 'taught' him to turn his attention instead to accidents. But the fruit that Traherne wants to glean is different. Accidents are material to our happiness not because they enable our mastery of nature, but because they contribute to 'Glory & Delight': indeed, 'all the Glory of Heaven & Earth is Derived therfrom' (II, p. 111):

---

[28]   See Robert Pasnau, *Metaphysical Themes 1274–1671* (Oxford, 2011), Part III: Accidents.

> Hony without its Sweetness is but Yellow Mire. Gold without its Yellowness & Consistence is a Shadow, & without its Price a Stone. What would a Rose be without its Redness, an Ey without its Sight, a Star without its Splendor? Accidents are the very Robes of Glory. (II, p. 112)

Gold is not praiseworthy by being gold, but for its qualities. Indeed, the value of the procedure of 'reducing [accidents] to Order in nine Predicaments' is not better logic, but that it

> giv[es] us an Occasion to Observ both the Widenes & Discretion of the Soul [...] by this we see that the Soul, like a Bee flying in a Garden, from flower to flower; can rove over all Eternitie, from Creature to Creature, from Region to Region, & see the Limits of Existence & Possibilitie [...] The Discretion of the Soul is Apparent in Dissevering into Kinds, & reducing into Order, all Accidents, which are seen promiscuously Scattered over all the World: & in this the Empire of Mans Understanding. (II, p. 116)

The last sentence is close to Bacon's advocacy of the physique of abstracts, in which discrimination is able to analyse the integrity of concrete things, and recognise through accidents 'the unity of nature beneath the surface of materials which are very unlike'. This ability to see the order of the accidental world is an occasion for the demonstration of the glory of man's understanding, and thus, ultimately, of God.

Traherne's redefinition of 'Accident' thus parallels Bacon's rethinking of things. Both reverse the Aristotelian priority between substance and accident; both assert an initially counter-intuitive realism. And both attempt, though in different ways, to reorient their readers' interpretation of the world, to draw attention away from things conceived as substances, to accidents conceived as things.

THE THINGS THEMSELVES?

It is also evident, however, that while in sympathy with Bacon's ontological reorientation of attention, Traherne's purpose is different: accidents are an opportunity for the exercise of esteem, gratitude and praise, rather than the advancement of learning. This can be seen in the form taken by Traherne's explicit sympathy with the new natural philosophy. In *The Kingdom of God*, Traherne cited several 'Modern Divines and Philosophers', including 'Copernicus, [...] Descartes, Gassendus, [...] Dr Charleton, Dr Willis, [...] my Lord Bacon, Sr Kenelm Digby and the Incomparable Mr Robert Boyl' (I, p. 377). That modern categories would not identify these as 'Divines' shows Traherne's sense that the new philosophy, in all its novelty, was a kind of theological investigation, the

study of the made world as an opportunity for gratitude and the glorifi-
cation of God.

This is clear in Traherne's most unambiguous engagement with the
Royal Society, in his references to Robert Hooke's *Micrographia*. Hooke's
volume famously presented engravings of images seen through a microscope, revealing a hitherto unsuspected level of detail, intricacy, and
animation at levels below perception. Hooke's aim was, explicitly, to
further the Baconian project of advancement: he hoped to be useful to 'a
reformation in Philosophy', for which all that was required was 'a *sincere
Hand*, and a *faithful Eye*, to examine, and to record, the things themselves
as they appear'.[29]

The theological valence – and italicisation – of '*reformation*' and
'*faithful*' indicate that Hooke saw a devotional quality in microscopic
observation. It is this note that Traherne finds resonant. In *The Kingdom
of God*, the revelations of the microscope are praised for their discovery of
the dazzling incorrigible plurality of the animate world:

> living Creatures upon living Creatures, and many Hundred somtimes
> Conceald upon one is a Token of the Value, and Amiableness of Life, as those
> Myriads of Imperceptible Movers are, that by the Help of the Microscope are
> found in Liquors of evry Kind […] The Creation of Insects affords us a Clear
> Mirror of Almighty Power, and Infinit Wisdom. (I, pp. 421–2)

Correspondingly, the *Commentaries* contain an entry devoted to 'Ant',
cross-referred to an entry on 'Insect' that does not survive (III, p. 93). The
ant is of course a prompt to praise: 'a great Miracle in a litle room: a feeble
Creature made to be an Ornament of the Magnificent Univers […] Its Lims
and members are as miraculous, as those of a Lion or Tygre' (III, p. 93).

However Traherne does not allow the eye to stop in wonder: as with his
appropriation of Bacon, there is a lesson here about ways of seeing. The
ant, Traherne writes, is 'never truly seen till it is seen in its Original uses
services Relations and Ends' (III, p. 93). Those five terms name typical
subsections of Traherne's entries in the *Commentaries*. They each imply
that true seeing, undistorted by the vagaries or inadequacies of human
perception, involves thinking not of the thing in itself, as a substance, but
conceived in the category of relation, with an understanding of its efficient
and final cause, its purpose, its utility. Thus Traherne defines the 'Original'
and 'Ends' of the ant: it 'proceedeth from GOD to GOD. It was made by his
Power, and endeth in his Glory' (III, p. 93). The trope of circulation recurs:
in 'The Demonstration', 'All things from Him to Him proceed' (p. 52, 83).

---

[29]   Robert Hooke, *Micrographia* (London, 1665), sig. a2v.

For Traherne, 'Only tis GOD above,/ That from, and in himself doth live' ('The Circulation', p. 47, 78–9). These examples show the work done by prepositions in Traherne's prose and poetry, which assert different vectors of relationship, articulating the reciprocities of grace and gratitude, origin and end that are necessary for true seeing of things.

In a guide to meditation from which Traherne excerpted in his Commonplace Book, Thomas White offered a 'definition of Divine Meditation': 'it is a serious solemn thinking and considering of the things of God, to the end we might understand how much they concern us'.[30] The same motion, from meditating on things themselves to things in relation, appears in the poem 'Dumnesse': 'Sure Man was born to Meditat on Things,/ And to Contemplat the Eternal Springs/ Of God and Nature, Glory, Bliss and Pleasure' (p. 22, 2–4). In the *Centuries of Meditation*, 'It is the Glory of God to giv all Things to us in the Best of all possible maners. To Study Things therfore under the Double Notion of Interest and Treasure, is to study all Things in the best of all possible Maners' (I, p. 133). These are explicit accounts of Traherne's theory of things: not things in themselves, but things as they derive from God, as they concern us, and as they thus oblige us to render gratitude. Much of the burden of the *Centuries*, *Commentaries* and *The Kingdom of God* is precisely to recognise and participate in the economy of grace and gratitude.

This thus accounts for the aesthetic problem with which this essay began. On the one hand – as the *Thanksgivings* make clear – lists are not just enumerations of the various world, but an accounting of what is owed to God. In the entry of the *Commentaries* entitled 'Abridgement', Traherne asks 'What Man is there that will not hav a Terrier [survey or register] of His estate, an Inventory of His Riches, a Catalogue of Goods? [...] What Man is ther Especialy that would be Gratefull, that would be without an Inventory[?]' (II, p. 36). 'Abridgement' concerns epitomes that allow the proper contemplation of the glory of God in small. As such it acts as a justification for Traherne's cataloguing style, and especially for the *Thanksgivings*: they are the 'terriers', inventories, catalogues of the things of God in relation to man.

At the same time, however, these things are not to be considered or esteemed on their own terms. 'The Names of Things', Traherne states in 'Abridgement',

> are like the Titles only upon Apothecaries Boxes. Their first Ideas are but little more. There is as much difference between a familiar and perfect Apprehension of things, and their Names, as there is between A Childs Ey in seeing the Inscription, and a Physicians Soul in Knowing the Drugs. The

---

[30] Thomas White, *A Method and Instructions for the Art of Divine Meditation*, 2nd edn (London, 1672), p. 31.

one seeth only a Box and Painted Letters, the other is acquainted with the Color Consistence Properties and Virtues of the Thing within. (II, p. 36)

Traherne issues a direction to the reader not to take nouns for things: the 'Names of Things', the *signa rerum*, suggesting the priority of substance, conceal the significance of accidents, of 'Color Consistence Properties and Virtues', which are the thing's true value.

This is suggestive for how Traherne's lists and many of the poems should be read: as operating simultaneously in a horizontal and a vertical dimension. Each name or noun acts like the title on a box containing the materials of meditation. Thus the *Thanksgivings*, in particular, encourage an abrupted reading process that reads a list not sequentially, but as an invitation to open each box; which understands each word as shorthand for the accidental properties of colour, consistence, property and virtue that give it its character. Thus 'Abridgement shall at last be like so many Titles before thine Eys, by and through which thou Shalt enjoy a Prospect of all their [the things'] Excellencies' (II, p. 36). Traherne claimed that 'Mans Inclination to Meditate and Contemplate, makes all the Creatures to minister unto him, both food and Occasion for Praises and Thanksgivings' (III, p. 192). The things in Traherne's poems are thus tokens of a reality made up of accidents. This accounts for the apparent contradiction between the insistent deixis of Traherne's poems, and their vagueness about what in fact is being indicated. Attention is drawn to things themselves in order to draw attention away from them in themselves.

ALL AS IF ONE, ONE AS IF ALL

The structure of this meditative approach to 'Things' can be seen in Traherne's response to Bacon in the Early Notebook. There, Traherne found reason to quote and praise one of Bacon's opening compliments to James VI and I, an expansion of 1 Kings 4.29 ('And God gave Solomon wisdom and understanding exceeding much, and largeness of heart, even as the sand that is on the sea shore'):

> De Rege sapientissimo sacra perhibet scriptura. Cor Illi fuisse tanquam Arenam Maris: Cujus tanquam massa prægrandis, p[ar]tes tamen minutissimæ. Sic mentis indidit Deus Solomoni Crasin plane mirabilem, quæ etsi maxima quæque complectatur, minima tamen præhendat, nec sinat effluere: Cum p[er]difficile videatur, vel potius impossibile in Naturâ, ut idem instrumentum et Grandia opera, et pusilla, aptè disponat.[31]

---

[31] Traherne, Early Notebook (Oxford, Bodleian Library, MS. Lat. misc. f. 45), fol. 73. In the 1640 translation of *De augmentis* (Bacon, *Of the Advancement and Proficience*

Though Traherne usually adds his notes in the Early Notebook in English, here he comments on Bacon in Latin: 'Emphasis hujus exp[re]ssionis implicat, <u>universam</u> omnium, et <u>Distinctam</u> si[n]gulorum, cognitionem ita, ut Omnia Cognovit quasi singula, singula quasi sola.'[32] This, Traherne comments in English, is 'an Excellent praise & description of true Wisdome'.

For 'Omnia Cognovit quasi singula, singula quasi sola', Traherne uses a different hand to signal a quotation, a strategy used throughout his excerpts from Bacon in the Early Notebook. The phrase is a version of a tag attributed to Augustine: 'Curat universa quasi singula, & singula quasi sola.' Used of God, the phrase was translated by one of Traherne's near contemporaries as '*He Eyeth All as if one*, and *one as if all*.'[33] Providence attends at once to the whole course of the universal world and to the fall of the individual sparrow. In bringing together the Augustinian phrase with Bacon's praise of James as Solomon, Traherne sets up this simultaneous perception of many and one as a human aspiration, the 'Discretion of the Soul' in which human discrimination unifies the promiscuously scattered world, a double vision that can see at once the grain of sand and the seashore, the thing in itself and in its relation to the whole.

In this very early note, we can thus already see the metaphysical preoccupations that govern Traherne's later work. The final stanza of 'The Vision' begins with a rough paraphrase of the Augustinian tag: 'From One, to One, in one to see *All Things*' (p. 15, 56). The shift of capitalisation in 'The Vision' – if not a mere accident of the manuscript – signals a shift in the sense of 'one': from God conceived as the universal principle of unity, to God conceived as singular, from whom all things derive and to whom they are directed, to a solitary thing 'in' itself, from which the complexity of '*All Things*' can be inferred.

---

of Learning), the passage reads (p. 2): 'Wherefore as the sacred Scripture saith of the wisest King, *That his heart was as the sands of the sea*: which though it be one of the largest bodies, yet it consisteth of the smallest portions; so hath God given Your Majesty a composition of understanding exceeding admirable, being able to compass and comprehend the greatest matters, and neverthelesse, to apprehend the least, and not to suffer them to escape Your observation: whereas it should seem very difficult, or rather an impossibility in nature, for the same instrument to make it selfe fit for great and small works.' Traherne's transcription of Bacon's Latin is largely accurate, though where he has 'sinat' Bacon has the synonymous 'patiatur'; he also systematically removes direct references to James.

[32] 'The significance of this expression intertwines the universal cognition of all things, and the distinct cognition of individuals, just as he perceived all things as if they were individual, individuals as if they alone existed.' My translation.

[33] Christopher Ness, *A Compleat History and Mystery of the Old and New Testament* (London, 1696), p. 257.

The action of the whole process is made particularly clear in Traherne's discussion of the teeming insect world in *Kingdom of God*. Traherne begins with the *omnia*, the myriad variety of things: 'How many Thousand Insects flie in the Meadows, that we never dream of the Glory of whose lives and uses are unknown; How many Millions of Fishes are in the seas, and how many strange Varieties of Birds in the Air, I need not Mention' (I, p. 421). But this paraliptic evocation of profusion and multiplicity, of the infinite variety of the *omnia*, turns quickly to the *singulum*. I quoted above Traherne's praise of the 'Infinit Workmanship' and 'Exquisit Distinction' of the fly as a typical response to the intricacy revealed by the microscope. But the real purpose of the passage is a thought experiment in which Traherne conceives of the fly as the sole end of creation:

> Had but one of those Curious and High Stomachd Flies, been Created [...] That very Flie being made alone the Spectator, and Enjoyer of the Universe had been a little, but Sensible, King of Heaven and Earth [...] all the labours of the Heavens terminate in him, He being the only Sensible that was made to Enjoy them [...] So had he been the End of the Material World [...] God had done as much in little there, as he had done at large in the whole World. [...] The Heavens, and the Elements, and all Inanimates Trees, and Stones, and Fruits, and Flowers, Seeds, and Spices, all Minerals Gold, and Silver, and Precious Gems, yea The Sun and Moon, and Stars were made for the conservation of its Lims and Members. (I, pp. 422–3)

Here Traherne applies the principal of perceiving *universa, quasi singula, singula, quasi sola*: the 'quasi' of the meditative thought experiment makes the fly not only a singular thing in the centre of contemplative attention, but the only thing, to which the rest of the universal world is subordinate. But the purpose of this isolation is of course the reunion of the fly's singular perspective with the whole manifold world: 'If there are Innumerable other Creatures, this is not less, but more to be Esteemed, and as much to be admired, as if it were alone.' Conceiving the fly in itself, and then in relationship to the rest of the manifold world, allows meditation 'to adore the fulness of their Creator's Love, and revere the Height, and Depth, and Length, and Breadth of the Profound Abyss of his Wisdom, and Power, and Goodness in the smallest Life, that is in all Nature' (I, p. 423).

As in the insistence in the *Centuries* that, to esteem the world properly, you must 'Place yourself in it as if no one were Created besides your self' (I, p. 57) – another instance of the quasi or 'as if' – Traherne presents the consideration of all as one, and one as all, as the structure of meditation. The close of 'The Vision' makes the shift clear, in its two versions: 'Who all things finds conjoyned in Him alone,/ Sees and Enjoys the Holy one'; or 'Who *All Things* finds convey'd to him alone,/ Must needs adore *The*

Holy One' (p. 16, 62–3 and p. 103, 55–6). Though of course the changes in capitalisation and italicisation make significant differences to the precise meaning of the lines (whether 'he' is God or the individual; whether the enjoyment or adoration tends to the unity of all things, or the one who is holy), both versions play on a verbal shift that again enacts the Augustinian motion of divine intellection: from 'all things' to 'alone' to 'one', from *omnia* to *singula* and *sola*, and back again, in gratitude. The etymological pun in 'alone' is crucial: 'alone' means something single, solitary, and integral in nature, a thing in itself, but etymologically it is 'all one', part of the universal whole. Bacon, as we saw, called simultaneously for attention to the things themselves, and for a disintegration of the apparent integrity of things. Traherne, adapting Aristotle's ontology, and crossing Bacon's preoccupations with Augustine's, demands a simultaneous vision of the solitary individual thing, and of its difference and distinction subsumed in recognition of a deeper unity.

CONCLUSION: THOUGHTS AND THINGS

Traherne's major works use a variety of formal devices in order to effect this reorientation of attention, and, as Bacon put it, to return the commerce of the mind and things to its proper footing. The *Thanksgivings* work as an inventory of man's estate; the *Centuries of Meditation* adopt an exhortatory tone that insists on the reader learning how to 'Enjoy the World aright' (I, pp. 14 and ff). The *Commentaries* meanwhile reinterpret things in their uses, origins, ends and relations. The poetry combines these strategies of enumeration, exhortation and reinterpretation, issuing imperatives of the kind found in the *Centuries*: 'Giv but to things their tru Esteem', 'But give to Things their tru Esteem' ('Right Apprehension', VI, pp. 155–6, 1, 17). However, the most common device is a pattern of repetition and *metanoia* – literally 'change of mind', a rhetorical figure in which what has been said is contradicted and revised by the speaker – which, like the shape of 'Accident' and many entries in the *Commentaries*, starts from common usage and understanding to reverse expectation and effect new ways of seeing.

Analysis of a single poem will have to stand in for this frequent pattern of revision, and sum up Traherne's treatment of things.[34] 'Dreams' begins with an exclamation commenting on the oddity of sense experience without stimulus in dream states:

---

[34] For further examples, see Murphy, 'Thomas Traherne, Thomas Hobbes, and the Rhetoric of Realism', esp. 431.

> 'Tis strange! I saw the Skies;
> I saw the Hills before mine Eys;
> The Sparrow fly;
> The Lands that did about me ly;
> The reall Sun, *that* hev'nly Ey! (p. 179, 1–5)

The repetition of 'I saw' insists on the authenticity of experience even without external prompts. The 'reall Sun' makes an etymological gesture to things. If, in sleep, Traherne saw the 'reall' sun, its thingliness must not rely on what can be perceived by sense.

The stress on the real recurs later in the poem, with a typical turn to infant perception: 'My Childhood knew/ No Difference, but all was Tru,/ As Reall all as what I view' (p. 180, 24–6). The immediate sense in which childish perception knows 'No Difference' is that mental images in dreams, and actual stimuli in the world, are not distinguished; things seen in dreams are not disparaged in comparison with visible reality. But Traherne's refusal to qualify 'Difference' makes the statement general: the process of distinction, of parsing, which separates out one substance from another on the basis of *differentiae*, is alien to childhood. That this sense predominates is clear from the subsequent stanza:

> Till *that* which vulgar Sense
> Doth falsly call Experience,
> Distinguisht things:
> The Ribbans, and the gaudy Wings
> Of Birds, the Virtues, and the Sins,
> That represented were in Dreams by night
> As really my Senses did delight,
>
> Or griev, as those I saw
> By day. (p. 180, 29–37)

Before 'Experience Distinguisht things', dream sensation was as real as waking. There is again a straightforward and a logical sense in Traherne's attention to such discrimination: on the one hand 'Experience' separates 'real' things and mental things from one another; on the other, 'things' – substances – are seen distinguished from one another, 'in themselves', rather than as part of a manifold but single universe.

The phrase 'Distinguisht things' is the first time 'things' are explicitly, rather than etymologically, present in the poem; but in the remaining three stanzas, Traherne devotes himself to the commerce between the mind and 'things': to an opposition between 'Things' and 'Thoughts', as mental representations of things. 'Apparitions', says Traherne, 'seem'd as near/ As Things could be, and Things they were' (p. 180, 39–40). Initially, 'apparitions' only seem as real as 'Things'; 'Things' must mean objects actually existing in the world. But the second clause revises that sense, in an emphatic statement of realism: 'and Things they were'. If the first 'Things' are Aristotelian substances, the second 'Things' has the force of a statement of existence and reality. Anything that can be thought of is a thing, even if that thought does not represent something in the external world, and 'all [its] Being [were] founded in a Thought' (p. 180, 42).

As with the progression in 'Accident', this moment of equivalency between external and mental things starts to tip in favour of the latter. The penultimate stanza opens with a reiteration of thought's reality: 'O what a Thing is Thought!' This is at once an emphatic statement of thought's thingliness, a wondering exclamation, and a question – how can a thought be a thing, Traherne asks,

> Which seems a Dream; yea, seemeth Nought,
> Yet doth the Mind
> Affect as much as what we find
> Most near and tru! Sure Men are blind,
> And can't the forcible Reality
> Of things that Secret are within them see. (p. 180, 43–9)

Traherne vacillates between ascribing reality to the experienced stuff of the world, which we find 'most near and tru', and the 'forcible Reality' – etymologically, thingliness – of the stuff of thoughts and dreams. The poem ends with a clear statement of realism, and another example of the progressive, self-revisionary motion of Traherne's prose and poetry:

> Thought! Surely *Thoughts* are tru;
> They pleas as much as *Things* can do:
> Nay Things are dead,
> And in themselvs are severed
> From Souls; nor can they fill the Head
> Without our Thoughts. Thoughts are the Reall things
> From whence all Joy, from whence all Sorrow springs. (pp. 180–1, 50–6)

Like the pattern of 'Accident', Traherne begins with the common priority of the stuff of the world over the stuff of the mind, and then reverses its polarity, so that not only are 'Things [...] dead' without thoughts (or substances 'empty' or 'naked' without accidents), but the thoughts (or accidents) are the real things. Accidents exist only in thought: yet this increases their reality. The notion is frequently repeated: 'Imaginations *Reall* are', Traherne asserts in 'The Review II' (p. 194, 7); in another poem, with pertinently Aristotelian vocabulary, thoughts 'do all Substances Excell' ('The Influx', p. 67, 9). 'The Inference', in its two parts, systematically disparages substances and sense experience in comparison with the reality of thought:

'*Things* are indifferent' (part I, p. 181, 3); 'Thoughts are [...] such Valuable Things;/ Such reall Goods'(part II, p. 183, 5–6); 'Things are but dead: they can't dispense/ Or Joy or Grief: Thoughts! Thoughts the Sense/ Affect and touch'; thoughts are 'Reall things when shewn' (part I, p. 181, 17–19, 23). The doubleness of '*Things*' is particularly stark here: they can be dead and indifferent, or 'Reall'.

The etymological tautology of 'Reall things' – thingly things – highlights the ways in which Traherne exploits the ambivalence of 'things'. It also highlights the centrality of his realism both to the rhetorical structure of self-revision, and to his philosophy and theology. As Traherne explains, an accident 'is not a Substantial Material Thing Distinct from the Substance in which it lies, nor may it be seen as a Creature Distinct from the other by the Ey, but only by the Understanding. Yet it is a Being' (II, p. 111). It is only in the mind that an accident can be conceived as a thing; but if accidents are more real than substances, then thoughts must be more real than things. This would be anathema to Bacon, for whom thoughts were artificial, requiring careful abstraction from the things themselves to assure their accuracy. But for Traherne, in a way which, despite the earlier critical bafflement about his addiction to things, is intrinsically poetic, there can be no things, but in thoughts.

Chapter 3

THOMAS TRAHERNE AND 'FEELING INSIDE THE ATOM'

Cassandra Gorman

They are more necessary to us, then the Existence of Angels.
(*The Kingdom of God*, I, p. 347)

Thus Traherne concludes one of the chapters in his late study *The Kingdom of God*, the subject of which is not words of scripture, sacraments or prophets, but atoms. The chapter is remarkably prominent in the text, where it is positioned at the crux of meditations on elements of the spiritual and material cosmos. Traherne was fascinated with the atom as a connecting point between body and soul, time and eternity, humanity and the divine. He expands upon the topic of atomism yet further in another of his encyclopaedic works, the voraciously ambitious *Commentaries of Heaven*.[1] In the *Commentaries*, Traherne endeavours to investigate 'ALL THINGS' in an alphabetically ordered, sequential study of individual subjects – the resulting text runs over 300,000 words, though sadly it only fulfils its ambitions between the words 'Abhorrence' and 'Bastard'.[2] The section on the 'Atom' is by far the longest in the text. There was something inherent to the subject of atomism that fuelled Traherne's pen, leading him to close with two of the longest poems in the *Commentaries* and the editorial query of whether 'it be not best leav out some of these Poems' (III, p. 363).

This chapter will reveal how Traherne expands upon the common theological reception of seventeenth-century atomism to create a means for the obtainment of 'Felicitie' and grace. He muses on the 'indivisible' atom as

---

[1]   For the 'Atom' commentary, see Ross, III, pp. 333–63.
[2]   Traherne reveals his intention to unveil 'ALL THINGS' in the *Commentaries* on his frontispiece to the work, II, p. 3.

an image for the accommodation of divine mysteries, a rhetorical move that, though not entirely unusual in the latter half of the century, demands closer attention from the reader in the complexity of its interpretative possibilities. The driving force of his investigation is not so much on the atom as a means to deeper investigation of other unseen materials, but on the interior capacity of the atom itself. It is an entity that, rather like the intended final version of the *Commentaries*, encompasses 'ALL THINGS'. Traherne's 'Atom' is more than a distanced literary symbol for the recognition of mortal frailty, or the greatness of God: it comes to function as a model for the 'insatiable' Christian soul, which in Traherne's theology is ever seeking to explore 'All in All'.

I will examine the ways in which Traherne's personal corpuscular theories influenced the motives of his theology, and vice versa. In doing so, I challenge an enduring tendency to dismiss Traherne's natural philosophical knowledge as somewhat half-baked, ill-advised and outdated. For example, Carol L. Marks considered Traherne's presentation of the 'physical world' as a subject meriting 'study (such as the Royal Society supported and Traherne may have dabbled in)', implying that his interest in natural knowledge and experimentation was casual at the very least. She proceeds with the claim that there is 'slender evidence' of natural philosophical imagery in Traherne's works.[3] Marks constructed her argument prior to the discovery of further manuscripts in which the writer demonstrated his encyclopaedic philosophical knowledge with the greatest clarity. The claim that Traherne had only shallow knowledge of the contemporary material philosophies has nevertheless persisted, with Finn Fordham arguing that his writings 'frequently show a weak absorption of scientific discoveries'.[4] That these writings demonstrate any sort of 'weak absorption' I intend to disprove. Traherne was not merely a poet and a devotional writer occasionally commenting on areas outside of his expertise. His thoughts on the scientific discoveries of his period were intelligent and well-informed enough for him to formulate his own ideas and systems of knowledge. Critical work has focused on too narrow an examination of sources for Traherne's natural philosophical background, on the basis of which it has judged his limitations. As I will begin to show, he was familiar with the multiple cultural and theological responses to atomism that were live in the period, recycling common metaphorical frameworks and refiguring his own within the context of his works.

---

[3]   Carol L. Marks, 'Thomas Traherne and Cambridge Platonism', *PMLA* 7 (1966), 521–34, at 527.

[4]   Finn Fordham, 'Motions of Writing in the Commentaries of Heaven: The "Volatilitie" of "Atoms" and "ÆTYMS"', in *Re-reading Thomas Traherne*, ed. Jacob Blevins (Tempe, 2007), pp. 115–34, at p. 116.

Traherne's atomism was vitally important to the shaping of his polymathic oeuvre. His studious meditations on the atom inspired the use of hermetic, Neoplatonic, and Thomist images and terminologies, in addition to the vocabularies of contemporary European material philosophies. As a point of contraction, the 'Atom' also provides a sharp focus from which we can observe the coming together of many of Traherne's different philosophical and theological influences. This chapter will begin to tease out some of these layers of significance and, I hope, go some way toward demonstrating the crucial part Traherne's atomism had to play in the development of his most original theories about soul and self.

ATOMS AND MYSTERIES

Some thirty years before Traherne's birth, the mathematician Thomas Harriot wrote to the astronomer Johannes Kepler proposing the atomic system as a framework for philosophical thought. In his letter Harriot marvels at the benefits of the atomic hypothesis, not only as a means of understanding the construction of the natural world, but also, he implies, as a way of empathising with the hidden, spiritual truths that creation contains. He rounds off:

> I have conducted you to the doors of nature's house, where its mysteries lie hidden. If you cannot enter, because the doors are too narrow, then abstract and contract thyself mathematically to an atom, and you will easily enter, and when you have come out again, tell me what miraculous things you saw.[5]

The associations in Harriot's letter between the atom, knowledge of nature, and miracles anticipate some of the multiple ways the indivisible particle would become symbolic across the following century. According to the mid-seventeenth-century lexicographers Edward Phillips and Elisha Coles, an atom is, respectively, 'the smallest part of a body that can be *imagined*', and more simply 'the smallest part of anything'.[6] Within the context of early modern corpuscular matter theories, an atom represents the first element of all that is, the seed of matter in which all possible life

---

[5] Thomas Harriot, letter to Johannes Kepler, 2 December 1606. Quoted from Hans Christian von Baeyer, *Taming the Atom: The Emergence of the Visible Microworld* (New York, 1992), p. 12.

[6] Edward Phillips, *The New World of English Words* (London, 1658), sig. Dv; Elisha Coles, *An English Dictionary Explaining the Difficult Terms that are used in Divinity, Husbandry, Physick, Phylosophy, Law, Navigation, Mathematicks, and other Arts and Sciences* (London, 1677), sig. Dv. '*Imagined*' is italicised in Phillips's original text.

and action receives its origin and its ultimate state of contraction. It marks the beginning and end of all created forms: all existing things are moulded from atoms, and will be dispersed into the same, unchanged individuals at their corruption. The atomic perspective that Harriot proposes to Kepler, therefore, provides an insight into the secret operations of natural construction at a level of minute accuracy.

Yet as the allusion to 'miraculous things' implies, there is more to Harriot's advice than the wishful thinking of observing nature's atoms at work. The need to become an atom 'thyself' suggests the necessity for human empathy with the particle. There is likely of course to be a sense of humour and, possibly, a competitive streak of mockery coming into play here. Following his correspondence with Kepler on the formation of the rainbow, Harriot is declaring that his advice has gone as far as it can go: either Kepler desires to know something that would require a miracle to be made known, or he is being encouraged, in no subtle terms, to reconcile his views to Harriot's atomism in order to advance his study of nature.[7] On a more serious note, Kepler's need to 'contract' himself to an atom in order to enter the narrow doors of nature recalls the aphorism of the Gospels, that 'it is easier for a camel to pass through the eye of a needle than for a rich man to enter the gates of heaven'.[8] As it would more explicitly in theological and literary works across the seventeenth century, Harriot's atom comes to symbolise the spiritual benefits in actions that acknowledge the principles of Christian human humility. Hence the association in the letter between the impersonation of an atom and reception to natural secrets: meekness inspires blessing and the provision of discovery by the divine.

Writing decades later in the 1670s, Traherne delved into the subject of atomism when collecting material for the *Commentaries*. His notes on the atom not only intend to expand upon its worth as a metaphor for the accommodation of divine concepts, as it was being used with increasing frequency by contemporary theological writers. He is eager moreover to understand the actual, material presence of something so small yet so integral to the created world. Paralleling Harriot, Traherne is interested in the atom as a store of information, readily available to the human being who comes with the right approach to receive its knowledge. He applies by chance a very similar vocabulary to Harriot's when he considers how we might relate to something so unfathomable:

[7]   Baeyer, *Taming the Atom*, p. 12. I am grateful to Professor David Harris Sacks for pointing out the possible mockery in Harriot's invitation to Kepler in our conversation at the colloquium 'Crossroads of Knowledge: Literature and Theology in Early Modern England', University of Cambridge, 14 February 2015.

[8]   For the relevant passage, see Matthew 19.23–4, Mark 10.24–5 and Luke 18.24–5.

> I know not how, by reason of its Simplicitie it is Obscure, and inexpressible, and yet for that reason is the most easy to be apprehended in the whole World. Multiplicity breeds Distraction, but Singleness and Indivisibilite contract our Thoughts, and the Things are if not Known by Causes, felt by Intuition. And what we feel in an Atom (with our Minds) is the Matter of it. (III, p. 341)

Harriot and Traherne both hold the image of the singular atom as a means of exploring the mysteries of creation. In order to dwell on the 'Simplicitie' of the undividable particle the witness must empathise with its ultimate material poverty, which – as the image of the rich man facing the eye of the needle suggests – comes to inspire the state of humble being that makes closest contact with the divine. When Traherne refers to the 'Simplicitie' of the atom, he evokes primarily its status 'next to Nothing' (III, p. 343) in the scale of creation. It is utterly uncompounded and immune to corruption because 'it is already as litle as it can be' (III, p. 345). Traherne explains that 'All Corruption is a Dissolution, wherby the Thing Corrupted is Divided into its Elements' (III, p. 345). The word 'Element' in this context can be substituted for 'atom', literally 'that which cannot be divided', from which point no further diminishment is possible.[9]

The atom receives its status as divine entity and symbol from its immunity to corruption. As a result, the philosopher enquiring into natural secrets and the human creature desiring to enter the kingdom of heaven must be willing to become 'next to Nothing' to achieve their aims. Both Harriot and Traherne ask their reader to *feel*, to intuit, to enact in some sense the interior experience of an atom. While Harriot asks Kepler to adopt not just the theory but atomic size and vision to sharpen his focus on the operations of nature, Traherne goes somewhat further. He asks us to 'feel *in* an Atom (with our Minds)'. Though both writers speak of contraction, Traherne's perspective is not so much on using the atom as a means to deeper investigation of unseen materials – the finding of 'miraculous things' that can then be communicated – but on immersive experience within the atom itself; an essence, like the divine, that can be felt and known but not expressed. Harriot proposes the accommodative atom as a methodology, but Traherne views it as an end to knowledge and spiritual experience. At an earlier stage of the commentary, he describes how the atom forms a vessel for divine information:

> yet is there an unsearchable Abyss of Wonders contained in it; innumerable Difficulties, Uses, Excellencies and Pleasures concentering in its Womb, for

---

[9]   See the *OED* for the etymological history of the word 'Atom'.

our Information and Happiness; the clear Knowledge of which will make us Expert in the Chiefest Mysteries of GOD and Nature. (III, p. 333)

The 'Wonders' contained within the atom are 'innumerable' and piled within 'an unsearchable Abyss'; yet they exist for 'our Information and Happiness', and 'clear Knowledge' of them is considered possible. Framed as the ultimate object of enquiry, Traherne's 'atom' takes on an extraordinary level of spiritual importance as it provides a means to develop expertise in 'the Chiefest Mysteries of GOD'. What are the 'Wonders' encased within an atom, and how can they be 'unsearchable' and yet clearly known all at once?

Traherne implicitly acknowledges the roles the atom-image could play within the wider context of theological vocabularies, thus hinting at what sort of knowledge the primary particle of the created world might hold. By the 1650s atomism had made a distinct impact upon English society and culture. The proximity of the atom to nothingness, as the *minima materia* of the natural world, inspired a range of associations with mortal worthlessness and, consequentially, Christian humility. On the whole, however, these were negative analogies inspired by the threats atomic motion could pose to material order and stability. The dominant source for the development of atomic imagery in early modern Europe was Lucretius's didactic poem on the Epicurean philosophy, *De Rerum Natura*. Lucretius's description of a world governed by chance, subject to a violent 'swarm' of mutable atoms, brought an underlying microworld of disorder into contact with social, political and theological constructions.[10] Particularly within sermons, and notably those of non-conformist ministers, the frail and shifting forms of atomic construction could symbolise the precariousness of human existence. Atomism was seen to undermine the very nobility of human nature, as it required all corporeal beings to be composed of the same insensitive and inconsistent stuff. Thus Elisha Coles remarks that we are but 'atoms of clay animated' by God's breath; the logician Zachary Coke dismisses man as but a 'graine or an atom', and Bishop Joseph Hall despairs of what 'an insensible Atome man is, in comparison of the whole body of the Earth'.[11]

---

[10] For the passage relevant to the atomic 'swarm' see Book 3, lines 1409–10. Lucy Hutchinson produced what was likely to have been the first full English translation of the poem in the 1650s. See Reid Barbour and David Norbrook, *The Translation of Lucretius*, vol. II of *The Works of Lucy Hutchinson*, 4 vols (Oxford, 2012 –).

[11] Elisha Coles, *A Practical Discourse of God's Sovereignty* (London, 1673), p. 15; Zachary Coke, *The Art of Logick; or, The Entire Body of Logick in English* (London, 1657), sig. A3 (Address to 'THE ILLUSTRIOUS, His Excellency Oliver Cromwel'); Joseph Hall, *Select Thoughts, or Choice helps for a pious spirit* (London, 1654), p. 74. This usage is very common in the works of Hall: see also *A Sermon of Public Thanksgiving* (London, 1626), p. 8.

Meditations on the threatening presence of indivisible particles aside, the cultural association between the 'atom' and corporeal baseness continued in an etymological link with the word 'anatomy' – quite literally, 'an atomy'. The Greek word for 'anatomy' derives from the abstract noun 'ἀνατομή', which refers to 'cutting up' or 'dissection'.[12] Early modern literary references to the 'atomy' follow on from this history to gesture most frequently to a skeleton, or an emaciated body. When Mistress Quickly turns on the Beadle with the low insult 'Thou atomy, thou!' in *Henry IV 2*, the direct purpose of her curse is to compare its object with a withered corpse.[13] The outright comparison of a human being to an 'atom', or to a disordered swarm of particles, appears to have been a common insult – especially within seventeenth-century drama. Following the Neo-Epicurean developments of the mid century, the 'cutting up' of the anatomy had been taken so far that in John Corye's comedy *The Generous Enemies* (1672) a character receives the biting remark: 'You heap of Atoms kneaded into flesh!'[14] The insult plays on the irony that all humans, whatever their claim to personal integrity, are composed of a 'heap of Atoms' just like anything else.

Traherne suggests in his *Commentaries* that the atom is 'A good Emblem of Humility' (III, p. 345), but his reasons for viewing it thus are quite distinct from those of Coles, Coke, Corye and Hall. The description of the atom emblem as 'good' is telling. Traherne is enamoured with the idea of an atom. He observes its material poverty not with despair, but with joy in response to its 'great Miracle in a litle Room' (III, p. 333). More than a symbol for the Christian recognition of human frailty, and quite divorced from threat, Traherne's atoms demonstrate the *good* that a life of humility can achieve. The very reason the atom has become a symbol of humility, Traherne explains, is because 'the least things are the most secure' (III, p. 345). He uses the image as a metaphor for the ideal human individual, reinterpreting the consequences of the Lucretian 'swarm' to point out the stable immutability of the single atom amidst surrounding change. Its essence remains the same regardless of how it moves in the flux of the wider world. As Traherne writes in the second poem at the end of the commentary, despite the 'varietie' in sublunary things, the estates of atoms 'Are still the same: And which is very Strange,/ Without Change in themselvs, they all things change' (III, p. 358).

In holding out the atom as a metaphor for the ideal human individual, Traherne's interpretation is quite contrary to the dominant theological

---

[12]   See the entry in the *OED* for 'Atomy'.

[13]   *Henry IV.2*, Act 5, Scene 4, line 27. Quoted from *The Norton Shakespeare*, ed. Stephen Greenblatt (London, 2008), p. 1372.

[14]   John Corye, *The Generous Enemies, or, The Ridiculous Lovers* (London, 1672), p. 61.

discourse that dwells upon humanity's material frailty. The blessed human being is as constant in his or her faith as the unchanging interiority of an atom – constant in spite of the surrounding corporeal flux – and a person's spiritual capacity is comparably mysterious. Traherne even reinterprets the significance of shifting atomic matter in a way that further promotes the integrity of the individual within material, social and spiritual communities. Inverting the futility behind expressions such as 'atoms of clay', he marvels at the very power atoms have in their multitude to mould and remould created forms. Individually weak, atoms find strength in numbers and congregate together to enact change. Traherne comments more on the parallels between atomic union and Christian society in *The Kingdom of God*: 'Nothing is weaker then a single Atom', he explains, 'Nothing stronger then an Infinit Multitude' (I, p. 346). Quite unusually within seventeenth-century culture, Traherne combines the image of the singular atom with that of the congregational 'swarm' of particles to establish one positive symbol for the accommodation of spiritual life. The movement of his atoms is advantageous rather than threatening because it reflects the power that a community of pure individuals can possess. Plural atoms realise, on a physical and – following the consequences of their collaboration – macrocosmic basis, the divine potentiality of the single point of contraction.

The particle therefore is of tremendous physical and spiritual worth. Without atoms, there would be no physical world, nor – consequentially – access to 'the Chiefest Mysteries of GOD' from the mortal vantage point. As an entity, Traherne's atom coexists in material and metaphysical states of being, often indistinguishably: the weakest possible material particle is simultaneously the strongest metaphysical component of the cosmos, and it is never entirely clear as to whether the worth Traherne cherishes in the atom should be classed under the 'Created' or 'Increated' category of 'ALL THINGS'. A clear distinguishing factor between his interpretation of atomism and the other atomic theories of the century is his insistence that atoms are material, but not corporeal. As he writes in the *Commentaries*: 'An Atom being infinitly small is Incorporeal. For since the Essence of a Body is to be Extended, and to have Parts out of Parts, an Atom can be no Body' (III, p. 350). Traherne classifies the atom as a 'Material Spirit', a title that he also attributes to rays of light and 'Spirits' that 'move in the Blood' (III, p. 351). He then explains the location of these 'Material Spirits' within his universe:

> Material Spirits are the Mean or Clasp, between Immaterial Spirits and Material Bodies. for with Spirits they are void of Body, with Bodies they are full of Matter. (III, p. 351)

Traherne hints here at the information atoms may have in store for the faithful Christian. God created rays of light to reveal his presence, enable genesis and subsequently to establish contact between the terrestrial and the divine; 'spirits' within the blood enable the mingling of body and soul within the human individual.[15] The atom too is a 'Mean or Clasp' between the spiritual and the corporeal, but what it clasps, and how it follows that human contemplation of its essence is possible, remains unclear. There is a seeming discrepancy between Traherne's definition of the atom as a 'seed of Corporeitie' – a term he uses in *The Kingdom of God* (I, p. 342) – and an incorporeal, 'Material Spirit'. *The Kingdom of God* describes an atom as 'a Physical Monad, or an Indivisible and Tangible Realitie, of No Dimensions parts, or powers, but meerly passiv, and a Seed of Corporietie' (I, p. 342). Traherne makes no direct claim in this work to the incorporeal nature of the atom, but he does open the section by explaining that matter falls into two forms, physical and metaphysical: 'That which is Physical is Corporeal Matter; Metaphysical being any object, or Subject, whose Existence is the Ground work of its Form and Perfection' (I, p. 341). By his logic an atom, though a 'seed of corporeitie', is more metaphysical than physical. The constant, unchangeable presence of a single atom makes it the subject, or 'Ground work', of distinguishable material forms – if it were not for the movement and congregation of atoms, all matter would look the same; there would be no 'Form and Perfection' in the corporeal world, hence Traherne's trust in the positive consequences of atomic mutability. Reinterpreting Lucretian metaphor, the atom is a 'seed', designed to fulfil divine purpose by enabling the constant motion and evolution of the terrestrial world.[16] The end of this material and temporal motion is of course the state of 'Perfection' in God.

In the *Commentaries*, Traherne places greater emphasis on demonstrating the atom's metaphysical status, in the literal sense: he stresses that the particle is incorporeal and beyond the laws of nature. At the beginning of the 'Atom' commentary he acknowledges that we may treat the atom 'either Physicaly, or Metaphysicaly: the Metaphysical notion of

---

[15] For further information on the combined medical and theological significance of 'spirits' in the early modern period, see D. P. Walker, 'Medical Spirits in Philosophy and Theology from Ficino to Newton', *Arts du Spectable et Histoire des idées* (Tours, 1984), pp. 287–300.

[16] Traherne demonstrates further his direct knowledge of Lucretius in the first of his poems to conclude the 'Atom' section in the *Commentaries*. His reference to atoms dancing in the ray of light recreates the familiar Lucretian simile between atomic motion and motes in the sunbeam (see p. 354, lines 811–18). The image in Lucretius can be found in Book 2, lines 112–29.

it, helpeth much in the Mysteries of Felicitie, the Physical in the Secrets of Nature' (III, p. 333). Felicity is the blissful state of being toward which all of Traherne's writings are directed. The recognition of mankind's infinite capacity for knowledge and the divine blessing that this entails is necessarily intuitive, and it is in this context that feeling inside the atom –'with our Minds' – provides an opportunity by which these 'Mysteries' might encounter representation and experience. It is soon apparent, however, that there can be no clear distinction between a physical and metaphysical analysis of the atom. Even within its 'physical' definition, Traherne explains that it 'hath not its Three Dimensions', and has no extension of parts (III, p. 350). Rather, Traherne's physical theory of atomism directly provides the metaphorical lexis for accommodating spiritual truths and metaphysical obscurities, without any need to recreate the vocabulary in a separate context. Physical and metaphysical collapse into one point, the omnipresent 'Centre' of the atom:

> No Atom hath any Superfice, but it [is] all Centre, where it is toucht, it is wholy toucht. and cannot be touchd in one part, and untouchd in another. so that two Atoms having one between them, are as if they were immediatly together. (III, p. 350)

Traherne's recognition of the atom as a 'Centre', undividable and incorruptible, inspires his understanding of it as a vessel for divine spirit and eternity. It is not merely from the perspective of material experience that the atom is the 'Ground work' of all 'Form and Perfection': it also fulfils the creative intentions of the divine.

Though Traherne's spiritual reading into the atom image is extreme, he is not alone in the second half of the seventeenth century in developing such theories. When contemplation of the indivisible point meets theology, the atom – the original element of the natural world – takes on some of the characteristics of Julian of Norwich's hazelnut-sized ball that is 'all that is made'.[17] To borrow one of the titles in Traherne's *Commentaries*, an atom can be seen to contain 'All in All' (III, p. 11) in spite of its impossibly small size. It was not unusual, in theological writings, for the atom to become a mystical symbol encapsulating past, present and future. The ineffability of the atom, its liminal location within the material world and its vast longevity bestowed it with the characteristics of a near-immortal midpoint between the terrestrial and the divine. In a sermon on Ecclesiastes 12.1 from 1655, the churchman and historian Thomas Fuller meditates on the message 'Remember *now* thy Creatour' with the explanation: 'I say *now*,

---

[17]   See *Julian of Norwich: Revelations of Divine Love, and The Motherhood of God*, ed. Frances Beer (Cambridge, 1998), p. 29.

now is an Atome, it will puzzle the skill of an Angell to divide.'[18] Within the context of his theological exposition, Fuller refers to an atom as a minute unit of time, an accommodating object for the 'everlasting now' of Thomism.[19] Atoms represent the 'now' of the temporal present in as far as they gather together to formulate contingent entities, here today but gone tomorrow; a single atom represents the collapse of time into an eternal 'now' by its indivisible constancy.

For Traherne the link between the atom and eternity is more explicit. Divine power endows the atom with eternity, because God 'lodgeth his whole DEITIE,/ In one small Centre, yet is not confined' (*Commentaries*, III, p. 339). Prior to this conclusion, Traherne describes the atom as a 'means wherof all Things Past, Present, and to Come, may at once appear before the Understanding' (III, p. 338). The word 'means', common within the terminology of reformed religion and hearkening back to the recommended use of 'ordinary meanes' in the *Westminster Confession of Faith*, suggests that the believer should use the atom as a relatable object of assurance.[20] As Traherne admits when he recognises the 'Obscure [...] Simplicitie' of the atom in his *Commentaries*, such means can only be 'felt by Intuition'. The advice to 'feel inside an Atom', therefore, is no mere metaphorical construction. There is a degree of practicality in the logic behind its accommodation of 'ALL THINGS'. Physically and metaphysically, the atom is devoid of contents or characteristics, but it is the original element common to all matter, the 'Ground work' of all created form, the final particle into which all objects will fall and, throughout all this, a vessel into which the deity pours the essence of divine eternity. The obscurity of atomic simplicity necessarily defies definition, whether literal or figurative, thus enabling the concurrency of Traherne's multiple interpretations. His 'Atom' is both a sign of potentiality and growth – like a seed – and a point of contact between the terrestrial and the divine, on which material beings are reliant for their corporeal and spiritual source of life.

---

[18] Thomas Fuller, *A Collection of Sermons* (London, 1655), p. 29.

[19] This association between the atom and the indivisible present also owes much to a medieval significance of the word: from the early Middle Ages, the term 'atom' was used to refer to the smallest unit of measured time. According to the *OED*, there are 376 atoms in a minute and 22,560 in an hour. This usage was archaic by the early modern period, but lived on in literature, and merged rather strikingly with interpretations of Epicurean atomism to inspire new metaphors of indivisibility in the seventeenth century.

[20] For the relevant section of the Westminster Confession, see *The humble advice of the Assembly of Divines, now sitting at Westminster, concerning a Confession of Faith* (London, 1647), pp. 31–2.

On this note we can return full circle to Harriot's call for empathy with the atomic scale of being, a means by which the humble enquirer could seek out natural mysteries. In one of his most severe moments, Traherne claims that the mystical and paradoxical contents of the atom are only available to a certain kind of elect. He argues that it is '*Inter non Entia*, to a vulgar Soul. Common People cannot so much as Shape the Maner of its Existence' (III, p. 334).[21] When Traherne observes that atomic wonders remain unknown to a 'vulgar soul', he argues that the door – like the door of Harriot's nature, or the door of the heart at which Christ comes knocking – remains closed to the human being who approaches it without the necessary humility.[22] The witness must come empty and prepared to receive 'ALL THINGS'. Traherne's reflections on the atom lead him to conclude the prose part of the commentary:

> The Moral wherof is, that no Man should be full of himself, for fear of Eternal Emptiness: But void of it self, as the Soul is, that it might be full of All Things. (III, p. 351)

In drawing this moral, Traherne is unusually firm in distancing the accommodative image of the atom from his primary subject. The occasion that gives this cause is his use of the atom as a simile for the rational soul.

ATOMS AND SOULS

Traherne acknowledges the utility of the comparison in the *Commentaries*, explaining that 'Like the Soul, [the atom] is Empty in it self, and capable of all: but capable of all in an inferior maner' (III, p. 344). He interprets the ideal human soul as an infinite vessel to be filled with 'ALL THINGS', an essence of pure act that sustains its being through the insatiable quest for divine felicity. Like the atom, the soul is an undividable, individual unit and a model of material poverty: in order to be full of the wonders of the universe, it must be – as Traherne says – 'void of it self'. Atoms are nevertheless inferior, as their metaphysical significance is bound to their physical activity. Interpretation of the atom must take both its physical and metaphysical objectives into account, but Traherne perceives the soul as a pure capacity for divine wisdom and beneficence, unrestrained by the activity of the corporeal world. While material atoms are capable of 'all' only 'by contiguity and Union, Varietie of Companions, Seperation

---

[21] 'Inter non entia' can be translated as 'Non-existent, or without being'. See Ross, III, p. 334.
[22] For the relevant passage in the Bible, see Revelation 3.20.

and Division, Rest and Motion' (III, p. 344), the soul is in unity with itself.

Traherne moulds his simile to emphasise the superiority of the soul in the comparison. In this metaphorical model, the tenor and vehicle are plainly established and the atom provides an emblem for spiritual capacity. Similes between atoms and souls are not absent from late-seventeenth-century literature, though they are hardly pervasive.[23] The establishment of metaphorical equivalence between the two would be more problematic, in that conflating the materialist discourse of Epicurean atoms – wherein souls are corporeal and mortal – with the principles of spiritual immortality could have obvious tensions. Traherne, however, concludes his commentary by narrowing the metaphorical distance between atoms and souls and writing in his second poem:

> For Souls are Atoms too, and simple ones.
> Nay less then Atoms, not so firm as Stones,
> They are divested not of Bulk and Size
> Alone, but of all Matter too, and are
> So void, that very Nothings they appear.
> Yet for these Souls all Atoms were prepard
> They minister to these and these reward
> Them with their Looks. (III, p. 362)

The poem sheds some light on the extent of the reciprocity between atom and soul. Souls 'are Atoms' in the sense that the metaphysical definition of the indivisible particle – the 'Ground work' of 'Form and Perfection' – is also applicable to the rational soul. They are 'less then Atoms', however, because they are not only incorporeal but entirely immaterial. Less is more regarding the nature of 'self' in Traherne's theology. The empty, capacious being has the space and energy to pry into the mysteries of all things natural and divine. There is therefore another level on which souls 'are Atoms', though atoms cannot be equated with souls in turn. Traherne's soul is designed to take possession of 'ALL THINGS', whereupon it assumes the characteristics of all it encounters. The 'Looks' souls bestow upon material particles are acts of intimate absorbance rather than distanced studies. Atoms 'were prepard' for the insatiable activity of souls, which, by taking them in, 'are Atoms' in as far as they encapsulate and control all knowable matter. Like the atom, the soul contracts 'All in All' from past,

---

[23] An example can be taken from John Crowne's prose romance *Pandion and Amphigenia*, which imagines 'beatified Souls, that float like Atomes in the Sun-shine of [God's] resplendent glory'. See *Pandion and Amphigenia or, The history of the Coy Lady of Thessalia Adorned with Sculptures* (London, 1665), p. 215.

present and future; unlike the atom, Traherne urges it does so not within a multi-layered framework of divine, metaphysical and physical systems of knowledge, but in pure spiritual concentration. The second 'Atom' poem continues, in reference to the soul:

> But then their Essence they another Way
> Unknown to Atoms like them selvs enjoy
> And being Nothing, but a Power to see
> And Good for Nothing but Felicitie
> Their Nature and their Motion is to lov
> Their Being to behold their Life above.
> The Rest are Good for Nothing but to serv
> These Good for Nothing if from Bliss they swerv. (III, p. 363)

The 'Bliss' experienced by the soul is in a focused self-sufficiency, while atoms are made to 'serv'. Traherne emphasises the need for spiritual focus in his reference to the 'swerv' of inattentive souls. Recalling the Lucretian account of the 'swerve' to describe the motion of atoms in chaos, the metaphor accentuates the demarcating prerogative of the soul to remain concentrated in self-concentration. As they are 'Nothing' but the power 'to see' and, as was quoted earlier, 'very Nothings they appear', it would seem that souls come to 'appear' when they fulfil the act 'to see'. This circularity is heightened in the repetition of 'being' as verb and 'Being' as noun. Whilst the paradox of 'being Nothing' is strikingly oxymoronic, the tension is eased with the realisation that souls are required to 'lov/ Their Being' to understand the glories of celestial life. It is in the act of seeing, of experiencing and possessing knowledge, that souls fill the void and come to possess a 'Being' that shows them the 'Way' to spiritual ecstasy.

ATOMS AND ANGELS

'They are more necessary to us, then the Existence of Angels.' It is the very function of atoms 'to serv' the soul in its pursuit of felicity that drove Traherne to make this statement: by reconciling ourselves to the atom, he claims, we can come to know our soul and realise our spiritual purpose. Thomas Harriot's letter to Kepler anticipated the life of the image as an emblem for Christian humility and human empathy with the meek and impoverished. Harriot and Traherne, writing at either end of the seven-teenth century, gesture at a significant mystical side to atomism in the early modern period that has received little attention. Contrary to the criticism that has argued for the shallow inconsistency of Traherne's philosophy, the contents of the 'Atom' commentary and *The Kingdom of God* reveal how the author absorbed the terminology of contemporary matter theories to expand upon the purpose of familiar Platonic metaphors. His plural atoms are symbols of incorruptibility and endurance, quite opposed to the chaotic 'swarm' of atoms that originated in Lucretius and infested early modern literature. The singular atom represents virtuous humility and accommodates divine spirit. According to both a physical and metaphysical analysis, it stores information concerning the origin and end of material being but also, more importantly, the constancy of divine eternity. Made to 'serv' us, it is down to human responsibility to 'feel' inside this information. By the powers of Traherne's soul, anything is possible: as he explains with customarily hermetic language in *The Kingdom of God*, 'If it pleas, it can contract it self to the littleness of a Sand, to a Centre, and in a Moment dilate like a flash of Lightening over all the Heavens' (I, p. 465).

The infinite capabilities of the investigative soul enable the ultimate contraction of focus. According to Traherne, reflection on the atom reveals more than the 'miraculous things' of nature that Harriot suggested. More than a symbol of eternity, the atom is a contraction of eternity – a minute space in which the divine is lodged though not contained. In words from the section on 'Apprehension' in the *Commentaries*, 'Eternity is Essentialy present in evry Moment, and Immensitie filleth evry Point of Space Essentialy' (III, pp. 172–3). Nothing demonstrates this with greater resonance than the infinite potentiality of an atom.

Chapter 4

'CONSIDER IT ALL': TRAHERNE'S REVEALING OF THE COSMIC CHRIST IN *THE KINGDOM OF GOD*

Alison Kershaw

Traherne's contribution to seventeenth-century Christology has often been overlooked. Ever since his rediscovery in the early twentieth century, Traherne has been considered by many critics as a precursor of Blake, Wordsworth, Whitman, Jefferies and other 'nature mystics', and somehow ahead of his time.[1] Many have also perceived a lack of connection between Traherne's celebration of the world and his Christian philosophy – or even a disjunction between his identities as priest and poet. M. M. Ross, for example, laments the lack of traditional Eucharistic symbols in Traherne's poetry, which he links to a loss of a sense of the 'real presence' of Christ.[2] But as A. L. Clements notes, 'though one reads criticism to the contrary, Christ does pervade and inform the poems of the Dobell Folio, particularly if we see him as St. Paul did: the last Adam who is a quickening Spirit. Traherne refers to him sometimes overtly, most often subtly or indirectly.'[3] At the outset of the *Centuries*, Traherne promises to 'unfold' the 'Mystery, which from the beginning of the World hath been hid in GOD'. Just as that 'interior Beauty', so 'Strange, yet Common', so 'Incredible, yet Known' has

---

[1] For example George Harvey, 'A Precursor of Whitman', *North American Review* 185 (1907), 463–4; Edward Thomas, *Richard Jefferies* (London, 1978), p. 172; Gladys I. Wade, 'Traherne and the Spiritual Value of Nature Study', *London Quarterly and Holborn Review* 159 (1934), 243–5.

[2] Malcolm Mackenzie Ross, *Poetry and Dogma: The Transfiguration of Eucharistic Symbols in Seventeenth Century English Poetry* (New Brunswick, 1954), pp. 94ff. For a full discussion of Traherne's reception as a nature mystic and the perceived absence of Christ in his work see Alison Kershaw, 'The Poetic of the Cosmic Christ in Thomas Traherne's *The Kingdom of God*', Ph.D. thesis, University of Western Australia (2005), pp. 1–4.

[3] A. L. Clements, *The Mystical Poetry of Thomas Traherne* (Cambridge, MA, 1969), p. 185.

not been 'Esteemed' (*Centuries*, Ross, V, I.3), so the Christic presence in Traherne's writing has been overlooked, precisely because it is buried very deeply in the heart of it, suffusing his view of the whole creation.[4]

A close reading of a central chapter in one of his most recently discovered works, *The Kingdom of God*, confirms how Traherne's understanding of Christ is intimately bound not only to his intense feeling for the material world but also to his fascination with early modern science. Amid an ambitious and wide-ranging treatise on the divine attributes, the material universe, and the human soul, Traherne embarks upon an extraordinary catalogue of wonders as he imagines the sights, sounds and perfumes that would greet a 'Celestial Stranger' alighting upon earth. Christ's implicit presence, conveyed in the very texture of the language, is made explicit in the concluding passage that (in confirmation of Clement's observation) reprises St Paul's hymn to Christ by whom 'all things consist' (Colossians 1.15–19). By comparing interpretations of this Pauline passage with other seventeenth-century divines and considering the speculations regarding cosmology, light and atoms that appear elsewhere in *The Kingdom of God*, Traherne's Christology can be seen to be at once both orthodox and intrepid. Before embarking on the voyage of the Celestial Stranger, we first need to gain an overview of the notion of the Cosmic Christ in relation to Traherne and *The Kingdom of God*.

TRAHERNE AND THE COSMIC CHRIST

Traherne, I would argue, belongs to a tradition of cosmic Christology. Although the epithet 'cosmic' was first used of Christ in the twentieth century (growing out of nineteenth-century dialogues), cosmic Christology is not so much a modern theology as an ancient and persistent theology that has been recovered, defended, and extended over the course of centuries. As J. A. Lyons observes:

> the language pertaining to the Cosmic Christ posits Christ as 'the instrument in God's creative activity, the source and goal of all things, the bond and sustaining power of the whole of creation; he is called the head and ruler of the universe; and his redemptive influence and his body are considered to extend to the limits of the created order.

This language, he notes, appears in the New Testament and awareness of the Cosmic Christ might be attributed to 'patristic, medieval and other

---

[4]   Cf. Romans 16.25–7.

pre-nineteenth-century theologians'.[5] Cosmic Christology lies, as Joseph Sittler noted in a landmark address, 'tightly enfolded in the Church's innermost heart and memory'.[6]

A. A. Luce describes the Christ of the Pauline and Johannine texts as 'the embodiment of the cosmic relation'.[7] Traherne defends this primitive orthodoxy concerning the body of Christ not only against 'the Socinian Arian, &c.' but against a more pervasive loss of a sense of immanence in the Christian tradition (*Commentaries*, Ross, III, p. 286).[8] Although there are Platonic elements to his thought, he does not subscribe to what A. Hilary Armstrong describes as 'the Platonic representation of a universe on two levels' that has so influenced Augustinian Christianity. Armstrong observes that despite the 'rejection of cosmic religion', a 'sense of holiness, of an intimate and immediate presence of God in the world, has not been absent' from the Christian tradition. In a footnote he asserts: 'the best expressions of this sense of holiness of the world in Christian literature' are to be found in Thomas Traherne, who 'in some ways anticipates Teilhard de Chardin'– the twentieth-century Jesuit and palaeontologist who first advocated a radical integration of Christology and evolutionary science.[9] In a similar vein, William J. Wolf observes that Teilhard and Traherne share a 'mystical identification' with the created world 'based on the principle of the relatedness of all things'.[10] Graham Dowell also describes Traherne and Teilhard (and also Thomas Merton) as being among those 'notable exceptions' in not neglecting the 'cosmic dimensions of the Christian story'.[11] Traherne's 'anticipation' of such figures, however, needs to be seen within the context of his spirited engagement with his theological heritage and the debates and scientific conjectures of his age. We will now consider a

---

[5]   J. A. Lyons, *The Cosmic Christ in Origen and Teilhard de Chardin: A Comparative Study* (Oxford, 1982), pp. 1–2, n. 2.

[6]   Joseph A. Sittler, address to the Faith and Order Movement (New Delhi, 1961), published as 'Called to Unity', *The Ecumenical Review* 14 (1961–62), 177–87, at 183; see the comments by Lyons, *Cosmic Christ*, pp. 59–60; and Matthew Fox, *The Coming of the Cosmic Christ* (San Francisco, 1988), pp. 77–8, 83, 90, 221.

[7]   A. A. Luce, *Monophysitism Past and Present* (London, 1920), p. 7, cited in Lyons, *Cosmic Christ*, p. 34.

[8]   Traherne is scornful of how 'it cannot enter the fine and politick Noddle' of the Socinian 'how GOD should becom a Man, or how there should be three Persons in the same Divine and Eternal essence' (Ross, III, p. 286).

[9]   A. Hilary Armstrong, *St. Augustine and Christian Platonism*, The Saint Augustine Lecture 1966 (Villanova, 1967), pp. 13, pp. 16–17, p. 48, n. 17.

[10] William J. Wolf, 'The Spirituality of Thomas Traherne', in *Anglican Spirituality*, ed. William J. Wolf (Wilton, CT, 1982), pp. 49–68, at p. 62.

[11] Graham Dowell, *Enjoying the World: The Rediscovery of Thomas Traherne* (London, 1990), pp. 5, 9.

work not available to Armstrong, Wolf or Dowell, to explore how Traherne integrates an ancient cosmic Christology with the expanding cosmology of the seventeenth century.

THE KINGDOM OF GOD

In *The Kingdom of God* Traherne considers, in a typically ambitious 100,000 words and 42 chapters, every order of creation and the place of the human soul in the universal scheme. It is one of five works in a vellum-bound book unearthed by Jeremy Maule in the Lambeth Palace Library in 1997.[12] Maule describes the central chapters as an early work of physico-theology (between 1669 and 1674) and 'extremely typical of the natural philosophy of Reformed theology'. In studying the sun, moon and stars, the seas, rivers, trees, herbs, flowers, hills, mountains, rain, hail, snow, clouds and meteors, the work basically follows, he notes, Melanchthon's re-ordering of Aristotle, as well as lists from the Benedicite, Psalms and other works of praise. Like his contemporaries Ralph Cudworth and Henry More, Traherne is also keen to engage with all aspects of natural philosophy, including cosmology and anatomy, atomic theories and the nature of matter and light. Characteristically he moves from the contemplation of the smallest elements in creation, newly visible through the microscope, to the greatest; and considers the intricate relation of each wondrously constructed part to another. The glorious whole is seen to reveal the wisdom of God, and humanity is charged with completing the work of creation by observing, enjoying and giving thanks.[13]

While a substantial portion of *The Kingdom of God* might be described as physico-theology, it is not preoccupied with the argument from design that informs many works of that genre. Traherne does not posit a distant architect, but a living and integral relation between the material and the divine and he defines this Christic immanence against voluntarist and emerging 'mechanical' philosophies, delighting instead in the penetrative

---

[12] For a full description of Lambeth Palace, MS 1360, see Jeremy Maule, *Traherne and the Restlessness of God: The New Lambeth Discoveries* [audiotape] (Temenos Academy, 1998); Denise Inge and Calum MacFarlane, 'Seeds of Eternity: A New Traherne Manuscript', *TLS* (2 June 2000), 14; Ross, 'Introduction', *Works*, I, pp. xiii–xxiv.

[13] See C. J. Glacken, *Traces on the Rhodian Shore: Nature and Culture in Western Thought from Ancient Times to the End of the Eighteenth Century* (Berkeley, London, 1967), pp. 393–5; Ralph Cudworth, *The True Intellectual System of the Universe*, 3 vols (London, 1845), originally published 1678; Henry More, *An Antidote Against Atheism* (London, 1652); Maule also points to John Wilkins, *Of the Principles and Duties of Natural Religion* (London, 1675).

powers of 'Life it self' (*Kingdom of God*, Ross, I, p. 412). Nor does Traherne dwell on the millenarian associations of the 'Kingdom of God' that so engaged his age, being more concerned with the intrinsic nature of divine activity in this 'Glorious Kingdom' than with the transcendent will of a God who might decree the end of the world at any moment.[14]

The first eighteen chapters, as Maule notes, are in the tradition of commentaries on the Creed, describing attributes of the Deity such as Unity, Glory, Goodness and Infinitude. Traherne also discourses at length upon God as 'The Most Communicativ and Activ Principle That Is'. Describing Traherne's essentially Thomistic metaphysics, Paul Cefalu notes how he uses the word *act* in 'the now obsolete sense of both Reality and Active Principle'.[15] This contrasts with the Neoplatonic conception of the divine as the source of being that is itself beyond being. In the Thomist scheme, God's operations and laws cannot be divorced from the essence of God, which is simply 'to be'. So, far from being beyond being, Traherne's God commands an estate that can even be augmented by the activity of the divine Word.

Quoting the Elizabethan theologian Richard Hooker, Traherne thus delights that 'The Being of God is a Kind of Law to his Working' (*Kingdom of God*, p. 369).[16] Although impatient with the 'Drie and Empty Theames' of scholastic theology, Traherne is drawn to its core tenets (*Select Meditations*, Ross, V, III.30). Moreover, as his defence of the term 'Act' in *Commentaries of Heaven* demonstrates, he is gently resistant to the scorn of contemporaries such as his overseer, Bishop Herbert Croft.[17] Traherne would explore the essence of God and 'justly inquire' into the 'Quidditie of its Existence' (*Kingdom of God*, p. 316). By the mid sixteenth century, the term 'quidditie' had come to mean a quibble in reference to over-subtle scholastic argument.[18] Traherne, like the esteemed Hooker, however, persists in 'digging neer unto the root of things' to reach the 'haecceity' or 'thisness' of the world: 'All these things I speak concerning the Nature and Essence of God, becaus Evry one of them implies the perfection of the World' (*Kingdom of God*, p. 317). Traherne's assertion, in the context of a

---

[14] See Margaret C. Jacob, 'Millenarianism and Science in the Late Seventeenth Century', *Journal of the History of Ideas* 37 (1976), 335–41.

[15] Paul Cefalu, 'Thomistic Metaphysics and Ethics in the Poetry and Prose of Thomas Traherne', *Literature and Theology* 16 (2002), 248–69, at 252.

[16] Hooker described a universal natural law, seated 'in the bosom of God, her voice the harmony of the world', Richard Hooker, *Of the Laws of Ecclesiastical Polity* (1593–97), I, 16.8.

[17] Traherne, 'Act', *Commentaries*, II, especially under the heading 'An Observation', p. 173; Herbert Croft, *Naked Truth: the First Part, or the True State of the Primitive Church by an Humble Moderator* (London, 1680), p. 3.

[18] See *OED, s.v.* 'quiddity'.

piece of physico-theology, that 'God himself, and the Eternal Generation of his Son, are made Known by his Works', indicates a profoundly incarnational Christology (*Kingdom of God*, p. 259). Turning now to the journey of the Celestial Stranger that is fittingly placed in the heart of *The Kingdom of God*, we can see how Traherne pushes out from this solidly orthodox base to explore the quiddity of Christ incarnate in all things, enfleshing this expansive Christology in a poetic pulsing with the 'Most Communicativ and Active Principle That Is'.

THE JOURNEY OF THE CELESTIAL STRANGER

In the ecstatic prose of Chapter 25 of *The Kingdom of God*, Traherne brings to life a series of cosmological speculations concerning an infinite universe and the possibility of inhabited stars. Desire, curiosity, love, gratitude and transformation in Traherne are sparked by amazement, and his work abounds with stories of discovery and arrivals in 'this World' – 'How like an Angel came I down!/ How Bright are all Things here!' ('Wonder', Ross, VI, p. 4, 1–2). Here Traherne invites us to see the world anew by imagining the response, not of the infant stranger of 'The Salutation' and 'Third Century' (although he revisits this theme later), but of a 'Celestial Stranger' alighting upon Earth:

> Had a Man been allwayes in one of the Stars, or Confined to the Body of the Flaming Sun, or surrounded with nothing but pure Æther, at vast and prodigious Distances from the Earth, acquainted with nothing but the Azure Skie, and face of Heaven, little could he Dream of any Treasures hidden in that Azure vail afar off. or think the Earth (which perhaps would be Invisible to him, or seem but a Needle's Point, or Sparkle of Light) in any Measure capable of such a World of Mysteries as are comprehended in it.[19] (*Kingdom of God*, pp. 390, 388)

There are echoes of Dante's imagined journey through the seven spheres until he looks down upon 'this globe' and 'smiled' as it 'seemed so poor a thing'.[20] As the title of Chapter 25 indicates, however, Traherne telescopes from the perceived insignificance of the earth to its richness and bounty: 'Of the Globe of the Earth. Its Baseness, Its Litleness, its Dignity, its Glory. Its capacity and Greatness, Its fulness and varietie'. This is, in one sense, ironic, as Traherne's post-Copernican understanding of an infinitely expanded universe might have served to make the world seem even more

---

[19]   Cf. Traherne, 'The Salutation', VI, p. 4, stanza 7; *Centuries*, III.2.
[20]   Dante Allighieri, 'Paradise', *The Divine Comedy*, trans. Dorothy L. Sayers and Barbara Reynolds (Harmondsworth, 1962), vol. III, canto XXII, lines 133–5.

tiny and insignificant. Thomas Digges (the first astronomer to posit the infinity of space), for example, spoke of the 'litle darcke starre wherein we live' as being 'but as a poynct in respect of the immensity of that immoueable heaven'.[21] While Dante journeys upward to a still centre, Traherne's stranger descends. His impulse is to 'draw neer' and survey 'this globe of ours', where he discovers that what seemed so little is in fact very dignified, glorious, capacious and vibrating with life. As Poulet observes in comparing the poetry of Dante and Traherne (before the discovery of the Lambeth Manuscript):

> For Dante [...] the divine sphere was [...] composed of permanent marvels [...] which did not reveal themselves to the voyager until precisely the moment when he had finished his journeying to immobilize himself in the contemplation of the eternal beauties. With Traherne it is the very reverse which happens. He moves in the miraculous sphere; he therefore constantly changes its centre, and, at the same time, in his view, causes it constantly to change its aspect.[22]

Traherne's voyager who has been acquainted with nothing but the sky will find each object on earth, however humble, to be a miraculous centre of eternity.

From the silent world of the aether the stranger is catapulted, in a vertiginous zoom of focus, into a swirling mass of life. Once beamed down the man is immediately confronted with a myriad of experiences – he is bathed in what Teilhard was to call 'the ocean of matter' – overwhelmed by the 'the divine omnipresence in which we find ourselves plunged'.[23]

> Should he be let down on a Suddain, and see the sea, and the Effects of those Influences he never Dreamd of: such Strange Kind of Creatures; Such Mysteries and Varieties; such distinct Curiosities; Such never heard of Colors; Such a New and Lively Green in the Meadows; Such Odoriferous, and fragrant Flowers; such Reviving and Refreshing Winds; such Innumerable Millions of unexpected Motions; Such Lovely, Delicate, and Shady Trees; So many Brisk, and Beautifull, and melodious Birds; Such Fluent Springs, and silver Streams; Such Lions and Leopards, and foure footed Beasts; such innumerable Companies, and Hosts of Insects [...] (*Kingdom of God*, p. 388)

---

[21] Thomas Digges, *Perfit Description of the Cælestial Orbes* (1576–1605), cited in John Spencer Hill, *Infinity, Faith, and Time: Christian Humanism and Renaissance Literature*, McGill-Queen's Studies in the History of Religion (Montreal and Kingston, 1997), p. 29.

[22] Georges Poulet, *The Metamorphoses of the Circle* (Baltimore, 1966), pp. 9–10.

[23] Pierre Teilhard de Chardin, *Hymn of the Universe* (London, 1965), p. 65; Pierre Teilhard de Chardin, *Le Milieu Divin: An Essay on the Interior Life* (London, 1960), p. 111.

So begins the glorious catalogue that is in some ways the climax of the work. The treatise is itself a vast inventory containing many catalogues that, in their effusion and very form, embody the principle of augmentation. This catalogue is one of the most exhilarating. The prose is free-flowing, oiled with alliteration and repetition, and uninterrupted by periods or paragraph breaks. The exclamatory 'Such' expresses repletion and satisfaction, and together with the ensuing stream of plural nouns expresses a tangible if incalculable richness. This abundance is perceived with every bodily sense; the sights and smells of the earth delight, revive and promise to provide. The bucolic pastoral is varied with a voyage across the ocean where the stranger jumps back in surprise as whales and 'Syrens' leap out of the deep. The communication and stimulation is incessant, and as Maule observes 'generates a theology as well as acclamation'.[24] Traherne's poetic of repletion reflects the insatiable desire of the infinitely communicative Word, the incarnational fullness of the one who fills all in all.

The catalogue then moves seamlessly from creatures to humanity: 'Such Robes and Attires [...] Such Cities, and villages; Such Multitude of Boyes and Girles in the Streets'. The pattern is briefly broken and the pace accelerated by a rapid climb up the ladder of life: 'Such a Gradual Ascent from Sands to Spires of Grass to Insects, from those to Birds, from Birds to Beasts, from Beasts to Men, from Earth to Heaven'. Traherne continues to write breathlessly on the wing as one subject leads, either by suggestion or contrast, to the next: 'Such Bookes, and Universities; Such Colleges and Libraries; Such Trades and Studies; Such Occupations and Professions; Such Retirements and Devotions; Such Altars and Temples'. There is a small eddy in the stream when 'Such Holy Days, and Sabbaths' lead back, via vows, prayers, Joys, Pleasures, Solemnities, Songs and Praises, to return in reverse order to 'Such Sabbaths and Holy Days'. The list then resumes its course on through sermons, arts and sciences, oracles and miracles, and so on. All elements are prefaced with the ubiquitous 'Such', which by this stage of the catalogue has come to signify not only repletion but overflow. Traherne then plunges more deeply into the dark waters of life:

> Such Sufferings and persecutions; Such Deaths and Martyrdoms; Such Lov and fidelity; Such faith, and Hopes, and Desire; Such obligations, such Lawes, such Duties and Examples; Such Rewards and Punishments [...] (*Kingdom of God*, p. 388)

The prose is richly patterned with oppositions and, as we have noted, with alliteration and free-flowing word association. Such techniques, which

---

[24]   Maule, *Traherne and the Restlessness of God.*

in works such as *The Thanksgivings* also extend to the use of bracketed or parallel lists, 'conspire', notes Carl M. Selkin, 'to induce the reader to seek for some meaning which forges the identity between them'.[25] The catalogue form itself reflects the organising force of the pleroma – the Wisdom or Logos that, according to ancient Christology, informs all being, unites all contraries and justly resolves all imbalances. In Traherne's poetic of immanence, augmentation, repletion and rich patterning comprise a Christic consummation in which, as Teilhard would describe, 'the substantial *one* and the created *many* fuse without confusion in a *whole*'.[26] As Traherne reflects in an earlier chapter, 'Innumerable Millions of Objects [...] are represented in himself, in evry Point and Centre of his Immensity, without Confusion' (*Kingdom of God*, p. 355).

Traherne finally wraps up this sentence of many parts, and pauses for breath. He signals with a full colon the closure of the clause ('Should he be let down of a suddain, and see ...') that had unleashed this torrent, and concludes: 'He would think himself faln into the Paradise of God, a Phoenix nest, a Bed of Spices, a Kingdom of Glory' (*Kingdom of God*, p. 388). The pace is slackened and in the relative shortness of the phrase and truncation of 'fallen', there is a great sense of relief and abandonment. It is as though the stranger, after the excitement of his epic journey, has thrown himself onto a mass of exotic cushions; finding a peaceful and plentiful haven in the garden of paradise, the nest, the bed, at the heart of the Kingdom. The phoenix on her bed of spices traditionally alludes to the sacrifice and resurrection of Christ, and it is significant that Traherne has embedded this motif so centrally in his catalogue of creation. It evokes what is described in *Select Meditations* as the principle of Love and Goodness that is 'in its Highest Agonies, ever Dying, Expiring and Reviving every moment' (*Select Meditations*, II.77).

There is also an association with the beloved in the Song of Solomon to whom the lover goes as 'down into his garden, to the beds of spices, to feed in the gardens, and to gather lilies'.[27] The Christian allegorisation is extended by Traherne to imply not only Christ's love for the world, but the Celestial Stranger's love for Christ incarnate in the fragrant world that has so amazed him. The man rouses himself to reflect on how 'Those Heavens I was acquainted with, hav brought all their Joys hither, and here they are Enjoyed!' (*Kingdom of God*, p. 389). He then embarks on a second lengthy catalogue that counts the blessings of those who 'are conceived with

---

[25]   Carl M. Selkin, 'The Language of Vision: Traherne's Cataloguing Style', *English Literary Renaissance* 6 (1976), 92–104, at 95.
[26]   Teilhard de Chardin, *Le Milieu Divin*, pp. 110–12.
[27]   Song of Solomon 5.13, 6.2.

Pleasure, and come forth of the Womb to Innumerable Blessings'. They 'offer up themselves, their Souls and Bodies as a living sacrifice', as 'The Fruit of all in Heaven above, and here upon Earth is returned with Sweet Incense of Praise' (*Kingdom of God*, p. 390). The men and women in this 'Nest of Angels' are thus like the Christic phoenix, forever on fire with love (*Kingdom of God*, p. 389).

Again, the stranger comes to a brief point of rest, exclaiming:

> This litle Star so Wide and so full of mysteries! So capacious, and so full of Territories, containing innumerable Repositories of Delight, when we draw neer! Who would hav Expected, who could hav hoped for Such Enjoyments? (*Kingdom of God*, p. 390)

Some 1,500 words, mostly in the form of extended catalogues and raptures have elapsed since the Celestial Stranger first alighted. With satisfaction, Traherne enlists the voice of the Psalmist to draw the first half of Chapter 25 to a close, and to leave us in no doubt that 'to be let down' to earth is to be let into the heart of the Kingdom of God:

> Thus would a Celestial Stranger be Entertained in the World, and to this voyce we ought to reecho, Blessed is the Man whom thou Chusest, and Causest to approach unto thee, that he may dwell in thy Courts.[28] (*Kingdom of God*, p. 390)

In a corollary, Traherne grounds the fantastical voyage of the man from the stars with a veiled parallel reference to himself: 'I know a Stranger upon Earth in his Infancy' who upon learning the Earth is round and there are 'Stars also under his feet', is delighted to realise the world is:

> A Centre without Period, Limit, or Bound! The Similitude of his Endless Nature is impressed upon it, that Created the Same! He Sitteth upon the Circle of the Earth and the Inhabitants therof are as Grasshoppers; that stretcheth out the Heavens as a Curtain; and spreadeth them abroad as a Tent to dwell in.[29] Why this Earth is the Centre of the Heavens! (*Kingdom of God*, pp. 391, 392)

In this passage Traherne combines a 'modern' vision of an illimited universe and an ancient iconic one of the Creator sitting atop the closed spheres of creation. In doing so he addresses those that believed an infinite universe 'demolished', as Marjorie Nicolson observes, 'the circle of perfection' that characterised the old cosmology.[30] On the contrary, argues Traherne, the

---

[28] Psalm 65.

[29] Isaiah 40.22.

[30] Marjorie Hope Nicolson, *The Breaking of the Circle: Studies in the Effect of the 'New Science' upon Seventeenth-Century Poetry*, revised edn (New York, 1960), p. 165.

circle is perfected by its expansion. Poulet notes that the notion of God as a circle with its centre everywhere and its circumference nowhere, which first appeared in a twelfth-century pseudo-hermetic text and was popular with Nicholas of Cusa and 'other scholastics of the Middle Ages', was taken up in the sixteenth and seventeenth centuries by (among others) Bruno and Kepler, numerous Neoplatonists and mystics, metaphysical poets, and with particular enthusiasm by Traherne.[31] The image informs and serves Traherne's conception of divine goodness filling infinite space, the same glory found in an ant or atom communicated to the furthest reaches of the universe.

Traherne then expounds at length upon the carnal 'pleasures and Delights of [the] Marriage Bed' of Heaven and Earth, which are exponentially increased as he considers an infinite number of such centres of bliss:

> there may be (for ought we know) New Heavens, and other August and Magnificent WORLDS, wherin God delighteth as much as in this, tho he Seemeth to delight in this alone. (*Kingdom of God*, p. 392)

In the vast sweep of Chapter 25, Traherne thus follows in the Cusean tradition described by Poulet, expanding his 'imagination beyond measure', and also '[contracting] it in the extreme [… transporting] himself simultaneously both toward the circumference and toward the center'.[32] That this reflects an eternal Christic movement of incarnation, ascension and filling is made explicit in the concluding passage of Chapter 25, where Traherne focuses on what Teilhard terms the 'active centre' – the centre that informs all other centres – the simultaneously centralising and radiating, organising, incarnational force through which all worlds and all eternal and finite things are reconciled and consummated.[33]

THE CHRISTIC CENTRE OF ALL WORLDS

The Christic mystery that has been so deeply embedded in the heart of this chapter is now unfolded and made known in Traherne's concluding selection of verses from St Paul:

> By *faith we understand that <u>the Worlds</u> were framed* (saith the Apostle) *by the Word of God: so that things which are seen, were not made by things that do appear.*[34] And *God who at Sundry times, and in divers Manners, spake in*

---

31   Poulet, *Metamorphoses of the Circle*, pp. xi, xxiv.
32   Poulet, *Metamorphoses of the Circle*, p. xiii.
33   Teilhard de Chardin, *Le Milieu Divin*, p. 110.
34   See Hebrews 11.3.

time past unto us by the Prophets hath in these last Days spoken unto us by his Son, whom he hath appointed Heir of all things; by whom also he made the Worlds.[35] *Who being the Brightness of his Glory, and the Express Image of his Person, and upholding all things by the Word of his Power; when he had by himself purged our Sins, Sate down on the Right Hand of the Majestie on high.*[36] But yet all those will Continualy be one Univers: one GOD, one Lord, one Spirit, one Obedience, one End, one Original Cause, one Monarchie, one Blessedness throughout the Whole, and one Glory! One *Image of the Invisible GOD, Existing and Begotten in the Brightness of his Glory:* one infinit and Eternal Beginning; the Head of his Church, and *the first Born of Evry Creature! For by him were all things created that are in Heaven, and that are in Earth, visible, and Invisible; Whether they be Thrones, or Dominions, or Principalities, or powers: All things were Created by him, and for him. And he is before all things, and by him all things Consist. For it pleased the father that in him should all fullness dwell.*[37]

The universal Christ, Teilhard was to insist, 'must be understood with boldness, as St. John, and St. Paul and the Fathers saw it and loved it'.[38] These writers, he urged a friend, 'really present the *resurrected* Christ as being as vast as the World of all time. Have you read, for example, the beginning of the Epistle to the Colossians and tried to give it the full organic meaning it requires?'[39] It is with such boldness that Traherne turns to these verses to comprehend the journey of the Celestial Stranger, the richness of the earth and the infinity of the universe.[40] Like Teilhard, Traherne lived at a time when perceptions of the universe were undergoing a 'frightening enlargement', and he similarly resists an 'extrinsic and juridical' Christology, developing in its place an 'organic' understanding of Christ integrated with the 'totality of the cosmos'.[41] The extent of his boldness in relating an ancient Christology to the insights gained

---

[35] See Hebrews 1.1–2.

[36] See Hebrews 1.3.

[37] See Colossians 1.15–17, 19. This quotation of *The Kingdom of God* is from the manuscript, Lambeth Palace, MS 1360, fol. 263v, with Traherne's underlining as it appears in the manuscript and my italics for passages of scripture. The relevant page in Ross, I is p. 393.

[38] Pierre Teilhard de Chardin, 'Cosmic Life', *Writings in Time of War* (London, 1968), pp. 14–71, at p. 50.

[39] Pierre Teilhard de Chardin, *Letters to Two Friends 1926–1952*, cited in Ursula King, *Christ in All Things: Exploring Spirituality with Teilhard de Chardin*, Bampton Lectures 1996 (London, 1997), p. 72.

[40] Lyons, *Cosmic Christ*, p. 68; Colossians 1.15–19 is often referred to as a hymn.

[41] Pierre Teilhard de Chardin, 'Super-humanité, super-Christ, super-charité' (1943), cited in Christopher F. Mooney, *Teilhard de Chardin and the Mystery of Christ* (London, 1966), p. 78.

from both telescope and microscope can be measured by comparing the response of contemporary divines to these Pauline scriptures. As each verse is considered, Traherne's realisation of the Cosmic Christ becomes increasingly apparent.

Beginning with Hebrews, Traherne places Christ at the centre of all worlds: '<u>*The Worlds*</u> *Were Framed* (saith the Apostle) *by the Word of God*'. As the context and underlining suggest, *Worlds* is taken in a literal sense, and not simply as *ages* as assumed by Isaac Barrow.[42] 'I Should not Speak this, did I not Know that the Scriptures Mention a Pluralitie of them', says Traherne by way of introduction, having expanded upon 'other August and Magnificent WORLDS' (*Kingdom of God*, pp. 392, 393). Robert Gell, in his consideration of the same text, dwells on Christ as the Word and Wisdom of God, and also as the 'eternal Idea', or 'pattern [...] sufficient for the production of many worlds'.[43] While his conception of divine manifestation without exhaustion leaves open the possibility of an infinite universe, his primary concern is with the plurality of invisible worlds.[44] Traherne, however, seamlessly and eagerly links the underlying unity of the universe with the unity of God in Christ '*upholding all things by the Word of his power*' and bestowing 'one Blessedness throughout the Whole' (*Kingdom of God*, p. 393).

Traherne is also eager to link cosmic omnipresence with a cosmic understanding of the incarnation, elaborating with exclamation upon Colossians 1.15 and describing Christ as: 'one infinit and Eternal Beginning [...] *the first Born of Evry Creature!*' This echoes other images found in Colossians, Ephesians and John that reinforce the association of Christ with the pre-existent, eternally active and creative Wisdom of Proverbs; the Word, the brightness and glory of God.[45] In the context of this elaboration and in the wider context of the vibrant pageant that these verses bring to a close, the phrase 'The first born of Evry Creature' takes on a far more zestful and positive connotation than that ascribed by other commentators, who highlight a legalistic analogy. According to the non-conformist Thomas Manton, for example, the privilege accorded the first-born is granted to Christ as 'Reward, and recompense for the sorrows of his Humiliation'.[46]

---

[42] Isaac Barrow, 'His Onely Son', *The Works of Isaac Barrow, D.D.* (London, 1700), pp. 277–91, at p. 281.

[43] Robert Gell, *Gell's Remaines* (London, 1676), pp. 457–8.

[44] Gell, *Gell's Remaines*, pp. 454–5.

[45] Colossians 1.18; John 1.1; Proverbs 8.22–3; Ephesians 3.9.

[46] Thomas Manton, *Christs Eternal Existence and the Dignity of his Person Asserted and Proved in Opposition To the Doctrine of the Socinians In Several Sermons on Col. I. 17, 18, 19, 20, 21* (London, 1685), p. 51.

Similarly, Tobias Crispe writes, 'Christ hath purchased this preheminence, and he payd the father the uttermost farthing [...] and therefore he ought to have it.'[47] This legalistic interpretation was not limited to non-conformists. Robert Mossom describes the triumphant arrival of Christ in Heaven, having paid mankind's ransom, beholding 'the Father entertaining him, with a plenary grant of his Petition' bestowing the 'pre-eminence' of the 'first-born'.[48]

The term 'First Born' for Traherne, however, is inextricably and, as his exclamations suggest, joyfully linked to his sense of the divine incarnate in the material world. His acknowledgment that Christ '*had by himself purged our Sins,* [and] *sate down on the Right hand of the Majestie on high*' does not break the 'organic' connection to the 'lower' world. Immediately he interjects: 'But yet all those will Continualy be one Univers.' 'Christ', he says in an earlier chapter, is the 'first Born, and Beginning of Evry Creature', 'a Being [...] in which are hid all the Treasures of Wisdom, and Knowledge, all the Perfections of God, and all Possible Creatures' (*Kingdom of God*, p. 333).

With a further selection from Colossians 1, Traherne continues the theme of immanence and posits Christ as the source of being: '*For by him were all things Created that are in Heaven, and are in Earth, visible, and Invisible.*' As Chapter 25 has made abundantly clear, Traherne celebrates every order of creation in the marriage of heaven and earth; 'one Blessedness throughout the Whole'. For many other seventeenth-century theologians, however, life's journey was entirely orientated toward heaven. Nicholas Lockyer, for example, in his *Severall Lectures Painfully Preached Upon Colossians I*, sees earthly life as something of a torture to be endured before heavenly reward. Of the same text he writes, 'from Earth to Heaven is a Christians journey quite home':

> Earth is the slaughter house that belongest to hell; hearts that are made fat are killed on earth, and rosted in hell. We dwell in Gods kitchen and the devils slaughter-house, in earth [...] earth speaketh a lower room.

For theologians such as Lockyer, Christ's earthly work is chiefly that of redemption. While Lockyer states that 'being and disposition of being

---

47 Tobias Crispe, 'Christs Preheminence: Collos. I Ver. 18 That in All Things Hee Might Have the Preheminence', in *Christ Alone Exalted* (London, 1643), p. 140.

48 Robert Mossom, 'The Second Sermon Upon Coloss. I v. 18, 19', *The Preacher's Tripartite* (London, 1657), p. 131. From his quotation of verses 15–19 Traherne omits Colossians 1.18 ('And he is the head of the body, the church: who is the beginning, the first-born from the dead; that in all things he might have preeminence'), as he has incorporated elements of it into his elaboration and preamble – although the term 'preeminence' is not used.

are from Christ', he goes on to describe how 'pure persons are placed in Heaven, and impure in earth', 'the devil's heaven'.[49] Thomas Jackson, in a reflection that does not appear among the many selections from his work in Traherne's Commonplace Book, argues against the Lutheran belief that Christ's human nature is everywhere. He states instead that the Body of Christ must be looked for only in his heavenly sanctuary.[50]

On this point, Traherne is more in tune with thinkers such as Isaac Barrow, who in reference to the Colossians' text, writes that Christ 'was not only (as some heterodox Interpreters would expound it) to create a new moral, and figurative world; he should not only restore and reform mankind, but he of old did truly and properly give being to all things'.[51] Traherne's placing of the Christ hymn at the conclusion of a catalogue of earthly delights indicates a movement toward the further and ultimate conclusion of such a view; that, as Teilhard's correspondent Maurice Blondel was to express it, Christ is the bond that 'makes substantiation possible'.[52]

It is with this sense of Christ as the immanent giver of substance, that I feel Traherne understands the statement: *'by him all things Consist'.* Lockyer, by contrast, speaks only of 'supportation', 'disposition' or ordering, and the 'special providence' by which Christ steps in as peacemaker to save a world at war with itself:

> the whole world is a great body gnawing out it self, it hath gnawed it self to skinne and bones now, 'tis so old and torn, as is very sad to look upon, or live in, and it would have gnawed it self to nothing long ere this, if Christ had not upheld; in him hath the whole creation [...] a reconciliation of consistency.[53]

Thomas Manton, however, saw the consisting of all things in Christ as connoting 'Conservation and Providence',[54] sustenance and supportation; 'all things subsist by him' in the act of 'continued creation, or a continuance

---

[49] Nicholas Lockyer, *England Faithfully Watcht with, In Her Wounds: Or, Christ as a Father Sitting up with His Children in Their Swooning State: Which is the Summe of Severall Lectures Painfully Preached Upon Colossians I* (London, 1645), p. 86, pp. 94–5.

[50] Thomas Jackson, *Maran atha or Dominus Veniet: Christs Session at the Right Hand of God, and Exultation Therby. Commentaries Upon The Articles of the Creed* (London, 1657), pp. 3317ff (especially pp. 3319, 3325). The only section Traherne selects for his Commonplace Book is on the theme of 'Dominion' – noting that worldly authorities do not have ultimate dominion over men (Bodleian, MS Eng. poet. c. 42), fols 35v.2–36v.1.

[51] Barrow, 'His Onely Son', p. 281.

[52] Colossians 1.17.

[53] Lockyer, *England Faithfully Watcht*, pp. 117, 118, 120.

[54] Manton, *Christs Eternal Existence*, p. 79.

of being which God hath caused'.[55] Isaac Barrow also considered that Christ's divine work is 'to create [...] to sustain, and conserve things in being'.[56] Traherne is clearly aligned with such interpretations.

We might question, however, whether in Traherne we find an additional level of meaning at least hinted at. It seems orthodox for these seventeenth-century commentators to prefer to speak of how in Christ all things *subsist* rather than *consist* (as translated in the King James Bible). The two words, both current in the seventeenth century, have very similar meanings and, in the sense of 'having existence', may be used interchangeably. *Subsist* has the additional connotation of existing *in* something else, and of being supported. *Consist*, however, in the sense of 'hold together' (as translated in the New Revised Standard Version), implies less of dependency and more of inherency. This seems to be the import of the earlier chapters relating the eternally communicative nature and being of God to scientific speculations regarding the universe. In considering atoms and the 'Cohaesion' of matter, for example, Traherne embarks on yet another great cataloguing journey following the delight-filled passage of an atom through the universe, joining itself to other bodies without transmutation, enjoying an 'Infinit Libertie [...] Upon the Account of its Divine Original' (*Kingdom of God*, p. 349). So also Traherne understands the Word of God, the Exertion of Almighty Power, to be creative, communicative, of 'Matter' and the 'Realitie' of 'Solid Existence' – remaining entire in itself, yet the bond or vinculum of creation (*Kingdom of God*, p. 282).

In exploring this bond, and as evidenced in his Commonplace Book, Traherne was intrigued both by ancient theories about the Soul of the World and Henry More's thoughts on atoms (Commonplace Book, fol. 26v.2). In *The Kingdom of God*, however, he defines atoms as 'Material Spirits' and avoids the dualism of More and Robert Boyle. Where Boyle sees divine intervention in the ordering of physical particles, and More finds the material world to be held together by atoms of plastical spirit acting under the sway of a higher spiritual power, Traherne posits a nexus, rather than an ordering, interweaving or yoking together, of matter and spirit.[57] Similarly, he delights in the story of the Incarnation – '*And the Light was the Life of Men.* Thus Speaketh the Text of the holy Bible.' The possibly subconscious reversal of 'Life' and 'Light' in this quotation from the Gospel of John highlights how, for Traherne, 'a Divine and Eternal

---

55   Manton, *Christs Eternal Existence*, p. 94.
56   Barrow, 'His Onely Son', p. 285.
57   See Traherne, *Kingdom of God*, ch. 19. For a detailed discussion of Traherne's interest in notions of the Soul of the World and the holding together of matter, see Kershaw, 'The Poetic of the Cosmic Christ in Thomas Traherne's *The Kingdom of God*', pp. 113–39.

Mysterie' is 'painted out in a Temporal, and Visible, Created Wonder. For that which is Light in the open Air, is Life in Organised Bodies' (*Kingdom of God*, p. 350; John 1.4). It is not simply that Christ enlightens created life, but that the material light of the sun is the very means by which Christ creates and permeates all life – just as the Pythagorean fire 'diffuseth it self through the universe, and just as the Heart in Man's Body sheds abroad its Natural and Vivivick Heat into all the members' (*Kingdom of God*, p. 376).[58] 'The Matter', Traherne marvels, 'is so intricat, and deeply entangled' (*Kingdom of God*, p. 355).

Traherne, therefore, resists falling back into what Blondel terms a 'murderous symbolism', choosing instead to 'go forward towards a realism which is self-consistent throughout, towards a total reality which puts the metaphysics of Christianity in accord with […] mystical theology'.[59] Going with the flow of this 'realism', Traherne skips Colossians 1 verse 18 concerning the pre-eminence of Christ, to make an immediate association between the themes of consistency and fullness: '*For it pleased the father that in him should all fullness dwell.*' As Mooney observes, in Paul the 'fullness' dwelling in Christ indicates 'plenitude of being, both fullness of divinity and fullness of the universe, the whole of the cosmos filled with the creative presence of God'.[60] The fullness of Christ is connected in Traherne's text with the most tangible treasures of this 'little star' and all other 'Worlds'. Whereas other commentators understood there to be a communication of love and virtue 'defused to the creature', Traherne, I would argue, moves beyond this to imply an embodiment.[61]

An even greater contrast can be found in John Donne, whose Christmas Day sermon on Colossians 1.19–20 illustrates a 'murderous symbolism' tied to a harshly juridical understanding of atonement. Donne employs the images of rivers and seas, overflowings and deluges, not to describe, as Traherne does, a plenitude of being, but 'channels of concupiscencies'. Traherne describes the bodily organs as vessels of felicity, admitting a playful God that 'is hid in the Labyrinth of our Ears' and 'Strengthneth our Ankle Bones' (*Kingdom of God*, p. 313). Donne, by contrast, describes the body as a channel for sin, which 'hath found an issue at the ear', in the tongue and hands and feet:

---

[58] This section is heavily based on Theophilus Gale, *Court of the Gentiles, Part II, Of Philosophie* (Oxford, 1670), pp. 163–4.

[59] Pierre Teilhard de Chardin and Maurice Blondel, *Correspondence: Pierre Teilhard De Chardin, Maurice Blondel*, ed. Henri de Lubac (New York, 1967), p. 23.

[60] Mooney, *Teilhard de Chardin*, p. 147.

[61] Crispe, *Christ Alone Exalted*, pp. 119, 124, 130, 137; for similar sentiments see also Mossom, *Preacher's Tripartite*, p. 141.

when man's measure was full of sin, and God's measure full of wrath, then was the *fulness of time*; and yet then *complacuit*, it pleased the Father that there should be another fulness to overflow all these in Christ Jesus.[62]

In the hypostatical union of God and man in the body of Christ, there was for Donne 'not a dram of glory'. Christ's fullness in this regard is due to the fulsome greatness of God's gift and not to 'a propenseness, a disposition to goodness' in man.[63] Traherne, by contrast, rejoices in the infinite capacity of the soul to participate in the fullness of Christ, not least through a full exercise of the bodily senses.

Robert Gell observed of the word *fill* that 'according to the judgement of our Translators, and the harmony of the Reformed Churches, the word may be rendered, either to fill, as it is in the Text, or to fulfill, as in the Margin'.[64] William Nicholson, for example, preferred to deal with the marginal meaning, focusing exclusively on Christ fulfilling the law and prophecy of the written word, with no reference to the creative Word.[65] Gell, however, who was tutor to Henry More and inclined to a Cabalistic frame of mind, also considers 'how largely *all things* are here to be understood', and affirms the statement made in the Book of Wisdom, that 'God's Spirit filleth the earth'.[66] He goes on, however, to speak of how much more gloriously God fills the soul and the church.

The outspoken Robert South, whose popular sermons Traherne may well have encountered in Oxford, is more forthcoming. He accepts that Christ fulfils prophecies and fills the church with grace. However, he also argues, in terms similar to those deployed by Traherne in earlier chapters of *The Kingdom of God*, that Christ most importantly fills the universe through the

> omnipresence of his nature and universal diffusion of his Godhead. The Schools [...] make God to be in all things by repletion: that is, he is so *in them*, that they are rather *in him*; spreading such an immense fulness over all things, as in a manner swallows and folds them up within himself. Such a fulness has Christ as God, by which he fills, or rather overflows the universe, *et ad omnia praesentialiter se habet* [and he is present in all things].[67]

62   John Donne, 'Preached at St. Paul's, upon Christmas Day, 1622', *The Sermons of John Donne*, ed. Evelyn M. Simpson and George R. Potter (Berkeley, 1959), vol. IV, no. 11, p. 5.

63   Donne, 'Preached at St. Paul's, upon Christmas Day, 1622', pp. 7, 8.

64   Gell, *Gell's Remaines*, pp. 261–2.

65   William Nicholson, 'Of Christs Descent to Hell: Ephesians 4. 9, 10', *Exthesis Pisteos, or, Exposition of the Apostles Creed Delivered in Several Sermons* (London, 1661), Sermon 20, pp. 261–75, p. 273.

66   Wisdom 1.17.

67   Robert South, 'Ephesians 4: 10 He that Descended Is the Same Also That Ascended That

Furthermore, this 'omnipresential filling of all things always agreed to him'.[68] South then makes the somewhat contradictory distinction of another meaning of *filling all things* that only 'accrued to him upon and after his ascension, not before'. This refers to Christ's universal rule whereby 'He can command nature out of its course, and reverse the great ordinances of creation'.[69] As noted earlier, the suggestion of such voluntarism in Christ subverting natural law, and the perception of a historically dated rather than eternal governance of the universe, is largely absent in Traherne. In *The Kingdom of God* he applies with force what Gell refers to as the 'latitude' of the term *all things*. This latitude marks the ascension as an eternal filling of all things, the consummation of the incarnation, and the perfection of the creation.[70]

CONSIDER IT ALL

Traherne then, in company with some of his fellow divines, but in opposition to others, relates the fullness of Christ in whom all things consist to the concrete plenitude of the world, and indeed, all other 'Worlds'. Only 'timid minds', writes Teilhard, 'escape the awesome realism' of Paul's repeated statements'.[71] Traherne is perhaps bolder than many of his contemporaries in seeing 'Christ in all things and all things in Christ' in an essentially 'organic' sense.[72] This is the import of his placing of Paul's Christ hymn after the exhaustive survey of all worlds that comprises Chapter 25. 'These verses', said Joseph Sittler, 'sing out their triumphant and alluring music between two huge and steady poles – "Christ", and "all things" […] all things are permeable to his cosmic redemption because all things subsist in him'.[73] Chapter 25 is structured around these two poles, beginning with the Celestial Stranger's breathless wonder at the variety of 'all things' and concluding with a celebration of Christ as the element in whom they consist. Throughout his works, Traherne makes something of a Christic mantra of the Pauline phrases 'All Things' and 'All in All', to

He Might Fill All Things (Sermon I)', *Five Additional Volumes of Sermons Preached Upon Several Occasions* (London, 1744), vol. VII, p. 20.

[68] South, 'Ephesians 4: 10', p. 20.
[69] South, 'Ephesians 4: 10', pp. 23–4.
[70] Gell, *Gell's Remaines*, p. 261.
[71] Pierre Teilhard de Chardin, *Science and Christ* (1968), cited in King, *Christ in All Things*, p. 73.
[72] Ursula King sees this summation as touching 'the heart of Teilhard's vision', *Christ in All Things*, pp. 58, 70.
[73] Sittler, 'Called to Unity', pp. 184–6.

which he dedicates two entries in *Commentaries of Heaven*.[74] What Sittler says of Paul's 'expanded vocabulary' might also be said not only of the overflowing, energetic prose of the Celestial Stranger's great travelogue, but of Traherne's entire and wildly ambitious output: 'cosmic in scope, so vastly referential as to fill with Christic energy and substance the farthest outreach of metaphysical speculation [...] All is claimed for God, and all is Christic.'[75]

Just as Traherne finds the Light of the World to be 'deeply entangled' with the very atoms that comprise matter, so his Christology is woven into the very fabric of his poetry and prose – so ubiquitous as to be easily overlooked, yet boldly expressive of the insatiable desire and inexhaustible bounty of the ever incarnating Word. Traherne's exploratory prose is itself a form of Christic revelation. At the outset of *The Kingdom of God* he intrepidly undertook to 'Endeavour to rend the Vail' of Moses,

> that at least by a Chink, (if we remove it not wholly) we may See into the Beauty of Holiness, and admire the Secret of the most holy place: for that which discourages Timorous Spirits, animates the Couragious; and the very Incomprehensibleness of its Nature, which seemeth to reproov us, shall be the Allurement, Inviting us to Consider it all. (*Kingdom of God*, p. 258)

In considering all things, every sojourner and stranger on earth receives the fullness of Christ: 'when his Kingdom is received into the understanding, and dwelleth in us, we may be filled with all the fullness of GOD' (*Kingdom of God*, p. 260). And more than this, they that so enjoy the Kingdom themselves 'seem to be the fullness of him, that filleth all in all'[76] (*Kingdom of God*, p. 258). Each stranger becomes, as Traherne assures us at the conclusion of Chapter 25, coheirs with Christ to all possible Worlds:

> Whether Worlds are Glorious Enough Or no, to exist beyond the Heavens, I cannot tell; but of this I am sure, It pleased him to make us Coheirs with himself, and that Eyther these things or things Infinitly more Great, are beyond all Distances, prepared for us. (*Kingdom of God*, p. 393)

---

[74]   1 Corinthians 15.28; Ephesians 1.9–10, 22–3; Ephesians 4.10.
[75]   Sittler, 'Called to Unity', p. 178.
[76]   Cf. Ephesians 1.23.

II

PRACTICAL AND PUBLIC DEVOTION

Chapter 5

CROSSING THE RED SEA: *THE CEREMONIAL LAW*, TYPOLOGY AND THE IMAGINATION

Warren Chernaik

When my Soul is in Eden with our first Parents, I my self am there [...] I can
visit Noah in His Ark, and swim upon the waters of the Deluge.
(Centuries of Meditations, Ross, V, I.55)

The Ceremonial Law, a didactic poem by Traherne in heroic couplets,
discovered in 1997 and only recently published, is a commentary on
Genesis and Exodus, applying such episodes as the crossing of the Red Sea
and the manna in the wilderness to the lives of ordinary Christians.[1] In
this poem, unlike *Centuries of Meditations* and the poems in the Dobell
manuscript, the 'I' is clearly a representative figure with no autobiographical elements. Lines such as 'In Lands remote I see my self made
High' or 'I there behold a Tabernacle' ('Introduction', p. 197, 20, 30) do
not present a private, ecstatic experience but something readily available
to any Christian believer. The method of the poem is typological: passages
in the Old Testament not only can be seen as prefiguring the teachings of
Jesus in the New Testament, but are re-enacted in everyday life. As Barbara
Lewalski points out, such presentation of the experience of the Israelites as
'direct correlatives', 'being *ensamples* to us, and evident types of our estate

---

[1] Extracts from *The Ceremonial Law* are included in this essay by permission of the
Folger Shakespeare Library. I am grateful to the Folger Shakespeare Library for
providing me with a photocopy of Traherne's poem, Folger Shakespeare Library, MS
V.a.70. Page and line references are to Ross, Works, VI, published after this essay
was written. Substantial extracts from *The Ceremonial Law* were published by Julia
Smith in '*The Ceremonial Law*: A New Work', *PN Review* 25 (Nov/Dec 1998), 22–8;
see also Julia Smith and Laetitia Yeandle, '"Felicity disguised in fiery Words": Genesis
and Exodus in a Newly Discovered Poem by Thomas Traherne', *TLS* (7 November
1997), 17.

who live under the Gospel', was fairly common in seventeenth-century commentaries on Scripture.[2]

In 'A Reflexion', where the pronouns Traherne consistently uses are 'we' and 'our', Traherne comments on his typological method in terms of 'fit and Perfect Symmetrie', God's design made apparent in 'all the Parts of Time' (p. 218, 10–11). Citing the rather unlikely parallels of twelve apostles and twelve tribes of Israel (as well as twelve springs, twelve oxen, twelve thrones, and twelve loaves of bread in various biblical episodes), Traherne sees repeated 'Proportion' in 'Strange and Wonderfull' examples for our edification (p. 219, 55), made immediately discernible to anyone who can recognise the pattern:

> All which in His Proportions we may find
> Plainly Exhibited even to the Blind [...]
>   tis an Excellence
> As we may well Discern even by our sence. ('A Reflexion', 60–1, 102–3)

'The Church', as he uses the term in *The Ceremonial Law*, is the church militant, all believing Christians, wherever they may be, who, in their own lives, re-enact the experience of the Israelites. There are no polemics against dissenters or Roman Catholics, as in Traherne's *Select Meditations* and *Roman Forgeries*, and no claim that the ceremonial law of the Old Testament, with its 'imposition of strict laws', has been superseded, rendered invalid, by the 'better Cov'nant' of Grace, as Milton argues in contrasting 'shadowie Types' to 'Truth'.[3] Traherne's aim in this poem is to make the experience of the Israelites immediate and palpable to his readers, uniting past and present and transcending distances, and his use of the first person is a means toward that end.

> But that before my Birth I so should see
> New Joys in Old, prepard long since for me!
> Who would expect so strange a Wonder, who
> Would hope to such a Distant place to go? ('Moses Call', p. 203, 26–9)

---

[2] Barbara K. Lewalski, *Protestant Poetics and the Seventeenth-Century Religious Lyric* (Princeton, 1979), pp. 134–7, quoting William Perkins's commentary on Hebrews 11. See also Richard Douglas Jordan, 'Thomas Traherne and the Art of Meditation', *Journal of the History of Ideas* 46 (1985), 381–403.

[3] John Milton, *Paradise Lost*, ed. Barbara K. Lewalski (Oxford, 2009), XII.302–5. On the belief by Milton that the ceremonial law is abrogated by the Gospel (a view also held by Luther) see, e.g., *A Treatise of Civil Power*, in John Milton, *Complete Prose Works*, ed. Don M. Wolfe et al., 8 vols (New Haven, 1953–82), VII, pp. 259–60 (subsequent references to *CPW*). On the political element in Traherne's *Select Meditations*, see the editor's introduction to Thomas Traherne, *Select Meditations*, ed. Julia J. Smith (Manchester, 2009), pp. xix–xxi.

MEDITATION AND DIDACTICISM

Though the narrative element and the overt didacticism of *The Ceremonial Law* differentiate it from the *Centuries, Select Meditations*, and such poems as 'Shadows in the Water' or 'An Infant-Ey', it shares certain characteristics with these works. A book of private devotion, *The Ceremonial Law* is a series of occasional meditations, following the pattern for such meditation laid down by Joseph Hall and others by appealing to the eye of the imagination. According to Hall, 'no object should passe us without use [...] There is no creature, event, action, speech which may not afford us new matter of Meditation.'[4] As Traherne writes in *Centuries*, III.68, 'I saw moreover that it did not so much concerne us what Objects were before us, as with what Eys we beheld them; with what Affections we esteemed them [...] All men see the same Objects, but do not equaly understand them.'

In this recently discovered poem, the object of meditation, to be brought to life through the imagination, is a series of episodes from the first five books of the Old Testament, the 'ceremonial law' of Abraham and Moses. Thus, for example, Elim, a 'Haven of Repose' for the Israelites in their flight from Egypt through the 'Barren Sands' of the desert, is 'a Type & Representativ/ Of Canaan: Where we Desire to Live' ('Elim', pp. 213–14, 12, 30–1, 39). Similarly, 'We Noahs Rain Bow see [...] even in our Days' ('NOAHS RAINBOW', p. 201, 24–5). By an act of the imagination, Traherne suggests, the ordinary limits of time and space can be transcended. He makes a similar point in *Commentaries of Heaven*:

> The remotest Thing in rerum naturae is immediately near, because they are present not by any Extension of parts, but by an Act of understanding. Neither do they penetrate Distances by Degrees but surmount them in an Instant, without any Change of place. (II, p. 290)

Like others of Traherne's writings, *The Ceremonial Law* can be seen as a friendship offering, an act of communion. 'I' blends into 'we' and (for the Israelites) 'they': in this poem, as in many passages in the *Centuries*, the boundaries between first, second, and third person disappear. As Traherne puts it: 'We need Spectators; and other Diversities of Friends and Lovers, in whose Souls we might likewise Dwell [...] And as in many Mirrors we are so many other selvs, so are we Spitualy Multiplied when we meet our selvs more Sweetly, and liv again in other Persons' (*Centuries*, II.70). As Joan Webber has said, in commenting on the importance of communion in *Centuries of Meditations*, Traherne speaks 'to an ordinary "you" with

---

[4]   Joseph Hall, *Occasional Meditations* (London, 1630), sig. A11; Joseph Hall, *The Arte of Divine Meditation* (London, 1607), p. 20; quoted in Lewalski, *Protestant Poetics*, p. 151.

whom he wishes to share himself [...] Without reference to a "you", the "I" would be nothing.'[5] All experience must start with the self, and then widen out, in concentric circles. In *Select Meditations*, he speaks of his own experience in much the same way that, in the *Centuries*, he recommends as a spiritual exercise. The change of 'I' in the first passage to the imperative 'Place yourself in it' gives the later passage a didactic element, turning the individual and the ecstatic into the practical and generally applicable.

> In my Close Retirements I was some years as if no Body but I had been in the world. All the Heavens and the Earth are mine: mine a Lone. And I had nothing to do but walk with God, as if there had been non other but He and I. when I came among men I found them to be Superaded Treasures. and I am a Lone Still: The Enjoyer of all. But I have Greater work: To Glorifie God. O that I could do it, wisely, as I ought. (*Select Meditations*, Ross, V, III.69)

> If you desire Directions how to Enjoy it [the World], Place yourself in it as if no one were Created besides your self. And consider all the services it doth, even to you alone. (*Centuries*, II.2)

In his treatise *Inducements to Retirednes*, more conventionally, Traherne weighs up the advantages and disadvantages of society and solitude, concluding that though 'it is Infinitly Delightfull to pour out ones Soul into anothers Bosom', yet even the best of friends 'hav som Dissonancies, that Crack the Harmony, Discords towards us, and Defects in themselves' that render discourse 'Heavy and Unprofitable' (I, p. 14).[6] In several passages in *Select Meditations*, he speaks of himself as labouring under a calling, especially chosen in 'my work of calling others' (*Select Meditations*, III.67):

> to Thirst and love and bear, and long to reclaime! this is my portion under the Sun, and my task with God, wherein I am to Labor under as a fellow workman. (II.20)

> God hath use now for an Holy man [...] namely the Calling of those wonderfull ones to their Ancient possessions, to the Enjoyment of God, to their Inheritance of the world, to the Recovery of their Blessedness. (II.15)

The Ceremonial Law differs from Traherne's other writings in its explicit stance of patient elucidation: the use of 'we' is sometimes that of the

---

[5] Joan Webber, *The Eloquent 'I': Style and Self in Seventeenth-Century Prose* (Madison, 1968), pp. 224–9. Webber sees 'the creation of a multitude of personae', which 'meet and intermingle' in the *Centuries*, as imitating 'the universal communion of soul with soul [...] These personae, including the "you" of the reader, are all in a sense aspects of Traherne [...] as he sees in himself all mankind' (pp. 226–7).

[6] In *Centuries*, Traherne comments: 'Were all men Wise and Innocent, it were easy to be Happy [...] But he that would be Happy now must be Happy among Ingratefull and Injurious Persons' (*Centuries*, IV.20).

teacher addressing his students, the preacher addressing his flock ('But we/ Must other Meanings in this figure see', 'The Pascal Lamb', p. 211, 52–3). The poem 'contains straightforward ethical and spiritual instruction of a kind which he could have intelligibly preached to his rural congregation at Credenhill in Herefordshire'.[7]

For all the individuality of Traherne's voice in the more ecstatic passages of the *Centuries*, there is a sense in which all his writings can be seen as collaborative, engaged in a dialogue with actual or prospective readers. Bertram Dobell, who first published the *Centuries* in 1908, comments: 'That he intended it at first for one person only we may well believe: but that he must have seen as he went on that if it was fitted for the edification of his friend, it was equally well fitted for general use.'[8] *Centuries* includes a preface describing the book as a gift addressed to 'the friend of my best friend' (with the best friend being God). In all probability, the 'friend' to whom the work is addressed, to 'shew my Lov; To you, in Communicating most *Enriching Truths*' is Susanna Hopton, the author of several theological treatises, who lived near Traherne in Herefordshire, and whose niece was married to Traherne's brother Philip.[9] It is sometimes difficult to disentangle Susanna Hopton's religious prose works from related works by Thomas or Philip Traherne. Her *Daily Devotions* (1673), with the same publisher as Traherne's *Roman Forgeries*, contains at least one passage virtually identical with one in Traherne's unpublished *Church's Year-Book*, and of the three texts in Hopton's posthumously published *Collection of Meditations and Devotions* (1717), one exists in a second version, revised by Philip Traherne, and another, *Meditations on the Six Days of the Creation*, has been attributed both to Traherne and to Hopton, with no way of proving authorship to one or the other.[10] Nearly all of Traherne's works, left unpublished at his death,

---

7   Smith and Yeandle, 'Felicity disguised', 17. According to Julia Smith in her introduction to extracts from the poem, it is 'philosophically less complex than much of his other work, and is addressed to a less sophisticated audience, in a way which reflects his strongly didactic view of the purpose of art' (Smith, 'The Ceremonial Law: A New Work', p. 22).

8   Thomas Traherne, *Centuries of Meditations by Thomas Traherne, Now First Printed from the Author's Manuscript*, ed. Bertram Dobell (London, 1908), p. xiii. Dobell describes *Centuries* as 'a manual of devotion suitable for the members of the Church of England', a description that would also fit *The Ceremonial Law* (Dobell, p. xiii).

9   *Centuries*, prefatory poem (p. 6) and I.1. On Hopton, see *Susanna Hopton*, ed. Julia J. Smith, 2 vols (Farnham, 2010); see also Julia J. Smith, 'Hopton [née Harvey], Susanna (1627–1709)', *ODNB*. There is an extensive biographical introduction in [Susanna Hopton], *A Collection of Meditations and Devotions* (London, 1717).

10   See Cedric C. Brown and Tomohiko Koshi, 'Editing the Remains of Thomas Traherne', *Review of English Studies* 57 (2006), 769, 780–2; Catherine Owen, 'The Authorship of the "Meditations on the Six Days of Creation" and the "Meditations and Devotions on the Life of Christ"', *Modern Language Review* 56 (1961), 1–12. *Meditations on the*

have annotations by at least one other hand: with *The Ceremonial Law*, the comments go no further than 'I like this mightily but I pray prosecute it' to 'goe thorow the whole Sacred Story'.[11] In the Lambeth Manuscript the annotator goes further; entering into theological dispute with Traherne and at one point warning him that some of his speculations may be considered 'daingerous [...] if not Impious'.[12] The *ODNB* life of Traherne, pointing out that at least six other hands can be found in the Traherne manuscripts, suggests that 'writing was not a solitary activity for Traherne, and most of the manuscripts can be seen in some degree as communal productions'.[13] The most notorious example of collaboration, possibly unintended by Traherne, is Philip Traherne's rewriting of a number of his brother's poems: of the poems that do not appear in the Dobell manuscript, the revised Philip Traherne version is the only one we have.

One difference between *The Ceremonial Law* and Traherne's other writings is its narrative element, especially prominent in the section titled 'The Paschal Lamb'. Here the pronoun repeatedly used is 'they' (their, them): 33 times in 102 lines. 'We' is used only once until line 89, and then 9 times in the final lines of the section, where Traherne draws explicit conclusions, addressing his audience:

> This is the hidden sense
> That lurks behind their Nakedness. But we
> Must other Meanings in this figure see. ('The Paschal Lamb', p. 211,
>   51–3)

> But through this Blood we all resolv to go,
> No other Way to Heaven but this We know. (p. 213, 100–1)

In Traherne's narrative of the crossing of the Red Sea (Exodus 13 and 14) in 'The Paschal Lamb', he begins by emphasizing the desperate situation of the Israelites, with the prospect of death before and behind:

> The unrelenting Rocks and Mountains stand
> Unmovd, and close them in on either Hand.
> What shall they do? When all the World doth fail,
> And Death alone on evry side Assail ('The Paschal Lamb', p. 210, 10–13)

Creation is included in Ross, *Works*, IV as 'a work of uncertain attribution', about which 'the question of authorship may never be conclusively settled' (pp. xlvii–lii). Julia Smith attributes the work to Hopton; see Smith, *Susanna Hopton*, I, pp. xvii–xix.

[11] Ross, 'Introduction', in *Works*, VI, p. xxxii. See also Smith, 'The Ceremonial Law: A New Work', p. 22.

[12] See *Inducements to Retirednes*, in Ross, I, pp. 29–30.

[13] Julia J. Smith, 'Traherne, Thomas (*c*.1637–1674)', *ODNB*. On 'group activity' and 'collaborative production' as characterising the writing and circulation of Traherne's works, see Brown and Koshi, 'Editing the Remains of Thomas Traherne', pp. 780–1.

In depicting the miraculous parting of the seas, Traherne encourages the reader to participate in the scene, bringing out how what 'they see' enacted before them is a violation of the ordinary laws of nature, uniting opposites and giving unexpected access to things normally invisible. As Julia Smith says, in passages like this 'the voice of Traherne becomes indistinguishable from that of the Israelites', as narrator, audience, and the characters in the narrative seem to be caught up in a single experience.[14] In the passage that follows, the first 'they' refers to 'all the Waters', magically transformed, where the next four (all attached to active verbs – see, find, fetch, tread) refer to the Israelites, as Traherne seeks to convey what it might feel like to undergo such an experience.

> Like Ruby or like Chrystall Walls they stand
> Congealed by the Cold on either Hand.
> They see the Sands all red, the stones that pave
> The sea, the Rubbish under every Wave.
> Where Whales and Dolphins hertofore did play,
> They find an Uncouth strange Amazing Way
> Yet evry Step they fetch is life and Breath,
> They seem to tread and Trample upon Death. (p. 211, 30–7)

A passage in *Centuries*, beginning 'When my Soul is in Eden with our first Parents', quoted earlier as an epigraph, could serve as a prospectus for *The Ceremonial Law*, indicating both the completed sections of the poem and those initially projected.

> I can see Moses with his Rod, and the children of Israel passing thorow the sea. I can Enter into Aarons Tabernacle, and Admire the Mysteries of that Holy Place. I can Travail over the Land of Canaan, and see it overflowing with Milk and Hony; I can visit Solomon in his Glory, and go into his Temple. (*Centuries*, I.55)

In this section of the poem, along with the narrative, Traherne suggests 'other Meanings' (p. 211, 53), typologically appropriate to the everyday lives of his readers. 'A Bitter Wind' and the cold it brings, like any painful 'Affliction', may ultimately prove beneficial, 'Destructiv Things being made Preservative': 'What freezeth Water doth the Heart revive' (p. 212, 72, 76–8, 84). The pillar of cloud by day and the pillar of fire by night (Exodus 13.21–2), considered typologically, are an emblem of the distinction between those who recognize the true God and the reprobates and sinners, hearts hardened, blind and deaf to the manifestations of divine providence – 'all Joy' to the faithful but 'not understood' by 'their Foes' (59–61).

---

[14] Smith, '*The Ceremonial Law*: A New Work', p. 22.

The longest section of the poem, 'Elim', is based on one verse in Exodus, 15.27: 'And they came to Elim, where were twelve wells of water, and three-score and ten palm trees: and they encamped there by the waters.' From this very brief account, along with references to Exodus 15.22–4 (`and they went three days in the wilderness, and found no water'), Traherne finds the material for 130 lines of 'Elim', 50 lines of `Elim II', and 114 lines of 'A Reflexion'. In the opening lines of this section, the dominant pronoun is 'thou', addressing the 'Sacred Place' newly encountered by the Israelites: 'Thou Mine of Treasures!/ Thou little Eden of Delightfull Pleasures!' ('Elim', p. 213, 2, 12–13). The pronouns 'thou' and 'thee' occur 11 times in the first 13 lines, and 'I' 3 times, in a passage closer than any other part of the poem to the characteristic tone of the ecstatic vision of Edenic childhood in the Third Century, and in such poems as 'Eden', 'The Rapture', and 'Innocence'. In an extended apostrophe to Elim and its natural beauties, as providing sustenance to the parched, desiring soul ('Thou little centre of Desires!'), Traherne makes the discovery his own, as well as those of the Israelites:

> The Sweet and Chrystal Streams which flow from Thee
> To Quench, enflame my Soul: even while I see
> The glorious Beauty of the Donors face,
> Conceald and Painted in this lovly Place. ('Elim', p. 213, 4, 6–9)

The passage is characteristic of Traherne in presenting desires or wants as `the Fountains of Felicitie', simultaneously quenching and arousing thirst, and in seeing earthly beauties, in Neoplatonic terms, as shadows of a transcendent divinity.[15]

As in the *Centuries* and the poems in the Dobell manuscript, the enhanced vision of prophecy is contrasted with the clouded vision of those trapped in their material perspective, blinded by their false values. Traherne now moves from 'I' ('What sweet Refreshments do I find in Thee') to 'we', with the first person plural initially referring to 'corrupted Men', immured in darkness (p. 213, 14, 18). The pronoun 'we' and its variants occur 38 times in 'Elim': for most of the narrative, the Israelites are 'we' rather than, as in 'The Paschal Lamb', 'they'. As in the earlier section of the poem, Traherne in his narrative emphasises the sufferings of the Israelites in the desert, the apparent lack of hope in the hostile

---

[15] 'The Anticipation', p. 54, 72. On desire for the unknown as 'the Bands and Cements between God and us' (*Centuries*, I.51), see Denise Inge, *Wanting like a God: Desire and Freedom in Thomas Traherne* (London, 2009), pp. 25–41, 63–72; Louis L. Martz, *The Paradise Within: Studies in Vaughan, Traherne, and Milton* (New Haven, 1964), pp. 39–41, 61–2; and Warren Chernaik, 'Milton and Traherne: Paradise Recovered', in *Milton Through the Centuries*, ed. Gábor Ittzés and Miklós Péti (Budapest, 2012), pp. 225–7.

conditions: 'a Wilderness we found/ We Dreamt not of', a universe of death where 'Only Barren Sands appear' and 'evry Rock did seem like Open Graves' (35–6, 39, 43). 'We' here encourages identification, bringing out the physical pain of 'Raging thirst'.

> Three Days we travaild o'er Barren Sands
> And Squeezd the Clods for Water with our Hands
> Or suckt moist stones. The Raging thirst like fire
> Did wear us out, And evry step did tire
> Our Thirsty fainty Souls. (p. 214, 58–62)

When the Israelites arrive at Marah, where 'they could not drink of the waters [...] for they were bitter' (Exodus 15.22), Traherne brings out their disappointment in how 'the Waters which we hopd to Drink became/ More Sour and Bitter' (p. 215, 68–9). In commenting here on the typological meaning, Traherne uses the pronoun 'we' to make application to his Christian audience, while in the narrative itself 'we' consistently refers to the Israelites, subjected to experiences they are unable fully to understand:

> These are the Afflictions which on Earth we meet
> As long as here we mov our Pilgrim feet.[16] (p. 215, 70–1)

The pains and frustrations of the journey – 'But here we may not sojourn long, we must/ Away again' (84–5) – are brought out in the lines leading up to the sudden discovery of the paradisal Elim, with the pronouns 'we' and 'our' repeated 6 times in 8 lines. But at line 91 'we' suddenly becomes 'they' (5 times in 9 lines), as the Israelites, released from their suffering, are able to 'Drink with Eagerness' and delight in 'the long forgotten Verdure of Green Trees'.

> Beneath the Shade upon the Grass they Sit
> And Crowd together for the Benefit.
> The Beauties of the Place they here rehears,
> Call it the Ey of all the Univers.
> But first with Greediness they slake their Thirst. (p. 215, 93–8, 100)

With line 108, it is again 'We Drink' (p. 216), and until the end of 'Elim' the first person plural predominates (10 times in 24 lines), in the narrative and in homiletic conclusions drawn from the events narrated. As in the opening lines of the episode, Elim is associated with a recovered Eden, a

---

16 For similar passages, see 'Elim', p. 215, 79–82, where 'us' refers both to the Israelites and to the audience: 'Which here are Typd these Springs being understood./ They Pleas Allure and Promise fair being viewd /Far off: but neerer hand they us delude:/ And make us perish of a Double Death'.

'Relick of our Ancient Innocence' and for this reason it 'revives our sence' (p. 216, 112–13). The moral Traherne draws from the episode is that God's providence is evident at all times, even in distress, and that 'the Greatest Blessings' are 'Vain and Waste' unless we learn to appreciate and 'prize them' as emblems of 'our Blessedness' awaiting us in heaven (p. 216, 115, 129).

> Had GOD no other Caus but only this,
> For which he led us through this Wide Abyss
> Of Desert Horrors [...]
> It justifies His Wisdom and his Lov.
> [...]
> Unless we prize them and excite Esteem
> The Greatest Pleasures will but little seem. (p. 216, 120–2, 124, 126–7)

In *Christian Ethicks*, Traherne characterises the human condition as an 'Estate of Trial', in which 'Affliction and Vertue meet together': 'The Pain is necessary that is usd as a Remedie'.

> Our present Estate is not that of Reward, but Labour. It is an Estate of Trial, not of Fruition: A Condition wherein we are to Toyl and Sweat, and travail hard, for the promised Wages; an Appointed Seed Time, for a future Harvest; a real Warfare, in order to a Glorious Victory.[17]

The painful journey through 'a Desolat Accurst/ And Barren Wilderness' to the 'Pleasant Arbor' of Elim ('Elim II', p. 216, 2–6) can be seen as another version of the belief, central to Traherne, that the 'Eager Thirst' of desire, 'that did incessantly a Paradice/ Unknown suggest', is the necessary precondition of felicity ('Desire', p. 71, 3, 11–12). As he says in 'Manna II', 'want preceding makes us cleerly see/ Both End and Fountain of felicitie' (p. 223, 24–5).

> As Pictures are made Curious by Lights and Shades, which without Shades, could not be: so is Felicitie composed of Wants and Supplies, without which Mixture there could be no Felicity [...] Infinit Want is the very Ground and Caus of infinit Treasure.[18] (*Centuries*, I.41, 42)

The poem 'Desire', like several passages in *Centuries*, also suggests that the 'Fruits, Flowers, Bowers, Shady Groves and Springs' to be found on earth are in themselves but 'Dead Material Toys', since all objects only come to life as they are apprehended:

---

17 Traherne, *Christian Ethicks*, pp. 19, 185; see also 'Affliction', in *Commentaries of Heaven*, Ross, II, p. 305. On the 'estate of trial', see Inge, *Wanting like a God*, pp. 162–8.
18 On desire and the imagination in Traherne, considered from a Lacanian perspective, see A. Leigh DeNeef, *Traherne in Dialogue: Heidegger, Lacan, Derrida* (Durham, NC, 1988), pp. 115–24, 236–47.

> For not the Objects, but the Sence
> Of Things, doth Bliss to Souls dispence. (p. 72, 62–3)

Or, as Traherne says in 'The Inference I':

> Thoughts are alone by Men the Objects found
>   That heal or wound.
> Things are but dead: they can't dispense
> Or Joy or Grief.[19] (p. 181, 15–18)

Under the heading 'Apprehension' in *Commentaries of Heaven*, as in the poems in the Dobell manuscript entitled 'Thoughts' and 'My Spirit', Traherne makes a similar point: 'What were the Sun, or Stars, did ye not lie/ In me! And represent them there' ('Thoughts I', p. 63, 48–9). Material objects, he argues, are lifeless until subjected to 'Apprehension' and brought home to the individual 'Soul' reaching out to them.

> Whether all Desires are not Extensions, or the Stretching forth of the Soul to lay hold on its Object may be a Question. But certainly all are founded on Apprehension. Without which there could be no Life, nor no Valu in any Creature. (III, p. 174)

Like the Cambridge Platonists, Traherne rejects materialist epistemology, and sees the inward eye of the mind or the imagination, which 'made me present evermore/ With whatso ere I saw', as an active, creative agent ('My Spirit', p. 27, 38–9). According to his contemporary Ralph Cudworth:

> Sense is but the offering or presenting of some object to the mind, to give it an occasion to exercise its own inward activity upon [...] or knowledge is not a knock or a thrust from without, but it consisteth in the awakening and exciting of the inward active powers of the mind.[20]

As Traherne says in *Select Meditations*, there is 'no such world [...] nay not a Soul till we meditate upon it [...] They are there but not seen till the understanding Shine upon them' (IV.13).

---

[19] See the discussion of 'the animate and inanimate' in Traherne, in Gary Kuchar, 'Traherne's Specters: Self-Consciousness and its Others', in *Re-Reading Thomas Traherne*, ed. Jacob Blevins (Tempe, 2007), pp. 184–90.

[20] Ralph Cudworth, *A Treatise Concerning Eternal and Immutable Morality*, appended to *The True Intellectual System of the Universe*, 3 vols (London, 1845), III, pp. 564–6. On Traherne and Renaissance Platonism, see Carol L. Marks, 'Thomas Traherne and Cambridge Platonism', *PMLA* 81 (1966), 521–34; and S. Sandbank, 'Thomas Traherne on the Place of Man in the Universe', in *Studies in English Language and Literature*, ed. Alice Shalvi and A. A. Mendilow (Jerusalem, 1966), pp. 121–36.

TYPOLOGICAL APPLICATION: POINTING A MORAL

All but two of the sections of *The Ceremonial Law* are based on Exodus. 'Manna', with four separate sections, of 59, 96, 75 and 38 lines, is treated even more fully than 'Elim', though almost entirely in typological application, rather than narrative. In 'Manna I', only the first 18 lines are devoted to narrative, with the pronoun 'we' and its variants initially referring to the Israelites, as in 'Elim'. Here again, the emphasis is on the suffering of the Israelites, before they are relieved by the gift of manna:

> We meet with nothing but a desert ground,
> Where unrelenting Rocks and Sands are found.
> Our pale & witherd Cheeks, our famishd Eys,
> Our Dying Infants, & our Childrens Cries. ('Manna', p. 221, 6–9)

After the opening lines, narrative turns into typological commentary, and the complaints of the Israelites, who 'repind, and murmured' against Moses (as in Exodus 16.2–3), lead into a passage in which 'we' applies both to the Israelites and to 'weaker Spirits' among Traherne's audience. Here Traherne draws a moral lesson from the episode, showing how trial 'feeds our faith', while others, discouraged, show only 'our ill Nature', sinking under God's 'afflicting Rod' ('Manna', p. 221, 18, 21, 24–7, 36).

In 'Manna II' and 'Manna III', the emphasis is on the relationship between want and fulfilment. Those who live 'in Bondage' to the false pleasures of 'abundance' may be blinded by what Traherne in *Centuries* calls 'the outward Bondage of Opinion and Custom' (III.8):

> While in the midst of fulnesses we live,
> Which Natures Bounty only seems to give,
> Knowing not whence they came, we cannot see,
> The Donors Hand from which receivd they be.
> (Manna II, pp. 222–4, 12–15, 58, 61)

For this reason, Traherne says, addressing his readers, 'let us not in Egypt sit/ Continualy', but, like the Israelites under Moses' leadership, 'lets sojourn in the Desert Wilderness' ('Manna II', pp. 223–4, 56–7, 70), and learn by experiencing 'Distress'.

> Would you but sink into your low Estate,
> And feel your Wants ye then would know your fate.
> ('Manna III', p. 225, 24–5, 33)

Some of the lessons drawn here are highly conventional and not at all dependent upon the particular circumstances of the narrative. 'Moderation is a Sacred Thing', 'measure' and 'Temperate Care' are advisable at all times, and we should 'be content even with our daily Bread' ('Manna III', p. 226,

67, 70, 72, 76). Similar statements, equally conventional, can be found in Traherne's *Christian Ethicks*, Chapters 20, 22 and 23, 'Of Prudence' and 'Of Temperance'.[21] In the four sections of 'Manna', Traherne presents the gift of manna in the wilderness as illustrative of the workings of providence: 'Diviner Providence/ Doth cheaply give Sufficient, and the Land/ Affords whats necessary neer at hand' ('Manna III', p. 225, 9–11). Even the ordinary grains that spring from the earth – wheat, corn, rye – are 'as Great a Miracle as Manna is', evidence of God's providential care. Men, with their 'Bruitish souls', are 'Blind and Deaf' to a world 'rich in fruits', but, seeking after 'Novelties', fail to 'prize' the 'Common Benefits' offered them ('Manna II', p. 223, 37, 43, 52, 54).

In a number of passages in *The Ceremonial Law*, there is no element of narrative, as Traherne uses his typological method to make doctrinal points. Thus 'Israel', when it appears in 'Elim II', 'A Reflexion' and 'The Rock', at times typologically represents 'the church'. In 'Elim II', 'the Church', seeking and finding shelter, is contrasted with 'the World': the suggestion in many of these passages is that a body of believers is set apart from those with more worldly values:

> Yet Israel is the Church which hither came,
> That Drank the Springs, and from the Suns Bright Flame
> When twas too Scorching hid themselvs.[22] ('Elim II', p. 217, 34–6)

Traherne presents such a symbolic interpretation in 'A Reflexion' as part of God's design: 'that He by Elim did His church Design' and 'That Israel was the church which thither came' ('A Reflexion', p. 219, 46, 50). The 'church' in these passages would appear to refer to the community of Christian believers, the 'redeemed' ('A Reflexion', p. 219, 66). In 'The Rock', the church is explicitly identified with belief in Jesus Christ, in a section of the poem dedicated to showing, typologically, a number of ways in which 'The Rock was Christ: from whence the Water flows', quenching the believer's thirst and providing 'Refuge' ('The Rock', p. 228, 2, 10). There is an allusion here to Peter as the rock upon which Jesus will build his church (Matthew 16.18–19),[23] but no suggestion that 'the church' is an institution,

---

[21] Traherne, *Christian Ethicks*, pp. 152–60, 170–84; see Inge, *Wanting like a God*, pp. 41–9.

[22] For the contrast of 'the Church' and 'the World', see 'Elim II', p. 216, 6–7. Later Traherne comments on the 'Exactness in the Emblem' of 'the Church Secured from the Soultry Beams/ Of this Worlds Scorching sun' ('Elim II', p. 217, 39–41).

[23] 'And I say also unto thee, That thou art Peter, and upon this rock I will build my church; and the gates of hell shall not prevail against it' (Matthew 16.18). As a biblical proof-text, this passage has been interpreted in very different ways by Roman Catholics, Laudian Anglicans and Reformed Protestants. It is partly based on a pun on the name Peter (since the same word is used to mean 'rock').

an apostolic tradition, or associated with particular buildings or congregations, as in Traherne's poem 'Churches':

> Those stately Structures which on Earth I view
> To GOD erected, whether Old or New;
> [...]
> My Soul delight: How do they pleas mine Ey
> When they are fill'd with Christian Family![24]
> ('Churches I', p. 133, 1–2, 5–6)

Instead, in 'The Rock', the church consists of 'the Righteous', wherever they are found through 'all the Nations and the Ages' ('The Rock', p. 228, 18).[25] Traherne's language brings out the physicality of the experience of thirst satisfied and vividly evokes the bustling crowd, suggesting the natural cycles uniting humans and trees:

> The Righteous are like Trees whose thirsty Roots
> Suck in the Moysture they receive in fruits.
> And lo the Israelites those Thirsty Souls,
> Com crowding hither with their Cans and Bowls
> And Pots and Pails and Pitchers. ('The Rock', p. 228, 20–4)

In 'Moses Call', in contrast, the church is treated in terms similar to several passages in *Select Meditations*, in lines that appear to allude to the state of the church of England before the Restoration, seen as a kind of internal exile, reviled by 'the foolishness of sectaries' who would 'Abandon her and Lay her wast':

> Thy Church, she was a Bramble void of fruit,
> To which a Bush of Thorns did only suit.
> But now She Shines tho Barren, and she Bears
> Even in the midst of fire. What fruit? Her Tears.
> ('Moses Call', p. 203, 44–7)

A few lines later, 'thy church' again is presented as finding its only expression 'in Tears', in a 'vine [...] made of Thorns': 'and do no other fruits/ Flow from thy vine but Empty Tears? this suits/ Best with a barren Bush' (p. 204, 56–8).[26] The imagery of thorns, barrenness, and tears is traditional in devotional poetry: a parallel can be found in Herbert's 'The Collar':

---

[24] Ross writes, 'When they are fill'd with His Great Family!' following Philip Traherne's emendation of his brother's text.

[25] Milton, less orthodox in his theology, defines 'the universal visible church' as 'the whole multitude of those who are called from any part of the whole world, and who openly worship God [...] either individually or in conjunction with others': *De Doctrina*, I.29, *CPW*, VI, p. 568.

[26] See Traherne, *Select Meditations*, III.24, 25.

> Have I no harvest but a thorn
> To let me blood, and not restore
> What I have lost with cordial fruit?
> Sure there was wine
> Before my sighs did dry it: there was corn
> Before my tears did drown it.[27]

But in Traherne, the passage seems to have a topical dimension, with the church identified with the church of England, 'a National church [...] in which we walk under the Wings of Magistrates and the Protection of Laws', 'a church Established by Laws'. In *Select Meditations*, the barrenness and thorns are not those of the individual repentant sinner, but conditions inflicted by 'Ingratefull Phrarisies [...] and Selfe Conceited Holy ones', enemies of Traherne's beloved church of England, who have turned Zion, 'the vineyard of God', into 'a wilderness'. Israel, here as in *The Ceremonial Law*, serves as a model: the 'happieness to the church of Israel' was 'that all their Tribes were united into one, that She was a vine planted by God almighty [...] that Shee was rooted by Laws', and should it not be so 'to us'? (*Select Meditations*, I.85; III.23–5).

THE CEREMONIAL LAW AND THE GOSPEL

The relationship between the ceremonial law of the Israelites and the Gospel is a central concern in the last completed sections of Traherne's poem, 'The Rock', 'The Stone', 'Mount Sinai', 'The 10. Commandments', 'Moses in the Mount', 'Moses Face' and 'The Vail'. In *Select Meditations*, Traherne distinguishes between the 'kingdom of Legal Righteousness' and the 'kingdom of Evangelical Grace', seeing them as equally necessary for salvation, with no suggestion of one having been nullified or superseded by the other:

> Had there been no kingdom of Legal Righteousness there had been no King of Such a Kingdom. No place for Rewards or Punishments, no Goverment nor use of Laws, no Trial of Ingenuity and excellency [...] Had there been no kingdom of Evangelical Grace, The Incarnation of God, the Redemption of man, Mercy towards sinners [...] the truth of prophesies, the sight of wisdom in the ceremonial Law [...] our Labours and Travels and sweat in his service [...] had never been. (*Select Meditations*, III.37)

In one passage in 'The Vail', Traherne contrasts the limited vision of 'Carnal Jews' and their ceremonial law to the greater truth of the Gospel,

---

[27] 'The Collar', 7–12, in George Herbert, *Complete English Poems*, ed. John Tobin (London, 1991), p. 144.

and here he appears to some extent to share Milton's view that 'shadowie Types' may obscure or conceal truth, rather than revealing it.

> But Types and Shadows like a vail orespread
> Conceald that Glorious Brightness from the Dead
> And Carnal Jews, the Ceremonial Law
> In which the Patriarchs and the Prophets saw
> As in a Glass our Gospel Mysteries. ('The Vail', pp. 240–1, 12–16)

A few lines earlier, he speaks of 'Israels dimmer Sight' and later, developing the metaphor of the veil as barrier or impediment, says 'The Vail is don away in Christ, the Skreen/ Removd, the Cloud disperst' ('The Vail', pp. 240–1, 3, 28–9). But even in the lines about 'Types and Shadows', Traherne suggests that typologically the prophets of the Old Testament foreshadowed or even foresaw the truths of the Gospel.[28] Later in 'The Vail', the distinction is not between 'Carnal Jews' and Christians, but between 'the just and Wise', wherever they may be, and those who 'saw nothing' because of their inability or refusal to see. As in the crossing of the Red Sea and the pillar of fire, what is 'a Night to them' is 'a Day to us', as 'purer Israelites' are contrasted with benighted Egyptians:

> for they
> Saw nothing, where a World of virtue lay.
> And that we may not such Egyptians be,
> But purer Israelites made apt to see. ('The Vail', p. 241, 17, 20–3)

In 'The Stone', when Traherne descants on the various meanings of 'stone' in the narrative of Moses and the Israelites, he again speaks of 'the Carnal Jews' as not recognising the value of what is offered to them: 'the Stone of Stumbling to the Carnal Jews/ The Stone the foolish Builders did refuse' ('The Stone', p. 232, 68–9). Similarly, in 'Israel and Egypt', the truth of the Gospel is characterised both as hidden and as, once revealed, offering a new freedom, a new hope:

> So was the Gospel Hid from Ages, and
> Concealed only in the Jewish Land;
> Till Jesus came, and opened the Door
> To those Whose Sins much Wider then before
> The Breach in evry Age had made. ('Israel and Egypt', p. 209, 29–33)

---

[28] Cf. Milton, *Paradise Lost*, XII.300–6: 'So Law appears imperfet' [sic.] as compared to 'a better Cov'nant, disciplin'd/ From shadowy Types to Truth, from Flesh to Spirit/ [...] from servil fear/ To filial, works of Law to works of Faith'. In *De Doctrina*, Milton finds the Christian 'covenant of grace' to have been 'first announced, obscurely [...] by Moses and the Prophets' (*De Doctrina*, I.27, *CPW*, VI, p. 521).

Yet 'concealed in' does not mean 'rejected by', and the lines suggest that the truths of both the Old and New Testament, in 'the Hebrew Tongue', were not disseminated widely until the spread of Christianity (and, perhaps, translation of the Bible into the vernacular). The fundamental contrast here is between the faithful and 'the Injurious & Ingratefull', whether they are Egyptians, Jews or gentiles, who 'Despised the Old' (Testament) and 'New Mercies would not hear' ('Israel and Egypt', p. 209, 21, 34–5). In 'The Rock', the most ecumenical of the sections of *The Ceremonial Law*, where, as we will see, Traherne seeks to reconcile the Law with Love, Old Testament morality with the teachings of Jesus, 'Jews and Christians' are presented as essentially one, worshipping the same God:

> He is both Rock and Law, both Rod and Spring
> To Jews and Christians he is evry Thing. ('The Rock', p. 229, 78–9)

In this respect, Traherne differs profoundly from Milton, who considered the ceremonial law a 'childish and servile discipline' abrogated in its entirety by 'the new dispensation of the Covenant of Grace [...] written in the hearts of believers':

> The Mosaic Law was a written code, consisting of many stipulations, and intended for the Israelites alone. It held a promise of life for the obedient and a curse for the disobedient.[29]

Though Traherne concedes that 'by that Law no flesh is justified', since 'the justest by that Law must needs have died' ('Mount Sinai', p. 233, 28–9), he also characterises 'the Moral Law' of the Old Testament as 'enlightned with Divine/ And saving promises' ('The Vail', p. 240, 8–9): 'The Law was full of light when understood' ('Mount Sinai', p. 233, 40). In an interesting passage, developing a single metaphor for over twenty lines, Traherne compares the ceremonial law to hieroglyphics, which, in the manner of typology, both reveal and conceal 'Sacred Secrets'. We may not be able fully to comprehend the meaning of the signs in hieroglyphics, 'fair Types of Things' conveyed in 'Pictures', but eventually, through Jesus Christ, it will be possible to 'explain' the ceremonial law, deciphering what is partly hidden:

> As Hieroglyphicks on a Pyramid,
> The Secret Thoughts of the Egyptians hid,
> Whose fancies and conceits embodied were
> In Beasts and Birds and Trees engraven there.
> ('The Vail', p. 241, 50–3, 56, 70–1)

---

[29] Milton, *De Doctrina*, I.26 and 27, *CPW*, VI, p. 517, p. 522; see Maurice Kelley's notes, *CPW*, VI, pp. 521–2, p. 531. Traherne also disagrees with Milton and with the Reformed tradition in Luther, Calvin and others, in arguing for justification by works rather than by faith: see *Select Meditations*, III.38–42, 48–50.

In *Select Meditations*, Traherne characterises ancient Israel, under the ceremonial law, not as plunged into darkness because of ignorance of the Gospel, but as uniquely privileged:

> He hath Shewed his word unto Jacob, his Statutes and his judgments unto Israel: he hath not dealt so with any nation, and for his judgments they have not known them. This was the Joy and Glory of Israel, that She alone of all the nations in the whole world was acquainted with the wayes and judgments of the Lord. (III.17)

In 'Mount Sinai', 'Moses in the Mount' and 'Moses Face', Traherne emphasises 'the Terror of the Law'. 'Mount Sinai', the most heavily revised section of the poem, begins 'Long time the World had been without a Law': for two thousand years, the inhabitants of the earth wandered aimlessly, 'Without a Law promulgd, and knew not why', lacking an 'inward Law' to govern their conduct ('Mount Sinai', p. 232, 2, 15–16). When Moses ascended Mount Sinai, he was accompanied by 'devouring fire', arousing in all the beholders fear of 'direfull vengeance' from an angry deity.

> In Clouds, thick Darkness, Thunders, Lightnings, he
> The Terror of the Law did make them see.
> The Trumpets Sound did all the Mountain shake
> And make the Wilderness of Sin to quake.
> ('Mount Sinai', pp. 232–3, 22–5, 30, 33)

When Moses eventually descended, bearing the tablet with the Ten Commandments, 'transfigurd' with a face that 'did like the Burning Sun appear', those who saw him were terrified at the apparition:

> When Aaron came
> With joy to meet him, seeing a Man of flame
> Approach, he fled; and all his friends did flie
> His Presence, as a Dreadfull Prodigie.[30] ('Moses Face', p. 239, 8–9, 14–17)

And yet, characteristically, Traherne in these final completed sections of the poem seeks to reconcile Law and Love, a deity who punishes sinners and a deity 'who doth our Strength renew,/ On whom we feed, while we his Lov do view' ('Manna IV', p. 227, 24–5). In 'The Rock' and in 'Mount Sinai', 'that fiery Law which Scours away all Rust' is seen as a cleansing fire, 'all devouring', which spectators can approach only from a distance. In the thunder, lightning and fire marking Moses' ascent of Mount Sinai (Exodus 19:16), the Christian believer can find both 'Terror and Comfort',

---

[30] In *Paradise Lost*, Milton similarly emphasises the punishment threatened for disobedience under the Mosaic Law: 'the voice of God/ To mortal eare is dreadful' (*Paradise Lost*, XII.235–6).

illustrating how that 'our State' is 'intermixd' ('The Rock', p. 229, 68; 'Mount Sinai', p. 233, 60–1, 66). Similarly, in 'Moses Face', where again the onlookers are identified with the audience, addressed as 'we', the initial reaction to the extraordinary apparition of the transfigured Moses is 'Terror', but afterwards the 'Dread' is turned to 'Joy' ('Moses Face', p. 239, 30–5).

The term 'Love' occurs again and again in Traherne's paraphrase of the Ten Commandments: the Law is 'a pledge of Love', we must learn 'to practice Love on Earth', 'true Love' is 'The fountain head from whence all Duties mov' ('The 10. Commandments', pp. 234–6, 30, 79, 112–13). This treatment of love as the guiding principle of human conduct, the link between God and man, is central to Traherne's thought, expressed again and again in the *Centuries, Select Meditations*, poems and recently discovered tracts:

> GOD is present by Lov alone. By Lov alone He is Great and Glorious. By Lov alone He liveth and feeleth in other Persons. By Lov alone He enjoyeth all the Creatures [...] The Soul is shriveld up and Buried in a Grave that does not Lov.

> By Loving a Soul does Propagat and beget it self. becaus before it loved it lived only in it self: after it loved, and while it loveth it liveth in its object [...] the Soul without Extending, and living in its object, is Dead within it self. (*Centuries*, II.50, 56)

The Ceremonial Law presents the truths of the Gospel as not only compatible with, but foreshadowed in the Moral Law as embodied in the Ten Commandments: 'The Moral Law a Gospel did implie' ('The 10. Commandments', p. 234, 2). 'True Love', the love of the deity for his creatures, 'Is that the Law doth aim at'. As he says in the final couplet of 'The 10. Commandments':

> Love gave the Law, Love made the World, and Love
> The very Substance of the Law doth prove. (p. 237, 116, 122–3)

TRAHERNE AND THE TRADITION OF BIBLICAL COMMENTARY

Though the emphasis on a God of love is characteristic of Traherne's theology – one of the ways in which he dissents from Calvinist doctrines of predestination and reprobation – the lessons inculcated by *The Ceremonial Law* are for the most part conventional and uncontroversial. Traherne is not engaging in theological disputes, or, in his commentary on Exodus, seeking to elucidate knotty points of Scripture or unearth hidden meanings. The aim, common within the Reformed tradition as in the church of England to which Traherne adhered, was 'the application of all scripture to the self':

Christians were invited to perceive the events and personages of Old and New Testament salvation in history not merely as exemplary to them but as actually recapitulated in their lives in accordance with God's vast typological plan of recapitulation and fulfilments.[31]

Though no Calvinist, Traherne followed the practice of Calvin in his Commentaries on Genesis and Exodus, in combining narrative and moral observations. Calvin is commenting here on the structure of Exodus and the three books that follow it in the Hebrew Bible, but the remarks apply equally well to his commentary, and to others of its kind:

> These FOUR BOOKS are made up of two principal parts, viz., THE HISTORICAL NARRATIVE and THE DOCTRINE, by which the Church is instructed in true piety [...] as well as in the fear and worship of God; and thus the rule of a just and holy life is laid down, and individuals are exhorted to the performance of their several duties. This distinction MOSES does not observe in his Books, not even relating the history in a continuous form, and delivering the doctrine unconnectedly, as opportunity occurred.[32]

The habit of drawing practical lessons from Scripture and applying them to everyday life transcends doctrinal distinctions, as biblical commentaries by the influential Puritan theologian William Perkins and the conservative Anglican Henry Hammond illustrate.[33] On the crossing of the Red Sea, Perkins comments: 'In their example wee are taught the same dutie, to doe as they here did [...] When a man is past all hope of life, he must then believe and hope for life, as the Israelites did in the red sea, for preservation.' The Psalms, according to Hammond, 'will seldom miss to meet seasonable matter to worke on in any mans breast, which wants not devotion to discern and bring it home to him'. In reading, reciting, or meditating on the Psalms, we must be 'allwaies in a posture ready for them [...] by exciting in our selves the *same affections* which we discern to have been in *David* and in others at that time, *loving when he loves, fearing when he fears, hoping when he hopes, praising God when he praises*'.[34]

What distinguishes *The Ceremonial Law* from prose commentaries like that of Calvin, Perkins, or William Poole's *Annotations upon the Holy Bible* (1683) is Traherne's proliferating imagination, the profusion of the analogies

---

[31] Lewalski, *Protestant Poetics*, p. 131.

[32] John Calvin, *Commentaries on the Four Last Books of Moses*, trans. C. W. Bingham, 4 vols (Edinburgh, 1852–54), I. xv.

[33] See William Perkins, *A Cloud of Faithfull Witnesses, leading to the Heavenly Canaan: Or a Commentary upon the II. Chapter of the Hebrews* (London, 1608); and Henry Hammond, *A Paraphrase and Annotations upon the Book of the Psalms* (London, 1659).

[34] Perkins, *Cloud of Faithfull Witnesses*, pp. 453–4; Hammond, *Paraphrase and Annotations*, Preface, sig. c2v, c3v.

by which he seeks to deliver 'the doctrine unconnectedly, as opportunity occurred'.[35] Elim (Exodus 15.27) is scarcely mentioned in Poole or Calvin, but gives rise to nearly 300 lines in Traherne. For Poole, 'the *Israelites* are obliged and encouraged to the obedience commanded by being put into better circumstances than they were under in their last station', where for Calvin, commenting practically on the geographical conditions of Palestine:

> Moses here relates that a more pleasant station was granted to the people, when they were led to a well-watered spot, even planted with palm-trees, which do not usually grow in a dry soil.[36]

The incident of Moses' rod turning into a serpent (Exodus 4.1–5) gets a brief commentary in Poole and an extended one in Calvin, both emphasising the relevance of this miraculous occurrence to the situation of the Israelites and the Egyptians, as well as drawing a general moral about 'the divine power and goodness'. Poole and Calvin raise the question of whether 'the change of the rod into a serpent was real, and actual, or whether the outward form only was changed'. To Poole, Moses' rod 'was really changed into a Serpent, whereby it was intimated what and how pernicious his Rod shortly should be for the Egyptians', where for Calvin, 'God wished to shew him, that although his condition was abject and despicable, still he would be formidable to the king of Egypt.' 'What was to be hostile and injurious to his enemy, would be an assistance and safeguard to himself'.[37] Traherne, in 68 lines of commentary that include a paraphrase of the Twenty-Third Psalm and remarks on various meanings of 'rod' and shepherd, is more concerned with his seventeenth-century readers or parishioners than with the ancient Israelites. He draws a political moral, but one in accordance with his own conservative royalism, arguing that kings, like 'Gods, must be obeyd'. Here again the 'Type' suggests direct application of the biblical narrative to modern readers:

> This Rod of GOD being seen in Moses hand,
> Doth giv us, as a Type, to understand,
> That GOD to Mortal Men doth now commit
> His Kingly Scepter, for their Benefit. ('Moses Rod', p. 205, 34–7, 39)

In 'The Stone' (Exodus 17.8–16), Poole once more raises practical questions about the literal meaning of the Scriptural text, asking whether it would be possible for Moses, sitting on a stone, to raise his hands for an entire day and whether it was believable that when Moses held up his hand Israel prevailed in battle:

---

35   Calvin, *Commentaries*, I. xv.
36   William Poole, *Annotations upon the Holy Bible* (London, 1683), Exodus, Chap. XV, 27 (unpaginated); Calvin, *Commentaries*, I. 267.
37   Calvin, *Commentaries*, I. 86–7; Poole, *Annotations*, Exodus, Chap. IV, 3.

Not that both hands were erected and joined together, which was not a fit posture for one holding a rod in his hand, but that *Moses* shifted the rod out of one hand into the other when the former was weary [...] This [...] seems not to have been the gesture of one praying which is the lifting up of both hands, but of an Ensign-bearer.

To Calvin, the episode, in which Moses, 'wielding the rod of God', observed the battle from afar, shows the glory of the victory to be 'entirely attributed to the gratuitous favour of God'. Traherne, in the 78 wide-ranging lines of 'The Stone', agrees:

> Unseen, far off, in Secret Moses was,
> Yet got the Victory. As in a glass
> We here may see the force of prayer, made
> By holy Souls. (p. 231, 42–5)

But where Calvin is at pains to reject 'divers allegories [...] made of this place', in which in accordance with typological foreshadowing, Moses' associates Aaron and Hur 'present a figure of the Old and New Testament, on which the prayers of the saints must rest', Traherne, allowing his imagination free rein, throws out a seemingly endless number of analogies in consecutive lines.[38] Like Moses, Traherne suggests, making the biblical episode applicable to his seventeenth-century audience, we need the 'Support' of Faith 'to uphold our Weary hands' ('The Stone', p. 231, 56–8). As he rings the changes on the central metaphor of Christ as 'the Stone on which we sit', Traherne soon leaves the original biblical context far behind:

> But Christ alone
> Is the Square Root, the precious Corner stone
> [...]
> The Stone that Babylons proud Monarch saw,
> From which the Prophet did such Mysteries draw
> The little Stone, that grew, and fil'd all Lands,
> The Stone cut out without a Mortals hands.
> The Stone of Stumbling to the Carnal Jews
> The Stone the foolish Builders did refuse.
> A tried Elect and Precious Stone to them,
> That in the New and True Jerusalem
> Are on him built, like lively Stones, and make
> One Holy Temple for his Glory Sake.
> ('The Stone', pp. 231–2, 54, 60–1, 64–73)

---

[38] Poole, *Annotations*, Exodus, Chap. XVII, 111–12; Calvin, *Commentaries*, I. 293. In such allegorical readings, 'of more acuteness than solidity', Calvin says, 'the stone which they gave to Moses to sit upon was offered him because our faith is only founded upon Christ'.

MAKING THE WORLD VOCAL

What is evident here is what Traherne's contemporary John Dryden describes as 'the faculty of imagination', which in some respects can be considered 'wild and lawless':

> the faculty of imagination in the writer which, like a nimble spaniel, beats over and ranges through the field of memory, till it springs the quarry it hunted for; or, without metaphor, which searches over all the memory for the species or ideas of those things which it designs to represent.[39]

The emphasis on 'memory' as the source for the imagination's explorations fits Traherne's use of material from the Bible, as well as his use in many of his writings of a commonplace book. According to another of Traherne's contemporaries, the scientist Robert Boyle, the practice of occasional meditation can 'make the World vocal, by furnishing every Creature, and almost every occurrence, with a Tongue'. The habit of meditation available to anyone, by means of 'apt Similitude, pertinently appli'd', can simultaneously 'Instruct the Mind, and Warm the Affections':

> The mind of Man is so comprehensive, and so active a faculty, that it can force its passage into those imaginary spaces, that are beyond the outermost parts of the outermost Heaven, and can in a moment return back.[40]

Beyond the world of quotidian appearances, obscured by our petty, earthbound concerns, there is, Traherne maintains, a world of infinite possibility, available to the awakened imagination. Though *The Ceremonial Law*, a work by a minister addressing his congregation, is more explicitly didactic than the *Centuries* or *Select Meditations*, it shares with these works the desire to 'waken thy soul and stir it up', and through the awakened 'Imaginations and affections' (*Select Meditations*, III.84), unearth the hidden powers that we are not always aware we have.

> But Spirits in a Moment can commence
> An Endless Journey; and extend a Sence
> To any Object, which no Ey can see,
> Tho tis the furthest in Eternity.
> ('Of Israels coming out of Egypt', p. 207, 17–20)

---

[39] John Dryden, 'Of Dramatic Poesy' (1668), in *Of Dramatic Poesy and Other Critical Essays*, ed. George Watson, 2 vols (London, 1964), I, p. 8, p. 98.

[40] Robert Boyle, *Occasional Reflection upon Several Subjects*, 2nd edn (London, 1669), sig. b1v–b2; p. 4, p. 14.

Chapter 6

SECTARIANISM IN *THE CEREMONIAL LAW*

Carol Ann Johnston

Little thus far has been written about *The Ceremonial Law*, Traherne's curtailed epic poem in heroic couplets. The discovery of the poem was reported in the *TLS* on 7 November 1997; Laetitia Yeandle of the Folger Shakespeare library found the manuscript listed as an anonymous poem from the 1680s (Yeandle and Julia Smith subsequently redated the poem to the 1660s).[1] *The Ceremonial Law* had been in the library since the summer of 1958, bought from H. A. Hammelmann of Suffolk. This recent find, however, has left scholars with little time to reflect upon its contents in comparison to the manuscripts discovered in the late nineteenth century. Besides its late discovery, the reasons for the lack of attention to *The Ceremonial Law* are several: the bulk of the Traherne manuscripts reside at the Bodleian and the British Libraries. *The Ceremonial Law* and *Select Meditations* are the outliers, in the United States. Furthermore, the manuscript of the poem was only published for the first time in 2014, in the sixth volume of Jan Ross's *The Works of Thomas Traherne*. In addition to these logistical reasons, *The Ceremonial Law* maintains in some ways a different focus from other more familiar works by Traherne, and readers are still considering its place in his canon.

Traherne's distinctively Protestant use of typology in *The Ceremonial Law*, I will argue, allows him to experiment with sectarian ideas far afield from the Anglican orthodoxy scholars have read in his work. The current thinking that Traherne wrote the poem in the 1660s further suggests a comparison to another manuscript dated to the 1660s, the *Select Meditations*. Scholars have drawn conclusions about Traherne's politics based upon perceived levels of orthodoxy and loyalty to the national church, and therefore to the

---

[1] See Julia Smith and Laetitia Yeandle, "'Felicity disguised in fiery Words': Genesis and Exodus in a Newly Discovered Poem by Thomas Traherne', *TLS* (7 November 1997), 17.

royalist cause, that they read especially in *Select Meditations*. Yet Traherne's extreme Protestant views in *The Ceremonial Law* concerning individual Christians' agency, their ability to become one and the same as the Deity – with everyone serving as a king on Earth and in Heaven – suggests an affinity with more radical Protestant sects, and with politics nearer to sectarian beliefs. I will argue that we expand our understanding of Traherne's political and ecclesiastical loyalties when we read his work anew through the lens of his engagement with typology in *The Ceremonial Law*. His typological emphasis in the poem focuses upon images and characters prominent from the Exodus that are in radical Protestant writing. Further, the story of the Exodus has a history in a political – as well as a religious – typology. The liberation of the Israelites from Egyptian slavery resonates in any situation in which a group of Christians perceives itself under persecution and bondage. This narrative was especially resonant, John Coffey argues, in the English Civil War.[2] In addition, Traherne's unique embodiment of types, and ultimately of the Deity, in his lyrics and *Centuries* shows Traherne seizing a shared agency with God. James Block has argued that radical Protestants in England advocated for a shared agency between Christians and God, which accounted for making them uncontrollable by government.[3] This ultimately led to their political failure. Traherne's political activism – as well as the airing of his beliefs in print – has, until this volume of essays, been assumed to be nil. I understand Traherne as trying out broad theological ideas in his various manuscripts. In *The Ceremonial Law* these ideas resonate with radical sectarianism flourishing in the years prior to the Civil War through the Interregnum.

The Ceremonial Law takes Genesis and Exodus as its subject, with the majority of its sections dedicated to the Exodus narrative. The poem also features a narrator who places himself spatially and temporally in and among the scenes he relates from the Bible. The elements of verse form, subject matter, and narrative placement are at first glance anomalous in the Traherne canon, although we can see Traherne in writing *The Ceremonial Law* enacting his speaker's recollection of reading the Bible from the Third Century:

> When the Bible was read my Spirit was present in other Ages. I saw the Light and Splendor of them: the Land of Canaan, the Israelites entering into it. the ancient Glory of the Amorites, their Peace and Riches, their Cities

---

[2] See John Coffey, *Exodus and Liberation: Deliverance Politics from John Calvin to Martin Luther King Jr* (Oxford, 2014). All further references to this text will be cited in the text by page number.

[3] See James E. Block, *A Nation of Agents: The American Path to a Modern Self and Society* (Cambridge, 2002).

Houses Vines and Fig trees, the long Prosperity of their Kings, their milk and Honie, their slaughter and Destruction, with the Joys and Triumphs of GODs people all which Enterd into me, and GOD among them. I saw all and felt all in such a lively maner, as if there had been no other Way to those Places, but in Spirit only. this shewd me the Liveliness of interior presence, and that all Ages were for most Glorious Ends, Accessible to my Understanding, yea with it, yea within it. for without Changing Place in my self I could behold and Enjoy all those. Any thing when it was proposed, tho it was 10000 Ages agoe, being always before me. (*Centuries of Meditations*, Ross, V, III.24)

The narrator of *The Ceremonial Law* relates the biblical story outlined here, 'the Israelites entering into [the land of Canaan]'. He does so in the breathless fashion that the narrator of the *Centuries* intimates: 'I saw all and felt all in such a lively maner, as if there had been no other Way to those Places, but in Spirit only.' Traherne's speaker throughout his work argues for individual capaciousness, for the experience of 'All': here, 'Anything when it was proposed [...] being always before me'; elsewhere 'No Brims nor Borders, such as in a Bowl/ We see, My essence was Capacitie./ That felt all Things' ('My Spirit', Ross, VI, p. 26, 8–10). Critics have discussed Traherne's capacity in general largely in terms of subjectivity and objectivity through his quest to merge subject and object: 'The World was more in me, than I in it', he explains in 'Silence' (p. 26, 80).[4] Yet *The Ceremonial Law* shows the narrator internalising the biblical stories of the Exodus and of Adam and Eve even as he simultaneously embodies himself in these stories. 'Capacity' in *The Ceremonial Law* relates to time, as much as to space. The 'present' is synchronic. It is the narrator's moment in time, as well as the time of the biblical narration, and the reader's time. The narrator thus takes on the divine capacity of encompassing different moments while embodying them in an eternal present.

In the section of *The Ceremonial Law* entitled 'A Reflexion', the speaker draws out his understanding of time represented spatially, establishing a synchronicity of space in addition to time within his body. Milton most famously devises a synchronic sense of time for God in *Paradise Lost*, who comprehends all of history as a single moment. Milton argues as well for a synchronic paradise within all Christians as God promises Adam and Eve 'A paradise within thee, happier far'.[5]

---

[4] See, for example, the poet Forrest Gander's essay comparing Traherne with phenomenologists Husserl and Merleau-Ponty, and the theory of intersubjectivity: Forrest Gander, 'The Strange Case of Thomas Traherne', *Jacket* 32 (April 2007) <http://jacketmagazine.com/32/k-gander.shtml> [accessed December 2015].

[5] Quoted from *Milton: Paradise Lost*, ed. Alastair Fowler, 2nd edn (Harlow, 2007), XII.587, p. 674.

Traherne incorporates this conception into his speaker's mind with the important addition of the speaker's body. As the speaker's mind comprehends all ages temporally in Miltonic fashion, his body also contains them spatially. Importantly, the speaker recognises that his theory of the body, able to contain all ages, arises from his understanding of typology as 'GODs Design':

> That we no fiction make, but See the Thing,
> Which from the Type most realy doth Spring,
> We may by this Discern: by GODs Designe,
> All Ages closing in one Body shine
> They are a Glorious Fabrick, or a Tent
> Wher in the GODHEAD Dwells, a Monument
> Of Wisdom (Ross, VI, p. 218, 2–8)

He concludes this meditation with a comparison of 'all Ages closing in one Body' to 'a famous Tomb' wherein 'evry Part a Secret Beauty lends/ To all the Parts' (p. 218, 5–15). God's special brand of architecture creates this collapse of time into space, which is the principal means by which individuals are instructed in felicity: 'That after Ages might instructed be/ In all the Secrets of Felicitie' (p. 218, 26–7). Traherne's narrator embodies both temporal and spatial capacity, containing all historical time and events.

Given Traherne's interest throughout his work in the collapse of spatial and temporal boundaries, his engaging in the Old Testament narrative, and thus in typology – as witnessed in the above quotation – seems inevitable. Typology, the Christian technique of reading the Old Testament that sees the episodes and persons there as corresponding to the life of Christ, suggests a collapse of space and time. In typological readings, an event in the Old Testament is as a stamp on one side of a coin, which, when it is flipped, reveals a corresponding event from the New Testament. Thus these events may come to seem concurrent in the sense of God's knowing all events that happen as a synchronic gesture. The ceremonial laws in the Old Testament epitomise the Christian understanding of typology. Protestant thinkers such as Calvin and Luther divide the Old Testament law into three parts: ceremonial laws, civil laws, and moral laws.[6] These divisions in Protestant theology are not hard and fast, but help to classify how laws function in the Old Testament.[7] Ceremonial laws apply to 'the functioning of the sacrificial system, including tabernacle/temple operations, religious

[6]   See, for example, Jean Calvin, *Institutes of the Christian Religion*, trans. Henry Beveridge (London, 1845), 2.7 1–17 and 4.20 14–16.
[7]   See David W. Jones, *An Introduction to Biblical Ethics* (Nashville, 2013), p. 57.

festivals, and dietary regulations'.[8] Explaining the Christian perspective on these Judaic laws, David W. Jones says, citing John 8.56 and Hebrews 11.13: 'in retrospect, it is evident that the ceremonial laws prefigure the redemptive work of Jesus, a fact that New Testament authors note was evident to perceptive Jews [...] The ceremonial laws were fulfilled – not abrogated – by the advent and work of Christ.'[9] For Christians, Christ 'observed and embodied' the ceremonial laws, rather than replacing them, in his sacrifice of his body for their sins. Typology, then, is inherent in the writing of a poem based upon the ceremonial law.

Additionally, typology also lies at the centre of Traherne's identity as a Protestant. As Barbara Lewalski points out, Traherne's lyrics and *Centuries of Meditations* embody a uniquely Protestant use of typology: 'These figures and these states are not merely moral exemplars or analogies for Traherne, but are said to be actually repeated in him.'[10] Traherne 'becomes' Edenic Adam in such Dobell lyrics as 'Innocence', for example, and in Burney manuscript poems such as 'Adam', the speaker returns from his corrupt and sinful state by way of believing in – and embodying – Christ.[11] In a sense, Traherne's use of typology represents the ultimate endgame for Protestant belief: identification and self-examination draw the Christian ever closer to Old Testament types, from participating in scenes as the narrator does in *The Ceremonial Law*, to loss of the distance between sign and signifier in the lyrics and the *Centuries* as the narrator becomes Adam, and is King on the Throne in Heaven. These positions, Traherne asserts, are not merely the providence of his narrator, but are also available to all Christians.

My reading of typology and Traherne – and of representation in Traherne overall – continues the complication of Traherne's Protestant beliefs begun with the discovery of the Lambeth Palace manuscript. Traherne's religious allegiances after 1660 generally have been discussed as being to the national church. Critics from Gladys Wade to Stanley Stewart and Sharon Seelig see Traherne as a high Anglican (if such a person exists).[12] However, Jeremy Maule's discovery of four unpublished treatises

---

8   Ibid.

9   Ibid, p. 58.

10   Barbara K. Lewalski, *Protestant Poetics and the Seventeenth-Century Religious Lyric* (Princeton, 1979), p. 100.

11   As in stanza five of 'Innocence', for example: 'That Prospect was the Gate of Heav'n, that Day/ The ancient Light of Eden did convey/ Into my Soul: I was an Adam there,/ a little Adam in a Sphere/ Of Joys!' (p. 10, 53–8).

12   Wade initiates this notion: 'In the *Roman Forgeries* [...] and in the *Meditations* and very markedly in *The Book of Private Devotions*, Traherne appears constantly as an enthusiastic High Churchman, conscious of the continuity of the Anglican Church in doctrine

in the Lambeth Palace Library has begun to suggest a more complex picture of Traherne's theology. In her introduction to the manuscript, Jan Ross suggests that as one of the 'conforming clergy', Traherne was 'unaligned theologically'. This group of clergymen, attending university during the Interregnum, resists easy classification. 'Preoccupied with their pastoral office', she argues, 'they took "to heart the nation's superficial godliness and hypocrisy".[13] These clergymen would be less interested in parsing sectarian alliances – an activity that divided their country into war – and more interested in attending to their pastoral office and parishioners, a way to serve God authentically and without conflict. In reading *A Sober View of Dr Twisses his Considerations* from the Lambeth Manuscript, James Balakier sees a different aspect of sectarianism in Traherne from his affinity with 'high church' Anglicanism or being theologically unaligned. He reads 'a latitudinarian slant' in Traherne's thoughts on the Calvinist–Armenian disagreement on predestination.[14] Latitudinarians were referred to in the seventeenth century as 'low church', contrary to our initial view of Traherne's religious allegiances. Further complicating our understanding of Traherne's loyalties, his admission to the living of Credenhill in Herefordshire in 1657 was supported by certificates from some of the most well-known Presbyterian clergy, preachers at Hereford Cathedral who were dismissed after the Restoration.[15] Julia Smith finds that Traherne before the Restoration 'was not of rigid orthodoxy', as his ordination in the 1650s and continuation in the ministry after the Restoration certainly confirms.[16] Further, Traherne attended Brasenose College, Oxford, one of the colleges with the strictest Puritan enforcement. Eschewing representation, he writes in the preface to 'The Poems of Felicity': 'No curling Metaphors that gild the Sence/ [...] But real Crowns and Thrones and Diadems!' ('The Author to the Critical Peruser',

---

and ritual with the early apostolic Church, and proud to be an heir of its traditions.' Gladys I. Wade, *Thomas Traherne: A Critical Biography* (Princeton, 1946), pp. 64–5. See also Sharon Seelig, *The Shadow of Eternity: Belief and Structure in Herbert, Vaughan, and Traherne* (Louisville, 1981); Stanley Stewart, *The Expanded Voice: The Art of Thomas Traherne* (San Marino, 1970).

[13] Ross, I, p. xiii. She quotes John Spurr in *The Restoration Church of England, 1646-89* (New Haven, 1991), p. 13.

[14] James J. Balakier, *Thomas Traherne and the Felicities of the Mind* (Amherst, 2010), p. 166.

[15] They were William Voyle, William Lowe, Samuel Smith and George Primrose. See Richard Baxter and Edmund Calamy, *Abridgment of [... his] History of His Life and Times: With an Account of the Ministers, &c. Who Were Ejected After the Restauration of King Charles II*, 2 vols (London, 1713), II, p. 352.

[16] Julia J. Smith, 'Attitudes towards Conformity and Nonconformity in Thomas Traherne', *Bunyan Studies* 1.1 (1988), 26–35, at 26.

p. 84, 11–14).[17] As Julie Spraggon points out, the 'final violent outburst' of iconoclasm at Oxford occurred in 1651 with Prince Charles's defeat in Worcestershire; Traherne matriculated at Brasenose the following year.[18] In addition, Sir Robert Harley, the zealous head of The Committee for the Demolition of Monuments of Superstition and Idolatry, served as the MP for Herefordshire.[19] Traherne was a friend of his son, Edward, also an MP.[20] While I am not disagreeing with the association of Traherne with the national church, and by extension the royalist cause after the Restoration, I do think that he has every reason to be sympathetic to iconoclasm given these circumstances. Further, I understand Traherne's antagonism to Catholicism in *Roman Forgeries* (1673), while directed against the perceived changes in faith of Charles II, nevertheless to have a foundation in his early training and experiences during the 1650s. I find consistency in his position throughout his adult life in terms of iconoclasm and anti-Catholicism. Being iconoclastic and anti-Catholic during this period in Protestant England is, of course, not unusual, but coupled with his use of typology, his emphasis upon the Exodus story so resonant with English revolutionaries, and sense of shared agency with God, we see a Traherne engaged with radical Protestant ideology to a greater degree than critics have noted.

My questions about typology that will lead to this larger question of the nature of Traherne's Protestantism are twofold: first, what aspects of typology seem to be at work in the Protestant imagination, and second, what are the differences in the understanding of typology among Protestant sects? St Paul establishes the fundamental principles of typology in his letters to the church at Corinth. There he argues that Judaism, and the Old Testament, represent the initial step towards the fulfilment of God's

---

[17] In a previous context, I presented Traherne's abjuring images as part of a general anti-Petrarchan aesthetic and discuss this poem in the context of Herbert's *ars poetica* poems, 'Jordon (I)' and 'Jordon (II)'. See Carol Ann Johnston, 'Heavenly Perspectives, Mirrors of Eternity: Thomas Traherne's Yearning Subject', *Criticism* 43.4 (2001), 380–4. The idea of what exactly entails Puritan theology has been much discussed in recent scholarship. Dwight Brautigam, for example, shows how Laudian uses of the term Puritan, while 'responding to genuine tensions in the church and state [...] raised the level of discontent among the godly' and 'Helped bring down not only the Laudian Church of England but [also] the monarchy that it had so closely supported'. Dwight Brautigam, 'Prelates and Politics: Uses of "Puritan", 1625–40', in *Puritanism and Its Discontents*, ed. Laura Lunger Knoppers (Newark, 2003), pp. 49–66, at p. 62.

[18] Julie Spraggon, *Puritan Iconoclasm during the English Civil War* (Woodbridge, 2003), p. 249.

[19] Ibid, p. 84.

[20] See Julia J. Smith, 'Traherne, Thomas (*c.*1637–1674)', *ODNB*.

promises to individuals. These promises culminate in the birth and death of Christ. While Judaism is caught up in hewing to the laws set out in the Old Testament, Christians move beyond the law, Paul asserts, to embody Christ's spirit. 'The Letter killeth, but the spirit giveth life', Paul writes in II Corinthians 3.6. And in II Corinthians 3.15–16 he adds, 'But even unto this day, when Moses is read, the veil is upon their heart. Nevertheless when it shall turn to the Lord the veil shall be taken away.' In line with these Pauline assertions, Traherne's subtitle of *The Ceremonial Law* is 'after the vail'. Thus Traherne aims to end the poem with the typological answer to the narrative he has told; Christ replaces the ceremonial law. This veil refers to that curtain separating the Holy of Holies from sinners, first described with the details of Moses' tabernacle in Exodus 26. At Jesus' death, as three of the Gospel writers relate, the four-inch-thick veil was ripped in half from the top down. *The Ceremonial Law* ends with a reference to the 'vail' as Paul discusses it in Corinthians: 'The Vail is don away in Christ, the Skreen/ Removd, the Cloud disperst, when he is seen' (p. 241, 28–9).[21] The veil across the heart for Paul is endemic among those who don't believe in Christ. Paul's verses form the principle that the Old Testament prefigures the coming of the Messiah, as told in the New Testament. Put simply, a type is something that happens in the Old Testament, such as Jonah being in the belly of the whale for three days, which prefigures the antitype, Christ, who rose from the grave in three days. Writers after Paul developed typology into a complex practice. Typology evolved from Philo and Augustine into the medieval Catholic fourfold method of interpretation solidified in the twelfth and thirteenth centuries. This method is not especially enthralled with history, but rather taken with the literal and 'hidden' spiritual meaning of the text. Reading biblical texts typologically after the thirteenth century entails four levels of comprehension: the literal sense, which as such is the least important level; the allegorical sense (this is where typology resides, as the Old Testament is considered an allegory for the New Testament); the tropological sense, applying the Bible to the inner moral lives of individuals; and finally the anagogic sense, or what will happen in the life to come.[22]

Protestants generally rejected this fourfold method of reading. Instead, following Luther and Calvin, Protestants insisted that the meaning of the Bible was literal.[23] Luther writes in his 'Answer to [...] Goat Emser':

---

[21]   I am grateful to the Folger Shakespeare Library for allowing me access to the manuscript, and to Heather Wolfe and Jan Ross for discussions of Traherne's handwriting.

[22]   Isabel Rivers offers a thorough overview of the origins of typology in her chapter 'Biblical Exegesis and Typology', to which I am indebted. See Isabel Rivers, *Classical and Christian Ideas in English Renaissance Poetry*, 2nd edn (London, 1994).

[23]   Rivers, *Classical and Christian Ideas*, p. 142.

The Holy Spirit is the plainest writer and speaker in heaven and earth, and therefore his words cannot have more than one, and that the very simplest, sense, which we call the literal, ordinary, natural, sense. That the things indicated by the simple sense of his simple words should signify something further and different, and therefore one thing should always signify another, is more than a question of words or of language. For the same is true of all other things outside the Scriptures, since all of God's works and creatures are living signs and words of God, as St Augustine and all the teachers declare. But we are not on that account to say that the Scriptures or the Word of God have more than one meaning.[24]

And Milton in *Christian Doctrine* insists:

Each passage of Scripture has only a single sense, though in the Old Testament this sense is often a combination of the historical and the typological [...] No inferences should be made from the text, unless they follow necessarily from what is written. This precaution is necessary, otherwise we may be forced to believe something which is not written instead of something which is, and to accept human reasoning, generally fallacious, instead of divine doctrine, thus mistaking the shadow for the substance. What we are obliged to believe are the things written in the sacred books, not the things debated in academic gatherings.[25]

Neither of these writers contends that Protestants deny typological readings. Rather, they argue that for Protestants the typological *is* the literal. Breaking down further the category of seventeenth-century Protestantism, Isabel Rivers argues, 'Anglicans were much more inclined to draw on the allegorical tradition than Puritans.'[26] This is an important point in reading Traherne's use of typology in *The Ceremonial Law* – typological readings exist on a spectrum from more to less allegorical, from more to less 'high church'.

The general rejection of the fourfold method of reading pertains directly to Protestant emphasis upon life on earth. Unlike Augustine's focus upon the 'City of God' rather than the 'City of Man', Protestant belief, especially radical Protestant belief, comes to focus upon what Puritan John Winthrop en route to America famously called 'The City on the Hill', the

---

[24] Quoted from *Works of Martin Luther*, ed. Eyster Jacobs Henry and Adolph Spaeth, 6 vols (Philadelphia, 1930), III, pp. 310–401, at p. 350.

[25] John Milton, *On Christian Doctrine*, I.30, in *Complete Prose Works of John Milton*, ed. John Carey, 2nd edn, 8 vols (New Haven, 1980), VI, pp. 581–3. As with Luther, these issues are complex in Milton's work, and complete discussion of their views is beyond the scope of this paper. Milton asserts, for example, that some men are called by God to be prophets (as he sees himself) and therefore have greater authority in interpreting Scripture.

[26] Rivers, *Classical and Christian Ideas*, p. 142.

notion that individual Christians can proceed in a steady progress towards establishing heaven on earth.[27] Augustine explains the two cities in *The City of God*, Book 14, Chapter 28: 'Two loves therefore, have given original to these two cities: self-love in contempt of God unto the earthly, love of God in contempt of one's self to the heavenly; the first seeks the glory of men, and the latter desires God only as the testimony of the conscience, the greatest glory'.[28] Puritans, and other more radical Protestant sects, overall believed in a progressive model of history, which in its ultimate – and most radical – form would lead to heaven on earth, Winthrop's 'City on the Hill'. The idea of heaven on earth is consistent with Traherne's position in his lyric poems and *Centuries*: 'There are Christians', he writes, 'that place and desire all their Happiness in another Life, and there is another sort of Christians that desire Happiness in this.' He cannot see that 'the first sort be Christians indeed' (*Centuries*, IV.9). For Traherne, this is an unusually sharp boundary between those who are and are not 'Christian'.

In this context of Reformation uses of typology and of radical Protestant belief in material to spiritual evolution on earth, Traherne's exploration of typology in *The Ceremonial Law* appears quite compelling and raises a number of questions, many of them pertaining to the nature of his Protestant faith. As I have said, initially, most, if not all, Traherne scholars found that he identified with 'mainstream' Anglicanism after the Restoration. I believe that *The Ceremonial Law* challenges that assertion, and in so doing helps us to see Traherne's oeuvre in a different light. In their *TLS* article announcing the discovery of the poem, Julia Smith and Laetitia Yeandle argue that it was written after the Restoration, due to what they understand as its reference to the national church, which, according to Traherne, '"was a Bramble void of fruit" but is now restored'. They silently attach the word 'national' to 'church', but quickly add, however, 'in marked contrast to *The Select Meditations*, "The Ceremonial Law" does not make a significant use of Biblical allusion as a means of commenting on current affairs'.[29] By this they mean, I think, that they do not believe the poem has political overtones. Steven Zwicker argues, however, that in 'Reformation England' salvation and 'intensely partisan politics' were

---

27   Sacvan Bercovitch discusses the millennial expectations of Winthrop's colony in America in *The Puritan Origins of the American Self* (New Haven, 1975). Writers such as Winthrop, Cotton Mather, and here Richard Mather and William Thompson argue for the New Jerusalem: 'They needed only to "be patient for a while, for a very little while, for it [would] not be long afore the storm be over, and then [they would] have glorious daies" and "*Ireusalem* [...] come down from heaven"'. (Bercovitch, p. 91).

28   Augustine of Hippo, *The City of God*, trans. Marcus Dods (Edinburgh, 1913), p. 53.

29   Smith and Yeandle, 'Felicity disguised', 17.

ideologically related. 'Moreover', he adds, 'the language of types, a rhetoric of high spiritual authority in the early part of the century, was insistently used in Civil War, Commonwealth, and Restoration England to argue questions that seem to us exclusively political in nature.'[30] In my reading of Traherne, I am reversing Zwicker's logic: uses of typology that seem to be exclusively religious may also point to political allegiances. While the dating of *The Ceremonial Law* may seem reasonable for the moment, I will bracket and return to it along with the 'Bramble void of fruit' and its referent. First I will describe the poem.

The Ceremonial Law takes as its text Genesis and Exodus, primarily focusing upon Exodus as it narrates the Jews' plight in the wilderness. The Exodus story begins with the Israelites' flight from Egypt, and entails the perils of wandering in the wilderness before crossing over the Jordan River into Canaan. Typically of Traherne, the poem does not complete the story. Divided into nineteen sections, the poem begins with an introduction characteristic of the Traherne we know from the lyrics and *Centuries of Meditations*. In the introduction, the narrator explains that before he was born and two thousand years before Christ, God created great joys for him:

> Two thousand yeers before my Savior came,
> In *Hieroglyphick Laws* I see His Name.
> My GOD prepard, before my self was born,
> Great Joys wher with I might my Life adorn. (p. 197, 2–5)

The '*Hieroglyphick Laws*' are the Torah, the five books of laws in the Old Testament, and perhaps also a reference to Moses' tablets containing the Ten Commandments. Traherne asserts here that he will read these laws typologically, but not allegorically. That is, these 'types' in the laws anticipate the coming of Christ. This kind of reading is consistent with the Reformation Protestant application of typology, which slanted more towards the radical than the Anglican. After the Fall occurred, the narrator goes on to tell us, God prepared for Christ's coming by creating types in the Old Testament:

> Whom that I might more certainly descrie,
> With ancient Figures He did Beautifie,

Steven N. Zwicker, 'Politics and Panegyric: The Figural Mode from Marvell to Pope', in *Literary Uses of Typology from the Late Middle Ages to the Present*, ed. Earl Miner (Princeton, 1977), pp. 115–46, at p. 115. Zwicker adds 'the equation of David with Cromwell or David with Charles II assumes that Scripture contains not only types completed in Christ's life and recapitulated in the earthly pilgrimage of the individual soul, but also narrative and prophecy that would continue to apply to God's plan for his covenanted people until the millennium' (p. 116).

> And made those Types the pleasant Posies be
> Of His great Lov, and Kindness unto me.
> Wher in I might with Joy and Sacred Pleasure,
> His Goodness read, and see my Glorious Treasure. (p. 197, 10–15)

These 'types' have the effect of raising the speaker to 'A Princelike Heir of glorious Works' (p. 197, 28), a familiar position for the Traherne narrator to assume; he becomes divine royalty and inherits the entirety of God's creation. Every Christian, Traherne understands, becomes royalty for whom all of nature is a great treasure.

After the fifty-four-line introduction, the first section of *The Ceremonial Law*, 'Adam's Fall', focuses more closely on antecedents for Christ's coming. Only ten of thirty-two lines, however, are given over to an oblique description of Adam's fall. This section dwells instead upon the murder of Abel by Cain. Here is part of the description:

> In Curious Types He did Express His Care,[31]
> And shewd the Means His Wisdom did prepare.
> One Sind, another died: A Beast was slain;
> An Innocent was kild, a Foe doth reign.
> [...]
> This Blood first spilt doth cleans the World, and is
> An Embleme of the Way to Sinners Bliss. (pp. 198–9, 8–15)

These 'Curious Types' are Cain ('One Sind') and Abel ('another died [...]/ An Innocent was kild'). At one level, the concentration upon Abel and Cain is a simple typological focus – Cain is a precursor of Christ's death upon the cross. However, the most obvious precursor to Christ in the Genesis story is Adam; Christ is, after all, the 'second Adam', a frequent reference in Traherne's lyrics. Traherne's concentration upon Abel and Cain here remains consistent with what we know of him from his lyric poetry and *The Centuries of Meditations*, if we focus upon a historical understanding of what Cain represents. The Hellenistic Jewish philosopher Philo (20 BCE–50 CE) interprets Cain's name allegorically to

---

31 Paul J. Korshin argues for the 'seventeenth-century confusion of terminology which, in its narrowest range, cause typology to expand its area of reference'. He explains that 'seventeenth-century writers themselves were often indistinct in their application of types: sometimes the word "type" in a theological context, describes an emblem, a hieroglyphic, a heraldic device, a historical painting, a portion of a picture or portrait, and engraved title page, or a purely representative device like a symbol'. Korshin, 'The Development of Abstracted Typology in England, 1650–1820', in *Literary Uses of Typology from the Late Middle Ages to the Present*, ed. Earl Miner (Princeton, 1977), pp. 147–203, at pp. 14–9. Here 'type' means 'typology'. Elsewhere Traherne may substitute other terms, such as 'Hieroglyphick', also in reference to typological matters.

mean 'acquisition' and argues that he symbolically represents a tendency for humans to turn away from God and into the self. Traherne does not focus upon this aspect of Cain in his work. Essential for Traherne's work, however, Philo sees Cain's primary shortcoming as misunderstanding the concept of possession. He believed that all material things belonged to him, and not to God.[32] We could see how this reading of Cain as aberrantly possessive could present a problem for Traherne. His fundamental philosophy is nevertheless that all material things do belong to all human beings, though they share ownership with all other Christians, as well as with God. Ownership is never selfish for Traherne. The Roman Jewish scholar Josephus (37CE–100) expresses a historical interpretation of Cain that is in keeping with one of Traherne's obsessions. In the opening of Chapter 3 in *The Antiquitie of the Jews*, Josephus's introduction of Cain, like Philo's, explains that the name 'signifieth acquisition'.[33] Josephus explicates this meaning as he describes Cain's building the city of Enoch after murdering his brother: 'He overthrew that simplicity which men before that time had used in their mutual societies, by the inventions of measures and weights [...] He it was that first bounded the fields, and built the first Citie, and made wall and a rampire.'[34] Josephus's interpretation is based upon Cain's building the city of Enoch after murdering his brother. Cain focused upon boundaries and human capacity in Enoch, Josephus argues, by introducing weights and measures and putting walls around fields.[35] In Traherne's signature lyric, 'Wonder', among the things that 'Fled from the Splendor' of the speaker's 'Eys' as his soul entered his body at birth were 'Hedges, Ditches, Limits, Bounds' (p. 6, 59–60). Any sort of limit for Traherne is anathema, and thus Josephus's historical interpretation renders Cain the initiator of an endeavour Traherne most detests. Interest in a historical interpretation of Old Testament figures such as Cain and Abel squares not only with Traherne's concerns as a poet, but also with what I have identified as the Protestant understanding of typology. This view of Cain as establishing limits upon individuals is derived from fact and history, just as Reformation theologians argued the Bible should be read. The historical understanding of Cain indicates why Traherne would show him more interest here than he would Adam.

---

[32] John Byron, *Cain and Abel in Text and Tradition* (Boston, 2011), p. 213.

[33] Thomas Lodge, *The Antiquitie of the Jews* (London, 1602), sig. Aiij. The Lodge translation was the first and only English translation until that by William Whiston in 1732.

[34] Ibid.

[35] Louis H. Feldman, *Studies in Josephus' Rewritten Bible*, Journal for the Study of Judaism Supplement Series 58 (Leiden, 1998), p. 11.

After sections two and three of *The Ceremonial Law* reveal more of those 'Types that pleasant Posies be' – Abel's Lamb (not Abel) and Noah – Traherne narrates the Exodus story, which comprises the bulk of the poem. The narration begins in the fourth section of the poem (continuing the narrative until the poem ends abruptly in section nineteen) with the section entitled 'Moses Call'. Traherne moves quickly in the fourth section to a predominant image, Moses' burning bush. The burning bush maintains a long history in typological reading. Gregory of Nyssa in the fourth century found that the bush represented the Virgin Mary and this interpretation endured into early modern readings.[36] Traherne describes the bush with a similar understanding: 'She in this Bush is typified, & here/ Her Lord in Glory doth again appear./ In Her He lives who is a flaming fire' (p. 202, 10–12). Christ is inside the burning bush that represents Mary, just as he was a part of Mary before birth.

Thus far I have offered examples of Traherne's narrowly typological reading of Genesis and Exodus in *The Ceremonial Law*, which I have connected with a kind of reading more in tune with a radical faction of Protestants than with those welcoming the national church back after the Restoration. I will now push harder on a reading of Traherne as outside of mainstream Anglicanism, beginning with uses of Moses during the Interregnum to represent Cromwell. As Laura Knoppers argues, questions of how to represent a non-royal head of state become one of the difficulties of Cromwell's rule. Cromwell was 'remarkably passive in shaping a protectoral image' leaving others to do so.[37] In 1655 both John Moore, in *Protection Proclaimed*, and George Wither, in *The Protector* (a poem, like *The Ceremonial Law*, in heroic couplets) represented Cromwell as Moses.[38] In his poem Wither argues that Cromwell should eschew the title of 'king' and keep that of 'Protector', which Cromwell had accepted in 1653.[39] Drawing the comparison of Cromwell with Moses, Wither writes,

---

[36] David L. Jeffrey, *A Dictionary of Biblical Tradition in English Literature* (Grand Rapids, 1992), p. 115.

[37] Laura Lunger Knoppers, *Constructing Cromwell: Ceremony, Portrait, and Print 1645–1661* (Cambridge, 2000), p. 70.

[38] John Moore, *Protection Proclaimed (through the loving kindness of God in the present government) to the Three Nations of England, Scotland, and Ireland* (London, 1655); George Wither, *The Protector. A Poem Briefly Illustrating the Supereminency of That Dignity; And, Rationally Demonstrating, That the Title of Protector, Providentially Conferred upon the Supreme Governour of the British Republike, Is the Most Honorable of All Titles, And, That, Which, Probably, Promiseth Most Propitiousness to These Nations; If Our Sins and Divisions Prevent It Not* (London, 1655).

[39] In 1657, a group of MPs approached Cromwell with a new constitution, in which he was formally offered the crown. This would make his rule legal since elected individuals

> Observe the *Parallel: Divisions*, here,
> Have raised Factions, which, like *Mountains* are
> On each hand straightning us.
> 'Yet', he continues,
> > we have still a *Moses* in our *Camp;*
> And, those, on whom, there doth appear the stamp
> Of *A'rons* sanctity; and, (which is more)
> God, still, with us, abides as heretofore.[40]

Even though England may still be politically unsettled, Wither emphasises that Moses, in the figure of Cromwell, remains to lead the nation to the Promised Land, and many of his advisers could serve in the role of Aaron. The figure of Moses, moreover, had been conscripted for a kind of political typology centuries before Wither employs him to exemplify Cromwell. John Coffey points out that the fourth-century historian, Eusebius of Caesarea, followed Origen's typological association of Moses, but with a political figure, rather than with Christ. 'Following the conversion of the Emperor Constantine, Eusebius found himself in a context Origen could not have anticipated', Coffey explains. Needing a way to justify Christian war, Eusebius turned to Moses 'to legitimize the Constantinian revolution' (p. 5). As God intervened in political history during the Exodus, he would enter into history again to help his people. Associating Cromwell with Moses, then, draws upon political typology as well as biblical typology, a powerful connection indeed.

In his overarching argument, Coffey asserts that the Puritan Revolution was 'England's Exodus', an association he supports with important examples of Cromwell's comparison to Moses. For example, Thomas Goodwin, Puritan minister and president of Magdalen College, Oxford, delivered a sermon before Parliament in Westminster Abbey late in 1653 that epitomises the comparison. The text of the sermon is lost, but Cromwell summarised it in his speech to Parliament later that day:

> You had to-day in the sermon [...] Much recapitulation of Providence, much allusion to a State, and dispensation in respect of discipline and correction, of mercies and deliverances, the only parallel of God's dealing with us that I know in the world [...] Israel's bringing-out of Egypt through a wilderness, by many signs and wonders towards a place of rest: I say towards it. (Cromwell in Coffey, p. 25)

Cromwell's description emphasises that his primary narrative of the English Civil War and his subsequent government is parallel to the Israelites' bondage in Egypt, though Cromwell believes that the people

---

offered the title. Cromwell refused. See Charles S. Hensley, 'Wither, Waller and Marvell: Panegyrists for the Protector', *Ariel* 3.1 (1972), 5–16, at 11.

[40] Wither, *The Protector*, pp. 34–5.

have yet to find the Promised Land. They are moving 'towards it'. Indeed, as Coffey summarises, 'Throughout the 1640s and 1650s, no story captured the imagination of the godly quite like [the Exodus]' (p. 26).

Coffey continues in making his argument to explicate uses of the Exodus story in seventeenth-century England, asserting that English Protestants in general believed that God had delivered them to the Promised Land upon the Reformation and especially with the Elizabethan settlement, casting Catholics as traitors. Puritans, however, believed the deliverance from bondage to be incomplete, especially as the Laudian pressure upon the national church increased and with it persecution of Puritans (Coffey, p. 37). The Exodus narrative was particularly potent to Puritans leaving for America; Winthrop's 'City on a Hill' speech draws parallels between the migrating English and the people of Israel fleeing Egyptian bondage (Coffey, p. 38). The Exodus narrative, however, achieved its most firm purchase in the 1640s and 50s. The Puritan parliamentarian Sir Frances Rous, for example, implied that Charles I's 'Personal Rule had taken the nation back to Egyptian bondage' (Coffey, p. 39). The Exodus narrative, moreover, gained power among radical sects: the Diggers, the Ranters, the Fifth Monarchists, and the Quakers. The Diggers, for example, wanted a promised land without private property (a position that Traherne also embraces) (Coffey, p. 50); the Ranter Abiezer Coppe's interpretation of Exodus was centred on personal, rather than political liberation (Coffey, p. 51). The Quakers, like the Ranters, found that the Exodus narrative revealed a 'spiritual typology, and earthly foreshadowing of a spiritual reality' (Coffey, p. 51). The Fifth Monarchists, after the dissolution of the Rump Parliament in 1653, 'hailed Cromwell as the new Moses, whose appointed role in history was to overthrow earthly monarchies and replace them with the fifth monarch of God' (Coffey, p. 52). The most influential of the revolutionary radicals, John Milton, employed the Exodus story in service of his politics as well, most memorably in the final paragraph of *The Ready and Easy Way to Establish a Free Commonwealth*, from March 1660. Milton, certain of the restoration of the monarch, notes that the English people 'seem now chusing them a captain back for Egypt', referring to the return of the monarch as a leader who would take the English from the Promised Land, bringing the revolutionary use of the Exodus narrative full circle.[41]

In the charged air surrounding the Exodus story, linking Cromwell with Moses and the English Civil War to a fight for freedom from an enslaving monarchy, Traherne composes a poem on the ceremonial law, more than three quarters of which relates the story of the Exodus. Because this

---

[41] Milton, *Complete Prose*, VII, p. 463.

scripture comprises a story, it provides a flexible narrative frame in which to imply contemporary events, suggesting that God continually interacts with human beings – one of Traherne's essential principles. Traherne, as I have said, pointedly places himself in the scenes from Exodus that he retells. Coffey shows that such an exercise was common amongst Republicans:

> Parliamentarian preachers prompted their congregations to inhabit the biblical narrative. Hearers imagined themselves and their nation enduring Egyptian bondage, sharing the first Passover meal, being pursued by Pharaoh's army, crossing the Red Sea, murmuring against their deliverers, wandering in the Wilderness, camping at Mount Sinai, or standing on Mount Pisgah looking out over the Promised Land. (Coffey, p. 42)

Traherne, in the section of the poem he entitles 'On Isreals coming out of Egypt', places himself in one of the most dramatic scenes of the narrative:

> By Mighty Seas Divided here I seem,
> Yet there behold Things of Supreme Esteem. (p. 206, 3–4)

He pauses here in the narrative to exclaim,

> My Spirit present is in Ages! And
> There sees, there lovs, and there doth understand. (p. 206, 5–6).

It is impossible to know how well versed Traherne might have been in the political uses of Moses and the Exodus narrative. We do know, however, that Traherne read deeply in the work of Peter Sterry, the Cambridge Neoplatonist. In addition to his philosophical writing, Sterry, as Cromwell's chaplain, also penned *Englands Deliverance from the Northern Presbytery* (1656). When Cromwell won his battle against the Scottish Covenanters, Sterry suggested that England's delivery from the Scots held a place next to the foiling of the Gunpowder Plot, being saved from these 'Two Spiritual Egypts' (Sterry, in Coffey, p. 44). It is not possible, then, to conceive of Traherne's ignorance of the politically charged rhetoric that the Exodus narrative had become.

In his telling of the Exodus story that resonates with the Puritan Revolution, Traherne focuses notably upon the burning bush, which within the narrative represents the voice of God speaking to Moses. The burning bush is a prominent symbol in the reformed church, and as such Traherne's emphatic use of the image underscores the radical resonance within *The Ceremonial Law.* The burning bush was first used in the French reformed church in 1583, and remained a favourite symbol of the Huguenots.[42]

---

[42] John Hill Burton, *The History of Scotland: From Agricola's Invasion to the Extinction of the Last Jacobite Insurrection* (Edinburgh, 1873), p. 340.

Something similar seems to be represented in the seal of the Waldensian church that the Duke of Savoy tried to exterminate in 1655, which inspired a famous sonnet by Milton.[43] The emblem was moreover associated with the Scottish Presbyterian church from about 1635.[44] The association of the burning bush with these churches represents their survival of persecution – they were burned, but not destroyed. John Quick's dedication of *The Synodicon* (1692), an account of the activities of the 'reformed church in France', describes the seal as a

> *Hieroglyphick ... which was* Moses's *Miraculous Vision when he led his Flock under the Mount of God, viz.* A Bramble-Bush in a flaming Fire, having [...] this Motto, *Comburo non consumor, in its Circumference, I* burn but am not Consumed. *With this those venerable Councils Sealed all their Letters and Dispatches. A sacred Emblem of their past and present Condition.*[45]

The burning bush as an emblem of survival carries on the tradition of its interpretation in the *Glossa Ordinaria*, where it is understood as a representation of the church under persecution.[46] Traherne draws on this history of the 'burning bush' while writing *The Ceremonial Law*. He refers to the bush first as 'Thy Church, she was a Bramble void of fruit' suited only to a bush of thorns, but then the bush begins to bear fruit 'Even in the midst of fire' (p. 203, 44–7). The bush yields unusual fruit, the fruit of tears, which by its nature makes the bush shine. In the production of tears, Traherne again explicitly draws a comparison between the bush and the

---

[43] The sonnet is 'On the Late Massacre in Piedmont'. The Duke of Savoy was after the Waldensian sects in the remote sections of the Italian Alps, and this massacre was particularly gruesome.

[44] 'So far as we know the earliest use of the emblem in Scotland is on the title page of a book "Joy and Tears", published in 1635, where it is introduced with some reference to the troubles of the Kirk. It appears again as frontispiece to a pamphlet printed in London, 1642, and there are frequent allusions to the Burning Bush as a symbol of the suffering Church in Samuel Rutherford's "Letters". See Robert Cobain, 'The Burning Bush', *The Presbyterian Herald* (August 1987) <http://www.ballycarrypresbyterian.co.uk/history/bush1.html> [accessed December 2015].

[45] John Quick, *Synodicon in Gallia Reformata, Or, The Acts, Decisions, Decrees, and Canons of Those Famous National Councils of the Reformed Churches in France*, 2 vols (London, 1692), I, sig. A3.

[46] A collection of the glosses from the church Fathers and afterwards from the margins of the Vulgate, largely forgotten after the fourteenth century. Traherne refers to the bush as 'she', which is in line with the Patristic understanding that the bush is representative of the Virgin Mary, although he has referred to the church, which is represented by the bush, as 'she' as well. See Christopher Ocker, *Biblical Poetics Before Humanism and Reformation* Cambridge, 2002), p. 83.

church: 'So doth thy church confess,/ Her Enmity, and it in Tears express' (p. 203, 54–5).

In addition the bush bears other, abstract, fruits: 'Hope, Patience, Glory, Faith and Charity' (p. 204, 66). The poem continues:

> And while in Stranger fire she seems to burn
> She Joys conceivs, and Praises doth return.
> She burneth still, yet not consumes: her fire
> Calcines her only, while her flames aspire
> To Heaven and Thee. (p. 204, 68–72)

In this, the bush/church 'doth the World allure' (p. 204, 74). Later on in section twelve of the poem, 'The Rock', Traherne refers to the burning bush as the rock upon which the church is built. Other references to 'church' in the poem invoke the Israelites as God's church. Nowhere in the poem does the word 'national' appear in relation to the word 'church' or otherwise. Traherne's dwelling upon the description of the burning bush suggests not an identification of the restored national church, but rather an affinity with radical protestant imagery, specifically with the persecuted Scottish and Huguenot churches.

Referring to the church in the past as a barren bramble that in the present of the narrator and the reader has been renewed could be read as the restoration of the national church, as Smith and Yeandle see it.[47] But the association of the burning bush with radical imagery asks that we consider alternative readings. N. H. Keeble argues that among those attempting to reform the church, the true English church was the Celtic church: 'the wide spread belief in the purity of a British church which flourished before Augustine's mission readily inspired those seeking a more radical reformation and the abolition of episcopacy'.[48] The renewal of the church, then, could be for Traherne's narrator the return in the Protectorate to the pre-Augustinian, pre-Catholic church, the purist church imaginable on British soil. He opens the poem asserting that God inserted in '*Hieroglyphick Laws*' the name of Christ, also emphasising throughout the poem that the burning bush is upon a rock that becomes God's church. This church is greater than any inspiring mere sectarian allegiance. *The Ceremonial Law*, then, may fit into the pattern of radical Protestant uses of the Exodus story; the fact that Traherne's use of typology in the poem is narrowly historical, in the fashion that typified Protestant

---

[47] As I note above, Smith and Yeandle date the poem to the 1660s, emphasising Traherne's use of the burning bush as representing the national church.

[48] N. H. Keeble, *The Literary Culture of Nonconformity in Later Seventeenth-Century England* (Leicester, 1987), p. 2.

sectarian readings, rather than the allegorical readings that characterised the Anglican church, further supports the argument for radical affinities.[49]

The received wisdom, however, has been that Traherne at least began the Restoration as a staunch loyalist. Reading *The Select Meditations*, a manuscript as *The Ceremonial Law* also attributed to the 1660s, both Julia Smith and Nabil Matar have argued for Traherne's allegiance to the national church and Charles II after the Restoration. Matar, however, adjusts Smith's argument for Traherne's unchanging attitude towards the king and church by pointing out a reduction in his enthusiasm for the latter in his later work, after he becomes personal chaplain to Orlando Bridgeman (Charles II's Lord Keeper of the Seal, whom Charles dismissed for refusing to sign the Declaration of Indulgence).[50] In fact, most of Traherne's friends, including Bridgeman, were either non-conformists 'or were actively involved in attempts to comprehend them within the national church'.[51] In *The Select Meditations*, which Smith dates to the early Restoration, Traherne initially seems thrilled to have a church in alignment with the law.[52] Yet given his background, we might expect that he is not entirely orthodox in this volume, and that is the case – as Smith points out, he insists, for example, that everyone 'may be a King in that Kingdom' (*Select Meditations*, Ross, V, III.59), not exactly an endorsement of a religious conformity.[53] His praise for the national church thus comes across more as a great sigh of relief that conflict has ceased and the rule of law is firmly re-established in a central location. He seeks unity in the

---

[49] Knoppers points out that at the Restoration, some imagery was borrowed from Cromwellian iconography to represent Charles II. In so doing, however, royalists succeeded in keeping Cromwell in the public eye, something they presumably did not intend (*Constructing Cromwell*, pp. 168 ff). John Hale notes that 'Old Testament parallels had given trouble, since the King's side could use them too, with great effect.' However, it became clear that 'England after Cromwell had no Moses', so that particular parallel did not pertain: Hale, 'England as Israel in Milton's Writings', *Early Modern Literary Studies* 2.2 (1996), <http://extra.shu.ac.uk/emls/02-2/halemil2.html> [accessed December 2015].

[50] Bridgeman also presided at the regicide trials. The dates of Traherne's service to Bridgeman are currently under dispute, having been modified in the most recent entry in the *ODNB*. See Smith, 'Traherne', *ODNB*.

[51] Smith, 'Attitudes towards Conformity and Nonconformity', 33.

[52] 'Before the Restoration, there had been great anxiety over "the want of a lawfull magistrate", and it had not been at all clear what authority a law which worked by precedent had in the absence of a kin. The city of London felt, said John Ogilby, "inexpressible Happiness" at the restoration not only of their king to his thrown, but of "us His Subjects to our Lawes, Liberties, and Religion".' Quoted from Julia J. Smith, 'Thomas Traherne and the Restoration', *The Seventeenth Century* 3.2 (1988), 203–22, at 208.

[53] Smith, 'Attitudes towards Conformity and Nonconformity', 28.

Restoration, 'Religion received into a kingdom by kings, and Established by Laws' (III.19), and

> A Flourishing church, converted Citties, Religion Established by Laws, kings and Magistrats turned From Paganisme. the Freedom of the Gospel, and the Shining Light which a Golden candlestick giveth in a National church. (III.23)

Traherne, however, is Miltonic in his requirements for kings: 'the office of kings is exceeding Glorious whether they be Beloved or no: Provided they understand and Discharge their Duty' (III.11). Initially enthusiastic for the 'office of kings', he quickly qualifies his enthusiasm, just as he qualifies his acceptance of the national church earlier in *The Select Meditations*.[54]

We have, then, two Traherne manuscripts dated from the 1660s that seem to strain against one another in terms of his relationship to the national church. *The Select Meditations* mentions the church and the relief that Traherne feels that it has been reinstated. *The Ceremonial Law*, however, uses typology, especially from the Exodus narrative, in the manner of radical sects and employs imagery from the writings of the radical Protestant movement. Is the poem an anomaly, or is it Traherne's attempt to repurpose the language of the sectarian movement to the service of the national church? While either of these is a possibility, I suggest that his relationship to the national church is, as *The Select Meditations* indicates, one of relief at the return of stability, and, perhaps, one of survival in his chosen profession. Traherne would not desire to be removed from the ministry, as were those who wrote letters supporting his ordination. A clue to Traherne's deeper, more complex allegiances lies in *The Select Meditations*; in making the argument for his involvement in the church, as I pointed out, Julia Smith notes Traherne's unorthodoxy in asserting that everyone 'may be a King in that Kingdom' (III.59). This levelling notion of everyone as king, rather than being the exception to the rule in Traherne's other imaginative works, is the centrepiece of Traherne's conception of the relationship between Christians and God in all of his work. The focus of Traherne's spiritual autobiography in the lyrics and *Centuries* is upon the speaker's seeing as God sees and, equally important,

---

[54] Milton argues in *The Tenure of Kings and Magistrates*: 'A tyrant whether by wrong or right coming to the crown, is he who regarding neither law nor the common good reigns only for himself and his faction [...] And because his power is great, his will boundless and exorbitant, the fulfilling whereof is for the most part accompanied with innumerable wrongs and oppressions of the people, murders, massacres, rapes, adulteries, desolation, and subversion of cities and whole provinces', in *Complete Poems and Major Prose*, ed. Merritt Yerkes Hughes (Upper Saddle River, NJ, 1957), pp. 759–60.

upon God seeing as the speaker sees.[55] The lyric 'The Improvment', for example, opens with a riddle that points to God's organisation of creation for the purpose of human vision: ''Tis more to recollect, [to gather together] then make. The one/ Is but an Accident without the other' (p. 17, 2–3). This 'Improvment' and answer to the riddle entails God's reordering – improving – of creation for Christians' optimal vision; once Christians have an optimal point of view, God shares in that point of view as well. The idea that God and individuals share a point of view, that God wishes to stand in the Christian's shoes just as He wishes the Christian to stand in His, is Traherne's perspectival way of saying that everyone 'may be a King in that Kingdom'. That is the way that God designs it.

This blurring of points of view leads to a shared agency between Christians and God, and this shared agency is a legacy of what James Block sees as a transformation to a society of agency in sixteenth- and seventeenth-century England. Block argues that: 'Agency forms the core of a Protestant worldview' that erupted into a national movement and a revolutionary Commonwealth in England. The result was a group of 'self-authorizers' who ultimately could not be controlled by Protestant sects, since they gave no legitimacy to 'worldly hierarchies'.[56] Block's argument is built in part upon Christopher Hill's assertion that Traherne takes on the revolutionary idea of universally owned property. Traherne writes in the lyric 'Ease':

> That all we see is ours, and evry One
> Possessor of the Whole; that evry man
> Is like a God Incarnat on the Throne,
> Even like the first for whom the World began. (p. 34, 22–5)

Traherne also is akin to Cromwell's chaplain Peter Sterry in his Ranter period, whom Hill describes as one who 'believed that all men could become Sons of God and that God was potentially in all men, that all were perfectible and could attain on earth a Paradise within'.[57] These beliefs bring Traherne close to Block's society of agency. For preachers such as John Goodwin, a defender of unlimited atonement, individuals carried

'A sufficiency of means [...] to redeem themselves,' and each had God's

---

[55] The design of the *Poems of Felicity*, for example, is such that the reader is compelled through the sequence a second time, back to an infant's point of view after first reading, just as individuals must recapture their original vision as infants, when all saw the world from God's point of view.

[56] Block, *A Nation of Agents*, p. 27.

[57] Christopher Hill, *The Collected Essays of Christopher Hill: Writing and Revolution in 17th-Century England*, 3 vols (Amherst, 1985), I, p. 233.

'strongest ground of assurance' that 'upon a regular deportment of himself towards him, he shall receive protection and every good thing from him'.[58]

This development of the narrative of agency in Traherne's lyrics, the speaker's learning again to see from the divine perspective and then alongside God, with God also seeing from the speaker's point of view, also finds affinity with the influential sixteenth-century Puritan William Perkins's *A Treatise of God's Free Grace and Man's Free Will*. Perkins' work underscores my argument about Traherne's active subject as he places the subject position on a par with God:

> Now these actions are works of God in and by a man's will: and mans will is not only a subject of them, but also an instrument, a subject, in that God is the first and principal worker of these works in the will. An Instrument, because it pleases God to use the will, and to move it by his grace for the acting and effecting of the things which he appoints. And thus the will is not merely passive, but passive and active both: first passive, and then active [...] It is necessary indeed that God first regenerate us and make us his children and new creatures. And in this thing we do not Co-work with God, but stand as patients, that God may work upon us and reform us [...] Yet, after our regeneration, by truth [...] we begin to be Co-workers with the grace of God.[59]

Movement from the passive 'patients' of God to the active '*Co-workers*' of God transforms Christians into subjects with substantial agency. 'With the grace of God' reads as a hasty addition after establishing the individual as being on a par with the divine. For Christians in Traherne's work, the important perspectival plot in the Dobell lyrics – trying to achieve a point of view that satisfies both mortal and divine desire to see God's universe as He intended – engenders the evolution of passive to active agency resulting in a partnership with God. This plot is mirrored in the Burney lyrics as well as in the Third Century.

Traherne's speaker/subject is 'Possessor of the Whole', as he writes in 'Ease': a coherent subject with the ownership of 'all' within God's visual field. The reciprocal relationship between God and individual threads together several levels of Christian life. This similitude between God and individuals is based upon visual discourse – sharing a single point of view – and is the *sine qua non* for the relationship. It offers the individual Christian the kind of agency argued for in the radical Protestant movement, and as such further links Traherne to that movement. This

---

58   John Goodwin, quoted from Block, *A Nation of Agents*, p. 87. Goodwin was imprisoned along with Milton, but released because he had Arminian leanings.

59   William Perkins, quoted from Block, *A Nation of Agents*, p. 63.

linkage, along with Traherne's iconoclastic aesthetic, his early experiences and alliances, and the typological *The Ceremonial Law* and its emphases, suggests that our early understanding of Traherne as a 'high Anglican' was flawed, understandably, by too little information. We had not yet discovered *The Ceremonial Law* or the Lambeth Palace manuscript, with its complex theological treatises. We must also reconsider the dating of *The Ceremonial Law*. Smith and Yeandle date the poem based upon the mention of the church associated with the burning bush. However, since the burning bush metaphor has a tried and true association with the persecuted church, might *The Ceremonial Law* originate from earlier in Traherne's career, perhaps in the late 1650s? The stress upon the Exodus narrative further underscores the connection of the poem with radical sectarian thinking. This would be a politically savvy – or safer – enterprise, showing sympathy for the government in power. Whatever the case, *The Ceremonial Law* insists that we reconsider Traherne's sectarian explorations and loyalties during his lifetime.[60]

[60] I would like to thank those attending the *Future Directions for Traherne Studies* conference at Cambridge, especially C. E. Gorman; the Early Modern Writing symposium at Harvard; and the Traherne Association annual Jeremy Maule Memorial Lecture in Hereford for hearing early versions of these ideas and contributing significantly to their development. In memory of Sacvan Bercovitch.

Chapter 7

THOMAS TRAHERNE AND THE STUDY
OF HAPPINESS

Ana Elena González-Treviño

If any man Should ask me what God was doing before the world began? I would not Answer with Saint Austin: that He was makeing Hell For such Busy enquirers. But studying from Eternity to do all in the most Perfect manner. For all things are so perfect that they [are] worthy to be Seen For ever, and are in very Deed, the Product of Eternal Study.

(*Select Meditations*, Ross, V, III.89)

Felicity is a central theme in both the poetic and prose works of Thomas Traherne. The most evident example is the collection entitled *Poems of Felicity: Divine Reflections on the Native Objects of an Infant-Ey*.[1] This opens with an address to the reader announcing that the poems were written 'to th'end thy Soul might see/ With open Eys thy Great *Felicity*' ('The Author to the Critical Peruser', *Poems of Felicity*, Ross, VI, p. 84, 7–8) All of the *Poems of Felicity*, as well as the collection known as the Dobell poems, deal one way or another with the question of how felicity is attained, experienced, and enjoyed.[2] The same is true of the volume commonly known as the *Thanksgivings*, in which the

---

[1] The phrase appears on the title page of British Library, Burney MS 392, first published by H. I. Bell as *Traherne's Poems of Felicity* (Oxford, 1910). The title is apt, even though it was probably not coined by Thomas, but rather by Thomas's brother, Philip Traherne (or Traheron), in whose hand the manuscript is written, and who is believed to have altered the original considerably. See Thomas Traherne, *Centuries, Poems and Thanksgivings*, ed. H. M. Margoliouth, 2 vols (Oxford, 1958), I, pp. xiv–xvi.

[2] For an account of how Bertram Dobell first identified Traherne as the author of the manuscript (Bodleian Library, MS. Eng. poet. c. 42), see the introduction to *The Poetical Works of Thomas Traherne, B. D., 1636?–1674: Now First Published from the Original Manuscripts*, ed. Bertram Dobell (London, 1903).

154

condition of felicity is expressed in terms of gratitude.[3] On the title page of *Commentaries of Heaven*, Traherne announces that 'The Mysteries of Felicitie are opened and ALL THINGS Discovered to be Objects of Happiness' (*Commentaries*, Ross, II, p. 3). On several occasions within this manuscript, he speaks of a 'schole of happiness', or sometimes a university, as in the following lines:

> My Soul, a Graduate in Excellence
> Life vertu Wisdom Sence Felicitie
> In this Transcendent Universitie
> Heres Schole and Book and Doctor all in one
> And the Professors Chair's an Heavenly Throne.[4]
> ('Act II', *Commentaries*, II, p. 186)

In the most autobiographical section of the *Centuries of Meditations,* probably Traherne's best-known work, he tells the story of how the study of happiness became the sole purpose of his life, and how he attained it:

> When I came into the Country, and being Seated among silent Trees, had all my Time in mine own Hands, I resolved to Spend it all, whatever it cost me, in the Search of Happiness, and to Satiat that burning Thirst which Nature had Enkindled, in me from my Youth. (*Centuries*, Ross, V, III.46)

There is an analogous passage in *Commentaries of Heaven*:

> When I devoted my self to Study and spend my Days as consecrated to Felicitie, I neither Knew its Objects nor the maner of enjoying them. being therfore stark Blind, notwithstanding those Rays and Shreds of Learning I had gathered. ('Delights of Ages', *Commentaries*, II, pp. 340–1)

The idea of a search for happiness may seem ordinary enough; less familiar is the assumption that it can be acquired through study. A few meditations earlier in the *Centuries*, Traherne had described his disappointment at not finding it in the curriculum at Oxford: 'som things were Defectiv too. There was never a Tutor that did professely Teach Felicity: tho that be the Mistress

---

[3] The complete published title is *A Serious and Pathetical Contemplation of the Mercies of God, in several most Devout and Sublime Thanksgivings for the same*, published, also posthumously, by George Hickes in 1699. Although the author's name is not actually given, the work has been definitely attributed to Traherne. See Gladys I. Wade, *Thomas Traherne: A Critical Biography* (Princeton, 1946), pp. 145–56. This work is not in prose, but it is certainly not metrical poetry, being rather a form of free verse. Hickes described it as being 'composed in *Numbers*, or numerous Periods, which tho of the *freer* sort, are not so easy for an Author to express his thoughts in, as plain and unconfined Prose'. *A Serious and Pathetical Contemplation of the Mercies of God* (*Thanksgvings*), sig. A2r.

[4] See also 'Account', *Commentaries*, II, pp. 126–9.

of all other Sciences' (*Centuries*, III.37).[5] While regretting the lack of a course on felicity at university, Traherne also deplores the fact that every other subject was studied as what he calls *Aliena*, that is, as alien or extraneous knowledge, concepts and events that had occurred to other people in other places and ages. He was very enthusiastic indeed about learning logic, ethics, physics, metaphysics, geometry, astronomy, poetry, medicine, grammar, music, rhetoric, 'all kind of Arts, Trades and Mechanicismes that Adorned the World' because they were all part of felicity. Nevertheless, he is very critical of this educational model because it fails to involve students directly. He writes: 'We Studied to inform our Knowledg, but knew not for what End we so Studied. And for lack of aiming at a Certain End, we Erred in the Maner' (*Centuries*, III.37). In *Seeds of Eternity* he recounts how he perceived important drawbacks in humanist education:

> when I heard the Lectures of Humanitie in our Scholes, I was frustrated in my Expectation, and tho Aristotle hath written a book of the Soul, opening many Faculties and Powers in it, yet because he shewd not the uses of those Faculties at least not so as to make me see the Pith of that perfection and glory I expected, to me he was defective. he did not manifest the Designe of God from whom they came, nor the Sovereign End to which they tended: nor gave me those causes of Complacency in God which my Soul desired.[6]
> (*Seeds of Eternity*, Ross, I, p. 236)

Both his critical attitude towards institutionalised learning and the powerful nature of his own calling motivated him to devise his own method towards the achievement of happiness, while defining himself as its student. He pursues this method throughout the *Centuries*, and in different instances he claims to have succeeded in attaining felicity. In meditation IV.55 he admits that 'He was ten yeers Studying' before he could attain his goal, and in the conclusion of meditation III.46, he writes: 'And God was so pleased to accept of that Desire, that from that time to this I hav had all things plentifully provided for me, without any Care at all, my very Study of Felicity making me more to Prosper, then all the Care in the Whole World.' The notion reappears in *Christian Ethicks*, first printed in 1675, in the preface of which he actually presents his proficiency on the topic as a credential:

> My purpose is to satisfie the Curious and Unbelieving Soul, concerning the reality, force, and efficacy of *Vertue*; and having some advantages from the knowledge I gained in the nature of *Felicity* (by many years earnest and

---

[5]   Traherne was admitted at Brasenose College in 1653; he obtained a BA degree in 1656 and an MA in 1661. See *Centuries, Poems and Thanksgivings*, ed. Margoliouth, I, p. xxiv.
[6]   Traherne's view of Aristotle is a mixture of great admiration and reproach, especially as expressed in the entry dedicated to him in the *Commentaries*, III, pp. 188–96.

diligent study) my business is to make as *visible*, as it is possible for me, the lustre of its *Beauty, Dignity,* and *Glory.* (*Christian Ethicks*, p. 3)

The phrase 'by many years earnest and diligent study' has been rarely if at all questioned by Traherne scholars.[7] One must decide whether it is simply a figure of speech, or whether it is meant to be taken literally, and if so, what it entails exactly. Traherne insists on this so much that it is quite possible that he seriously endeavoured to create a curricular approach towards the attainment of happiness. The analytical methodology he follows in works such as *Commentaries of Heaven* would corroborate this, as would the proximity between his concepts of study and meditation. These could be based initially on books and reason but developed into a discipline of thought and emotion.[8] He was not alone in this, since analogous ideas occur as well in other devotional writings of the period.

In this period, the greater availability of printed books had made more widespread the personal pursuit of spiritual growth. A crucial part of what Christopher Hill has described as 'an ideology of self-help' and Patrick Collinson as 'a kind of do-it-yourself practical theology' was precisely the proliferation of manuals and instruction books that handed down to the individual the responsibility of procuring his or her own improvement through study and meditation to gain salvation.[9] The treatment given to this topic could vary widely according to the author's circumstances, education, experience and purposes, but the generic classification of these books was very similar nonetheless. The following titles of works from this period attest to this: *The Way to True Happiness*; *The Art of Happiness*; *A Discourse of True Happiness*; *The Way to Bliss*; *The Crown and Glory of Christianity, Or Holiness, The only way to Happiness*; *The Art of Contentment*; *The Happy Ascetick*; *Of Contentment, Patience and Resignation to the Will of God*; *Enquiry after Happiness*; *Jacob's Vow or Man's Felicity and Duty*; *Directions How to be Content*; *A Gentleman Instructed in the Conduct of a Virtuous and Happy Life.*[10] *The Anatomy of Melancholy,* of

---

[7] See for example, Carol L. Marks, 'General Introduction', *Christian Ethicks: Or, Divine Morality. Opening the Way to Blessedness, By the Rules of Vertue and Reason*, ed. Carol L. Marks and George R. Guffey, Cornell Studies in English 43 (Ithaca, 1968), p. xxxi.

[8] At least one critic has suggested that this work was Traherne's response to the absence of a course in felicity in academia. See Richard Douglas Jordan, 'Thomas Traherne and the Art of Meditation', *Journal of the History of Ideas* 46.3 (July 1985), 381–403, at 396.

[9] Christopher Hill, *Reformation to Industrial Revolution: The Pelican Economic History of Britain*, vol. II: *1530–1780* (Suffolk, 1969), p. 287; Patrick Collinson, *English Puritanism* (London, 1987), p. 36.

[10] Authors and dates of publication are here listed in the corresponding order: Ralph Venning (1655); Francis Rous (1656); Robert Bolton (1656); Elias Ashmole (1658);

course, occupies a prominent place in the group; it has a relatively lengthy subsection entitled 'A Consolatory Digression, containing the Remedies of all Manner of Discontents'.[11]

Happiness guidebooks did not exist as a separate, formal category but simply as a recognisable theme that was popular within devotional literature classified under the general heading of 'Divinity'. During the Stuart period, religious works occupied the greater part of the total output of new editions; by 1640 as much as 42% of the titles could still be counted as religious.[12] Twenty years later, in 1660, when bookseller William London printed the second supplement to his *Catalogue of the Most Vendible Books in England*, divinity was still the foremost and lengthiest category.[13] London would rather have presented himself as a provider of knowledge than a bookseller, so in the catalogue he characterises himself as one of his own potential pious clients, as someone who has personally benefited from his own product, an age-old marketing strategy.

London makes use of the traditional division between 'divine and humane' knowledge. First he distinguishes 'several parts of *Learning* and *Knowledg* [...] wherein first and principally, that of *God*, that *Divine knowledg treasured* in that sacred Book is chiefly to be studied'.[14] Then he proceeds to expostulate on the immeasurable benefits to be obtained through the knowledge afforded by this kind of printed material, which he describes as an aid to salvation itself:

> The *Knowledg of God* [... is] the *Summum bonum*, the chiefest of studies, which indeed is superlatively above all. [...] This is the knowledg that speeds our passage to Eternal Glory, that is the shortest cut to Immortal Happiness. [...] the Knowledg of God in Christ, is the Philosophers Stone in Divinity;

Thomas Brooks (1662); author of *The Whole Duty of Man* (1675); Anthony Horneck (1681); Isaac Barrow (1685); Richard Lucas (1685); John Cockburn (1686); Isaac Barrow (1704); George Hickes (1709). All were published in London except *The Art of Contentment* (Oxford). These are just a few examples. See also Ian Green's generic description of similar treatises in *Print and Protestantism in Early Modern England* (Oxford, 2000), pp. 216–25.

[11] Robert Burton, *The Anatomy of Melancholy, What it is, With all the kinds of causes, symptomes, prognostickes, and several cures of it [...]* (Oxford, 1628 [1621]), Part 2, Sect. III, Memb. I, Subsect. I, pp. 284–8.

[12] See Tessa Watt, *Cheap Print and Popular Piety, 1550–1640* (Cambridge, 1991), p. 69. Ian Green explains that the proportion of divinity books had fallen some twenty years later, but rose again in the 1690s and into the eighteenth century, remaining the largest single literary category: *Print and Protestantism*, pp. 13–14.

[13] William London, *A Catalogue of the Most Vendible Books in England (1657, 1658, 1660)*, ed. D. F. Foxon, facsimile edn, English Bibliographical Studies (London, 1965), Series 2, Catalogues of Books in Circulation.

[14] London, *A Catalogue*, sig. C3v.

by it we may turn all events into golden advantages to our souls. [...] The many advantages now in print, by *Learned, Reverend,* and *Holy Ministers,* will be one day a witness against such as make it not their chief study to train up themselves, and relations therein.[15]

London's presentation is based on the view, proposed by the devotional books he sells, that the purpose of human existence is to search always the superlative good, that this good is to be found only through the knowledge of divine matters, as portrayed in books, and that their study 'speeds our passage to Eternal Glory' and 'is the shortest cut to Immortal Happiness'.[16] He makes use of the alchemical promise that, with this knowledge, 'the Philosophers Stone in Divinity', everything will turn into 'golden advantages to our soul'.

Religious books varied considerably in range and purpose. Among the main types, we may count prayer books, psalters, catechisms, sermons and treatises, meditations, versified biblical paraphrases, prose commentaries, moralising pamphlets and handbooks to devotion.[17] Many were addressed to a knowledgeable readership in order to offer them methods or 'ways' to achieve happiness, a legitimate purpose in life, and a natural consequence of godliness. When carried into practice, these books contributed to the shaping of social identities both through outward behaviour and inward self-examination.

Guidebooks to holiness and happiness in general have a close connection with books of remedies for discontent; many authors wrote both kinds. Robert Bolton, for example, wrote both *A Discourse of true Happiness* and also *Instructions for a right comforting afflicted consciences.* Francis Rous wrote *The Art of Happiness* and *The only remedy that can cure a people.* William Strong wrote *Holiness, the only way to Happiness* and *The Sick Mans Salve.* Richard Lucas's *Enquiry after Happiness* deals with the causes of unhappiness, and his *Religious Perfection* describes how to achieve happiness.[18] The connection between happiness and remedy books highlights the contiguity between the two kinds of manuals: they are two sides of the same coin. The subtle difference in focus conveyed by the title would only serve to channel expectations in slightly different ways. What

---

[15] London, *A Catalogue,* sig. D2r.
[16] For the philosophy underlying this notion see, for example, Henry More's description of the *boniform* faculty of the soul: 'that part of the Will which moves towards that which we judge to be absolutely the best'. Henry More, *An Account of Virtue: Or, Dr Henry More's Abridgement of Morals, put into English,* trans. Edward Southwell (London, 1690), p. 6.
[17] See Watt, *Cheap Print,* p. 69.
[18] Also from London's catalogue; all these books were published in 1657, except for Rous's *Art of Happiness,* of 1656, and Lucas's works of 1685 and 1696, respectively.

matters is that happiness is again and again described not as a state to be reached, but as an art to be learned, as knowledge to be acquired.

Many of Traherne's works share some characteristics with guides to happiness; for example, *Christian Ethicks*. The full title of the 1675 edition is *Christian Ethicks: Or, Divine Morality, Opening the Way to Blessedness, By the Rules of Vertue and Reason*. It has been suggested that Traherne, who died shortly before the book was published, probably did not coin this title.[19] In 1962, Margaret Bottrall edited the volume, borrowing from the early edition the phrase *The Way to Blessedness* as an alternative title. Debatable though this may be, its adequacy is apparent in the light of other contemporary publications such as Nicholas Byfield's *Way to Holiness*, Samuel Crooke's *The Guide unto true blessedness*, Alexander Grosse's *The Fiery Pillar [...] or the way to a blessed life*, Henry Mason's *Hearing and Doing, the ready way to blessedness*, and even *The Way to Bliss*.[20]

This circumstance alone would align *Christian Ethicks* with the guide-books I have alluded to; however, there is much stronger evidence in the content of the work itself. The first academic editor of the *Ethicks*, Carol L. Marks, agrees that the original title is inappropriate and suggests that a more adequate one would have been *Christian Virtue* on the grounds that contemporary books on ethics and moral philosophy took into account not only the virtues, but also passions, vices and 'the powers of the soul', whereas Traherne deals almost exclusively with virtue.[21] One of Traherne's key models for this work was the *Ethica* by Eustache de Saint-Paul, first published in Paris in 1609 and going through several reprints in England, including the 1658 London edition. The important first part of Eustache's *Ethica* is dedicated to the analysis of happiness.[22] In the prefatory note 'To the Reader' of *Christian Ethicks*, Traherne states that the 'design of his Treatise' is

> to elevate the *Soul*, and refine its Apprehensions, to inform the Judgment, and polish it for Conversation, to purifie and enflame the Heart, to enrich

---

[19] The 1675 printer included the following note after Traherne's preface: 'The Author's much lamented Death happ'ning immediately after this Copy came to the Press, may reasonably move the Readers charity, to pardon those few Errata's which have escaped in the Printing by so sad an occasion.' *Christian Ethicks* (London, 1675), sig. a8v. For the argument, see *Christian Ethicks*, ed. Marks and Guffey, pp. xxxi–xxxii; and Wade, *Traherne*, pp. 138–9.

[20] Byfield (1656); Crooke (1657); Grosse (1650); Mason (1657); Ashmole (1658). *The Way to Bliss* is an alchemical treatise.

[21] It must be emphasised here that the relationship between happiness books and remedy books does not apply to vice and virtue. In seventeenth-century religious discourse, vices are far from being the only causes of discontent, whereas virtues are the only way to happiness. For Marks's proposal see *Christian Ethicks*, ed. Marks and Guffey, pp. xv–xxii.

[22] *Christian Ethicks*, ed. Marks and Guffey, pp. xix–xx.

the Mind, and guide Men (that stand in need of help) in the way of *Vertue*
[…] and so at last to lead them to true Felicity, both here and hereafter.
(*Christian Ethicks*, p. 3)

The central importance of the study of happiness to the *Ethicks* is stated
recurrently. In the first chapter he even explains that virtue is desirable
only because it is necessary in 'the Way to Felicity'. Later he adds, 'whatever
Varieties of Opinion there are concerning Happiness, all conclude and
agree in this, that Mans last End is perfect Happiness' (*Christian Ethicks*,
pp. 13, 14).

Traherne's *Select Meditations* was discovered in 1964 but not published
until 1997. In spite of being a series of meditations in the style of the
Centuries, it has some sections with a guidebook format; notably a list of
twelve 'Instructions Teaching us how to Liv the Life of Happieness' (*Select
Meditations*, III.31). Louis Martz has defined *Centuries of Meditations* as 'a
treatise of instruction, an introduction to the devout life'.[23] This work, besides
the title announcement, also has certain formal characteristics in common
with happiness manuals, the most evident of which is the fact that entries
very often include a series of aphoristic 'Instructions'.[24] The *Inducements
to Retiredness* contain similar sections, although in this case they are called
'Resolutions' or 'Resolves' (*Inducements to Retiredness*, Ross, I, pp. 9, 19).

In an entry entitled 'Arithmetick' in the *Commentaries of Heaven*, the
proximity between Traherne's work and happiness textbooks is made
evident. He explains: 'For our Designe is only to supply the Defects of
Learning as much as possible […] for the immediate Instruction of Man
in felicitie' (*Commentaries*, III, p. 208). 'Assistance' is also revealing because
it contains his philosophy of teaching. The mission of a spiritual teacher
is eminently altruistic: 'All Assistances must proceed from Love, and end,
or design to end in the Happiness of the Person' (*Commentaries*, III, p.
268). Love itself is didactic, and the teaching profession enjoys in his eyes
an exceptionally high dignity, insofar as teachers 'instruct or (well truly
may they be said to) inform the World with Diviner Order, and Celestial
Knowledg'. Their mission of improving standards and bringing them closer
to heavenly order is only the beginning. What 'assistants' actually manage to
do is to help people take right possession of all instead of seeing it as alien:

The Inward and Eternal Services they [assistants] do are unconceivable:
They help us to see, Lov, rejoyce, Prize, Praise and Enjoy, not only as Exterior
Actors on the Stage of the World doing that beside us, in other Places, which

---

[23]   Louis L. Martz, *The Paradise Within: Studies in Vaughan, Traherne, and Milton* (New
       Haven, 1964), p. 58.
[24]   'Instructions' in the *Commentaries of Heaven* are too many to be cited individually.

we cannot do but as Single Persons in our selvs: but as Objects exciting us as Obligations Engaging us, as Crowns Rewarding us, and to speak all in a Word as Assisting Formes inwardly Aiding and Strengthening, Awakening and Quickening Widening and Enlarging hightening and Perfecting our Powers. for as two Drops of Water touching mingle into one, yet the parts of either are all Intire so, two Souls, but without any Segregation of Parts may inhabit and inspire each other. (*Commentaries*, III, p. 273)

The teacher's mission entails the purest form of communication between individuals, a veritable 'marriage of true minds' that Traherne shall seek to achieve not only in his pursuit of happiness and in his teaching of felicity, but also as a direct result of that achievement. The question of how to communicate most effectively is derived directly from the theme of happiness because happiness is essentially communicative. As Traherne puts it: it is not the possession but the communication of happiness that makes us happy, and 'He most Happy that is Infinitly [communicative]' (*Select Meditations*, III.65). Therefore, the teacher of happiness is joyfully obliged to teach in order to preserve his own happiness.

Not everybody shared the view that happiness was man's most natural and ardent desire, or that it had anything to do with transcendent pursuits. Atheism and 'infidelity' were two of the most important sources of anxiety for the teachers of virtue and happiness, and against them would they direct many of their attacks. Epicurean atomism, as understood in the seventeenth century, was the source of atheism since it proposed a random universe of atoms in motion, without any ulterior purpose or guiding principle, thereby obliterating the distinction between vice and virtue. In this period, the atheistic 'perversion' to which atomism led was incarnated in the views of the arch-materialist Thomas Hobbes, who provided the champions of happiness and virtue with a direct target for invectives and ample subject for controversy. Refuting the ideas of Hobbes was a rhetorical performance that came to be standard in both moral and scientific treatises.[25] The irony is that the figure of Hobbes unwittingly helped to define the position of his adversaries by giving them occasion for passionate denial and refutation of a materialist threat, which in reality already permeated much contemporary thought. In addition, Hobbes paradoxically provided them with a methodology and set of references they felt forced to adopt.

For Hobbes the mere suggestion of learning or studying happiness would have been absurd. In the first part of *Leviathan*, 'Of Man', he writes

---

[25] See Richard S. Westfall, *Science and Religion in Seventeenth-Century England* (Yale, 1970), pp. 108–9.

'Of the Natural Condition of Mankind as concerning their Felicity and Misery', where he presents what he considers the fundamental cause of human discontent or misery, which invariably leads humanity to war: their natural self-destructiveness, which makes it imperative that some power 'keep them all in awe'. For him, the very search for happiness is only the cause of further unhappiness. Without an agreed external governing power, the natural tendency of humanity is war, and in war there is no difference between vice and virtue.[26]

Furthermore, virtue itself is relative because it is 'valued for eminence; and consisteth of comparison'; the same is valid for good and evil, because they merely depend on whether an object is said to be desired (appetite) or hated (aversion). For Hobbes, felicity has nothing to do with virtue and even less with personal effort; he defines it, along with other 'passions', as the 'continual success in obtaining those things which a man from time to time desireth'. According to him, it bears no relationship whatsoever to any existential or transcendent purpose, but is rather proof of humanity's weakness because it evidences their enslavement to sporadic appetites. In the same passage, he discards the notion of a '*beatifical vision*' because the term is for him a linguistic fallacy as incomprehensible as the supposed felicity preordained by God for men.[27]

In Bishop Gilbert Burnet's *History of His Own Time*, he describes the impact of Hobbes's ideas when they were first published:

> He seemed to think that the universe was God, and that souls were material, Thought being only subtil and unperceptible motion. He thought interest and fear were the chief principles of society: And he put all morality in the following that which was our own private will or advantage. He thought religion had no other foundation than the laws of the land. [...] And this set of notions came to spread much. The novelty and boldness of them set many on reading them. The impiety of them was acceptable to men of corrupt minds, which were but too much prepared to receive them by the extravagancies of the late times.[28]

While Hobbes certainly figures as the main antagonist of certain moral positions, it must be reiterated that he was often used as a mere figurehead who would get the brunt of self-righteous indignation. He embodied historical anxieties about a morality that felt increasingly threatened, the most dangerous of his concepts probably being the abolition of the absolute

---

[26] Thomas Hobbes, *Leviathan*, ed. J. C. A. Gaskin (Oxford, 1996), p. 63.

[27] Hobbes, *Leviathan*, p. 23, pp. 29–30.

[28] Gilbert Burnet, *Bishop Burnet's History of His Own Time*, 2 vols (London, 1724, 1734), cited in Isabel Rivers, *Reason, Grace and Sentiment: A Study of the Language of Religion and Ethics in England 1660–1780*, 2 vols (Cambridge, 1991, 2000), I, p. 45.

distinction between vice and virtue. The fearful figure of the gigantic Leviathan, with all its pessimistic, deviant and cynical implications, is perhaps one of the reasons why many of the divines and moral philosophers who wrote about happiness often recur to images of monstrosity to illustrate their outrage against such prospects. Isaac Barrow, theologian and Newton's mathematics professor, expostulated against 'the monstrous paradox [...] that all men naturally are enemies one to another'.[29] Edward Southwell, who translated Henry More's *Enchiridion Ethicum* from Latin (1668), reports that 'the Doctor [i.e., Henry More] laments to see the World so abound with Monsters, who even deride this Blessing of Virtue, and upon all occasions expose it for a mere Imaginary Thing'.[30] Richard Lucas, several years later, is openly emphatic. The controversy still fresh towards the end of the seventeenth century, he sees in the 'Hobbist' threat a lamentable retrogression:

> What gross and monstrous absurdities are these? shall we now after the Improvement of so many Ages [...] dispute whether Vice or Vertue be the better guide of Humane Actions, or the more serviceable to Humane Life? shall Sloth and Luxury be thought to conduce as much to the prosperity and decency of our Lives, as Industry and frugal Temperance? shall Ambition, Pride, and Choler be now judg'd as instrumental to promote or preserve the Peace and repose of our Minds and States, as Modesty, Meekness, and Charity?
>
> [...] this were a God [*sic*] fit for a *Hobbist*, one who can discern no difference between Vertue and Vice, between Good and Evil, between Love or Charity and Devillishness.[31]

In a very similar tone, Traherne expostulates in *Christian Ethicks*:

> LET those Debauched and unreasonable men, that deny the Existence of Vertue, contemplate the Reality of its Excellency here, and be confounded with shame at their Prodigious Blindness. Their Impiety designs the Abolishment of Religion [...] while they pretend the Distinction between Vertue and Vice to be meerly feigned, for the Awing of the World; and that their Names have no foundation in Nature but the Craft of Politicians and the Tradition of their Nurses. [...]
>
> Those things by which a man is made serviceable to himself and the World, they think not to be Vertues, but imagine Chimeraes which they cannot see, and then deny they have any Existence. A man is capable of far more Glorious Qualities then one of them: And his Courage it self may

29 Isaac Barrow, *Theological Works*, IV, Sermon XXVIII (Oxford, 1830), p. 79.
30 More, *An Account of Virtue*, sig. A2v. For a detailed account of the philosophical opposition between Hobbes's materialism and Henry More's Neoplatonism, see Samuel I. Mintz, *The Hunting of Leviathan: Seventeenth-Century Reactions to the Materialism and Moral Philosophy of Thomas Hobbes* (Cambridge, 1969), pp. 80–109.
31 Richard Lucas, *Enquiry after Happiness* (London, 1685), p. 68, p. 112.

be raised to far higher Ends and purposes then Buffoons and Thrasonical Heroes can dream of. (*Christian Ethicks*, p. 163)

Like Lucas, Traherne sees in the obliteration of morality a serious interruption to social progress, resulting in the rule of unreason. The Hobbesian reduction of virtue to a linguistic delusion leads to the tragic inability to perceive and aspire to felicity, friendship and transcendence. Blindness to all things invisible (i.e., spiritual) is at the core of the materialistic error:

> *Vertues* are listed in the rank of *Invisible things;* of which kind, some are so blind as to deny there are any existent in Nature: But yet it may, and will be made easily apparent, that all the *Peace* and *Beauty* in the World proceedeth from *them*, all *Honour* and *Security* is founded in them [...] Were there nothing in the World but the *Works* of *Amity*, which proceed from the *highest Vertue*, they alone would testifie of its Excellency [...] Were there no *Blindness*, every Soul would be full of Light, and the *face* of *Felicity* be seen, and the *Earth* be turned into *Heaven*.[32] (*Christian Ethicks*, p. 4)

Traherne, as well as Lucas, made a special point regarding the source of peace among humanity, which he purposefully based on virtue by contrast with Hobbes's peace based on fear of the governing power. The fundamental distinction between these principles and Hobbes's is the consideration of humanity's moral and spiritual perfectibility; in other words, that they may acquire virtue and aspire to felicity through learning. For Hobbes, even learning is linguistically determined and ruled by belief, so he cannot bring himself to equate mere words with 'real' virtues. For

---

[32] For other examples of Traherne associating atheism with the inability to see the invisible, see 'Atheist', *Commentaries*, III, p. 329; as well as 'Accusation', II, p. 141 ('What is invisible by ruder Minds can Hardly be Enjoyed'; 'Acknowledggement', II, p. 162 ('Foundations are unseen, and roughly laid', invisible and therefore despised; to acknowledge God is not inconvenient as the Atheist supposes, but delightful); 'Affliction', II, p. 311 ('Only the blind & Infidels are miserable'); 'All Things', II, p. 409 ('this very Ignorance of mine, methinks should tend much to the Conviction and Satisfaction of Atheists'); 'Ascension', III, pp. 241–5 (p. 243, 'for the Satisfaction of a few Abominable Atheists'); 'Assimilation', III, p. 260 (atheists think 'that Nothing but what is visible is real'); 'Atom', III, p. 334 ('Which sufficiently displays the Realitie of Things invisible to the Conviction of Atheists'). A text in which this concept occupies a central position is Joseph Hall, *The Invisible World, Discovered to Spirituall Eyes, and reduced to Usefull Meditation* (London, 1659). In spite of this and other instances of disagreement between Traherne and Hobbes, there are certain important notions they shared. For example, Traherne also rejected the notion that man's inclinations were naturally good, a tenet crucial to his pedagogical practice. See *Christian Ethicks*, p. 260, and Stanley Stewart, *The Expanded Voice: The Art of Thomas Traherne* (San Marino, CA, 1970), p. 61.

him, it is belief that hinders learning, and only the strictest of methods can sift out its errors, but even then assurance will be relative.[33]

Despite their sonorous protestations, there is no question that the champions of virtue and happiness felt the need to justify faith by employing rationalistic discourse, by formulating emphatically logical arguments about the compatibility of reason with religion.[34] The role of reason towards the achievement of happiness had to be defined in order to make it clear that it *could* be studied and learnt. To illustrate this I shall refer to several passages drawn from moral treatises and happiness guide-books in order to sample the rhetorical texture of different authors. First, here is an excerpt from Henry More's *Account of Virtue*:

> [Marcus Aurelius said that] *to act according to Nature or according to Reason, is in a rational Creature the same thing.* Wherefore all pravity [*sic*] is repugnant to human Nature. But that Virtue is natural to human Nature, and born as a Twin therewith, is manifest, as well because Man's Soul is a rational Being, as because Righteousness or perfect Virtue (as we are told *by Divine Revelation*) is immortal; and that it was Sin only that brought Death into the World. For since the State of Innocence was to have been eternal, this plainly shews, that such a state was most perfect and most natural. And therefore that Restitution unto such a State must be the most intrinsick and peculiar Pleasure.[35]

Here, reason and virtue are both regarded as innate qualities, the argument being a refutation of Hobbes's ideas. More is drawing here on the Aristotelian notion of pleasure (in Southwell's rendition, a '*restitution of every Creature from a state imperfect, or preternatural, unto its own proper Nature*'), which, in this pure state, is equal to happiness. The innate quality of virtue here described is tempered by the notion of 'restitution', which may imply a self-earned achievement. In another passage, he adds yet another ingredient to this definition: 'Happiness *is that pleasure which the mind takes in from a Sense of Virtue, and a Conscience of Well-doing;*

---

[33] Hobbes, *Leviathan*, pp. 18–22. An entirely different opposition to the idea of teaching virtue came from the notion that virtue could be innate. Robert Ferguson, in *Moral Virtue*, observed that if one accepted Plato's idea that virtue is infused, then it could not be inferred that 'Vertue was teachable'. See *Christian Ethicks*, p. 316, Carol Marks's notes to p. 25, 11–25. Traherne felt it was 'far more conducive to our Felicity' that we should study to acquire virtue than that it was simply infused, because this is how glory became 'ours', *Christian Ethicks*, p. 25.

[34] On the origins of 'the religion of reason' – especially as a reaction against materialism, enthusiasm and superstition – within latitudinarian discourse, see Rivers, *Reason, Grace and Sentiment*, I, p. 34.

[35] More, *An Account of Virtue*, p. 6; compare John Milton, *Paradise Lost* (London, 1668), Book I, lines 1–3.

and of conforming in all things to the Rules of both.'[36] What he calls 'a conscience of well-doing', at the risk of being confused with self-right-eousness, is the translation of rational thought into action, which is going to be crucial in Traherne's own account of happiness as evidence that it can be learnt.[37]

Another solution to the dilemma was conceived by John Cockburn, the Scottish divine and author of *Jacob's Vow or, Mans Felicity and Duty*, who expresses the view that it is not reason but religion that distinguishes human beings from beasts:

> Some considering the *Natural pronness* of Men to the Worship of a GOD, have defined Man to be *Animal Religiosum*, and have made *Religion* and not Reason the difference betwixt him and other Creatures: And indeed we never shew so much Reason or Act so much above the *Inferiour Creatures*, as when we are taken up in the Exercise of Vertue and Religion; all other Actings are but Sense, and *Animal motions*, in which there be many Brutes who do often outdoe us. But when our Reason doth exerce it self in Religion, it is so far above their reach that they cannot offer at an imitation.[38]

Even though he places religion above reason in his concept of an *animal religiosum*, alluding to the commonplace of man as a rational animal, he then adds that religion is exalted *because* it is a rational act: 'we never shew so much Reason [...] as when we are taken up in the Exercise of Vertue and Religion'. It is evident that the entire argument aims to answer the reason-religion question. Cockburn is careful to place emphasis on the exercise of virtue and religion, an exercise that constitutes a public, observable conduct or display, and establishes man's inimitable rational identity. He manifests no doubts regarding the truthfulness of the 'shew', so the learning would come, perhaps, after the doing, and this would have some ritualistic or initiatory implications. Anxiety in this example, however, comes from the ghost of the bestiality to which non-virtuous, non-religious, non-rational humans are reduced.

Other interesting examples are afforded by the more philosophic divines, especially those who, like Traherne, had affinities with Neoplatonism. Nathanael Culverwel constructs a rhetorically percussive text in his attempt to establish the compatibility of reason and religion.

> [God's] commands are all rational; His word is the very pith and marrow of reason; His Law is the quickening and wakening of men's reason; His

---

[36]   More, *An Account of Virtue*, pp. 4, 5.
[37]   For a summary of the distinctions between More and Traherne, see Stewart, *The Expanded Voice*, p. 209.
[38]   John Cockburn, *Jacob's Vow, or, Man's Felicity and Duty in Two Parts* (Edinburgh, 1696), pp. 167–8.

> Gospel, 'tis the flowing out of His own reason; 'tis the quintessence of
> wisdome from above; His spirit is a rational agent. [...] By all this you see
> that God is the eternal Spring and Head of reason.[39]

Culverwel's procedure is simply to map onto theological discourse some
of the terms associated with reason, culminating with a doctrinal yet
emphatically logical conclusion: 'By all this you see ...' Whereas Cockburn's
perspective went from humanity to God, Culverwel's goes, as it were, from
God to humanity. The cue to action is given through God's law and the
agency of His spirit; the recognition of its divine origin should be enough to
move humanity towards the achievement of happiness. Learning here would
be obtained through recognition, or, to use his terms, 'the quickening and
wakening of men's reason'. Henry More, a Neoplatonist himself, had held that
Christianity had a 'special Prerogative' in 'that it dares appeal unto Reason'.[40]

Traherne's views on reason and religion are highly complex, and shall
not be dealt with in detail here. A few indications, however, shall be useful.
He shares some conventional notions with other thinkers, such as the idea
that reason confirms faith and faith perfects reason, or that reason has
certain limitations when it comes to the boundless appetite of the soul:
'The Soul of Man by Instinct of Nature inclines to more then his illuminated Reason dares approve' (*Christian Ethicks*, p. 225).[41] Whereas Henry
More's statement indirectly places religion slightly below reason in 'that it
dares appeal' unto it, in this extract by Traherne we see the reverse, reason
not 'daring' to approve of all the soul's instincts. The 'Instinct of Nature',
possibly related to Cockburn's idea of a natural proneness to worship,
reveals the commonplace that reason, even illuminated reason, is not
allowed into certain realms.

While emphasising the compatibility between the two parts of the
argument, Traherne does draw the fundamental distinction between
knowing and *believing*. At the same time, he clarifies what More meant by
appeal, and that is the fact that reason is merely instrumental and not an
end in itself. That is why there are numerous instances of reason presented
as doing service to religion, not substituting for it, as religious moralists
emphatically claim. The most important operation, however, will consist

---

[39] Nathanael Culverwel, *An Elegant and Learned Discourse of the Light of Nature* (London,
1652), pp. 120–1. The metaphoric dimension of Culverwel's argument as exemplified
here is probably the reason why Hobbes could never understand the relationship
between language and what he heard others call spiritual experience. Samuel Mintz
says that he was 'by temperament, impervious to mysticism': Mintz, *The Hunting of
Leviathan*, p. 82.

[40] Henry More, *A Collection of Several Philosophical Writings* (London, 1662), p. vi.

[41] See also 'Appetite', *Commentaries*, III, p. 144.

in the actual coupling of the two. In this case, learning would be that very action (or act of faith) of voluntary rational appropriation that Traherne repeatedly calls 'right apprehension'.[42] Without faith there can be no true learning; bare rational learning is still partly blind. Traherne defines a 'Tru Apprehension' as 'a Thought bearing the Similitud of what it apprehends'; the iconic resemblance between thought and its objects is what warrants the representational validity of rational processes. Man originally enjoyed this type of rightful thinking, but after the fall, apprehension was 'broken to pieces by contrary Examples' ('Activity', *Commentaries*, II, p. 204). One of the express purposes of the *Commentaries* is to restore right apprehension to non-believers by discovering the mysteries of religion to 'the Ey of Reason', one word at a time. Reason comes forth as an unassailable common *language* that naturally reinstalls religion in its pre-eminent position and unfailingly leads to happiness:

> There being such an Infinit union between Truth and felicitie, that it is impossible to see the Face of Truth fully, but we must see the Lineaments and features of felicity: and such an union between the sight of felicity and Infallibility, that when felicity is seen Infallibility is seen. So that while under all Words placed in their order, we open the nature of all Things, we shall even by Nature Discern all Things, clearly relate to Happiness, and in that to Religion. [...] Nature and Religion, faith and Reason, Truth and Blessedness being Married together. ('Acknowledgement', *Commentaries*, II, pp. 157–8)

In the end, it is a problem of assurance, as the concept of infallibility suggests. What is remarkable is Traherne's insistence that certainty is the fruit of study, hence the justification of human endeavour that is self-perpetuating indeed, but delightfully so: 'By much Labor and Study tis [assurance] attained, and when attained it inclines the Mind to more Labor and Study, but with more Delight and Desire' ('Assurance', *Commentaries*, III, p. 298). Traherne's own method of disquisition is to establish chains of causality based on strict logic. This passage from *The Kingdom of God* is typical in that sense:

> we must be Beloved, that we may Lov. And lov, that we may be Glorious. We must be Infinitly Glorious, that it may be seen apparently that we are Infinitly Beloved. And of This Circle does the sphere of felicitie Consist. This is the Circuit of Heaven, against which there is no Inchantment: this the communion between God and us, this the Cause and End of all. (*Kingdom of God*, Ross, I, p. 279)

Along the same lines, Isaac Barrow underlines the value of reason as the means to acquire virtue and, consequently, the assurance of salvation,

---

[42] See Ian Green, *The Christian's ABC: Catechism and Catechizing in England c.1530–1740* (Oxford, 1996), pp. 321–2.

i.e., unconditional happiness: '[Virtue] is an art, with which we are not born, no more than with any other art or science; the which, as other arts, cannot be acquired without studious application of mind, and industrious exercise.'[43] From here, there is only one step towards our original premise: '[Contentment] is certainly a most excellent piece of learning; most deserving our earnest study: no other science will yield so great satisfaction, or good use; all other sciences, in comparison thereto, are dry and fruitless curiosities.'[44]

It is therefore not surprising in this context that Traherne affirmed that his vocation was the study of felicity. The notion abounds in the devotional literature of the period, and was used with great liberality by preachers who, in this sense, speak as teachers, encouraging their disciples, the congregation, in the study of this peculiar subject. The conclusion of Dr Thomas Jacob's exposition entitled 'How Christians may learn in every State to be content' is exemplary in the use he makes of classroom terminology.

> My Brethren, will you fall upon the studying of this excellent lesson of Contentment? You have learnt nothing in Christianity till you have learnt this: you are no better than *Abecedarians* in Religion if you have not mastered this great piece of practical knowledg [*sic*]. You have *heard* much, *read* much of contentment, but have you *learnt* it so as to live in the daily practice of it? Pray take up with nothing short of that.[45]

Traherne expresses the same distinction between mature wisdom and infantile ignorance, the traditional opposition between 'babes and men', when he writes about 'Old Babes, that will never be men' until they find felicity through study, 'till they are acquainted with the Mysteries of all Ages, and enter into Eternity and Gods omnipresence by their Meditations' ('Babe', *Commentaries*, III, pp. 438, 439). The need for study is another consequence of the fall, because originally 'the Mystery of Happiness [...] was not a Mystery in the Estate of Innocency, but is made a Mystery by our Iniquity' ('Second Adam', *Commentaries*, II, p. 228). On the other hand, 'study' is also a sacred activity because God himself does it all the time; the entire creation is the result of divine and infinite deliberation. God in his sphere is ever 'Compounding and Dividing Examining and Comparing what things so

---

43 Isaac Barrow, *Of Contentment, Patience and Resignation to the Will of God. Several Sermons* (London, 1685), p. 43. Many authors use 'contentment' as a synonym for 'happiness', which is why they are included here. Traherne, however, sometimes makes a distinction, even to the degree of deriding contentment as 'a sleepy thing', the opposite of infinite avarice and ambition, which are the only way to attain real happiness. See Traherne, *Christian Ethicks*, ed. Marks and Guffey, p. 217.

44 Barrow, *Of Contentment*, p. 44.

45 Thomas Jacob, Sermon 26 in Samuel Annesley, *A Supplement to the Morning-Exercise At Cripplegate: or, Several more cases of Conscience Practically Resolved by sundry Ministers*, 2nd edn (London, 1676), p. 668.

ever it pleaseth in Time or Eternity' ('Activity', *Commentaries*, II, p. 200).[46] By imitating God in this, human beings get closer to forging godly thoughts, in which joy resides. Study is therefore a mental and emotional discipline through which 'right apprehension' is cultivated, thus creating value and joy: 'Nothing can truly be Apprehended but it must needs be Aprehended [*sic*] as Treasure and Inter[e]st' (*Select Meditations*, III.6).

Even when Traherne shares with other divines similar aspirations expressed through similar language, he is the only one of them all to actually claim that his study of felicity *has* been successful. Among the others, it is only he that is able to announce, at the end of his 'Instructions Teaching us how to Liv the Life of Happieness':

> The seeds of all wisdom Happiness and Glory are here Included. And these Instructions So Great, that I would have given in my childhood Millions of worlds to have met with one teaching them, so earnestly did I Long after them. How much therfore am I bound to Bless God for haveing Satiated my soul and Replenished me with Good Things. It makes us see the face of Religion as Bright as the Sun, as Fair as the Heavens, as Real as the world.
>
> It discovereth an Infinit weight and Depth of concernment in evry work in evry Person. And Lifts a Holy Man above Thrones and Kingdoms, as much as Stars are a bove Sands or Angels a bove Pismires.
>
> It maketh a man at home in his own Kingdom. And even as a Pilgrim here to Liv in Heaven.
>
> It Sheweth the Infinit Dreadfullness of any crime: and with what profound affections we ought on all occasions to walk with God.
>
> It Shews the infiniteness of the Love of God in the contemplation of which we ought to Liv For ever. (*Select Meditations*, III.31)

To conclude, since Traherne had affirmed that there can be no happiness without communication, then the works of Traherne, the successful student, acquire new significance. Books such as the ones he wrote become indispensable to *his* own happiness because study involves both reading and writing, and they are the continuous expression that is necessary for the perpetuation of that state. Books are also the constant teachers that banish the forgetfulness of the learner who is writing them, and they aim towards an ever-vigilant, ever-effulgent memory. Happiness is perfect sight, eternal reading and, inevitably, endless teaching and writing, in the eternal cycle of study.[47]

---

[46]   See also, in *Select Meditations*, III.89, the epigraph to this chapter.

[47]   On the more traditional aspects of writing as religious duty, see Nigel Smith, *Perfection Proclaimed: Language and Literature in English Radical Religion, 1640–1660* (Oxford, 1989), p. 23; and Jordan, 'Thomas Traherne and the Art of Meditation', 383–4, 392, on Baxter and the duty of writing. On the 'notebook culture' see Peter Beal, 'Notions in Garrison: The Seventeenth-Century Commonplace Book', in *New Ways of Looking at Old Texts*, ed. W. Speed Hill (Binghampton and New York, 1993), pp. 131–48, at pp. 131–3.

Chapter 8

'INNOCENCY OF LIFE': THE INNOCENCE OF THOMAS TRAHERNE IN THE CONTEXT OF SEVENTEENTH-CENTURY DEVOTION

Elizabeth S. Dodd

This chapter is concerned with Traherne's afterlives. It addresses an underlying yet persistent assumption in Traherne criticism: the ongoing association of Traherne's idea of innocence with a caricature of the Romantic ideal of the child. It argues that reading Traherne in the light of seventeenth-century devotion presents a very different picture of innocence; one neither derivative of, nor dependent upon, the child as its primary model. A contextual interpretation divests Traherne of the connotations that surround the Romantic picture of the child and that have been formative for Traherne criticism: the taint of nostalgia and of sentimentality, and the idealisation of the child.

My intention in this chapter is not to deny the importance of the child image in Traherne's works or his use of the child as a figure of Adamic innocence, which have been extensively described in previous literature.[1] Rather, I seek to explore the hitherto neglected wider semantic field of

---

[1] Compare, for example, the biographical interpretation of Gladys I. Wade, *Thomas Traherne: A Critical Biography* (Princeton, 1944), pp. 169–71; the historical literary-criticism of Leah Marcus, *Childhood and Cultural Despair: A Theme and Variations in Seventeenth-Century Literature* (Pittsburgh, 1978), pp. 42–93; the psycho-phenomenological approach of Franz K. Wöhrer, *Thomas Traherne: The Growth of a Mystic's Mind. A Study of the Evolution and the Phenomenology of Traherne's Mystical Consciousness* (Salzburg, 1982), pp. 99–135; the Piagetian child in Robert Ellrodt, *Seven Metaphysical Poets: A Structural Study of the Unchanging Self* (Oxford, 2000), p. 91, pp. 93–4, pp. 97–8; and the literary symbol of Adamic perception in Sharon Cadman Seelig, *The Shadow of Eternity: Belief and Structure in Herbert, Vaughan and Traherne* (Louisville, 1981), p. 146, p. 161.

his language of innocence, in light of a fresh reading of his devotional hinterland. This chapter focuses upon seventeenth-century devotional literature rather than on the entire corpus of Traherne's sources, which limits the scope of what would otherwise have been a much longer chapter. It also illustrates the importance of the devotional culture that shaped the ways in which Traherne wrote about innocence, which in its literal sense is primarily a moral and spiritual term that denotes harmlessness, guiltlessness and holiness. It outlines several forms of the contemporary devotional language of innocence that are found in Traherne's works. Its treatment is not comprehensive, but should be sufficient to indicate the importance of providing an alternative intellectual framework to the illusory genealogy that has identified Trahernian innocence as a precursor to the Romantic ideal. While concurring with previous criticism on the significance of innocence as a concept for Traherne, this paper concludes that the scriptural, ethical, sacramental and devotional models of innocence that influenced his works portray not a lost and yearned-for infant paradise, but an 'innocency of life' that is part of the life of faith.

THE ROMANTIC LEGACY AND THE IDEAL OF CHILDLIKE INNOCENCE IN TRAHERNE STUDIES

First, it is worth outlining the pervasiveness and persistence of post-Romantic readings of Traherne's idea of innocence, and their implications for critical understandings of Traherne. The association between Traherne and the Romantics goes back to the first publication of his *Poetical Works* by Bertram Dobell in 1903. His poems, 'Eden', 'Wonder' and 'Innocence', and *Centuries of Meditations* III.1–3, have been frequently compared to William Wordsworth's *Immortality Ode* and William Blake's *Songs of Innocence*.[2] This comparison is understandable, given the haunting reminiscences between Traherne's 'little Adam in a Sphere/ Of Joys' ('Innocence', Ross, VI, p. 10, 57–8) and Wordsworth's 'Child of Joy'. In Traherne's declaration, 'How like an Angel came I down' ('Wonder', p. 4, 2), one can see Wordsworth's divine child 'trailing clouds of glory'. Wordsworth reminds his readers that 'Heaven lies about us in our infancy', while Traherne's child is able to 'see beneath, as if I were abov the Skies' (*Centuries*, Ross, V, III.4). Wordsworth describes everything 'Apparell'd in celestial light', while Traherne's 'Infant-Ey' sees everything in the 'ancient Light of Eden'

---

2   See *The Poetical Works of Thomas Traherne, B.D., 1636?-1674: Now First Published from the Original Manuscripts*, ed. Bertram Dobell (London, 1903), pp. lxxvii–lxxxi.

('Innocence', p. 10, 55). This primitive innocence is corrupted by what Wordsworth refers to as 'dialogues of business, love, or strife', and Traherne terms the 'Bondage of Opinion and Custom' (*Centuries*, III.8).[3]

The ways in which Traherne has been likened to the Romantics have gone much deeper than surface comparisons such as these. For critics influenced by the work of T. E. Hulme, Traherne became the forerunner of the 'Romantic Heresy' of Pelagianism; an assertion of the natural innocence of childhood that represented a modern shift away from the orthodox Augustinianism of original sin.[4] These comparisons meant that by the mid twentieth century Traherne, alongside Henry Vaughan, was established as an exemplar of a pre-Romantic praise of childhood and precursor to a Romantic ideal of innocence, within the field of childhood studies.[5]

This early association with the Romantics elevated Traherne's status within the corpus of early modern British literature, but it also led to critiques of his work. Douglas Bush compared Traherne unfavourably with William Blake by arguing that in his naivety and positivity, Traherne 'never graduated from songs of innocence to songs of experience'.[6] More importantly, the identification of Traherne as a pre-Romantic anchors his notion of innocence to post-Romantic critiques of the Romantic ideal of innocence, most notably accusations of nostalgic social conservatism, sentimentalism, and the idealisation of childhood.[7] Such critiques implicitly draw upon more recent concerns over the fetishising of childhood innocence in contemporary culture.[8]

Despite the significance of the historical turn in Traherne criticism, through the work of Julia Smith, Nabil Matar and others, more recent studies

3   William Wordsworth, 'Immortality Ode', *The Collected Poems*, ed. Antonia Till (Ware, Hertfordshire, 1994), lines 34, 65, 67, 4, 99.
4   Keith William Salter, 'Thomas Traherne and a Romantic Heresy', *Notes and Queries* 200 (1955), 153–6; T. E. Hulme, 'Romanticism and Classicism', in *Speculations: Essays on Humanism and the Philosophy of Art*, ed. Herbert Read (London, 1936), pp. 111–40.
5   See, for example, George Boas, *The Cult of Childhood* (London, 1966), p. 45; Alan Richardson, *Literature, Education and Romanticism* (Cambridge, 1994), pp. 9–10.
6   Douglas Bush, *English Literature in the Earlier Seventeenth Century, 1600–1660*, 2nd edn revised (Oxford, 1962), p. 158.
7   See, for example, Judith Plotz, *Romanticism and the Vocation of Childhood* (New York, 2001), pp. xiii–xvi; Charles John Sommerville, *The Rise and Fall of Childhood* (London, 1982), pp. 131–2; Hugh Cunningham, *The Children of the Poor: Representatives of Childhood since the Seventeenth Century* (Oxford, 1991), pp. 151–63.
8   See, for example, Joanne Faulkner, 'The Innocence Fetish: The Commodification and Sexualisation of Children in the Media and Popular Culture', *Media International Australia* 135 (May 2010), 106–17; Kerry H. Robinson, *Innocence, Knowledge and the Construction of Childhood* (Abingdon, 2013), pp. 61–3.

continue to base their interpretations of Traherne's innocence upon post-Romantic frameworks.[9] For example, in their attempt to move Traherne criticism away from shallow comparisons with the Romantic poets, Denise Inge and Edmund Newey reveal the tenaciousness of post-Romantic ideas and assumptions surrounding the ideal of innocence. They both defend Traherne the theologian against post-Romantic critiques of the Romantic ideal of childhood by de-emphasising the centrality of childlike innocence to Traherne's thought. Inge does not list innocence among Traherne's childlike qualities, and Newey is at pains to show that Traherne's child represents the whole life of the soul and not merely its innocent beginnings.[10] However, this defence comes out of a reading of Traherne's notion of childlike innocence that is founded upon post-Romantic assumptions. In arguing for the central place of post-lapsarian grace in Traherne's theology, Inge identifies the prior estate of innocence with the lost estate of childhood: 'His memory of innocence, however bright, is essentially a memory lost.'[11] This echoes the post-Romantic critique of nostalgia and sentimentalism in literature on childhood innocence. In his keenness to present Traherne's child not as a figure of innocence alone but an 'icon of the whole human condition', Newey reflects post-Romantic anxieties over a two-dimensional idealisation of childhood.

The most effective response to the anachronism of these post-Romantic comparisons and frameworks must be a contextual one. This is not to deny that there are links between Traherne's poetic raptures on infancy and those of Wordsworth and Blake. The similarities outlined above suggest a subterranean legacy of mystical Christian Platonism and its transcendentals of beauty, truth and goodness, which in the works of Traherne, Wordsworth and Blake are expressed in the ideal human being in the form of the infant. However, since Traherne's poetic and meditative works remained lost until 1896–97, this intellectual genealogy cannot be more than implicit, and there is not space to develop this argument here. Traherne's idea of innocence was also embedded within the devotional culture of his time. It drew upon contemporary biblical scholarship, popular works of ethics and moral theology, published debates on the spiritual life and sacramental

---

[9]   See, for example, Julia J. Smith, 'Thomas Traherne and the Restoration', *The Seventeenth Century* 3.2 (1988), 203–22; Nabil Matar, 'The Anglican Eschatology of Thomas Traherne', *Anglican Theological Review* 74.3 (Summer 1992), 289–303.

[10]   Denise Inge, *Wanting Like a God: Desire and Freedom in the Thought of Thomas Traherne* (London, 2009), pp. 63, 100, 150–1, 187–8, 193–4; Edmund Newey, '"God Made Man Greater When He Made Him Less": Traherne's Iconic Child', *Literature and Theology* 24.3 (2010), 227–41.

[11]   Inge, *Wanting like a God*, pp. 162–3, 183.

theology, and texts for private and public devotion. In order to illustrate the formative role of this wider context on Traherne's idea of innocence it is important for the moment to ignore the theme of childlike innocence, to leave space to consider the additional models that are present in his works. This can be no more than a representative selection, but will indicate several ways in which Traherne, in the context of seventeenth-century devotion, wrote about innocence.

THE CONTEXT OF SEVENTEENTH-CENTURY DEVOTION

The language of innocence in seventeenth-century devotion was varied and nuanced, as illustrated by the popular *Christian Dictionary* of Thomas Wilson. This was the first dictionary of the Bible in English, but was explicitly derivative of the 'most approved Authours, both Ancient and Modern', especially the sixteenth-century Catholic work, Petrus Ravanellus's *Bibliotheca Sacra*.[12] The dictionary provides a good working vocabulary for seventeenth-century devotional understandings of innocence, as it was expanded by other hands, revised and reprinted eleven times in the seventeenth century alone following its first publication in 1612. Given its patchwork construction, Wilson's Reformed theology need not be considered overly determinative for the work, although it should naturally be taken into account.[13]

The 1661 edition, the most contemporaneous with Traherne's active period of writing, has not one but three definitions of 'Innocency'. The first is 'A meer voydnesse of fault, and freedome from all sin. In this estate *Adam* was created. This is perfect innocency by creation.'[14] This is the original innocence of Eden, which in Traherne's poetry is echoed by the infant's purity. The second definition of innocence is 'A certain measure of this estate in all regenerate persons, who indevour to serve God in innocency of life, having also Christs innocency imputed to them.' Innocence is not therefore confined to humanity's original estate, but is

---

[12] Thomas Wilson, *A Complete Christian Dictionary*, ed. J. Bagwell and A. Simson, 7th edn (London, 1661 [1612]), title-page.

[13] On Wilson and the *Dictionary* see Ian Green, *The Christian's ABC: Catechisms and Catechizing in England, c.1530–1740* (Oxford, 1996), pp. 746–7; Stephen Wright, 'Wilson, Thomas (1562/3–1622)', *ODNB*; Kathleen Curtin, 'Jacobean Congregations and Controversies in Thomas Wilson's *Christian Dictionary* (1612)', *The Seventeenth Century* (2010), 197–214; Leif Dixon, 'Calvinist Theology and Pastoral Reality in the Reign of King James I: The Perspective of Thomas Wilson', *The Seventeenth Century* 23.2 (2008), 173–97, at 175.

[14] Wilson, 'Innocence', *Dictionary*, p. 336.

an element of Christian living, albeit in a diminished sense. This second innocence is twofold: the moral 'innocency of life' that the believer offers to God through holy living, and the imputation of Christ's righteousness that is the gift of grace through baptism and faith. The third definition of innocence is 'Uprightnesse in some speciall or particular cause'. This is the innocence of 'the innocent'; those who may be unjustly accused, persecuted or afflicted, but who are vindicated in the sight of God and honoured in heaven. None of these three definitions of innocence mentions childhood as its particular model; all are explicitly founded in scripture (Genesis 1.26–7 and Genesis 2, Psalm 26.6,11, and Psalm 7.8 or Daniel 6.22). All of these definitions and more can be found in devotional writings from the period. Wilson's threefold definition provides the basis upon which to look for different ways in which Traherne employs the language of innocence, informed by contemporary devotion.

SCRIPTURAL DEVOTION, *THE CEREMONIAL LAW* AND THE SACRIFICE OF 'THE INNOCENT'

An example of Wilson's third definition of innocence, the persecuted uprightness of 'the innocent', is evident in Traherne's typological epic, *The Ceremonial Law*.[15] This biblical poem, based on Genesis and Exodus, demonstrates the scriptural models behind Traherne's devotional poetry. In its heroic couplets, its often lamentatory tone and its themes of trial and purgation, it follows the scriptural models of epic poetry used in early modern Protestant poetics, as identified by Barbara Lewalski, recalling especially the book of Job.[16]

Three of the poems within the sequence contain references to the sacrifice of an 'innocent', more specifically, an innocent lamb or beast. The first appears in 'Adams Fall', referring to the first beast that was killed in order to clothe Adam and Eve's nakedness. The second is 'Abels Lamb', the first blood sacrifice to God and an early type of Christ's sacrifice that has been repeated in every animal sacrifice since. The third reference is in the title of the poem, 'The Paschal Lamb'. This poem curiously makes no explicit reference to the sacrifice of Exodus 12.5–11. Instead, in this typology the sacrificial lamb is the church, which is 'A Simple flock of unexperienc'd sheep', naked in its dependence upon God's providence

---

[15] On *The Ceremonial Law*, compare the chapters by Carol Ann Johnston and Warren Chernaik in this volume.

[16] See Barbara K. Lewalski, *Protestant Poetics and the Seventeenth-Century Religious Lyric* (Princeton, 1979), pp. 7–10, 97, 387.

(Ross, VI, p. 211, 43). The sacrificial 'innocent' is also found in the waters of the Red Sea, which represents the 'Ocean of our Saviors Blood', through which Israel or the church must walk towards salvation (p. 212, 89). Compare this with Giovanni Diodati's commentary on the lamb of Exodus 12.5 as one '*Without blemish]* A figure of Christs perfect justice and innocency: Heb 9. 14. 1 Pet. 1. 19'.[17] It was common in protectorate-era royalist defences of Anglicanism to liken the church to the suffering innocents of the Hebrew Bible. For example, Edward Sparke, in *Scintilla Altaris*, refers to the church as '*Ruddy* in thy *Shame,* in thy *Labours,* in thy *Sufferings*! but *white* in thine *Innocence,* in thy *Patience,* in thy *Deliverance*'.[18] Although the imagery is similar and the message is the same – that victory comes through affliction – Traherne's poem does not explicitly reference these political concerns. While Carol Ann Johnston presents a compelling argument for the influence of sectarian politics in *The Ceremonial Law*, this influence is implicit.[19] 'The Paschal Lamb' focuses explicitly not on contemporary politics but on the church militant through the ages, its ongoing need for grace, and the provision of grace through the purgative waters of baptism.

In all its appearances in this poem, the suffering innocent has a Christological point of reference. The strength of the Christological typology is evident in 'Abels Lamb', where an emendation of the text results in a more explicit identification of the first sacrifice with that of Christ:

> ~~A Lamb!~~ The Lamb of GOD, that takes away our Sin,
> Is slain, even when the World doth first begin.[20]

The first model of post-lapsarian innocence, both in historical terms and in terms of priority, is the sacrificial lamb, which is a type of Christ. Christ in this typology may be the implicit 'Cosmic Christ' that Alison Kershaw has convincingly argued for as a feature of Traherne's poetics.[21] However, the typology is so explicit as to leave no room for doubt that Traherne is referring to Christ, and moreover to the historical event of the crucifixion in the light of eternity, rather than to the eternal presence of the Logos.

---

[17] Giovanni Diodati, *Pious Annotations Upon the Holy Bible* (London, 1643), p. 24.
[18] Edward Sparke, *Scintilla-Altaris* (London, 1660), p. iv.
[19] See the chapter by Carol Ann Johnston in this volume.
[20] Quoted from the manuscript of the poem (Folger Shakespeare Library, MS V.a.70, fol. 5r). The relevant lines in Ross are p. 199, lines 4–5.
[21] See Alison Kershaw's contribution to this volume, and Alison Kershaw, 'The Poetic of the Cosmic Christ in Thomas Traherne's *The Kingdom of God*', Ph.D. thesis, University of Western Australia (2005).

This indicates the importance of Christ as a model of innocence for Traherne, perhaps even above Adam.

It is the innocence of the innocent sacrifice that makes it effective.[22] Traherne declares the meek lamb a more proper sacrifice than bears or tigers:

> But GOD and Lov all these for man Despise,
> His Altar wils no Guilty Sacrifice.
> Tis strange, what He lovs best our GOD doth make,
> His only Sacrifice for Sinners sake. ('Abels Lamb', p. 200, 20–23)

This 'strange' motif provides an Abrahamic inversion of the story of Abel, which turns the sacrifice in question from an offering by humanity to God into God's provision for humanity. Not concerned with the first and best of the flock that Abel chose, Traherne intimates that God chooses the innocence that God 'lovs best' as a sacrifice for sinners. Traherne is not alone in the implication that the sacrifice of Christ is 'innocence itself'. William Austin, for example, in *Devotionis Augustinianae Flamma*, which Traherne quotes in the *Church's Year-Book*, describes the annunciation of Mary in the following terms: '*when* the *holy Ghost* came upon her, [her flesh] was *wholy cleansed,* and made fit for *Innocence* it selfe to weare, before he put it on*'.*[23] The appearance of this motif in *The Ceremonial Law* indicates that the innocence of Christ is central to Traherne's soteriology.

The mystery of innocent sacrifice is further expressed through Traherne's use of paradox, a popular device in early modern Protestant poetics and in Traherne's work.[24] Both Adam's beast and Abel's lamb emblematise the commonplace paradox of 'the innocent' who is punished as if they were guilty in order that the guilty might be treated as innocent. In 'Adams Fall' this paradox is described thus:

> One Sind, another died: A Beast was slain;
> An Innocent was kild, a Foe doth reign. (p. 198, 10–11)

In 'Abels Lamb', it is expressed through the wonder that:

> An Innocent, that from all Blemish free,
> Owning no Sin, might aptly Die for me. (p. 199, 6–7)

---

[22] Denise Inge has made this point in *Happiness and Holiness: Thomas Traherne and His Writings* (Norwich, 2008), p. 147.

[23] William Austin, *Devotionis Augustinianae Flamma* (London, 1635), p. 20.

[24] See Rosalie Littell Colie, *Paradoxia Epidemica: The Renaissance Tradition of Paradox* (Princeton, 1966).

This paradox reflects a soteriology that contains elements of satisfaction or scapegoat salvation theories, in which innocence and guilt are exchanged and the transaction is completed through the guilt-ridden death of the innocent. The Cambridge Platonist Benjamin Whichcote conformed to this soteriological structure: 'Christ, who was Innocent, was dealt withal, as if he were Faulty; that we, who are Faulty, might be dealt withal, as if we were Innocent.'[25] The 'as if' of that transaction is a clear element in Traherne's spirituality of imputed innocence. For him, the infant who sees the light of innocence lives '*As if* there were nor Sin, nor Miserie' ('The Preparative', p. 12, 55; my italics). Traherne does not argue that their life is indeed void of misery, but their innocence is an imagined existence, a form of play-acting. This principle also informed Traherne's view of proper ethical conduct. In the *Select Meditations* he instructs the reader that 'Towards thy neighbor thou must behave thy Selfe with as much Candor and Sweetness as if He were an unspotted Angel. Becaus He is the Redeemed of christ' (Ross, V, IV.53). Regardless of the effects of original sin or apostasy upon those one meets, the paradoxical sacrifice of the Innocent both permits and necessitates that they be treated as innocent. This paradoxical soteriology wherein the guilty are treated as innocent may provide resources for Traherne to address internal tensions within his thought between the Reformed soteriology of the Thirty-Nine Articles and its emphasis on original sin, and Renaissance humanist ideas of the potential for human goodness.

THE *CHRISTIAN ETHICKS* AND INNOCENT ACTIVITY

In seventeenth-century works of moral theology innocence could be read as a quality of public virtue, as the 'innocent activities' of the righteous. For example, Richard Allestree's popular ethics *The Whole Duty of Man*, a major work with which Traherne's *Ethicks* is inevitably compared, exhorts his reader to 'keep thy self always busied in some innocent, or virtuous employment'.[26] Traherne uses innocence in this sense occasionally to denote an activity that is without malice, addition or corruption, and which has a sincere intent, such as the 'Humble and Innocent Discharge' of duty (*Inducements to Retirednes*, Ross, I, p. 20).

---

[25] Benjamin Whichcote, *Moral and Religious Aphorisms*, ed. W. R. Inge (London, 1930), #401.

[26] Richard Allestree, *The Practice of Christian Graces, or, The Whole Duty of Man* (London, 1658), p. 172; see Kevin Laam, 'Thomas Traherne, Richard Allestree, and the Ethics of Appropriation', *Re-Reading Thomas Traherne: A Collection of New Critical Essays*, ed. Jacob Blevins (Tempe, 2007), pp. 37–64.

At the same time there is in seventeenth-century Protestant ethics a concern for unity between external actions and the hidden spirit; between what Paul Cefalu has identified as the moral poles of 'practical morality' and the *habitus* of infused dispositions.[27] This concern was manifest in critiques of hypocrisy and in exhortations to sincerity.[28] Sincerity of heart was an important element of virtue. Benjamin Whichcote, for example, stated that 'Sincere *Intention* is Evangelical Perfection'.[29] Allestree further states that 'if there were the perfectest innocence in our tongue, and hands, yet if there be not this purity of heart, it will never serve to acquit us before [God]'.[30] Innocence in the sense of purity of heart is a status to be kept, preserved or maintained; as Allestree says, 'as ever thou wouldst keep thy self innocent from the great offence, guard thee warily from all such inlets, those steps and approaches towards it'.[31]

For Traherne, this act of preservation is a priority in the ethical life, as he states in the *Ethicks*: 'THE more Honor and pleasure we enjoy, the Greater and more Perfect is our present Happiness: Tho many times in the Way to Felicity, we are forced to quit all these, for the Preservation of our Innocence' (*Christian Ethicks*, p. 18). Innocence is preserved through keeping the heart pure or the intentions honest. Traherne outlines this principle in the *Centuries of Meditations* in a maxim for enjoying the world: 'he had but one thing to do, and that was to order and keep his Heart which alone being well guided, would order all other things Blessedly and Successfully' (IV.40). This principle is explicitly inspired by Proverbs 4.23, '*In all thy Keeping Keep thy Heart, for out of it are the Issues of Life and Death*' (IV.41). Innocence of the heart or sincere intention was an important ethical principle, and was to be preserved by the ordering and guiding of the affections.

The sceptical moral philosophy of Pierre Charron, an important source for Traherne's *Ethicks*, was dismissive of this act of preserving innocence. Charron considered the preservation of purity to be a 'cowardly and idle innocencie, *quae nisi metu non placet!* Thou keepest thy selfe from

---

[27] Paul Cefalu, *Moral Identity in Early Modern English Literature* (Cambridge, 2004), pp. 3, 16, 192.

[28] See, for example, John Tillotson, *Of Sincerity and Constancy in the Faith and Profession of the True Religion* (London, 1695), pp. 3, 27–8; compare Jeremy Taylor, 'Of Christian Simplicity', *The Whole Works of the Right Rev. Jeremy Taylor*, ed. Reginald Heber, 15 vols (London, 1822), vol. VI, p. 141, on the 'sincerity of an honest, and ingenuous, and a fearless person'.

[29] Whichcote, *Aphorisms*, #815.

[30] Allestree, *Whole Duty*, p. 262.

[31] Allestree, *Whole Duty*, p. 220.

wickednesse, because thou darest not be wicked.'[32] Traherne seems to be aware of such critiques, and to respond to them in the *Ethicks* by exalting courage as the foundation of 'the Essence of a man', and by revelling in the masculine connotations of the Latin etymology of 'virtu' (*Christian Ethicks*, p. 192). Lancelot Andrewes's *Holy Devotions* resolves the tension between idle innocence and active virtue, providing a source for the unification of outward actions with inner holiness and of the preservation of purity with active righteousness. Andrewes's influence on Traherne is particularly evident in the Ramist prayer structure adopted in the *Thanksgivings*, but is also seen in his approach to the ethics of innocence. In *Holy Devotions*, Andrewes translates Psalm 37.37, following the Douay-Rheims version, as an injunction to 'Keep innocence, and behold justice.'[33] His interpretation of the divine law draws the preservation of innocence and the pursuit of righteousness together, as equal partners in the holy life. To reinforce the point, he goes on to describe God's dual commandment to humanity as '*1. To keep innocency, and to do that which is right [Psal. 37.38]. 2. And to do no evil [Eclus 7.10]*.'[34] In this passage, keeping innocence is united to righteousness, and distinguished from a mere abstention from evil, which saves it from Charron's critique of the passivity of innocence. Traherne echoes Andrewes's sentiment in his discussion of prudence in the *Ethicks*. He cites 1 Peter 3.10–13:

> He that will love Life and see good Days, let him refrain his Tongue from Evil, and his Lips that they speak no Guile: let him eschew Evil, and do Good, let him seek Peace and ensue it, for the Eyes of the Lord are over the Righteous: And who is he that will harm you, if ye be followers of that which is Good?' (*Christian Ethicks*, p. 157)

In accordance with the *Ethicks*' focus on virtue over vice, Traherne omits verse 12b, 'but the Face of the Lord is against them that do evil'. For him, the prudent life is one that both preserves the innocence of the heart and seeks to perform innocent activities. Innocence is thus not only an object of preservation but also of pursuit, a feature of 'manly' virtue and a key aspect of Traherne's moral theology.

---

32 Pierre Charron, *Of Wisdom Three Bookes*, trans. Samson Lennard (London, 1608), p. 288.
33 Compare the King James Bible, which translated the verse thus: 'Marke the perfect man, and behold the upright.'
34 Lancelot Andrewes, *Holy Devotions with Directions to Pray*, 5th edn (London, 1663), p. 15; compare Thomas Aquinas, *Summa Theologica*, trans. Thomas Gilby (Cambridge, 1964–1981), IIB.79.i, on doing good and avoiding evil as 'Quasi-Integral Parts of Justice'.

PRIESTLY DEVOTION: WASHING ONE'S HANDS IN INNOCENCE

The motif of washing one's hands in innocence reveals another aspect of ethical discourse on innocence, one that also speaks of the art of meditation and the duties of a priest. The image of the washing of hands had varying connotations in seventeenth-century devotional literature. It could be interpreted as the unity of outward actions and inner sincerity. Ainsworth's *Annotations* on Genesis 20.5 ('in the integrity of my heart and innocency of my hands have I done this') interprets innocent hands as denoting both righteous action and a pure heart: '*Innocence of my hands/* or, *cleannesse of my palmes:* the *palmes of the hands* are named, as wherein filthinesse might be hidden: so purging himselfe even from secret crime.'[35] For Andrewes, washing hands in innocence indicates a will to preserve purity, 'a steadfast purpose of keeping our selves cleane.'[36] In Wilson's *Dictionary*, Psalm 26.6 is quoted at the end of the entry on regenerate innocence and so signifies both an 'indevour to serve God in innocency of life', and an imputation of 'Christs innocency'. Wilson's quotation suggests that, through the act of washing, the organs of innocent action are bathed in the imputed innocence of Christ that justifies them.[37]

This variety and depth of meaning underlies Traherne's use of the phrase in *Inducements to Retirednes* and *Thanksgivings*, when he paraphrases Psalm 26.6, 'I will wash my hands in Innocency: so will I compass thine Altar, O LORD.' Although the ethical connotations of the unity of purity and righteousness described above are clearly relevant here, it is perhaps the devotional and cultic interpretations of the text that are most informative for Traherne's explicit use of the verse. In *Inducements*, Traherne quotes it as part of a compilation of verses from Psalms 84 and 26. This concludes a section which exhorts the reader to meditate on the things of God, and to think like God in order to be drawn closer to God. To wash one's hands in innocence in order to encompass God's altar may therefore be interpreted as focusing the thoughts on God in order to be drawn into glory: 'For as the same Thoughts must proceed from the same Principles, so must they End in the same Glory' (*Inducements*, p. 8). This usage is easily comparable to that of Joseph Hall, who in his *Art of Meditation* used the verse to stress the importance of purgation and preparation of the will before meditation: 'The soule must therefore bee purged, ere it can profitably meditate. [...]

---

[35]   Henry Ainsworth, *Annotations upon the Five Bookes of Moses, the Booke of the Psalms, and the Song of Songs* (London, 1627), p. 78.

[36]   Lancelot Andrewes, *XCVI Sermons by the Right Honourable and Reverend Father in God, Lancelot Andrewes, Late Lord Bishop of Winchester* (London, 1629), p. 744.

[37]   Wilson, *Dictionary*, p. 336b.

First, saith *David*, I will was my hands in innocencie, then I wil compass thine altar.'[38]

There are obvious cultic connotations to this verse, which continues, unquoted by Traherne: 'so will I compass thine altar, O Lord: That I may publish with the voice of thanksgiving, and tell of all thy wondrous works'. These associations are clear in Traherne's 'Thanksgivings for the Body'. In this work Traherne cites Psalm 26 as part of a prayer of dedication that follows a lament for his guilt and estrangement from God. So it takes the imperative tense: 'Enable me to wash my hands in Innocency. That I may compass thine altar about' (*Thanksgivings*, Ross, IV, p. 332). As one approaches the altar of the Lord with clean hands, it implies, so innocence is the precondition for true praise and knowledge of God. This interpretation of the passage echoes the cultic character-istics of innocence in the theology of the patristic theologian Lactantius. For Lactantius, innocence is the condition for and the content of true worship. Humanity was created 'that we might with pure and uncor-rupted mind worship Him who made the sun and the heaven', for which 'nothing more than innocence alone' is sufficient.[39] This cultic interpre-tation of innocence coheres with the worshipful trajectory of Traherne's devotional works, which, like each section in *Inducements* and like many of the entries in the *Commentaries of Heaven*, frequently conclude in prayers of thanksgiving. Understood in the light of Psalm 26, such acts of praise are not private prayers but declarations of God's goodness before the whole congregation.

This interpretation conforms to Traherne's evident concern with his priestly duty. Although *Inducements* is directed towards a general audience, his ascetic recommendations clearly reference his own single life and the work contains a description of the priestly role in terms of the Levitical duty of praise and sacrifice (Ross, I, pp. 16, 21). The particular priestly role of washing one's hands in innocence is described in Anthony Sparrow's protectorate-era defence of *The Book of Common Prayer*, which quotes Psalm 26.6 in defence of the symbolic action of washing hands in prepa-ration for the consecration of the Eucharistic elements. Sparrow interprets

---

[38] Joseph Hall, *The Art of Divine Meditation Profitable for all Christians to Knowe and Practise* (London, 1606), p. 25.

[39] Lactantius, 'Of the Worship of the True God, and of Innocency, and of the Worship of False Gods', *The Divine Institutes*, trans. William Fletcher, in *Ante-Nicene Fathers*, vol. VII, ed. Alexander Roberts et al. (Buffalo, NY, 1886), revised edn Kevin Knight, New Advent, <http://www.newadvent.org/fathers/07016.htm> [accessed July 2011], VI.1; compare Psalm 51.17 and James 1.27; also Whichcote, *Aphorisms*, #762, where the state of innocence is spiritual worship of God.

this as a symbol 'that those that are to do these holy Offices should have a special care of purity'.[40] Traherne clearly had a sense of this priestly 'special care'. As he described it in the *Church's Year-Book*, the priest's authority is dependent upon his purity: 'one Blemish so fatal and Destructiv therto, keep me Pure and Spotless, that I may win and save thy People' (Ross, IV, pp. 170–1). For Traherne therefore, to wash one's hands in innocence connotes not only inner and outer purity, but also being drawn closer to God through meditation and repentance, and the priest's particular duty to lead the church in worship through purity.

DEVOTIONAL DEBATES: RETIREMENT FROM THE WORLD

Innocence could be a contested term in the context of seventeenth-century disagreements over proper devotion. The pamphlet debate between John Evelyn and Sir George Mackenzie that provides the backdrop to Traherne's *Inducements to Retirednes* reveals the disputed language of innocence in discussions over the relative virtues of retirement.[41] In *A Moral Essay, Preferring Solitude to Public Employment* (1665), Mackenzie argues that Adam's 'congenial innocence' made it good for him to have company, but that Adam was unable to live one day with company and to remain innocent.[42] He believes that through retirement to isolation in the countryside, humanity is 'restor'd to that primitive innocence' lost since Adam.[43] Mackenzie therefore extols the virtues of rural life, where 'old age crowns, with innocence's livery, these who have innocently improven their youth'.[44] Evelyn responds in *Publick Employment and an Active Life Prefer'd to Solitude* (1667), that it is equally possible to find sincere and virtuous people in the city as in the country, 'And to be so innocent *there*, where there is so much *temptation*, is so much the greater merit.'[45] Traherne agrees with both Mackenzie and Evelyn, partly by altering the terms of the debate, and partly through an irenic *via media*. He defines retirement not in terms of town and country, but in terms of 'Retirement from the

---

[40] Anthony Sparrow, *A Rationale Upon the Book of Common Prayer of the Church of England* (London, 1672), p. 218.

[41] On the possible dating of the manuscript and Traherne's position within these debates, see Ross, *Works*, II, p. xxi.

[42] George Mackenzie, *A Moral Essay, Preferring Solitude to Publick Employment* (Edinburgh, 1665), p. 40.

[43] Mackenzie, *Moral Essay*, p. 107.

[44] Mackenzie, *Moral Essay*, p. 106.

[45] John Evelyn, *Publick Employment and an Active Life Prefer'd to Solitude* (London, 1667), p. 40.

World for the better Introversion of Spirit' (*Inducements*, p. 4). This spiritu-alisation of the debate connects it with discourses on meditation and the ascetic life rather than on social ethics, and provides a means of combining the two contrasting models of the innocent life.[46]

Traherne agrees with Mackenzie that retirement is, in Traherne's words, 'A Cheap Estate, Safe, and easy to be attained', akin to the easy innocence of Adam in Eden (*Inducements*, p. 22). This is the model of Adamic innocence that has been noticed so frequently in Traherne's lyric poems, although it is here recapitulated in prayer and meditation rather than through a praise of infancy. Retirement is easy because there is plenty of space in the world to retire to, safe because to be alone is to be spared from temptation and protected from danger by the angels, and cheap because solitude costs nothing (p. 22). This is not to devalue the virtues of retirement, since Traherne is at pains, as he is in the *Centuries* and elsewhere, to assert 'That things excellent are most common, cheap and precious' (p. 11). The virtues of an Adamic innocent state are that, 'Were all men innocent, Exposures would be far more safe and Happy then they are. there would be less in them either of Danger or Temptation' (p. 13). The Adamic innocence of retirement is the security of the pure heart.

The security of Adamic innocence is to be contrasted with the glory of innocence hard won through exposure to the world. Elsewhere, Traherne agrees with Evelyn that 'Purchase and Triumph' is preferable to Adam's 'Quiet Possession of the World innocently' (p. 32). He resolves this apparent dichotomy by arguing that retirement is a preparation and not an end in itself. Retirement is preferable to the companionship of friendship or marriage, but only in the sense that it expands the soul to love the whole world equally and 'in a more immediat and clear manner', rather than focusing its affections upon a single object (p. 7). Retirement is a prepa-ration for activity in the world (p. 12). Following the 'GREAT EXEMPLAR' Christ, who remained in retirement for thirty years and preached for three, so retirement is preparation for public ministry (p. 14). In this argument we detect once again Traherne's concern with the priestly vocation. In an irenic turn Traherne concludes that both private and public living, both retreat and exposure to the world are desirable, and he aims for a 'Sweet Mixture of these Extremes, and a Wise Improvement of both' (p. 20). The innocent life may therefore be found both in the security of retirement from the world and in victorious encounters with the world.

---

[46]   See Traherne, *Inducements*, p. 25.

SACRAMENTAL THEOLOGY: *A SOBER VIEW* AND SACRAMENTAL INNOCENCE

The area of sacramental theology brings this chapter closer to debates that have hitherto dominated Traherne criticism on the extent and orthodoxy of his apparent claims to infant innocence.[47] There is not space to go into these fully here, but there is room to introduce a neglected idea into these debates: the notion of sacramental innocence. Traherne's views on sacramental innocence are set out most clearly in *A Sober View of Dr Twisses His Considerations*, which is his contribution to contemporary discussions on the doctrine of election, and in his entry on 'Baptism' in the *Commentaries of Heaven*.

Sacramental innocence provides an answer to the question of the source of regenerate innocence. Wilson's Reformed definition, discussed above, suggests that innocence is restored only through the imputation of Christ's righteousness. Traherne adopts a Lutheran standpoint in arguing that the process through which this occurs is the sacrament of baptism. Traherne's theology of baptism is relatively polemical. It is situated in defence of pædobaptism against Socinian and Quaker critiques, and is directed particularly against the Anabaptist John Tombes of nearby Leominster.[48] Its central theme is the defence of sacramental regeneration against its critics; as he argues, 'so is evry one Regenerated, that is Baptized, in a Sacramental Maner' ('Baptism', *Commentaries*, p. 450).[49]

---

[47] See, for example, William H. Marshall, 'Thomas Traherne and the Doctrine of Original Sin', *Modern Language Notes* 73.3 (1958), 161–5; George Robert Guffey, 'Thomas Traherne on Original Sin', *Notes and Queries* 14 (1967), 98–100; Franz K. Wöhrer, 'The Doctrine of Original Sin and the Idea of Man's Perinatal Intimations of the Divine in the Work of Thomas Traherne', *Yearbook of Studies in English Language and Literature 1982/83* (Vienna, 1984).

[48] Thomas Traherne, 'Baptism', *Commentaries*, Ross, III, p. 451, note on line 92 (deleted section, see p. 522); see John Tombes, *Anti-Pædobaptism*, 3 vols (London, 1652, 1654, 1657); Tombs was assistant to the Herefordshire commission on 29 September 1657 (Traherne was admitted on 30 December that year), and remained in Leominster until his ejection in 1662, see Julia J. Smith, 'Tombes, John', *ODNB*; compare A. B. Chambers, *Transfigured Rites in Seventeenth-Century English Poetry* (Columbia, 1992), pp. 48–58, who thinks that the Restoration Anglican controversy over baptism lies behind Traherne's commitment to internal rites of spiritual regeneration over outward sacramental acts.

[49] For a near-contemporary defence of baptismal regeneration against Reformed critiques, see Cornelius Burges, *Baptismall regeneration of Elect Infants* (London, 1629); see also 'On the Salvation of Mankind', *Certaine Sermons or Homilies Appointed to be Read in Churches in the Time of Queen Elizabeth I* (London, 1623), ed. Mary Ellen Rickey and Thomas B. Stroup, facsimile edn, 2 vols (Gainesville, FL, 1968), I, sermon 3, p. 13, on the baptised as 'washed by this sacrifice from their sinnes, in such sort, that there remaineth

Thus the sacrament of baptism is essential to a proper understanding of Traherne's theology of regenerate innocence.

Luther describes sacramental regeneration as the entrance into a divine and glorious innocence: 'It is as if the sponsors, when they lift the child up out of baptism, were to say, "Lo, your sins are now drowned, and we receive you in God's Name into an eternal life of innocence."'[50] The 'washing of regeneration' is more than purification, but an inauguration into a new life.[51] This is an innocence of the entire life of faith from birth to resurrection, conferred by the grace of God through the imputation of the innocence of Christ, the model and measure of a Christian innocence of life. For Traherne, sacramental regeneration is the status of being a child of God, which is conferred on all the baptised.[52] Although the promises made in baptism must be fulfilled in order to be effective for salvation, the sacrament of baptism is the means of this regenerate innocence.[53] Andrewes expressed a similar sentiment by styling innocence alongside peace, sincerity and patience, as one of the '*virtutes Baptismales*, the very virtues of our Baptisme.'[54]

If innocence is conferred through baptism then this has implications for Traherne's idea of infant innocence. *The Book of Common Prayer* liturgy for baptism reports how Christ 'exhorteth all men to follow their [children's] innocency', but the question of whether this is a pre- or post-baptismal innocence is left unclarified. In his theological works Traherne appears less concerned with the soteriological status of the unbaptised infant than

---

not any spot of sinne, that shall be imputed to their damnation'; Aquinas, *Summa*, III.69.i–iv, on baptism's removal of sin, guilt and penalties, and its regeneration of the believer through incorporation into Christ.

[50] Martin Luther, 'The Holy and Blessed Sacrament of Baptism, 1519', in *Luther's Works*, ed. E. Theodore Bachmann and Helmut T. Lehmannm (Philadelphia, 1960), vol. XXXV: 31; compare John Calvin, 'Of Baptism', *Institutes of the Christian Religion*, trans. Henry Beveridge (London, 1953), Book IV, ch. 15.

[51] Luther, 'Of Baptism', section III.

[52] See Traherne, *A Sober View of Dr Twisses His Considerations*, Ross, I, p. 80, citing the 'Thanksgiving appointed after Public Baptism', *Book of Common Prayer*. While agreeing with him, Traherne's commentator notes that sacramental regeneration was not uncontroversial, p. 81; compare Cranmer's interpretation of sacramental regeneration as a 'sign', Cranmer, PS, I. P.124, cited in Geoffrey W. Bromiley, *Baptism and the Anglican Reformers* (London, 1953), p. 114; on this debate see Brian D. Spinks, *Reformation and Modern Rituals and Theologies of Baptism: From Luther to Contemporary Practices* (Aldershot, 2006), pp. 66–73; see also Luther, 'Of Baptism', section V.8: 'Man, therefore, is altogether pure and guiltless, but sacramentally ['rein und unschuldig, sakramentlich'], which means nothing else than that he has the sign of God.'

[53] Traherne, *Sober View*, p. 81.

[54] Andrewes, *XCVI Sermons*, p. 681.

with their status after baptism. Baptism lays a duty on the infant not to be apostate from this faith:

> In Baptism vow I will [...]
> Do all that GOD doth by his Law require:
> I surely then must set the World on fire [...]
> But then I must, if to triumph I mean
> Keep Soul and body, washt in Baptism, clean. ('Baptism', p. 454–5)

So the sins of the child are not the sins of nature but of apostasy: 'a Heathen cannot, but an Infant Baptized may become an Apostate' ('Baptism', p. 453).[55] The innocence of the infant after baptism is not the natural innocence of Adam but the regenerate innocence of the Christian. This regenerate innocence is, arguably, more significant than the innocence of nature as a model for the life of faith.

THE *CHURCH'S YEAR-BOOK* AND INNOCENCE IN PUBLIC PRAYER

The ways in which innocence was referred to in written prayers are indic-ative of its place in seventeenth-century devotional thought. Traherne's use of the language of innocence in set prayers might appear striking in the light of contemporary arguments for the simplicity of extemporary worship against defences of the magnificent corporate ritual of authorised liturgies.[56] However, claims to the innocent sincerity of true worship were not the preserve of supporters of extemporary prayer alone, but were used on both sides of the debate. Anthony Sparrow defended *The Book of Common Prayer* in these terms, arguing that there is not 'A more innocent, blameless form, against which there lies no just exception'.[57] Traherne's *Church's Year-Book*, as an edited compilation of set prayers and liturgies organised according to the festivals of the church year, also defends the innocence of authorised public worship. It begins with a meditation on the joy of the Resurrection and of Christ's church, which took 'Production from his Blood, Life from His Death, Health from His Wounds, and now Establishment, as well as Growth from his Resurrection, rejoicing in it' (IV, p. 7). Here, the establishment of the national church is clearly a cause for praise. Later on he defends the observance of Holy Days as, among other things, 'The Relicks of Eden, and superadded Treasures. [...] Wherin we

---

55 Compare Traherne, 'Apostasie', *Commentaries*, III, pp. 124–7.
56 Horton Davies, *Worship and Theology in England*, vol. II: *From Andrewes to Baxter and Fox, 1603–1690* (Princeton, 1975), V, 'Style in Worship: Prestigious or Plain?'.
57 Sparrow, *Book of Common Prayer*, p. 81.

are restored to the Joys of Heaven. [...] Heavenly Perspectives wherin we behold the Mystery of Ages' (p. 233). Here Traherne defends the rituals of the national church through his own characteristically hermetic mysticism.

Innocence has a recognised place in set and commonplace prayers from this period. It appears particularly with reference to Christ, such as in prayers on the Annunciation, the Festival of the Circumcision, Good Friday and Easter Day.[58] Innocence is also used in the context of the death of martyrs – especially the Holy Innocents, John and Stephen, whose festivals fall near to each other and whose innocence is a type of Christ's, as Sparkes describes them: 'all three making *Christ* as Cant. 5. white and rudy, the chiefest of ten thousand'.[59] Traherne references innocence in similar contexts in the *Church's Year-Book*.[60] His reference to the innocence of the Holy Spirit in prayers for the festival of the baptism of Christ after Epiphany reveals just how deeply his language of innocence was incorporated into contemporary devotional culture. Jan Ross attributes the source of Traherne's prayer on the Holy Spirit descending as a dove to Daniel Featley's *Ancilla Pietatis: or, The Hand-Maid to Private Devotion*, as it is situated within a longer paraphrase of Featley's work. However, it might just as easily have been inspired by similar prayers from other sources. Featley's prayer states:

> O Eternall and infinite *Holy Ghost*, the love of the Father and the Sonne, who diddest *descend* upon our Saviour in the *likenesses of a Dove*, without gall, purge out of my conscience all *gall* of malice and *bitternesse*, and grant that with *meekenesse I may receive the ingraffed Word which is able to save my soul.*[61]

Traherne's adaptation prays: 'Giv me the Properties of a Dov; Mildness, Meekness, Innocence, Purity, Chastity, Constancy, yea Diligence and Swiftness' (*Church's Year-Book*, pp. 148–9). This long catalogue of dovelike properties is characteristic of Traherne, but a comparable list can be found in Henry Ainsworth's *Annotations* on Leviticus 1.14, for whom 'The *Dove*

[58] See, for example, Sparke, *Scintilla Altaris*, pp. 65, 136–7, 222.
[59] Sparke, *Scintilla Altaris*, pp. 106–7.
[60] See Traherne, *Church's Year-Book*, p. 17 on the Resurrection 'as full of Honor as it is of Innocency'; pp. 167 and 172 on John's 'Innocency of his Silence!' and his 'Innocency of a Virgin'; p. 228 on the Holy Innocents.
[61] Daniel Featley, *Ancilla Pietatis: or, The Hand-Maid to Private Devotion* (London, 1647), p. 476. NB pp. 476–8 are paraphrased in Traherne, *Church's Year-Book*, IV, pp. 148–9 (Ross only quotes Featley, *Ancilla Pietatis* pp. 477–8, in *Works*, IV, pp. 288–9); see also Featley, 'Prayer for Ascension Day', *Ancilla Pietatis*, pp. 461–6, paraphrased in Traherne, *Church's Year-Book*, IV, pp. 104–6 (Ross, *Works*, IV, p. 279, notes only Featley, *Ancilla Pietatis*, pp. 461–3).

[an emblem of the people of God] is a creature sociable, innocent, chaste, mournfull, quiet, fearfull, given to meditation.'[62] A request for the innocence of the descending and ascending dove appears similarly in a prayer from Francis Quarles: 'Lord, give my soul the milk-white innocence/ Of Doves, and I shall have their pineons too'.[63] William Birchley makes the same request in a prayer based on Psalm 40: 'Give me, O Lord, the innocence of Doves; and fill my soul with thy mild spirit:/ Then shal I need none of their wings; since heav'n it self wil dwel in my hart'.[64] Traherne expands upon and clarifies this theme, in line with Featley's prayer, by arguing that the Holy Spirit's descent as a dove signifies 'the Innocence and fecundity of Good works, in those whom He Inspireth; as well as His own Meek and Excellent Nature' (*Church's Year-Book*, p. 129).[65] Not a divine attribute alone, innocence is also a gift of the Spirit and a feature of the Christian life. Traherne's adaptation of set prayers reveals elements of his distinctive spirituality, but they are also embedded in commonplace usage through which the language of innocence weaved its way into seventeenth-century devotion.

INNOCENCE OF LIFE

The genres of seventeenth-century devotional literature discussed above – scriptural interpretation, ethics and moral theology, theological treatises and polemical tracts, liturgies and prayers – all refer to innocence in different ways. However, the various uses of the language of innocence manifest in Traherne's works may be summarised as portraying a concern with what Wilson called 'innocency of life' or regenerate Christian innocence. Christ is the primary model of the innocent life, as seen in Edward Stillingfleet's exhortation to his readers to 'take *notice* of the *unspotted innocency* of his *life*'.[66] The innocent life is what leads to the

---

62 Henry Ainsworth, *Annotations upon the Five Bookes of Moses*, p. 8; compare Peter Sterry, 'To The Honorable House of Commons', *The Clouds in which Christ Comes Opened in a Sermon before the Honourable House of Commons* (London, 1648), p. 10, offers to them 'a Payre of Turtle Doves; Simplicity, and Sweetnesse; or, an Innocent Integrity with an Humble Meekenesse'.

63 Francis Quarles, *Emblemes Divine and Moral* (London, 1635), V.13, pp. 296ff.

64 William Birchley, *Devotions in the Ancient Way of Offices* (London, 1668), p. 47.

65 Traherne also humanises and personalises divine attributes by misquoting Featley, *Ancilla Pietatis*, p. 466, in *Church's Year-Book*, IV, p. 106, changing 'This Day Thou didst Transport *thy* Body into Heaven', to 'This Day Thou didst Transport *my* Body into Heaven' (my italics).

66 Edward Stillingfleet, *Origines Sacræ, or a Rational Account of the Grounds of Christian Faith* (London, 1662), p. 288.

sacrifice of the innocent, as Willet's commentary on Genesis intimates, asserting that the story of Cain and Abel shows 'why the righteous are hated of the wicked, is for their innocent life'.[67] The one with innocent hands leads an innocent or righteous life; as defined by Wilson, innocent hands 'signifie a righteous life, or actions rightly framed, free from wrong, deceit, blood and violence'. The sacrament of baptism is an inauguration into the innocent life, as described by Luther. Finally, innocence of life was a primary concern for the priest, who at his ordination service would have heard the following prayer: 'so replenish them with the truth of thy Doctrine, and adorn them with innocency of life, that, both by word and good example, they may faithfully serve thee in this Office, to the glory of thy Name, and the edification of thy Church'.[68] This theme of the innocent life rests on the definition of innocence outlined in my introduction, as harmlessness, guiltlessness, purity and holiness, rather than the naivety, simplicity or inexperience of the child.

Traherne's use of the language of innocence reflects this rich diversity of influences but is also shaped by the particular themes and concerns of his work, which include: meditation upon the innocent and effective sacrifice of Christ; exhortation to and celebration of sincerity, purity and virtue; reflection upon the role of a priest and his duty to live innocently; allurement of the reader into meditation and the pursuit of an innocent life; and a poetic trajectory towards praise and worship conducted with a pure heart. The significance of innocence of life both for Traherne's priestly role and for the devotional life more generally suggests that for Traherne, as for Augustine, 'The whole of righteousness, therefore, is reduced to the one word, innocence'.[69]

---

[67]   Andrew Willet, *Hexapla in Genesin & Exodum: That is, a Sixfold Commentary upon the First Bookes of Moses* (Cambridge, 1605), p. 63.

[68]   'The Form and Manner of Ordering of Priests', *The Book of Common-Prayer* (London, 1662).

[69]   Augustine, *Expositions on the Book of Psalms, A Library of Fathers of the Holy Catholic Church, Anterior to the Divisions of the East and West*, 6 vols (Oxford, 1847–57), vol. IV, Psalm 101.2, para. iv, p. 483.

AFTERWORD

Jacob Blevins

Nearly 120 years after he was rediscovered and reintroduced to the world by Bertram Dobell, Thomas Traherne still fascinates us. When his poems and centuries re-emerged at the turn of the twentieth century, there was an explicit attempt by scholars to find a place for this new voice that had been pulled from the dusty shelves of the forgotten. Traherne's centuries and poems offered readers a strikingly personal series of meditations on the spiritual growth of an individual: there was the celebration of childhood, of nature, of happiness, of God, and of humankind itself; it was a poetic and theological voice that seemed out of place, or without place, upon initial reading. Scholars just did not know exactly what to do with it.

Much of the early scholarship on Traherne tried to find 'the place' for his work. There were attempts to define him as a proto-Romantic, hearkening toward writers like Wordsworth, Emerson, Whitman and Blake.[1] He was also viewed as the poetic representation of a new Platonism, one corresponding with a group of Cambridge thinkers, including Benjamin Whichcote, Henry More and Ralph Cudworth, amongst others.[2] He was a mystic, part of a long tradition of mystical interaction with nature and Godhead.[3] He was perhaps a metaphysical poet, one whose voice

---

[1] The early critics who discuss Traherne's 'Romanticism' and compare him to Wordsworth are too many to cite. Even Dobell in his first edition of Traherne makes the comparison between the two writers: see *The Poetical Works of Thomas Traherne, B.D., 1636?-1674: Now First Published from the Original Manuscripts*, ed. Bertram Dobell (London, 1903), pp. lxxvii–ix. And for the first half of the twentieth century, nearly every critic writing on Traherne mentions his Proto-Romantic qualities.

[2] See, for example, T. O. Beachcroft, 'Traherne and the Cambridge Platonists', *The Dublin Review* 186 (1930), 278–90, and Gladys Wade, 'Thomas Traherne as "Divine Philosopher"', *Hibbert Journal* 32 (1934), 400–8.

[3] Again, many early studies associated Traherne with the mystic tradition. For two very notable studies, see Itrat Husain's 'Thomas Traherne, The Mystical Philosopher', *The Mystical Element in the Metaphysical Poets of the Seventeenth Century* (London and

belonged in the tradition of Donne, Herbert and Vaughan.[4] For years, scholars tried to situate this voice somewhere, in some tradition, to find a literary, intellectual, and theological place from which to begin understanding the relevance of Traherne's work. However, there were also others who did not even try. Traherne could be read and understood in a spiritual vacuum, a writer who simply provided a kind of inspiration and model for living a moral life and celebrating the beauty of creation, all creation; a man of God who was testifying right in front of us, there on the page.

Despite important contributions from numerous early scholars, none of these approaches was wholly satisfying. Traherne did sound different than other seventeenth-century writers, but there were also substantial echoes of much else that we had read or felt before in other places. As new work emerged (somewhat miraculously) throughout the twentieth century, a much more comprehensive understanding of Traherne began to develop. His was not the seemingly isolated voice we heard – or wanted to hear – in the centuries and poems; his work was part of a complex dialogue of philosophical, theological, political, and scientific discourse that existed during the seventeenth century. His voice could not be separated from the voices around him. Prominent Traherne critics, like Julia Smith and Nabil Matar, began to see just how much a part of the seventeenth century Traherne really was.[5] More about his life, his politics and theology began to emerge, and this changed our understanding of Traherne. He was indeed responsive to many elements of seventeenth-century intellectual thought, but at the same time his work in its entirety was strange and unique; it was still *his* voice we heard, but it was a voice that took influence from many others.

This current volume marks a culmination, a climax, of our new understanding of Traherne's place in seventeenth-century thought. Many of the essays here revisit old contextual topics, but they offer more nuanced

---

Edinburgh, 1948), pp. 264–300, and A. L. Clements's 'On the Mode and Meaning of Traherne's Mystical Poetry: "The Preparative"', *Studies in Philology* 61 (1964), 500–21.

4   See Husain, *Mystical Element*; J. B. Leishman, *The Metaphysical Poets: Donne, Herbert, Vaughan, Traherne* (Oxford, 1934); Margaret Willy, *Three Metaphysical Poets* (London, 1961); also Louis L. Martz, *The Paradise Within: Studies in Vaughan, Traherne, and Milton* (New Haven, 1964).

5   See Nabil Matar's 'A Note on Thomas Traherne and the Quakers', *Notes and Queries* 226 (1981), 46–7; 'Prophetic Traherne: "A Thanksgiving and Prayer for the Nation"', *Journal of English and Germanic Philology* 81.1 (1982), 16–29; 'Thomas Traherne's Solar Mysticism', *Studia Mystica* 7.3 (1984), 52–63; 'Mysticism and Sectarianism in Mid-17th Century England', *Studia Mystica* 11.1 (1988), 55–65; 'The Anglican Eschatology of Thomas Traherne', *Anglican Theological Review* 74 (1992), 289–303; and 'The Political View of Thomas Traherne', *The Huntington Library Quarterly* 57 (1994), 241-53. For Julia J. Smith, see 'Attitudes Toward Conformity and Non-Conformity in Thomas Traherne', *Bunyan Studies* 1.1 (1988), 26–35; and 'Thomas Traherne and the Restoration', *The Seventeenth Century* 3.2 (1988), 203–22.

examinations of Traherne and his place in intellectual and historical discourses of the period. For example, Kathryn Murphy moves beyond the common tendency to align Traherne with Cambridge Platonism, and shows not just that Traherne was also influenced by Aristotelianism, but that his Aristotelianism was negotiated within contemporary scientific inquiry. Even Traherne's attitudes toward the human soul and the nature of Christ are tied up into contemporary natural philosophy and experiences of the body, as Phoebe Dickerson, Alison Kershaw and Cassandra Gorman variously demonstrate. Traherne's interaction with these different discourses has been touched upon previously, at least superficially, but the scholars of this volume – both as individuals and as a group – have more closely identified the complexities of Traherne's influences: his voice is revealed to be an intricate dialogic construction, integral to the various strains of seventeenth-century intellectual history and yet also very much outside any single discursive or intellectual tradition. He is neither a Cambridge nor an Oxford Platonist, but rather a manifestation of both. He is both an Aristotelian and a Neoplatonist, but his engagement with science, and the incarnate body, undermines both philosophical traditions in substantial ways.

Part II of this volume challenges the early perception of Traherne (again, largely based on the centuries and poems) that his was an isolated voice, more personal than public; that his attitudes about felicity, childhood, and even the church were primarily the result of inward meditation rather than an active engagement with contemporary discourse. Elizabeth Dodd takes one of Traherne's most privileged themes – innocence – and shows us a seventeenth-century context for Traherne's persistent valorisation of innocence and childhood, as opposed to the anachronistic positioning of Traherne within Romantic or Pre-Romantic ideologies in which so many early scholars engaged. Similarly, Ana Elena Gonzales-Treviño shows us that Traherne's views of felicity were in fact engaged with other writings about happiness. Contrarily to the common position that Traherne's felicity was located within, felicity, Gonzales-Treviño asserts, is attained primarily through engagement with society itself. This is furthered by Warren Chernaik's claim that Traherne's meditative mode contains a very public element, and Carol Ann Johnston's belief that, beneath Traherne's surface Anglicanism, there is a more radical Protestant undercurrent that challenges the church and its theological orientation. Once again, these particular essays pick up on past critical trends in Traherne studies, but they expose previous misunderstandings that resulted from a lack of appreciation of the complexities of seventeenth-century thought, and just how the various currents of that thought made their way into Traherne's work.

The contributors here have several advantages over many of the earlier Traherne critics. With the enormous amount of newly discovered material, the works in this volume are able to be far more comprehensive in their assessment of the author. The earliest work discovered by Dobell did seem isolated, meditative, and subject to frequent eccentricities. As new works came to light, however, that seemingly personal, meditative voice of Traherne began to find context as these newer works more explicitly demonstrated his dialogue with distinct areas of seventeenth-century intellectual thought. The foundations for the present collection were undeniably laid by previous scholarly attempts to recognise Traherne's place in some of these contemporary movements, but what we have here is a completely new level of critical insight that both complicates and illuminates Traherne the man, his work, his theology, his aesthetics, and his vision of the natural world.

By itself, saying Traherne is part of his age is not saying much. Finding 'sources' for Traherne's thought is interesting but does not give us substantial insight into him. True and new insight comes through recognising the significance of those sources and the contemporary trends of which he was a part. The present volume does that. By complicating Traherne's 'reading' of other discourses, his own voice becomes even more prominent. The voice of the early work is no longer idiosyncratic; it proves to be a processed result of a complex array of discourses converging on and within Traherne, a voice that manifests itself as a new expression of seventeenth-century thought. Mikhail Bakhtin believed that all utterances were dialogic, a continual process of constructing our own voices out of the multitude of voices that surround us. We are in constant dialogue with all the other dialogues that have (and even have not) been uttered before. We respond, we question, we anticipate all voices that are or could be possible. Our own voices are not isolated – ever. They are necessary components of larger dialogues of which we are necessarily a part. Of course Traherne was a part of seventeenth-century thought, but this collection demonstrates just how dialogic his work is, just how complex and sophisticated his vision and intellect really are.

But, of course, our own critical dialogue with Traherne and with each other does not end here. This volume, with its specific insights into Traherne's place in his own time, is a major contribution to the field of Traherne studies. Cassandra Gorman and Elizabeth Dodd have put together a group of essays that both clarify and complicate. Readers will leave this, as I have, with a much more solid grounding in just how much of Traherne's presence in the seventeenth century has been lost on previous work. Ultimately, however, what this book gives us is a grounded licence to continue delving into all aspects of Traherne's historical context. One does not need that context to read Traherne, but the contexts that these contributors provide will prove to be essential to the next phase of Traherne scholarship. There is so much more that Traherne can offer us, and this volume is the necessary facilitator to that offering.

CHRONOLOGY OF TRAHERNE'S LIFE AND CONTEMPORARY INTELLECTUAL DEVELOPMENTS

1543	Copernicus, *De Revolutionibus Orbium Coelestium* (*On the Revolutions of the Celestial Spheres*) presents a heliocentric model of the universe
1573	Thomas Digges, *Alae Seu Scalae Mathematicae* defends Copernicus's theories in English
1584	Giordano Bruno, *De L'infinito Universo et Mondi* (*On the Infinite Universe and Worlds*) asserts the infinity of the universe
1593–98	Richard Hooker, *Of the Laws of Ecclesiastical Polity*. It will prove a significant text in the development of Anglican self-understanding, based upon scholastic notions of natural and divine law
1605	Francis Bacon, *The Advancement and Proficience of Learning Divine and Human*, a foundational text in the development of experimentalist or empiricist method
1610	Galileo Galilei publishes *Sidereus Nuncius*, which is based upon observations through a telescope
1620	Francis Bacon, *Novum Organum Scientiarum* (*New Method*)
1624	Book one of Pierre Gassendi, *Exercitationes Paradoxicae Adversus Aristoteleos*, which defends atomist matter theories
1633	Benjamin Whichcote becomes a fellow of Emmanuel College, Cambridge. This is often considered a significant moment in the birth of the Cambridge Platonist school, which sought a return to Christian Platonism in response to scholastic Aristotelianism
1633	George Herbert, *The Temple*, a collection of metaphysical poems that would influence Traherne's spirituality and style
c.1637	Traherne is born in Hereford

1637	René Descartes, *Discourse on the Method of Rightly Conducting One's Reason*, presents a rationalist philosophical method
1642–49	Civil War. Hereford is pro-royalist but changes hands several times and is finally taken by the parliamentarians on 18 December 1645
1649	Execution of Charles I
1649–60	Britain is ruled as a Commonwealth and Protectorate under Oliver and Richard Cromwell
1651	Thomas Hobbes's *Leviathan* asserts that humanity's natural state is to be at war
1 March 1653– 13 October 1656	Traherne attends Brasenose College, Oxford. The Early Notebook was probably written during his student days, the Ficino Notebook perhaps some time later
30 December 1657	Traherne made rector of Credenhill, Herefordshire
1660	Samuel Pepys begins his Diary
	Restoration of the monarchy, Charles II crowned
20 October 1660	Traherne episcopally ordained deacon and priest
28 November 1660	First meeting of the Royal Society, which received a royal charter in 1662
1661	Robert Boyle, *The Sceptical Chymist*, provides a key contribution to the scientific revolution
6 November 1661	Traherne is made MA in Oxford
18 August 1662	Traherne subscribes to the Act of Uniformity (requiring episcopal ordination and use of *The Book of Common Prayer*). Possible early works such as the *Select Meditations, Inducements to Retirednes* and *A Sober View* may date from the early to mid 1660s
24 August 1662	St Bartholomew's Day ejections of dissenting clergy
1665	Robert Hooke, *Micrographia*, displays the wonders of the world through the modern microscope
1666	John Bunyan, *Grace Abounding* published
1667	John Milton, *Paradise Lost* is first published, often considered both the zenith and final word in a flowering of literature on the primordial paradise
1667–68	Failure of draft comprehension bill, which had been supported by Sir Orlando Bridgeman, for inclusion of Presbyterians in the Church of England
1668	John Dryden becomes Poet Laureate

1669	Traherne attains his BD in Oxford. Major works such as the *Centuries of Meditations*, *Commentaries of Heaven*, *The Kingdom of God* and *Christian Ethicks*, as well as many of his poems, may have been written during a prolific period in the final five years of Traherne's life
15 March 1672	Royal Declaration of Indulgence towards dissenting religious groups, one of the catalysts for the loss of favour of Traherne's patron Orlando Bridgeman, Lord Keeper of the Great Seal
1673	1672 Declaration of Indulgence revoked
	Test Act passed, requiring all officeholders to receive Anglican Communion, and leading to the resignation of the Duke of York as Lord High Admiral
	Traherne's *Roman Forgeries* is published, an anti-Catholic polemic dedicated to Orlando Bridgeman
September–October 1674	Traherne dies in Teddington, where he had been chaplain to Orlando Bridgeman, and is reputedly buried under the reading desk in the church
1675	Traherne's *Christian Ethicks* is posthumously published
1699	Traherne's *A Serious and Pathetical Contemplation* (*Thanksgivings*) is posthumously published
1717	Traherne's contested *Meditations on Creation* is published as part of *A Collection of Meditations and Devotions*, a posthumous collection of Susanna Hopton's works
1896–97	Traherne's Dobell MS (poems and Commonplace Book) and *Centuries of Meditations* are discovered by William T. Brooke and later published by Bertram Dobell as Traherne's (1903 and 1908)
1899	Dobell purchases the *Church's Year-Book*
1910	H. I. Bell publishes Traherne's *Poems of Felicity*. Bell also identified Traherne's Ficino Notebook
1935	Bertram Dobell's son purchases the Early Notebook
1964	The *Select Meditations* are identified as Traherne's
1981	The *Commentaries of Heaven* are identified as Traherne's, after having been pulled from a burning rubbish heap c.1967
1996–97	*The Ceremonial Law* and the Lambeth Palace MS 1360 (containing *Inducements to Retirednes*, *A Sober View*, *Seeds of Eternity* and *The Kingdom of God*) are identified as Traherne's

BIBLIOGRAPHY

PRIMARY WORKS

MANUSCRIPTS

Traherne, Thomas, *Commentaries of Heaven. Wherein the Mysteries of Felicitie Are Opened, and All Things Discovered to Be Objects of Happiness*, British Library, MS Add. 63054.
—— Commonplace Book, Bodleian, MS Eng. poet. c. 42.
—— Early Notebook, Bodleian, MS Lat. misc. f. 45.
—— *Poems of Felicity*, British Library, MS Burney 392.
—— *The Ceremonial Law*, Folger Shakespeare Library, MS V.a.70.
—— *The Kingdom of God*, Lambeth Palace, MS 1360, fols 148r–366r.

PRINTED WORKS

Ainsworth, Henry, *Annotations upon the Five Bookes of Moses, the Booke of the Psalms, and the Song of Songs* (London, 1627).
Allestree, Richard, *The Practice of Christian Graces, or, The Whole Duty of Man* (London, 1658).
Allighieri, Dante, *The Divine Comedy*, trans. Dorothy L. Sayers and Barbara Reynolds, 3 vols (Harmondsworth, 1962).
Andrewes, Lancelot, *Holy Devotions with Directions to Pray*, 5th edn (London, 1663).
—— *XCVI Sermons by the Right Honourable and Reverend Father in God, Lancelot Andrewes, Late Lord Bishop of Winchester* (London, 1629).
Anon., 'A Rediscovered Poet', *Living Age* 237 (1903), 696–9.
Annesley, Samuel, *A Supplement to the Morning-Exercise At Cripplegate: or, Several more cases of Conscience Practically Resolved by sundry Ministers*, 2nd edn (London, 1676).
Aquinas, Thomas, *Summa Theologica*, trans. Thomas Gilby (Cambridge, 1964–81).
Augustine of Hippo, *The City of God*, trans. Marcus Dods (Edinburgh, 1913).
—— *Expositions on the Book of Psalms, A Library of Fathers of the Holy Catholic Church, Anterior to the Divisions of the East and West*, 6 vols (Oxford, 1847–57).
Austin, William, *Devotionis Augustinianae Flamma* (London, 1635).
Bachelard, Gaston, *The Poetics of Space*, trans. Maria Jolas (Boston, 1994).
Bacon, Francis, *Novum Organum*, ed. and trans. Graham Rees (Oxford, 2004).
—— *Of the Advancement and Proficience of Learning [...] IX Bookes*, trans. Gilbert Wats (Oxford, 1640).

Barrow, Isaac, 'His Onely Son', *The Works of Isaac Barrow, D.D.* (London, 1700).

—— *Of Contentment, Patience and Resignation to the Will of God. Several Sermons* (London, 1685).

—— *Theological Works* (Oxford, 1830).

Baxter, Richard and Edmund Calamy, *Abridgment of … [his] History of His Life and Times: With an Account of the Ministers, &c. Who Were Ejected After the Restoration of King Charles II*, 2 vols (London, 1713).

Birchley, William, *Devotions in the Ancient Way of Offices* (London, 1668).

Boyle, Robert, *Occasional Reflection upon Several Subjects,* 2nd edn (London, 1669).

Burges, Cornelius, *Baptismall regeneration of Elect Infants* (London, 1629).

Burton, Robert, *The Anatomy of Melancholy, What it is, With all the Kinds of Causes, Symptomes, Prognostickes, and Several Cures of it* (Oxford, 1628 [1621]).

Calvin, John, *Commentaries on the Four Last Books of Moses*, trans. C. W. Bingham, 4 vols (Edinburgh, 1852–54).

—— *Institutes of the Christian Religion*, trans. Henry Beveridge, 3 vols (London, 1845).

Certaine Sermons or Homilies Appointed to be Read in Churches in the Time of Queen Elizabeth I (London, 1623), ed. Mary Ellen Rickey and Thomas B. Stroup, facsimile edn, 2 vols (Gainesville, FL, 1968).

Charron, Pierre, *Of Wisdom Three Bookes*, trans. Samson Lennard (London, 1608).

Cockburn, John, *Jacob's Vow, or, Man's Felicity and Duty in Two Parts* (Edinburgh, 1696).

Coke, Zachary, *The Art of Logick; or, The Entire Body of Logick in English* (London, 1657).

Coles, Elisha, *An English Dictionary Explaining the Difficult Terms that are used in Divinity, Husbandry, Physick, Phylosophy, Law, Navigation, Mathematicks, and other Arts and Sciences* (London, 1677).

—— *A Practical Discourse of God's Sovereignty* (London, 1673).

Corye, John, *The Generous Enemies, or, The Ridiculous Lovers* (London, 1672).

Crakanthorpe, Richard, *Logicæ Libri Quinque*, 2nd edn (London, 1641).

Crashaw, Richard, *Steps to the Temple* (London, 1646).

Crispe, Tobias, 'Christs Preheminence: Collos. I Ver. 18 That in All Things Hee Might Have the Preheminence', in *Christ Alone Exalted in Fourteene Sermons Preached in, and Neare London, by the Late Reverend Tobias Crispe* (London, 1643).

Croft, Herbert, *Naked Truth: The First Part, Or the True State of the Primitive Church by an Humble Moderator* (London, 1680).

Crowne, John, *Pandion and Amphigenia or, The history of the Coy Lady of Thessalia Adorned with Sculptures* (London, 1665).

Cudworth, Ralph, *The True Intellectual System of the Universe*, 3 vols (London, 1845).

Culverwel, Nathanael, *An Elegant and Learned Discourse of the Light of Nature* (London, 1652).

Davies, John, *The Muses Sacrifice* (London, 1612).

Diodati, Giovanni, *Pious Annotations Upon the Holy Bible* (London, 1643).

Donne, John, *The First Anniversarie An Anatomie of the World* (London, 1612).

—— 'Preached at St. Paul's, upon Christmas Day, 1622', *The Sermons of John Donne*, ed. Evelyn M. Simpson and George R. Potter (Berkeley, 1959), vol. IV, no. 11.

Dryden, John, *Of Dramatic Poesy and Other Critical Essays*, ed. George Watson, 2 vols (London, 1964).

Evelyn, John, *Publick Employment and an Active Life Prefer'd to Solitude* (London, 1667).

Featley, Daniel, *Ancilla Pietatis: or, The Hand-Maid to Private Devotion* (London, 1647).

Fuller, Thomas, *A Collection of Sermons* (London, 1655).

Gale, Theophilus, *Court of the Gentiles, Part II, Of Philosophie* (Oxford, 1670).

Gell, Robert, *Gell's Remaines : Or, Several Select Scriptures of the New Testament Opened and Explained : Wherein Jesus Christ, as Yesterday, Today, and the Same for Ever, Is Illustrated, in Sundry Pious and Learned Notes and Observations Thereupon*, ed. R. Bacon (London, 1676).

Goclenius, Rudolph, *Lexicon Philosophicum* (Frankfurt, 1613).

Green, Ian M., *The Christian's ABC: Catechisms and Catechizing in England, c.1530–1740* (Oxford, 1996).

Hammond, Henry, *A Paraphrase and Annotations upon the Book of the Psalms* (London, 1659).

Hall, Joseph, *The Art of Divine Meditation Profitable for all Christians to Knowe and Practise* (London, 1606).

—— *The Invisible World, Discovered to Spirituall Eyes, and Reduced to Usefull Meditation* (London, 1659).

—— *Select Thoughts, or Choice helps for a pious spirit* (London, 1654).

—— *A Sermon of Public Thanksgiving* (London, 1626).

Herbert, George, *Complete English Poems*, ed. John Tobin (London, 1991).

—— *The Temple* (London, 1633).

Hobbes, Thomas, *Leviathan*, ed. J. C. A. Gaskin (Oxford, 1996).

Hooke, Robert, *Micrographia* (London, 1665).

Hooker, Richard, *Of the Laws of Ecclesiastical Polity* (London, 1593–97).

Hopton, Susanna, *A Collection of Meditations and Devotions* (London, 1717).

—— *Susanna Hopton*, ed. Julia J. Smith, 2 vols (Farnham, 2010).

Hutchinson, Lucy, *The Translation of Lucretius*, ed. Reid Barbour and David Norbrook, vol. II of *The Works of Lucy Hutchinson*, 4 vols (Oxford, 2012–).

Jackson, Thomas, *Maran atha or Dominus Veniet: Christs Session at the Right Hand of God, and Exultation Therby. Commentaries Upon The Articles of the Creed* (London, 1657).

Julian of Norwich, *Julian of Norwich: Revelations of Divine Love, and The Motherhood of God*, ed. Frances Beer (Cambridge, 1998).

Lactantius, 'Of the Worship of the True God, and of Innocency, and of the Worship of False Gods', *The Divine Institutes*, trans. William Fletcher, *Ante-Nicene Fathers*, vol. VII, ed. Alexander Roberts et al. (Buffalo, NY, 1886), revised edn Kevin Knight, New Advent <http://www.newadvent.org/fathers/07016.htm>.

Lockyer, Nicholas, *England Faithfully Watcht with, In Her Wounds: Or, Christ as a Father Sitting up with His Children in Their Swooning State: Which is the Summe of Severall Lectures Painfully Preached Upon Colossians I* (London, 1645).

Lodge, Thomas, *The Antiquitie of the Jews* (London, 1602).

Lucas, Richard, *Enquiry after Happiness* (London, 1685).

Luther, Martin, *Luther's Works*, ed. E. Theodore Bachmann and Helmut T. Lehmannm, 55 vols (Philadelphia, 1960).

—— *Works of Martin Luther*, ed. Eyster Jacobs Henry and Adolph Spaeth, 6 vols (Philadelphia, 1930).

Mackenzie, George, *A Moral Essay, Preferring Solitude to Publick Employment* (Edinburgh, 1665).

Manton, Thomas, *Christs Eternal Existence and the Dignity of His Person Asserted and Proved in Opposition to the Doctrine of the Socinians in Several Sermons on Col. I. 17, 18, 19, 20, 21* (London, 1685).

Milton, John, *Complete Poems and Major Prose*, ed. Merritt Yerkes Hughes (Upper Saddle River, NJ, 1957).

—— *Complete Prose Works*, ed. Don M. Wolfe et al., 8 vols (New Haven, 1953–82).

—— *Complete Prose Works of John Milton*, ed. John Carey, 2nd edn, 8 vols (New Haven, 1980).

—— *Milton: Paradise Lost*, ed. Alastair Fowler, 2nd edn (Harlow, 2007).

—— *Paradise Lost* (London, 1668)

—— *Paradise Lost*, ed. Barbara K. Lewalski (Oxford, 2009).

Moore, John, *Protection Proclaimed (through the loving kindness of God in the present government) to the Three Nations of England, Scotland, and Ireland* (London, 1655).

More, Henry, *An Account of Virtue: Or, Dr Henry More's Abridgement of Morals, put into English*, trans. Edward Southwell (London, 1690).

—— *An Antidote Against Atheism* (London, 1652).

—— *A Collection of Several Philosophical Writings* (London, 1662).

Mossom, Robert, 'The Second Sermon Upon Coloss. I V. 18, 19', *The Preacher's Tripartite* (London, 1657).

Ness, Christopher, *A Compleat History and Mystery of the Old and New Testament* (London, 1696).

Nicholson, William, 'Of Christs Descent to Hell: Ephesians 4. 9, 10', *Exthesis Pisteos, or, Exposition of the Apostles Creed Delivered in Several Sermons* (London, 1661).

Perkins, William, *A Cloud of Faithfull Witnesses, leading to the Heavenly Canaan: Or a Commentary upon the II. Chapter of the Hebrews* (London, 1608).

Phillips, Edward, *The New World of English Words* (London, 1658).

Poole, William, *Annotations upon the Holy Bible* (London, 1683).

Quarles, Francis, *Emblemes Divine and Moral* (London, 1635).

Quick, John, *Synodicon in Gallia Reformata, Or, The Acts, Decisions, Decrees, and Canons of Those Famous National Councils of the Reformed Churches in France*, 2 vols (London, 1692).

Sanderson, Robert, *Logicæ Artis Compendium*, 2nd edn (Oxford, 1640).

Shakespeare, William, *The Norton Shakespeare*, ed. Stephen Greenblatt (London, 2008).

Sidney, Philip, *The Defense of Poesy* (London, 1595).

South, Robert, 'Ephesians 4: 10 He That Descended Is the Same Also That Ascended That He Might Fill All Things (Sermon I)', *Five Additional Volumes of Sermons Preached Upon Several Occasions* (London, 1744).

Sparke, Edward, *Scintilla-Altaris* (London, 1660).

Sparrow, Anthony, *A Rationale Upon the Book of Common Prayer of the Church of England* (London, 1672).

Sterry, Peter, *The Clouds in which Christ Comes Opened in a Sermon before the Honourable House of Commons* (London, 1648).

Stillingfleet, Edward, *Origines Sacræ, or a Rational Account of the Grounds of Christian Faith* (London, 1662).

Taylor, Edward, *Edward Taylor's 'Gods Determinations' and 'Preparatory Meditations': A Critical Edition*, ed. Daniel Patterson (Kent, 2002).

Taylor, Jeremy, *The Whole Works of the Right Rev. Jeremy Taylor*, ed. Reginald Heber, 15 vols (London, 1822).

Tillotson, John, *Of Sincerity and Constancy in the Faith and Profession of the True Religion* (London, 1695).

Traherne, Thomas, *Centuries of Meditations by Thomas Traherne, Now First Printed from the Author's Manuscript*, ed. Bertram Dobell (London, 1908).

—— *Christian Ethicks* (London, 1675).

—— *Christian Ethicks: Or, Divine Morality. Opening the Way to Blessedness, By the Rules of Vertue and Reason*, Cornell Studies in English, vol. XLIII, ed. Carol L. Marks and George R. Guffey (Ithaca, 1968).

—— *Select Meditations*, ed. Julia J. Smith (Manchester, 2009).

—— *A Serious and Pathetical Contemplation of the Mercies of God, in Several Most Devout and Sublime Thanksgivings for the Same* (London, 1699).

—— *The Poetical Works of Thomas Traherne, B.D., 1636?–1674: Now First Published from the Original Manuscripts*, ed. Bertram Dobell (London, 1903).

—— *Thomas Traherne: Centuries, Poems and Thanksgivings*, 2 vols, ed. H. M. Margoliouth (Oxford, 1958).

—— *Traherne's Poems of Felicity*, ed. H. I. Bell (Oxford, 1910).

—— *The Works of Thomas Traherne*, ed. Jan Ross, 6 vols (Cambridge, 2005–14).

Tombes, John, *Anti-Pædobaptism*, 3 vols (London, 1652, 1654, 1657).

Westminster Assembly, *The humble advice of the Assembly of Divines, now sitting at Westminster, concerning a Confession of Faith* (London, 1647).

Whichcote, Benjamin, *Moral and Religious Aphorisms*, ed. W. R. Inge (London, 1930).

White, Thomas, *A Method and Instructions for the Art of Divine Meditation*, 2nd edn (London, 1672).

Willet, Andrew, *Hexapla in Genesin & Exodum: That is, a Sixfold Commentary upon the First Bookes of Moses* (Cambridge, 1605).

Wilson, Thomas, *A Complete Christian Dictionary*, ed. J. Bagwell and A. Simson, 7th edn (London, 1661 [1612]).

Wither, George, *The Protector. A Poem Briefly Illustrating the Supereminency of That Dignity; And, Rationally Demonstrating, That the Title of Protector, Providentially Conferred upon the Supreme Governour of the British Republike, Is the Most Honorable of All Titles, And, That, Which, Probably, Promiseth Most Propitiousness to These Nations; If Our Sins and Divisions Prevent It Not* (London, 1655).

Wordsworth, William, *The Collected Poems*, ed. Antonia Till (Ware, Hertfordshire, 1994).

SECONDARY WORKS

Akers, Matthew P., 'From the Hexameral to the Physico-Theological: A Study of Thomas Traherne's *Meditations on the Six Days of the Creation* and *The Kingdom of God* Focusing upon the Cosmological Controversy', Ph.D. thesis, Drew University, Madison, NJ (2008).

Allchin, A. M., 'The Sacrifice of Praise and Thanksgiving', in *Profitable Wonders:*

Aspects of Thomas Traherne, ed. A. M. Allchin, Anne Ridler and Julia Smith (Oxford, 1989), pp. 22–37.

Allchin, Donald, *Participation in God: A Forgotten Strand in Anglican Tradition* (London, 1988).

Allitt, John Stewart, *Thomas Traherne: Il Poeta-Teologo della Meraviglia e della Felicità* (Milan, 2007).

Ames, Kenneth John, *The Religious Language of Thomas Traherne's Centuries* (New York, 1978).

Anon., 'A Newly-Discovered Poet', *TLS* (27 March 1903), 94–5.

Anon., 'A New, Old Poet', *Harper's Weekly* (3 November 1906), 1559.

Anon., 'A Rediscovered Poet', *The Academy* 64 (1903), 359–60.

Armstrong, A. Hilary, *St. Augustine and Christian Platonism*, The Saint Augustine Lecture 1966 (Villanova, 1967).

Ayers, Michael and Daniel Garber, eds, *The Cambridge History of Seventeenth-Century Philosophy* (Cambridge, 1998).

Baeyer, Hans Christian von, *Taming the Atom: The Emergence of the Visible Microworld* (New York, 1992).

Balakier, James J., *Thomas Traherne and the Felicities of the Mind* (Amherst, 2010).

—— 'Thomas Traherne's Concept of Felicity, the "Highest Bliss," and the Higher States of Consciousness of Maharishi Mahesh Yogi's Vedic Science and Technology', *Modern Science and Vedic Science* 4.2 (1991), 137–75.

—— 'Thomas Traherne's Dobell Series and the Baconian Model of Experience', *English Studies* 70 (1989), 233–47.

—— 'Thomas Traherne's "Thoughts" Poems and the Four Levels of Speech in Vedic Poetics', *Consciousness, Literature and the Arts* 7.3 (December 2006).

Barnstone, Willis, 'Two Poets of Felicity: Thomas Traherne and Jorge Guillén', *Books Abroad* 42.1 (Winter 1968), 14–19.

Beachcroft, T. O., 'Traherne and the Cambridge Platonists', *The Dublin Review* 186 (1930), 278–90.

—— 'Traherne and the Doctrine of Felicity', *Criterion* 9 (1930), 291–307.

Beal, Peter, *Index of English Literary Manuscripts*, 2 vols (London, 1987–93).

—— 'Notions in Garrison: The Seventeenth-Century Commonplace Book', in *New Ways of Looking at Old Texts*, ed. Speed Hill (Binghampton and New York, 1993), pp. 131–48.

Bercovitch, Sacvan, *The Puritan Origins of the American Self* (New Haven, 1975).

Birnbaum, Antonia, 'To Exist Is to Exit the Point', in Jean Luc-Nancy, *Corpus*, trans. Richard A. Rand (New York, 2008), pp. 145–50.

Blevins, Jacob, 'Finding Felicity through the "Pythagorean Eye": Pythagoreanism in the Work of Thomas Traherne', *Classical and Modern Literature* 25.1 (2005), 41–51.

—— 'Infinity is Thine: Proprietorship and the Transcendental Sublime in Traherne and Emerson', *ANQ* 25.3 (2012), 186–9.

Blevins, Jacob, ed., *Re-Reading Thomas Traherne: A Collection of New Critical Essays* (Tempe, 2007).

Block, James E., *A Nation of Agents: The American Path to a Modern Self and Society* (Cambridge, 2002).

Brautigam, Dwight, 'Prelates and Politics: Uses of "Puritan", 1625–40', in *Puritanism and Its Discontents*, ed. Laura Lunger Knoppers (Newark, 2003), pp. 49–66.

Brown, Cedric C. and Tomohiko Koshi, 'Editing the Remains of Thomas Traherne', *Review of English Studies* 57 (2006), 766–82.

Boas, George, *The Cult of Childhood* (London, 1966).

Bottrall, Margaret, 'Traherne's Praise of the Creation', *Critical Quarterly* 1 (1959), 126–33.

Bromiley, Geoffrey W., *Baptism and the Anglican Reformers* (London, 1953).

Burton, John Hill, *The History of Scotland: From Agricola's Invasion to the Extinction of the Last Jacobite Insurrection* (Edinburgh, 1873).

Bush, Douglas, *English Literature in the Earlier Seventeenth Century, 1600–1660*, 2nd edn revised (Oxford, 1962).

Byron, John, *Cain and Abel in Text and Tradition* (Boston, 2011).

Cefalu, Paul, *Moral Identity in Early Modern English Literature* (Cambridge, 2004).

—— 'Thomistic Metaphysics and Ethics in the Poetry and Prose of Thomas Traherne', *Literature and Theology* 16 (2002), 248–69.

Chambers, A. B., *Transfigured Rites in Seventeenth-Century English Poetry* (Columbia, 1992).

Charleton, James, *Non-dualism in Eckhart, Julian of Norwich and Traherne* (London, 2012).

Chernaik, Warren, 'Milton and Traherne: Paradise Recovered', in *Milton Through the Centuries*, ed. Gábor Ittzés and Miklós Péti (Budapest, 2012), pp. 219–28.

Clements, A. L., 'On the Mode and Meaning of Traherne's Mystical Poetry: "The Preparative"', *Studies in Philology* 61 (1964), 500–21.

—— *The Mystical Poetry of Thomas Traherne* (Cambridge, MA, 1969).

Clucas, Stephen, 'Poetic Atomism in Seventeenth-Century England: Henry More, Thomas Traherne and "Scientific Imagination"', *Renaissance Studies* 5 (1991), 327–40.

Cobain, Robert, 'The Burning Bush', *The Presbyterian Herald* (August 1987), <http://www.ballycarrypresbyterian.co.uk/history/bush1.html>.

Coffey, John, *Exodus and Liberation: Deliverance Politics from John Calvin to Martin Luther King Jr* (Oxford, 2014).

Colby, Frances L., 'Thomas Traherne and Henry More', *Modern Language Notes* 62 (1947), 490–2.

Colie, Rosalie Littell, *Paradoxia Epidemica: The Renaissance Tradition of Paradox* (Princeton, 1966).

—— 'Thomas Traherne and the Infinite: The Ethical Compromise', *Huntingdon Library Quarterly* 21.1 (1957), 69–82.

Collinson, Patrick, *English Puritanism* (London, 1987).

Connor, Steven, 'A Skin That Walks', paper given at the Humanities and Arts Research Centre, Royal Holloway University of London, 13 February 2002 <http://stevenconnor.com/skinwalks.html>.

Cunningham, Hugh, *The Children of the Poor: Representatives of Childhood since the Seventeenth Century* (Oxford, 1991).

Curtin, Kathleen, 'Jacobean Congregations and Controversies in Thomas Wilson's *Christian Dictionary* (1612)', *The Seventeenth Century* (2010), 197–214.

Davies, Horton, *Worship and Theology in England*, vol. II: *From Andrewes to Baxter and Fox, 1603–1690* (Princeton, 1975).

Davis, Dick, *Selected Writings of Thomas Traherne* (Manchester, 1988).

DeNeef, A. Leigh, *Traherne in Dialogue: Heidegger, Lacan, Derrida* (Durham, NC, 1988).

Dixon, Leif, 'Calvinist Theology and Pastoral Reality in the Reign of King James

I: The Perspective of Thomas Wilson', *The Seventeenth Century* 23.2 (2008), 173–97.

Dobell, Bertram, 'An Unknown Seventeenth-Century Poet', *Athenaeum* 3780, 3781 (7, 14 April 1900), 433–5, 466.

Dowell, Graham, *Enjoying the World: The Rediscovery of Thomas Traherne* (London, 1990).

Eliot, T. S., 'Mystic and Politician as Poet: Vaughan, Traherne, Marvell, Milton', *The Listener* 3.2 (April 1930), 590–1.

Ellrodt, Robert, *Seven Metaphysical Poets: A Structural Study of the Unchanging Self* (Oxford, 2000).

Faulkner, Joanne, 'The Innocence Fetish: The Commodification and Sexualisation of Children in the Media and Popular Culture', *Media International Australia* 135 (May 2010), 106–17.

Feldman, Louis H., *Studies in Josephus' Rewritten Bible*, Journal for the Study of Judaism Supplement Series 58 (Leiden, 1998).

Fitzgerald, W. B., 'A Literary Resurrection', *London Quarterly Review* 107 (1907), 312–23.

Fleming, W. K., *Mysticism in Christianity* (London, 1913).

Ford, David, *Christian Wisdom: Desiring God and Learning in Love* (Cambridge, 2007).

Fordham, Finn, 'Motions of Writing in the Commentaries of Heaven: The "Volatilitie" of "Atoms" and "ÆTYMS"', in *Re-reading Thomas Traherne*, ed. Jacob Blevins (Tempe, 2007), pp. 115–34.

Fox, Matthew, *The Coming of the Cosmic Christ: The Healing of Mother Earth and the Birth of a Global Renaissance* (San Francisco, 1988).

Garnier, Marie-Dominique, 'The Mythematics of Infinity in the *Poems* and *Centuries* of T. Traherne: A Study of its Thematic Archetypes', *Cahiers Élisabéthains* 28 (1985), 61–71.

Gander, Forrest, 'The Strange Case of Thomas Traherne', *Jacket* 32 (April 2007), <http://jacketmagazine.com/32/k-gander.shtml>.

Glacken, C. J., *Traces on the Rhodian Shore: Nature and Culture in Western Thought from Ancient Times to the End of the Eighteenth Century* (Berkeley and London, 1967).

Golz, David, 'Thomas Traherne and the Zen Poet of "On Believing in Mind"', *Studia Mystica* 13.1 (1990), 56–66.

Grandvoinet, Renée, 'Thomas Traherne and the Doctrine of Felicity', *Études de Lettres* 13 (1939), 164–77.

Grant, Patrick, *The Transformation of Sin: Studies in Donne, Herbert, Vaughan and Traherne* (Montreal, 1974).

Green, Ian, *The Christian's ABC: Catechism and Catechizing in England c.1530–1740* (Oxford, 1996).

—— *Print and Protestantism in Early Modern England* (Oxford, 2000).

Guffey, George Robert, 'Thomas Traherne on Original Sin', *Notes and Queries* 14 (1967), 98–100.

—— *Traherne and the Seventeenth-Century English Platonists, 1900–1966*, Elizabethan Bibliographies, Supplements, No. 11 (London, 1969).

Hale, John, 'England as Israel in Milton's Writings', *Early Modern Literary Studies* 2.2 (1996) <http://extra.shu.ac.uk/emls/02-2/halemil2.html>.

Harvey, George, 'A Precursor of Whitman', *North American Review* 185 (1907), 463–4.

Hawkes, David, 'Thomas Traherne: A Critique of Political Economy', *Huntington Library Quarterly* 62 (1999), 369–88.

Hensley, Charles S., 'Wither, Waller and Marvell: Panegyrists for the Protector', *Ariel* 3.1 (1972), 5–16.

Hill, Christopher, *The Collected Essays of Christopher Hill*, vol. I: *Writing and Revolution in 17th-Century England* (Brighton, 1985).

—— *The English Bible and the Seventeenth-Century Revolution* (London, 1993).

—— *Reformation to Industrial Revolution: The Pelican Economic History of Britain*, vol. II: *1530–1780* (Harmondsworth, 1969).

Hill, John Spencer, *Infinity, Faith, and Time: Christian Humanism and Renaissance Literature*, McGill-Queen's Studies in the History of Religion (Montreal and Kingston, 1997).

Howarth, R. G., '"Felicity" in Traherne', *Notes and Queries* 193 (1948), 249–50.

Hulme, T. E., 'Romanticism and Classicism', in *Speculations: Essays on Humanism and the Philosophy of Art*, ed. Herbert Read (London, 1936), pp. 111–40.

Husain, Itrat, 'Thomas Traherne, The Mystical Philosopher', in *The Mystical Element in the Metaphysical Poets of the Seventeenth Century* (London and Edinburgh, 1948), pp. 264–300.

Hutton, Sarah, 'Platonism in Some Metaphysical Poets: Marvell, Vaughan and Traherne', in *Platonism and the English Imagination*, ed. Anna Baldwin and Sarah Hutton (Cambridge, 1994), pp. 163–77.

Inge, Denise, *Happiness and Holiness: Thomas Traherne and His Writings* (Norwich, 2008).

—— *Wanting like a God: Desire and Freedom in Thomas Traherne* (London, 2009)

—— and Calum MacFarlane, 'Seeds of Eternity: A New Traherne Manuscript', *TLS* (2 June 2000), 14.

Jacob, Margaret C., 'Millenarianism and Science in the Late Seventeenth Century', *Journal of the History of Ideas* 37 (1976), 335–41.

Jeffrey, David L., *A Dictionary of Biblical Tradition in English Literature* (Grand Rapids, 1992).

Johnston, Carol Ann, 'Heavenly Perspectives, Mirrors of Eternity: Thomas Traherne's Yearning Subject', *Criticism* 43.4 (2001), 377–405.

Jones, Rufus M., *Spiritual Reformers in the Sixteenth and Seventeenth Centuries* (London, 1914).

Jones, Susan E., 'Fighting Words: Clashes of Discourse in Three Seventeenth-Century Anglican Writers: Henry Vaughan, Jeremy Taylor, and Thomas Traherne', Ph.D. thesis, University of Florida (1997).

Jordan, Richard Douglas, *The Temple of Eternity: Thomas Traherne's Philosophy of Time* (Port Washington, 1972).

—— 'Thomas Traherne and the Art of Meditation', *Journal of the History of Ideas*, 46 (July 1985), 381–403.

Keeble, N. H., *The Literary Culture of Nonconformity in Later Seventeenth-Century England* (Leicester, 1987).

Kershaw, Alison, 'The Poetic of the Cosmic Christ in Thomas Traherne's *The Kingdom of God*', Ph.D. thesis, University of Western Australia (2005).

King, Ursula, *Christ in All Things: Exploring Spirituality with Teilhard De Chardin*, Bampton Lectures 1996 (London, 1997).

Knoppers, Laura Lunger, *Constructing Cromwell: Ceremony, Portrait, and Print 1645–1661* (Cambridge, 2000).

Korshin, Paul J., 'The Development of Abstracted Typology in England, 1650–1820', in *Literary Uses of Typology from the Late Middle Ages to the Present*, ed. Earl Miner (Princeton, 1979), pp. 147–203.

Koshi, Tomohiko, 'The Rhetoric of Instruction, and Manuscript and Print Culture in the Devotional Works of Thomas Traherne', Ph.D. thesis, University of Reading (2004).

Koyré, Alexander, *From a Closed World to the Infinite Universe* (Baltimore, 1957).

Kuchar, Gary, *Divine Subjection: The Rhetoric of Sacramental Devotion in Early Modern England* (Pittsburgh, 2005).

—— '"Organs of thy Praise": The Function and Rhetoric of the Body in Thomas Traherne', in *Religion in the Age of Reason: A Transatlantic Study of the Long Eighteenth Century*, ed. Kathryn Duncan (New York, 2009), pp. 59–81.

—— 'Traherne's Specters: Self-Consciousness and its Others', in *Re-Reading Thomas Traherne*, ed. Jacob Blevins (Tempe, 2007), pp. 184–90.

Laam, Kevin, 'Thomas Traherne, Richard Allestree, and the Ethics of Appropriation', in *Re-Reading Thomas Traherne*, ed. Jacob Blevins (Tempe, 2007), pp. 37–64.

Lane, Belden C., 'Thomas Traherne and the Awakening of Want', *Anglican Theological Review* 81.4 (Autumn 1999), 651–64.

Lehrs, Ernst, *Der Rosenkreuzerische Impuls im Leben und Werk von Joachim Jundius und Thomas Traherne* (Stuttgart, 1962).

Leishman, J. B., *The Metaphysical Poets: Donne, Herbert, Vaughan, Traherne* (Oxford, 1934).

Lewalski, Barbara K., *Protestant Poetics and the Seventeenth-Century Religious Lyric* (Princeton, 1979).

Lobsien, Verena Olejniczak, *Transparency and Dissimulation: Configurations of Neoplatonism in Early Modern English Literature* (Berlin, 2010).

Lock, Walter, 'An English Mystic', *Constructive Quarterly* 1 (1913), 826–36.

London, William, *A Catalogue of the Most Vendible Books in England* (1657, 1658, 1660), ed. D.F. Foxon, facsimile edn, English Bibliographical Studies (London, 1965).

Love, Harold, *Scribal Publication in Seventeenth-Century England* (Oxford, 1993).

Low, Anthony, 'Thomas Traherne: Mystical Hedonist', *Love's Architecture: Devotional Modes in Seventeenth-Century English Poetry* (New York, 1978), pp. 259–93.

Lyons, J. A., *The Cosmic Christ in Origen and Teilhard De Chardin: A Comparative Study* (Oxford, 1982).

MacClintock, W. D., 'A Re-Discovered Poet', *Dial* 34 (1903), 395–8.

Maitland, Peter Kennedy, 'Thomas Traherne's Path to Felicity: The Missing Christ', M.A. thesis, Carleton University (1994).

Marcus, Leah, *Childhood and Cultural Despair: A Theme and Variations in Seventeenth-Century Literature* (Pittsburgh, 1978).

Marks, Carol L., 'Studies in the Reading of Thomas Traherne', unpublished B. Litt. thesis, University of Oxford (1962).

—— 'Thomas Traherne and Cambridge Platonism', *PMLA* 81 (1966), 521–34.

—— 'Thomas Traherne and Hermes Trismegistus', *Renaissance News* 19.2 (1966), 118–31.

—— 'Thomas Traherne's Commonplace Book', *Papers of the Bibliographical Society of America* 58 (1964), 458–65.

—— 'Thomas Traherne's Early Studies', *Papers of the Bibliographical Society of America* 62 (1968), 511–36.

—— 'Traherne's Church's Year-Book', *Papers of the Bibliographical Society of America* 60 (1966), 31–72.

Marshall, William H., 'Thomas Traherne and the Doctrine of Original Sin', *Modern Language Notes* 73.3 (1958), 161–5.

Martz, Louis L., *The Paradise Within: Studies in Vaughan, Traherne, and Milton* (New Haven, 1964).

Matar, Nabil, 'The Anglican Eschatology of Thomas Traherne', *Anglican Theological Review* 74 (1992), 289–303.

—— 'Mysticism and Sectarianism in Mid-17th Century England', *Studia Mystica* 11.1 (1988), 55–65.

—— 'A Note on Thomas Traherne and the Quakers', *Notes and Queries* 226 (1981), 46–7.

—— 'The Political Views of Thomas Traherne', *The Huntington Library Quarterly* 57 (1994), 241–53.

—— 'Prophetic Traherne: "A Thanksgiving and Prayer for the Nation"', *Journal of English and Germanic Philology* 81.1 (1982), 16–29.

—— 'Thomas Traherne's Solar Mysticism', *Studia Mystica* 7.3 (1984), 52–63.

Maule, Jeremy, 'Five New Traherne Works: The Lambeth Manuscript', unpublished paper, delivered at the Thomas Traherne Conference, Brasenose College, Oxford, 30 July 1997.

—— *Traherne and the Restlessness of God: The New Lambeth Discoveries* [audiotape] (Temenos Academy, 1998).

McAdoo, Henry R., *The Spirit of Anglicanism: A Survey of Anglican Theological Method in the Seventeenth Century* (London, 1965).

McColley, Diane Kelsey, *Poetry and Ecology in the Age of Milton and Marvell* (Aldershot, 2007).

McFarland Ronald E., 'Thomas Traherne's Thanksgivings and the Theology of Optimism', *Enlightenment Essays* 4.1 (1973), 3–14.

Miller, Justin, 'Love and Pain in the Poet of Felicity', *Historical Magazine of the Protestant Episcopal Church* 49.3 (September 1980), 209–20.

Mintz, Samuel I., *The Hunting of Leviathan: Seventeenth-Century Reactions to the Materialism and Moral Philosophy of Thomas Hobbes* (Cambridge, 1969).

Mooney, Christopher F., *Teilhard De Chardin and the Mystery of Christ* (London, 1966).

Murphy, Kathryn, '"Aves Quaedam Macedonicae": Misreading Aristotle in Francis Bacon, Robert Burton, Thomas Browne and Thomas Traherne', Ph.D. thesis, University of Oxford (2009).

—— 'Thomas Traherne, Thomas Hobbes, and the Rhetoric of Realism', *The Seventeenth Century* 28.4 (2013), 419–39.

Mussell, Gordon, *English Spirituality: From Earliest Times to 1700* (London, 2001).

Nancy, Jean-Luc, 'On the Soul', in *Corpus*, trans. Richard A. Rand (New York, 2008), pp. 122–35.

Newey, Edmund, '"God Made Man Greater When He Made Him Less": Traherne's Iconic Child', *Literature and Theology* 24.3 (2010), 227–41.

Nicolson, Marjorie Hope, *The Breaking of the Circle: Studies in the Effect of The 'New Science' Upon Seventeenth-Century Poetry*, revised edn (New York, 1960).

Norford, Don Parry, 'Microcosm and Macrocosm in Seventeenth-Century Literature', *Journal of the History of Ideas* 38.3 (1977), 409–28.

Ocker, Christopher, *Biblical Poetics Before Humanism and Reformation* (Cambridge, 2002).

Osborn, James M., 'A New Traherne Manuscript', *TLS* (8 October 1964), 928.

Osmond, Percy, *The Mystical Poets of the English Church* (New York, 1919).

Owen, Catherine, 'The Authorship of the "Meditations on the Six Days of Creation" and the "Meditations and Devotions on the Life of Christ"', *Modern Language Review* 56 (1961), 1–12.

Parry, Graham, *Seventeenth-Century Poetry: The Social Context* (London, 1985).

Pasnau, Robert, *Metaphysical Themes 1274–1671* (Oxford, 2011).

Plotz, Judith, *Romanticism and the Vocation of Childhood* (New York, 2001).

Ponsford, Michael, 'The Poetry of Thomas Traherne in Relation to the Thought and Poetics of His Period', Ph.D. thesis, Newcastle Upon Tyne University (1984).

—— 'Traherne's Apostasy', *Durham University Journal* 76 (1984), 177–85.

Poulet, Georges, *The Metamorphoses of the Circle* (Baltimore, 1966).

Pritchard, Allan, 'Traherne's *Commentaries of Heaven* (With Selections from the Manuscript)', *University of Toronto Quarterly* 53 (1983), 1–35.

Quiller-Couch, Arthur, *Felicities of Thomas Traherne* (London, 1934).

Rambuss, Richard, *Closet Devotions* (Durham, 1998).

Richardson, Alan, *Literature, Education and Romanticism* (Cambridge, 1994).

Rivers, Isabel, *Classical and Christian Ideas in English Renaissance Poetry*, 2nd edn (London, 1994).

—— *Reason, Grace and Sentiment: A Study of the Language of Religion and Ethics in England 1660–1780*, 2 vols (Cambridge, 1991, 2000).

Robinson, Henry H., *Innocence, Knowledge and the Construction of Childhood* (Abingdon, 2013).

Rose, Elliot, 'A New Traherne Manuscript', *TLS* (19 March 1982), 324.

Ross, Janice C.B., 'The Placing of Thomas Traherne: A Study of the Several Seventeenth-Century Contexts of his Thought and Style', Ph.D. thesis, University of Cambridge (1983).

Ross, Malcolm Mackenzie, *Poetry and Dogma: The Transfiguration of Eucharistic Symbols in Seventeenth Century English Poetry* (New Brunswick, 1954).

Russell, Angela, 'The Life of Thomas Traherne', *Review of English Studies* 6.21 (1955), 34–43.

Salter, Keith William, *Thomas Traherne. Mystic and Poet* (London, 1964).

—— 'Thomas Traherne and a Romantic Heresy', *Notes and Queries* 200 (1955), 153–6.

Sandbank, S., 'Thomas Traherne on the Place of Man in the Universe', in *Studies in English Language and Literature*, ed. Alice Shalvi and A. A. Mendilow (Jerusalem, 1966), pp. 121–36.

Sauls, Richard Lynn, 'Traherne's Hand in the Credenhill Records', *The Library* 24 (1969), 50.

Sawday, Jonathan, *The Body Emblazoned: Dissection and the Human Body in Renaissance Culture* (London, 1995).

Schoenfeldt, Michael, '"That Spectacle of Too Much Weight": The Poetics of Sacrifice in Donne, Herbert and Milton', in *Seventeenth-Century British Poetry, 1603–1660*, ed. John P. Rumrich and Gregory Chaplin (New York, 2006), pp. 890–907.

Seelig, Sharon Cadman, *The Shadow of Eternity: Belief and Structure in Herbert, Vaughan, and Traherne* (Louisville, 1981).

Seetaraman, M. V., 'The Way of Felicity in Thomas Traherne's "*Centuries*" and "The Poems"', in *Critical Essays on English Literature*, ed. V. S. Seturaman (Bombay, 1965), pp. 81–104.

Selkin, Carl M., 'The Language of Vision: Traherne's Cataloguing Style', *English Literary Renaissance* 6 (1976), 92–104.

Sherer, Gertrude Roberts, 'More and Traherne', *Modern Language Notes* 34.1 (1919), 49–50.

Sherrington, Alison, *Mystical Symbolism in the Poetry of Thomas Traherne* (St Lucia, Queensland, 1970).

Sicherman, Carol Marks, 'Traherne's Ficino Notebook', *Papers of the Bibliographical Society of America* 63 (1969), 73–81.

Sittler, Joseph A., 'Called to Unity', *The Ecumenical Review* 14 (1961–62), 177–87.

Skeen, James, 'Discovering Human Happiness: Choice Theory Psychology, Aristotelian Contemplation, and Traherne's Felicity', *Quodlibet Journal* 5.2–3 (2003), <http://www.quodlibet.net/articles/skeen-choice.html>.

Smith, Julia J., 'Attitudes towards Conformity and Nonconformity in Thomas Traherne', *Bunyan Studies* 1.1 (1988), 26–35.

—— 'The Ceremonial Law: A New Work', *PN Review* 25 (November/December 1998), 22–8.

—— 'Hopton [née Harvey], Susanna (1627–1709)', *ODNB*.

—— 'Thomas Traherne and the Restoration', *The Seventeenth Century* 3.2 (1988), 203–22.

—— 'Tombes, John', *ODNB*.

—— 'Traherne, Thomas (c.1637–1674)', *ODNB*.

—— and Laetitia Yeandle, '"Felicity disguised in fiery Words": Genesis and Exodus in a Newly Discovered Poem by Thomas Traherne', *TLS* (7 November 1997), 17.

Smith, Nigel, *Perfection Proclaimed: Language and Literature in English Radical Religion, 1640–1660* (Oxford, 1989).

Sommerville, Charles John, *The Rise and Fall of Childhood* (London, 1982).

Spinks, Brian D., *Reformation and Modern Rituals and Theologies of Baptism: From Luther to Contemporary Practices* (Aldershot, 2006).

Spraggon, Julie, *Puritan Iconoclasm during the English Civil War* (Woodbridge, 2003).

Spurgeon, Caroline F. E., *Mysticism in English Literature* (Cambridge, 1913).

Spurr, Barry, 'Felicity Incarnate: Rediscovering Thomas Traherne', in *Discovering and (Re)covering the Seventeenth Century Religious Lyric*, ed. Eugene R. Cunnar and Jeffrey Johnson (Pittsburgh, 2001), 273–89.

Spurr, John, *The Restoration Church of England, 1646–89* (New Haven, 1991).

Steadman, J., 'Felicity and End in Renaissance Epic and Ethics', *Journal of the History of Ideas* 23.1 (1962), 117–32.

Stewart, Stanley, *The Expanded Voice: The Art of Thomas Traherne* (San Marino, 1970).

Stewart, Susan, *Poetry and the Fate of the Senses* (Chicago, 2002).

Teilhard de Chardin, Pierre, 'Cosmic Life', in *Writings in Time of War* (London, 1968).

—— *Hymn of the Universe* (London, 1965).

—— *Le Milieu Divin: An Essay on the Interior Life* (London, 1960).

—— and Maurice Blondel, *Correspondence: Pierre Teilhard De Chardin, Maurice Blondel*, ed. Henri de Lubac (New York, 1967).

Thomas, Edward, *Richard Jefferies*, intro. Roland Gant (London, 1978).

'Thomas Traherne 1637–74', in *The Cambridge Guide to Literature in English*, ed. Dominic Head, 3rd edn (Cambridge, 2006).

'Thomas Traherne (1637–74)', in *The Concise Oxford Companion to English Literature*, ed. Dinah Birch and Katy Hooper, 4th edn (Oxford, 2012).

'Thomas Traherne (1637–74)', in *The Oxford Companion to British History*, ed. John Cannon (Oxford, 2009).

'Thomas Traherne (1637–74)', in *The Oxford Companion to English Literature*, ed. Dinah Birch, 7th edn (Oxford, 2009).

Thompson, Elbert N. S., 'Mysticism in Seventeenth-Century English Literature', *Studies in Philology* 18.2 (1921), 170–231.

—— 'The Philosophy of Thomas Traherne', *Philological Quarterly* (1929), 97–112.

Towers, Francis, 'Thomas Traherne: His Outlook on Life', *The Nineteenth Century* 87 (1920), 1024–30.

Underhill, Evelyn, *The Mystics of the Church* (London, 1925).

Wade, Gladys I., *Thomas Traherne: A Critical Biography* (Princeton, 1946).

—— 'Thomas Traherne as "Divine Philosopher"', *Hibbert Journal* 32 (1934), 400–8.

—— 'Traherne and the Spiritual Value of Nature Study', *London Quarterly and Holborn Review* 159 (1934), 243–5.

Walker, D. P., 'Medical Spirits in Philosophy and Theology from Ficino to Newton', in *Arts du Spectable et Histoire des idées* (Tours, 1984), pp. 287–300.

Watson, Robert N., *Back to Nature: The Green and the Real in the Late Renaissance* (Philadelphia, 2006).

Watt, Tessa, *Cheap Print and Popular Piety, 1550–1640* (Cambridge, 1991).

Webber, Joan, *The Eloquent 'I': Style and Self in Seventeenth-Century Prose* (Madison, 1968).

Westfall, Richard S., *Science and Religion in Seventeenth-Century England* (New Haven, 1970).

White, Helen C., *The Metaphysical Poets: A Study in Religious Experience* (New York, 1936).

Willcox, Louise Collier, 'A Joyous Mystic', *The North American Review* 193.667 (1911), 893–904.

Willy, Margaret, 'Thomas Traherne: "Felicity's Perfect Lover"', *English* 12 (Autumn 1959), 210–15.

—— *Three Metaphysical Poets* (London, 1961).

Wöhrer, Franz K., 'The Doctrine of Original Sin and the Idea of Man's Perinatal Intimations of the Divine in the Work of Thomas Traherne', *Yearbook of Studies in English Language and Literature* 1982/3 (Vienna, 1984).

—— *Thomas Traherne: The Growth of a Mystic's Mind: A Study of the Evolution and the Phenomenology of Traherne's Mystical Consciousness*, Salzburg Studies in English Literature (Salzburg, 1982).

Wolf, William J., 'The Spirituality of Thomas Traherne', in *Anglican Spirituality*, ed. William J. Wolf (Wilton, CT, 1982), pp. 49–68.

Wright, Steven, 'Wilson, Thomas (1562/3–1622)', *ODNB*.

Zhelezcheva, Tanya, 'The Poetics of the Incomplete in the Works of Thomas Traherne (ca. 1638–1674)', Ph.D. thesis, Northeastern University (2011).

Zwicker, Steven N., 'Politics and Panegyric: The Figural Mode from Marvell to Pope', in *Literary Uses of Typology from the Late Middle Ages to the Present*, ed. Earl Miner (Princeton, 1977), pp. 115–46.

INDEX

Abraham: 109, 179
Accommodation (in language): 25, 70, 72, 76, 79
Act (Action, Activity): 6, 20, 24, 26–7, 33, 35, 43–4, 57–8, 80–2, 88–9, 109, 117, 152, 155, 167–71, 180–4, 186
Adam: xiii, 18, 40, 84, 132, 134, 141–2, 170, 172–3, 176, 179, 185–6, 189
Agency: 20, 131, 136, 151–2, 168
Ainsworth, Henry: 183, 190–1
Allegory: 3, 92, 128, 137–8, 140–1, 149
Allestree, Richard: 180–1
   The Whole Duty of Man: 180
Allighieri, Dante: 89–90
'All in All': 25, 70, 78, 81, 91, 102, 103
'All Things' (*see also* Things): 1–2, 4, 7, 9, 16, 18, 20, 25, 45–6, 49, 57–8, 60–1, 63–5, 69–70, 75–6, 79–81, 85, 86, 89, 95–99, 101–3, 132, 154–56, 165, 169
Anabaptist: 8, 187
Anatomy: 32, 75, 87
Andrewes, Lancelot: 182–3, 188
Angels: 2, 23, 43, 69, 82, 93, 171, 186
Annotations: 17, 112
Aquinas, Thomas (*see also* Thomism): 182, 188
Aristotle (Aristotelianism): 6–8, 13, 16, 22–3, 25, 49–50, 52–9, 65, 67, 87, 156, 166, 195
   Categories: 25, 53–4, 56–7
   De Anima: 6, 156
   Metaphysics: 57
Arminianism: 5, 152
Atheism: 162, 165
Assurance (*see also* Means): 27, 79, 152, 166, 169
Atom (Atomism): xix, 2, 7–9, 13, 18, 21, 25, 69–83, 85, 87, 94, 99, 103, 162, 165

Atonement: 8, 100, 151
Augustine of Hippo: 6, 22–3, 63, 65, 86, 137–9, 148, 192
Avarice (see Covetousness, Desire, Insatiability, Possession): 19, 170

Bachelard, Gaston: 41
Bacon, Francis (*see also* Experimentalism): xix, 8, 13, 16, 22, 25, 49, 55–60, 62–3, 65, 68
   De Dignitate et Augmentis Scientiarum: 25, 55, 62
   Novum Organum: 55–6
   Of the Advancement and Proficience of Learning: 56, 59, 62–3
Bakhtin, Mikhail: 196
Barrow, Isaac: 96, 98–9, 158, 164, 169–70
Baxter, Richard: 4, 135, 172, 189
Birchley, William: 191
Blake, William: xiii, 84, 173–5, 193
Body: 5–6, 15–16, 24, 31–47, 51, 69, 71, 75–7, 85–6, 98, 100–1, 110, 132–4, 142, 184, 189, 191, 195
Bonaventure: 23
Book of Common Prayer, The: 184–5, 188–9
Borders (Boundaries): 14, 17–18, 20–1, 24, 33, 41, 44–6, 132–3, 142
Boyle, Robert: 99, 129
Brasenose College: 10, 52, 55, 135–6, 156
Bridgeman, Orlando: 149
Browne, Thomas: 4, 16
Buddhism: 14
Burnet, Gilbert: 163
Burning bush, the: 26, 143, 146–8, 153
Burton, Robert: 16, 158

Cain and Abel: 141–3, 177–9, 192
Calvin, John (for Calvinist, *see* Reformed): 123, 126–8, 133, 137, 188

Capacity: 8, 20–1, 42, 46, 70, 76, 78, 80–1, 89, 101, 132–3, 142
Catalogue: 48, 61, 85, 91–3, 98, 190
Catholicism: 7, 108, 119, 136–7, 145, 148, 176
Celestial Stranger: 8, 25, 85, 89–94, 95, 102–3
Centre: 8, 18–19, 78–9, 83, 90, 92–6, 114
Chalcidius: 6
Charles II: 136, 140, 149
Charron, Pierre: 181–2
Child (Childhood, Infancy, Infant): xiii–iv, xvi, 10, 15, 20, 26–7, 33, 38, 66, 114, 151, 170, 172–7, 180, 187–9, 192, 193, 195
Christ (Christology; *see also* Incarnation): 18, 20, 25–7, 80, 84–103, 119, 123, 128, 133–4, 137, 140–1, 143, 148, 177–80, 183, 186–8, 190, 192, 195
    Cosmic: 25, 84–103, 178
    Skin of: 24, 36–8
Church, the (*see also* National church): 12, 26, 101, 108, 111, 119–21, 125–26, 130, 134–6, 139, 143, 145–50, 153, 178, 189–90, 195
Circle (*see* Sphere): 19, 93–4, 110, 169
Civil War: 131, 140, 144–5
Cockburn, John: 158, 167–8
Cognition: 52, 54, 63
Coke, Zachary: 74–5
Coles, Elisha: 71, 74–5
Communication (*see also* Relation, between matter and spirit): 91, 100, 162, 171
Community (Society): 5, 26, 76, 110, 119, 151, 195
Copernicus: 3–4, 59
Corye, John: 75
Cosmology: 18, 25, 85, 87, 93
Covetousness (*see also* Desire, Insatiability, Possession): 19–20
Crakanthorpe, Richard: 52–3
Crashaw, Richard: 11, 24, 36
Creation (Creator): 3, 26, 64, 71, 73, 78, 85, 87, 92–3, 97–102, 141, 151, 170, 176, 194
Credenhill: 10, 12, 111, 135

Crispe, Tobias: 97, 100
Cromwell, Oliver: 140, 143–6, 149, 151
Crowne, John: 81
Cudworth, Ralph: 87, 117, 193
Culverwel, Nathaniel: 167–8

David (King): 8, 126, 140, 184
Davies, John (of Hereford): 37, 39
Digges, Thomas: 90
Denise (St): 6
Descartes, René: 59
Desire (*see also* Covetousness, Insatiability): xx, 5, 18–20, 23, 33, 38, 50–1, 89, 91, 103, 114, 116, 129, 139, 156, 162, 169
Devotion: 5, 8–9, 12, 17, 19, 23–7, 36–7, 60, 91, 109, 111, 120, 157–9, 170, 172–3, 176–7, 183–5, 189–92
Dictionaries: 8, 27, 71, 143, 176, 183
Didacticism: 10, 24, 26, 31, 74, 107, 109–11, 129, 161
Diggers, the: 145
Dobell, Bertram: 10–11, 40–1, 84, 107, 111–12, 114, 117, 134, 152, 154, 173, 193, 196
Donne, John: 11, 33, 100–1, 194
Dryden, John: 129
Dualism (Non-Dualism): 15–16, 99

Ecstasy: 3, 45, 82, 110–11, 114
Eden (*see also* Paradise): xiii–iv, 22, 107, 113–15, 134, 174, 176, 186, 189
Ego (*see also* Inwardness, Retirement, Self): 14, 43–4
Election (The Elect): 5, 80, 187
Elim: 109, 114–19, 127
Emerson, Ralph Waldo: 20, 193
Empiricism: 16
Enlightenment (*see also* Romanticism): 15, 22
Epicureanism (Epicurus): 7, 74–5, 79, 81, 162
Eschatology: 12, 22–3
Essence (*see also* Quidditie): 9, 45–6, 73, 75–80, 82, 86, 88, 132, 182
Eternity (*see also* Time): 19, 21, 23, 26, 33, 69, 78–9, 83, 90, 154, 170–1, 179
Ethics: 24, 27, 111, 156, 160, 173, 176, 180–3, 186, 191

Eucharist (*see also* Sacrament): 84, 184
Eusebius of Caesarea: 144
Eustache de Saint-Paul: 160
Eve: 132, 177
Evelyn, John: 185–6
Evil: 23, 163–4, 182
Experimentalism (*see also* Bacon,
    Francis): 13, 22, 25

Fall, the: 19, 140–1, 169–70, 177
Featley, Daniel: 190–1
Felicity (Happiness): xiii–xiv, 5, 7, 9,
    14–15, 19, 21–7, 58, 69, 74, 78, 80,
    82, 100, 110, 114, 116, 121, 133,
    139, 154–71, 181, 193, 195
Fifth Monarchism: 145
Freedom (Liberty): 5, 8, 19–20, 42, 122,
    145, 176
Free will: 5, 152
Friendship: 6, 8, 109–11, 165, 186
Fuller, Thomas: 78–9

Gale, Theophilus: 7–8, 15, 54, 100
Gell, Robert: 96, 101–2
Goodwin, John: 151–2
Goodwin, Thomas: 144
Grace: 8, 25, 27, 43, 61, 69, 101, 108,
    121–3, 152, 175, 177–8, 188
Gregory of Nyssa: 6, 19, 143

Hall, Joseph: 74, 109, 165, 183–4
Hammond, Henry: 5, 126
Happiness (*see* Felicity)
Harley, Robert: 136
Harriot, Thomas: 71–3, 80, 82–3
Herbert, George: 9, 11, 24, 37–8, 120–1,
    136, 194
Hereford (Herefordshire): xix, 10, 111,
    135–6, 187
Hermeticism (Hermetism, *see also*
    Trismegistus, Hermes): 17, 26, 71,
    83, 94, 190
Hieroglyphics: 123, 140–1, 147–8
Hobbes, Thomas: xix, 16, 27, 55, 57,
    162–8
    Leviathan: 162–8
Holiness: 14, 21, 23–4, 27, 86, 103, 157,
    159–60, 173, 182, 192
Holy Spirit: 138, 190–1

Hooke, Robert: 60
    Micrographia: 60
Hooker, Richard: 88
Hopton, Susanna: ix, 111–12
Huguenots, the: 146, 148
Humanism: 13, 20, 22, 156, 180
Humility: 72, 74–5, 80, 82–3
Hypostasis: 101

Iconoclasm: 136, 153
Imagination: 19, 67, 94, 107, 109,
    116–17, 126, 128–9, 136, 145
Immanence (*see also* Transcendence): 41,
    86–7, 92, 97–8
Incarnation: 8, 15, 18, 25–6, 89–103, 121,
    151, 195
Indivisibility: 19, 69, 71, 73, 75, 77–9, 81
Ineffability: 78
Infant, Infancy (see Child)
Infinity: 4, 8, 14, 18–21, 23, 25–6, 36,
    39–47, 50–1, 58, 60, 64, 76, 78, 80,
    83, 88–96, 99, 101, 116, 129, 162,
    169–71
Inge, Denise: 4–5, 23, 114, 175, 179
Innocence: xiii–xvi, 5, 21, 24, 27, 40–1,
    110, 116, 134, 141, 166, 170,
    172–92, 195
Insatiability (*see also* Covetousness,
    Desire, Possession): 8, 18, 25, 50–1,
    70, 80–1, 91, 103
Interregnum: 131, 135, 143
Intuition: 20, 73, 78–9
'Inward Ey', the: 23, 117
Inwardness: (*see also* Ego, Retirement,
    Self) 34–5, 40, 44, 47
Israel, the Israelites: 3, 26, 107–9,
    112–15, 118–29, 131–2, 140, 144–5,
    148, 178

Jacomb, Thomas: 170
Jackson, Thomas: 15, 98,
Jerome (St): 6
Josephus: 142
Julian of Norwich: 16, 78
Justin Martyr: 6

Kepler, Johannes: 71–3, 82, 94
Knowledge, attitudes toward: 2, 4, 8, 16,
    70–4, 78, 82, 97, 117, 156–60, 184

Lactantius: 184
Latitudinarianism: 11–12, 135, 166
Levellers, the: 20
Liberty (*see* Freedom)
Lists (*see* Catalogues)
Lockyer, Nicholas: 97–98
Logic: 52–7, 156, 166, 169
Logos (*see also* Word): 92, 94–6, 99, 138,
    179
Lucretius: 9, 74, 77, 83
Luther, Martin: 98, 108, 123, 133, 137–8,
    187–8, 192
Lyric: 1, 9, 24, 37, 131, 134, 139–42,
    150–2, 186

Mackenzie, George: 185–6
Macrocosm: 19, 76
Manna: 107, 116, 118–19, 124
Manton, Thomas: 96, 98–9
Marvell, Andrew: xx,
Materialism (materialist, materialistic):
    xvi, 5, 81, 117, 162, 164, 165, 166
Material philosophy: 18, 70, 71
Material spirits: 18, 76–7, 99
Material World: 13, 15–16, 25, 64, 97, 99
Mathematics: 71, 164
Matter: 3, 8, 14–17, 24, 33, 45, 71, 73, 76,
    77, 79, 81, 82, 87, 90, 99, 100, 103,
    109, 126
Maule, Jeremy: xvii, 5, 87–8, 91, 134, 153
Means (*see also* Assurance): 24, 25, 32,
    35, 43, 69, 70, 71, 73, 74, 79–80,
    100, 108, 129, 133, 139, 141, 151,
    169, 186, 188
Mechanical Philosophy: 87,
Meditation: 4, 6, 7, 10, 26, 27, 34, 37, 43,
    44, 46, 61–2, 64, 69, 71, 75, 78, 108,
    109, 117, 126, 129, 133, 157, 159,
    170, 172, 175, 183, 185, 186, 189,
    191, 192, 193, 195–6
Meister Eckhart: 16,
Metaphysics: 25, 57, 88, 100, 156
Metaphysical Poetry: xiv, 11, 12, 94, 193
Microscope: 60, 64, 87, 96
Millenarianism: 88, 139, 140,
Milton, John: xx, 9, 40, 108, 120, 122–4,
    132–3, 138, 145, 147, 150, 152
    De Doctrina Christiana: 120, 122–3

'On the Late Massacre in Piedmont':
    147
Paradise Lost: 40, 108, 122, 124, 132,
    166
*The Ready and Easy Way to Establish a
    Free Commonwealth*: 145
Mind: 6, 16, 23, 25, 33, 45, 53, 55, 65, 66,
    67, 68, 73, 78, 101, 102, 117, 129,
    133, 161–6, 169, 170, 184
Moore, John: 143
More, Henry: 87, 99, 101, 159, 164, 166,
    168, 193
Moses: 26, 103, 108–9, 113, 118, 120–2,
    124–8, 137, 140, 143–7, 149
Mysticism: 1, 11, 14, 15, 23, 168, 190,
    194
    Medieval: 14, 23
    Nature (*see also* Natural Philosophy,
        Nature, Physico-Theology): 15, 25,
        26, 84

Naked (nakedness): 17, 25, 32, 45–7, 58,
    67, 112, 177, 178
Nancy, Jean-Luc: 24, 35–6, 39–40, 42–4,
    46–7
Narrative (*see also* Story): 26, 109, 112–5,
    118–9, 122, 126–7, 131, 133, 137,
    140, 143–6, 150, 152–3
National Church (*see also* Church, the):
    12, 121, 130, 134, 136, 139, 143,
    145, 148–50, 189–90
Nature (*see also* Mysticism (Nature),
    Natural Philosophy, Physico-
    Theology): 5, 15, 19, 20, 25, 35, 42,
    54, 55, 56, 58–9, 61, 63–5, 71–4,
    77–8, 80, 82–3, 88, 93, 98, 99, 101,
    102, 103, 113, 118, 141, 155, 156,
    164, 165, 166; 168–9, 189, 191, 193
Natural philosophy: 2, 25, 59, 70, 87, 195
Nicholas of Cusa: 94
Nominalism: 56–7

Omnipresence: 78, 90, 96, 101–2, 170
Ontology: 25, 52, 54, 56–7, 59, 65
Origen: 144
Original sin: 174, 180, 187
Ornament (physical and poetic): 32, 38,
    60

Oxford: 10, 15, 52, 55, 101, 135–6, 144, 155, 195

Pantheism: 15, 25,
Paradise (*see also* Eden): 4, 22, 23, 40, 89, 92, 115, 132, 151, 173
Paradox: 9, 17, 35, 36, 37, 39, 42, 48, 49, 80, 82, 162, 164, 179–80
Patristics: 19, 85, 147, 184
Pelagius: 22, 174
Perkins, William: 108, 126, 152
Phillips, Edward: 71
Philo of Alexandria: 137, 141–2
Phoenix: 92–3
Physico-theology (*see also* Mysticism (Nature), Natural Philosophy, Nature): 87, 89
Plato: 6, 166,
Platonism: 12, 15, 18, 193
    Cambridge: 22, 117, 180, 195
    Christian: 12, 175
    Neo: 15, 22, 71, 88, 94, 114, 146, 164, 167, 168, 195
    Oxford: 15, 195
    Renaissance: 117
Plotinus: 6, 19
Politics: xvi, xvii, xviii, xix–xx, 1, 6–7, 12, 18, 26, 74, 86, 108, 127, 130–1, 139–40, 144–6, 153, 164, 178, 194
Poole, William: 126–7
Possession (*see also* Covetousness, Desire, Insatiability): 3, 20, 39, 81, 110, 142, 161, 162, 186
Poverty: 50, 75, 80
Presbyterianism: 135, 146, 147
Proclus: 6,
Providence: 63, 98, 113, 116, 119, 134, 143, 144, 178
Psychology: 14–15, 21–2, 38
Pythagoreanism: 13, 100

Quakerism: 12, 20, 145, 187
Quarles, Francis: 31–2, 35, 191
Quick, John: 147
Quidditie (*see also* Essence): 88–9

Radical religion: xix, 5, 10, 12, 14, 20, 26, 86, 131, 136, 138–40, 143, 145–6, 148–50, 152–3, 195
Ramism: 182

Ranters: 145, 151
Rationalism (*see also* Reason): 166–9
Realism: 16, 48–68, 100, 102
Reason (*see also* Rationalism): 27, 138, 157, 160, 165–9
Redemption (*see also* Salvation): 97, 121
Red Sea, the: 107–30, 146, 178
Reformed: 37, 79, 87, 101, 119, 123, 125, 146–7, 176, 180, 187
Regeneration: 152, 177, 183, 187–9, 191
Reification: 50, 57
Relation, between matter and spirit, parts and the whole (*see also* Communication): 14–18, 35–6, 39–40, 53, 58, 60–61, 63, 64, 65, 87, 152, 159
    Cosmic relation: 86
Republicanism: 146,
Restoration, the: xiv, xix, 12, 120, 135–6, 139–40, 143, 149–50, 175, 187
Retirement (*see also* Ego, Inwardness, Self): 5–6, 8, 23, 185–6
Rhetoric: 22, 32, 49, 51, 52, 65, 68, 70, 140, 146, 156, 62, 166, 167
Right Apprehension: 54, 65, 169, 171
Romanticism: 11, 27, 172–5, 193, 195
Royalism: 12, 127, 131, 136, 149, 178
Royal Society, the (*see also* Boyle, Robert): 2, 49, 60, 70

Sacrament (sacramental, sacramentalism, *see also* Eucharist): 15–16, 27, 69, 173, 176, 187–9, 192
Sacrifice: 10, 27, 37, 92, 93, 133, 134, 177–80, 184, 187, 192
Salvation (*see also* Redemption): 5, 10, 27, 36, 38, 121, 126, 139, 157, 158, 159, 169, 178, 180, 188
Sanderson, Robert: 5, 52, 53
Scholasticism (*see also* Aristotelianism): 13, 16, 22, 88, 94
Sectarianism (Sectarian, *see also* Radical Religion): 10, 27, 37, 120, 130–53, 178
Self (*see also* Ego, Inwardness, Retirement): 3, 6, 7, 8, 14, 16, 24, 26, 27, 34–40, 42–6, 57, 63, 64, 67–8, 71–2, 80–3, 92–4, 98, 100, 101, 103, 107, 110, 121, 125, 127, 132, 139, 140, 142, 155, 165, 179–81

'Self-authorizers': 151
Self-destructiveness: 163
Self-earned: 166
Self-examination: 134, 159
'Self-help': 157
Self-love: 138
Self-righteous: 163, 167
Senses: 38, 46, 54, 65–8, 86, 91, 101, 112, 117, 167
Sidney, Philip: 13,
Sin: 19, 38, 39, 66, 95, 97, 122, 124, 141, 166, 178–80
Skin (*see also* Christ; skin of): 24, 31–9, 42–7, 98
Society (*see* Community): xv, 5, 74, 76, 110, 151, 163, 195
Socinianism (Socinian): 8, 86, 187
Solitude (*see* Retirement): xiii, 5, 7, 50, 54, 110, 185–6
Soteriology (Soteriological, *see also* Redemption, Salvation): 179–80, 188
Soul: xiv, 3–6, 8, 9, 14, 16–20, 24–5, 31–3, 35–47, 59, 61, 63, 67, 69–71, 77, 80–83, 85, 87, 93, 99, 101, 107, 109–10, 113–15, 117, 119–20, 125, 128–9, 134, 140, 142, 154–6, 159–60, 162–3, 165–6, 168, 171, 175, 183, 186, 189–91, 195
South, Robert: 101
Sparke, Edward: 178, 190
Sparrow, Anthony: 184–5, 189
Sphere (*see also* Circle): 18–20, 26, 42, 89, 90, 93, 134, 169, 171, 173
Spirit: 14–18, 20–21, 24, 33, 36, 39, 41, 45–6, 76–8, 83, 84, 95, 99, 101, 103, 117–18, 122, 129, 131–2, 137–8, 146, 168, 181, 186, 190–1
Sterry, Peter: 146, 151, 191
Stillingfleet, Edward: 191–2
Story (*see also* Narrative): 9, 86, 99, 112, 131–2, 136, 140, 141–3, 145–6, 148, 155, 179, 192
Sublime: 20
Substance and Accident: 25, 45, 53–4, 56–60, 62, 66–8, 98, 103, 125, 138

Taylor, Edward: 42–3
Taylor, Jeremy: 13, 181

Tillotson, John: 181
Teilhard de Chardin: 25, 86, 90, 92, 94–5, 98, 100, 102
Things (*see also* 'All Things'): 13, 15, 17, 21, 25, 32, 40, 43, 45–6, 48–68, 72, 73, 75, 83, 88, 94, 99, 103, 113, 117, 123, 129, 138, 142, 146, 152, 154, 155, 163–5, 171, 181, 183, 186, 189
'miraculous things': 71–3, 83
Thomism (*see also* Aquinas, Thomas): 79
Time (*see also* Eternity): 1–2, 4, 6, 11–12, 19, 20, 22, 27, 53, 58, 69, 79, 84, 95, 108, 109, 116, 118, 132–3, 155, 171
Tombes, John: 187
Traherne, Philip: 111–12, 120, 154
Traherne, Thomas
    As mystic: xiii, 1, 11–12, 14–16, 21, 23, 25–6, 53, 78, 80, 82, 84, 86, 100, 175, 190, 193
    As poet: xiv, xix, 1, 8–13, 16, 19, 24, 26, 33, 34, 39, 41, 46, 48, 49, 51, 54, 61, 65, 67, 68, 70, 84, 89, 90, 91, 103, 120, 141, 142, 154, 155, 156, 175–9, 192, 193
    As priest/clergyman: 1, 6, 24, 27, 84, 135, 183–6, 192
    As philosopher: xvi, xviii, 2, 4, 9, 12, 15, 22, 24, 25–6, 40, 43, 49, 54, 57, 59–60, 68, 70–1, 73–4, 82, 84, 87, 142, 159, 161, 181, 194–5
    As teacher: 111, 155, 161–2, 170–1
    As theologian: xviii, xix, 1–5, 7–8, 10, 14–15, 18, 22, 24–6, 59–60, 68, 69–72, 74–5, 78–9, 81, 85–7, 91, 100, 112, 125–6, 131, 133, 135, 153, 175, 182, 187–8, 191, 193–6
    Works, Rediscoveries of: xiii–xv, 11, 17, 84, 193
    Centuries of Meditations: xiii–xv, xx, 2–5, 8, 10–11, 18–19, 23, 27, 38–9, 41, 49, 61, 64–5, 84–5, 89, 107, 109–11, 113–16, 118, 125, 129, 131–2, 134, 139–40–1, 150, 155–6, 161, 173–4, 181, 186, 193–5
    The Ceremonial Law: xvii, 5, 9, 10, 20, 23, 26–7, 107–29, 130–53, 177–80
    Christian Ethicks: xiii, xv, 10, 24, 27, 44, 54, 116, 119, 156–7, 160–1, 164–6, 168, 170, 180–5

Church's Year-Book: xv, 27, 111, 179, 185, 189–91

Commentaries of Heaven: xvi, 2, 4, 7–10, 16–18, 20, 27, 49–50, 54, 57, 60–1, 65, 69–70, 72, 75–80, 83, 86, 88, 103, 109, 116, 117, 155–7, 161–2, 165, 168–71, 184, 187, 189

Commonplace Book: xv, 2, 8, 61, 98, 99, 129

Dobell Poems: xiii, 5, 10–11, 32, 40, 41, 48, 84, 107, 112, 114, 117, 134, 152, 154, 173, 196

Early Notebook: xv, 5, 55, 62–3

Inducements to Retirednes: 5–6, 18, 23, 27, 110, 112, 161, 180, 183–6

The Kingdom of God: 2–5, 7–8, 18–19, 23, 25, 45–6, 49, 51, 59–61, 64, 69, 76–7, 82–3, 84–104, 169

Poems of Felicity: xiii, 5, 10, 21, 27, 40, 41, 48, 135, 151, 154

Seeds of Eternity: 5–6, 16, 18, 33, 156

Select Meditations: xvii, 1, 8, 10, 18, 26–7, 88, 92, 108–10, 117, 120–1, 123, 125, 129–31, 139, 149–50, 154, 161–2, 171, 180

A Sober View of Dr Twisses His Considerations: 5–6, 20, 27, 135, 187–9

Thanksgivings: xv, 10, 27, 51, 61–2, 65, 92, 154–6, 182–4

Transcendence (*see also* Immanence): 88, 108, 109, 114, 155, 162, 163, 165, 175

Treasure: 3, 4, 10, 20, 61, 89, 97, 100, 110, 114, 116, 141, 158, 171, 189

Typology: xix, 3, 9–10, 20, 26–7, 107–29, 130–1, 133–4, 136–45, 148, 150, 153, 177–8

Westminster Confession of Faith: 79

Whichcote, Benjamin: 180–1, 184, 193

White, Thomas: 61

Whitman, Walt: xiii, 84, 193

Wilderness: 3, 23, 107, 114–16, 118–19, 121, 124, 140, 144, 146

Wilson, Thomas: 27, 176–7, 183, 187, 191–2

Winthrop, John: 138–9, 145

Wisdom: 3, 60, 62–4, 80, 87, 92, 96–7, 101, 116, 121, 133 141, 149, 155, 168, 170, 171

Wither, George: 143–4

Word (*see also* Logos): 17, 34, 4, 45, 46, 53, 57, 62, 88, 91, 94–6, 99, 101, 103, 124, 138, 162, 169, 190, 192

Wordsworth, William: xiii, 84, 173–5, 193

Vanity: 24, 32

Vaughan, Henry: 11, 24, 174, 194

Vedic poetics: 14, 23

Veil: 69, 122, 137,

Virtue: 19–20, 23–4, 62, 66, 83, 100, 111, 122, 157, 160–7, 170, 180–2, 185–6, 188, 192

INDEX OF BIBLICAL REFERENCES

Genesis: 9, 107, 126, 131, 140, 141, 143,
   192
  1.26–7: 177
  2: 177
  20.5: 183
Exodus: 9, 107, 118, 125, 125, 131–2,
   136, 140, 143–6, 148, 150, 153, 177
  4.1–5: 127
  12.5–11: 178
  13–14: 112
  13.21–2: 113
  15.22–4, 27: 114, 115, 127
  16.2–3: 118
  17.8–16: 127, 128
  19.16: 124
  26: 137
Leviticus 1.14: 190
1 Kings 4.29: 62
Job: 177
Psalms: 8, 87, 93, 126, 183
  7:8: 177
  23: 127
  26: 183–4
  26.6, 11: 177, 183–4
  37.37: 182
  40: 191
  51.17: 184
  65: 93
  84: 183
  101.2: 192
Proverbs: 96
  4.23: 181
  8.22–3: 96
Ecclesiastes 12.1: 78

Song of Solomon 5.13, 6.2: 92
Isaiah 40.22: 93
Daniel 6.22: 177
Jonah: 137
Matthew
  16.18–19: 119
  19.23–4: 72
Mark 10.24–5: 72
Luke 18.24–5: 72
John: 96, 99
  1.1: 96
  1.4: 100
  8.56: 134
Romans
  7.24: 31
  16.25–7: 85
1 Corinthians 15.28: 103
2 Corinthians 3.6, 15–16: 137
Ephesians: 96
  1.9–10, 22–3: 103
  1.23: 20, 103
  3.9: 96
  4.9–10: 101–3
Colossians 95, 96
  1.15–19: 85, 95–8, 100
Hebrews
  1.1–3: 95
  11: 108
  11.3: 94
  11.13: 134
James 1.27: 184
1 Peter 3.10–13: 182
Revelations 3.20: 80

Studies in Renaissance Literature

Volume 1: *The Theology of John Donne*
Jeffrey Johnson

Volume 2: *Doctrine and Devotion in Seventeenth-Century Poetry*
Studies in Donne, Herbert, Crashaw and Vaughan
R. V. Young

Volume 3: *The Song of Songs in English Renaissance Literature*
Kisses of their Mouths
Noam Flinker

Volume 4: *King James I and the Religious Culture of England*
James Doelman

Volume 5: *Neo-historicism: Studies in Renaissance Literature,*
History and Politics
edited by Robin Headlam Wells, Glenn Burgess and Rowland Wymer

Volume 6: *The Uncertain World of* Samson Agonistes
John T. Shawcross

Volume 7: *Milton and the Terms of Liberty*
edited by Graham Parry and Joad Raymond

Volume 8: *George Sandys: Travel, Colonialism and Tolerance*
in the Seventeenth Century
James Ellison

Volume 9: *Shakespeare and Machiavelli*
John Roe

Volume 10: *John Donne's Professional Lives*
edited by David Colclough

Volume 11: *Chivalry and Romance in the English Renaissance*
Alex Davis

Volume 12: *Shakespearean Tragedy as Chivalric Romance:*
Rethinking Macbeth, Hamlet, Othello, and King Lear
Michael L. Hays

Volume 13: *John Donne and Conformity in Crisis in the Late Jacobean Pulpit*
Jeanne Shami

Volume 14: *A Pleasing Sinne:*
Drink and Conviviality in Seventeenth-Century England
Adam Smyth

Volume 15: *John Bunyan and the Language of Conviction*
Beth Lynch

Volume 16: *The Making of Restoration Poetry*
Paul Hammond

Volume 17: *Allegory, Space and the Material World in the Writings of Edmund Spenser*
Christopher Burlinson

Volume 18: *Self-Interpretation in* The Faerie Queene
Paul Suttie

Volume 19: *Devil Theatre: Demonic Possession and Exorcism in English Drama,
1558–1642*
Jan Frans van Dijkhuizen
Volume 20: *The Heroines of English Pastoral Romance*

Sue P. Starke

Volume 21: *Staging Islam in England: Drama and Culture, 1640–1685*
Matthew Birchwood

Volume 22: *Early Modern Tragicomedy*
edited by Subha Mukherji and Raphael Lyne

Volume 23: *Spenser's Legal Language: Law and Poetry in Early Modern England*
Andrew Zurcher

Volume 24: *George Gascoigne*
Gillian Austen

Volume 25: *Empire and Nation in Early English Renaissance Literature*
Stewart Mottram

Volume 26: *The English Clown Tradition from the Middle Ages to Shakespeare*
Robert Hornback

Volume 27: *Lord Henry Howard (1540–1614): An Elizabethan Life*
D. C. Andersson

Volume 28: *Marvell's Ambivalence: Religion and the Politics of Imagination
in Mid-Seventeenth-Century England*
Takashi Yoshinaka

Volume 29: *Renaissance Historical Fiction: Sidney, Deloney, Nashe*
Alex Davis

Volume 30: *The Elizabethan Invention of Anglo-Saxon England:
Laurence Nowell, William Lambarde, and the Study of Old English*
Rebecca Brackmann

Volume 31: *Pain and Compassion in Early Modern English Literature and Culture*
Jan Frans van Dijkhuizen

Volume 32: *Wyatt Abroad: Tudor Diplomacy and the Translation of Power*
William T. Rossiter